GREECE WITHOUT COLUMNS

GREECE
WITHOUT COLUMNS

The Making of the Modern Greeks

by

DAVID HOLDEN

FABER AND FABER
3 Queen Square
London

First published in 1972
by Faber and Faber Limited
3 Queen Square London WC1
Printed in Great Britain by
Latimer Trend & Co Ltd Plymouth
All rights reserved

ISBN 0 571 08372 2

Consider: is not to dream just this, whether a man be asleep or awake, to mistake the image for the reality?

(PLATO)

FOR RUTH

who started it and suffered it

CONTENTS

PREFACE

*The uppermost idea with Hellenism is to
see things as they really are.*

(MATTHEW ARNOLD)

Books should speak for themselves and this one is quite long enough
already without burdening it with a lengthy introduction. A few
things, however, should be said. Firstly, that although the following
pages are essentially about the politics of modern Greece they were
not inspired by and are not only about those current rulers of Greece
collectively known as 'the colonels'. On the contrary, the idea of the
book came into my mind two or three years before the colonels
appeared on the Greek scene, when I had spent enough time in the
country to discover for myself that a great screen of mutual misunderstanding seemed to hang between Greece and the western
world. I thought then that I might perform a service, if only to myself,
by trying to pierce a few holes in that screen with a book that sought
to explain why modern Greece is the way it is—to take a leaf out of
Matthew Arnold's book of 'Hellenism', so to speak, and see things
in Greece as they really are, without our customary, western preconceptions. That turned out to be a more presumptuous exercise
than I had supposed, but it has remained the guiding thought; and
the fact that the colonels happened to interpose themselves between
the idea and the actual attempt at its fulfilment made little difference
to what I thought needed saying—although it did persuade me that
I should try all the more to say it as soon as I could find the time and
the nerve for the attempt. Secondly, although the book is political
in that it is addressed mainly to aspects of the Greek political
situation, it is not and in the nature of things cannot be exclusively
about politics. Much of it, in fact, is about the character of Greece
and the Greeks and their interaction with the world around them,
out of which Greek politics have acquired their distinctive shape and
process. Thirdly, although I am greatly indebted to many other
people, some of whom are individually acknowledged elsewhere,
most of what I have written is either directly based upon or in some

way confirms my personal experience of Greece, both as journalist and traveller, going back now for more than a decade. Fourthly, I had better say here and now that I am not, in the usual sense of the word, a philhellene. To me, philhellenism is a love affair with a dream which envisions 'Greece' and the 'Greeks' not as an actual place or as real people but as symbols of some imagined perfection. I have never experienced that sensation. I happen to like Greeks, on the whole, and I have a number of treasured Greek friends who will, I hope, forgive me if some of what I say disappoints or angers them. I enjoy Greek sunshine, I can usually stomach Greek food and I readily acknowledge that the Parthenon is a noble sight. I also suspect, however, that a good deal of the Parthenon's appeal may be due to its state of ruin and I am perfectly certain that, if the alleged 'reconstructions' of the archaeologists are anything to go by, I should have disliked the place intensely in its original form. For it must surely have been a thing of some vulgarity in its heyday, covered as it was, apparently, in gaudy paint, surrounded by statues of the gods in every size and shape and with its interior dominated by a jewelled and gilded statue of Athene whose pictorial likenesses suggest to me that its disappearance is one of history's more supportable depredations. Fifthly, and arising out of this preamble, it must be clear that this book is not at all about the Greece which countless volumes have put before us and which the tourist advertisements nowadays continue to sell to us as a land of marvellous temples and antique memories of perfection. That is not my Greece nor, I believe, was it ever Greece at all except in the world of mental imagery. The Greece I know is a far more human place, as full of tragedy as of joy, of viciousness as well as humour, of pettiness as much as magnanimity and, I fear, of rather more shabbiness than glory. It is a Greece, as one might say, without columns—without, that is to say, those grand, upstanding, solidly-rooted things that hold up the roof of the temple. For the temple in Greece has always rested on unsure foundations, the columns are more often ruined than not and the roof has too often fallen in.

London, 1971

YUGOSLAVIA

●Sofia

BULGARIA

ALBANIA

●Skopje

Bari

Tirana

ITALY

MACEDONIA

Kavalla●

●Salonika

GREECE

CORFU

Mt.Olympus

●Ioannina

Igoumenitsa

EPIRUS

Larissa

THESSALY

SPORADES

EUBOEA

Ionian
Sea

IONIAN ISLANDS

Missolonghi

Patras●

ATHENS

PELOPONNESE

Corinth●

Nauplion

Piraeus

Kalamata

Sparta

Bay of
Navarino

Methoni●

●Monemvasia

THE GREEKS AND BYZANTIUM

Venice●

Odessa

WESTERN ROMAN

Rome●

f l

EMPIRE

EASTERN ROMAN
EMPIRE (BYZANTIUM)

Khania

●Constantinople

Smyrna

Athens

●Antioch

CYPRUS

Alexandria● ●Jerusalem

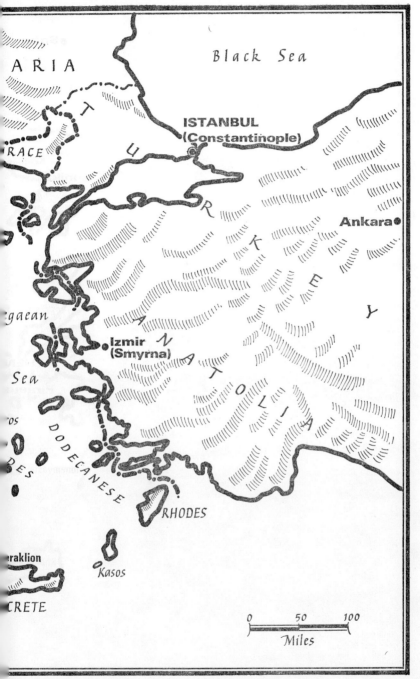

Black Sea

ARIA

TURKEY

RACE

THRACE

ISTANBUL
(Constantinople)

Ankara

Aegean

Izmir
(Smyrna)

ANATOLIA

Sea

DODECANESE

ros

RHODES

DES

Heraklion

Kasos

CRETE

0   50   100
Miles

B

PART I

QUESTIONS OF IDENTITY

Chapter 1

THE DOUBLE-BORN SOUL

*I . . . struggle to distinguish the two great
currents which constitute the double-born
soul of Greece.*

(NIKOS KAZANTZAKIS)

To begin, I have discovered, is the great difficulty with Greece. For how do you begin with something that only truly exists as a permanent oscillation between opposites? It is like trying to pin down a butterfly; you can do it only at the cost of destroying the movement that is the creature's essence.

The comparison is not altogether fortuitous, for the characteristic motions of a butterfly and of Greece have much in common. Both are simultaneously flowing and jerky, continuous and discontinuous to a remarkable degree. Observe a Greek in conversation and you will see at once what I mean. Hear the frequent and dramatic changes of pitch in the voice from the confidential whisper, say, to the scornful roar. Watch the accompanying gestures equally contrasted, from the sidelong glance that goes with the forefinger quietly massaging one side of the nose, to the sudden clap of the fingers of one hand against the base of the opposite palm. Each of these is as clearly defined, and as apparently unrelated to the others, as the sudden swoops, jigs and pirouettes of a butterfly's flight. Yet, as you watch, there emerges from the Greek performance—as from the butterfly's —an overall continuity. Just as the butterfly never really pauses in its apparently inconsequent and faltering flight, so the Greek in conversation subtly links each outrageous change of voice and gesture, becoming both fluid and spasmodic at the same time. The whole thing is, so to speak, an exercise in motion that creates its own significance. For the butterfly the destination seems to matter less than the manner of the journey. For the Greek the substance of the conversation is apparently less important than the style. For both it is the process, not the achievement, that counts.

If this is true for individual modes of Greek expression it seems equally characteristic of the collective Greek identity which has assumed so many different and sometimes contradictory forms over the last two or three thousand years and yet has retained an astonishing constancy of outlook and behaviour. The inconstancy of the form is a matter of record, both historical and geographical. Territorially, Greece has hardly ever been stable from one century to the next and very often—as in modern times—it has fluctuated in size and shape literally from decade to decade.

Even the present piece of impoverished Near Eastern real estate that we call 'Greece'—some 50,000 square miles between Corfu and the Dodecanese, Crete and the Balkan mountains, with a population of nearly nine millions and a seat at the United Nations—even that cannot safely be regarded as the final territorial expression of the idea of Greece, at least for as long as the ultimate fate of Cyprus remains unsettled. Looking backwards, it is only a quarter-of-a-century yet since Greece's current frontiers were established, when Italy transferred to her the Dodecanese Islands as part of the peace settlement after the Second World War. It is only half-a-century since Greek troops were marching happily into Anatolia in the ill-fated attempt to establish a new empire of Byzantium, and not much more than that since most of what is now northern Greece was wrested from Turkish hands in the Balkan wars.

Further back still, beyond the War of Independence, when the modern nation-state of Greece came into being for the first time, the whole concept of Greece as a geographical entity begins to blur before our eyes, so many and various were its shapes and meanings. For nearly four centuries under Turkish rule Greece ceased to have any independent political existence whatever; and for most of the thousand years of the Byzantine empire before that the peninsula to which we now attach the name of Greece was viewed by Greek leaders as a stagnant province, unfit to set beside the truly Greek glories of Constantinople. Like modern Greece, too, Byzantium had no stable boundaries, for the Turks, the Slavs, the Arabs, the Venetians or the Franks were forever hammering at its gates, often advancing, sometimes retreating, but rarely standing still. And when, still further back, we come to the Hellenistic world of Alexander and the Greek diaspora we are scarcely dealing with a territorial concept at all, but rather with a string of cultural and commercial communities stretching from the mouth of the Mediterranean to the plains of northern India. It is only when we reach Periclean Athens, and the supposedly golden age of classical Greece, 2,500 years ago, that peninsular Greece is once more central to the idea of Greek-ness and then, as a collection of quarrelling city-states, it is structurally so different from peninsular Greece today that we can hardly identify it as the same place in any but the most limited, material sense of the item.

But if geography can offer us no stable idea of Greece, what can? Not race, certainly; for whatever the Greeks may once have been, when Homer and Agamemnon lived and cloud-gathering Zeus leaped from his Cretan birthplace upon the ancient world, they can hardly have had much blood-relationship with the Greeks of the peninsula we know today. Serbs and Bulgars, Romans, Franks and Venetians, Turks, Albanians, Germans and Italians in one invasion after another have made the modern Greeks a decidedly mongrel race. Not politics either; for in spite of that tenacious western legend about Greece as the birthplace and natural home of democracy, the political record of the Greeks is one of singular instability and confusion in which, throughout history, the poles of anarchy and despotism have played roughly equal parts, and a decently modulated freedom has very rarely appeared. Not religion; for while Byzantium was Christian, ancient Hellas was pagan; and although the Eastern Orthodox Church has been closely associated with the Greeks for the last sixteen centuries it has never been their exclusive possession. Not even language will quite do, for although it brings us a good deal nearer than the others to some overall coherence in the forms of Greek identity, it has also been a source of much Greek division in modern times. The current demotic, or spoken, language is certainly derived from the classical Greek, but has become markedly different from it, while the official language of the state, called *katharevousa*, or 'pure', is an artificially imposed adaptation of the classical tongue; and since 1901, when a Greek Government fell because of riots over a translation of the New Testament into demotic, the language question has divided more Greeks than it has united.

Yet however often and radically the forms of Greece have shifted —and few national concepts, surely, have experienced upheavals so numerous and traumatic—a constant Greek spirit seems to have prevailed. Like the flight of the butterfly, it is something both ephemeral and persistent, blown willy-nilly by anarchic breezes, yet never losing its individual style. As Dr. William Miller, the acute correspondent of the London *Morning Post*, observed at the turn of the present century: 'It always seems to me that the average Greek of classical times must have had most of the characteristics of the modern hellenes. I say advisedly "the average Greek", because, owing to the circumstances of our classical education, we are unconsciously led to believe that all the ancient Greeks were men of extraordinary genius—a mistake as absurd as to suppose that all the contemporaries of Shakespeare were men of his standard. I suspect that the average Athenian, whom Aristophanes knew and drew, was not very different from the modern frequenter of . . . Constitution Square.'[1]

Indeed, the spiritual and practical correspondence does seem quite remarkable. Certainly there is hardly an aspect of modern Greek politics that does not have its antique parallel. Internal factionalism and personal jealousy combined with a proud Greek unity against all outsiders; a recurrent swing between efficient but detested despots and popular but incompetent democracies; a conspiratorial cunning along with much naïve gullibility; an intense curiosity and political awareness grappling with a love of talk and rhetorical gesture for their own sakes that often outruns all reason—all these and more can be discovered both now and then, amply documented in the historical and literary records. Equally striking is the persistence of what the ancients called *hubris*—that overweening pride that is at the core of so many classical Greek tragedies and that, as we shall see elsewhere, has continued to flourish with characteristically fatal results in practically every modern Greek statesman from the War of Independence until now. That Greeks make good servants but poor masters is an old saying, and some might think a harsh one; but it is amply justified by the record, both ancient and modern, for it is hard to think of another people whose leaders have been quite so regularly and speedily unbalanced by the feel of power.

The tenacity of these general traits of character and behaviour is easily illustrated. There is St. Paul, for instance, on Greek curiosity, remarking 2,000 years ago, according to the Acts of the Apostles, that 'all the Athenians and strangers which were there spent their time in nothing else, but either to tell, or to hear, some new thing'. Who has not heard of travellers in Greece today returning from the wilds of Crete or the Pindus mountains with tales of the loneliest shepherds displaying an equal passion? 'One's health, one's income, one's children, one's sex-life,' wrote Mr. Osbert Lancaster, twenty-five years ago, 'are all matters in which [the Greeks] are prepared to take a burning and perfectly genuine interest and on which deliberately to withhold information would be considered churlish.'[2] On the Greek passion for politics—and its often unhappy results—there is an embarrassment of comment. Here, for example, is Dr. Miller again: 'Politics are the morning and evening pabulum of Athens, and the debates are minutely followed in the papers. But intensely amusing as Greek politics are as a game, vividly as they recall the discussions of the Athenian democracy, they are, considered as a serious business, fatal to the real progress of the country.'[3] Yes, indeed—as the apparently endless series of unstable governments has revealed in the seventy or so years since that was written. But were things much different in the age of Pericles? Apparently not, as a more recent commentator tells us: 'The danger of Athenian democracy was that the power of the spoken word sometimes drove out reason. . . . The temperamental versatility of the Athenians was their greatest danger; the history of the later [Peloponnesian] war years demonstrates this clearly, as segments of the populace are urged first one way, then the other, and any continuity of diplomatic activity is rendered impossible.'[4] The corollary of which was, as Plato warned his countrymen in the *Republic*, that 'the excess of liberty, whether in States or individuals, seems only to pass into excess of slavery'. But the Greeks in their enthusiasm have never heeded that.

On cunning and shiftiness in the Greek character, and a general tendency to cheat all officialdom if possible, so often attributed by philhellenes (and Greeks) to the brutalizing effects of Turkish rule, we have the British historian, H. A. L. Fisher, describing a typical embarrassment of Byzantine administration in the reign of the emperor Justinian, 1,000 years before the Turks appeared on the scene: 'The Government was cheated by all its agents. Two-thirds of the revenue extorted from the taxpayers failed to find its way to the Treasury. The evil was apparently incurable. . . .'[5] Compare with the Frenchman, Edmond About, writing in 1852 of a similar problem: 'In Greece the law is never that intractable being so familiar to us. The officials pay heed to the taxpayers. There is always a way of reaching an agreement when people speak to each other in the familiar form of address and call each other brother . . . that abstract entity called the State is almost unknown to them. After all, the tax-collector is a careful man; he knows that no one is to be offended, that he has stretches of rough territory to cross before he gets home, and that an accident is swift to happen.'[6] Little has changed since then, except that Greece has got bigger and its problems more acute. The tax-collectors may not run quite the same risk of accident nowadays, when modern communications have enabled law and order of a sort to reach further into Greece's darker corners; but they do not stand much better chance of collecting and forwarding the taxes

officially due to them, and if they did so they would probably be
materially poorer men. Witness the fact that in 1964 it was estimated that two-thirds of all income-tax in Greece was evaded by one
means or another, and as far as I know there was no recorded case
of a collector being reduced to indigence, in spite of the notoriously
low salaries they received. Even military dictatorships do not necessarily overcome the intractable Greek spirit in matters such as these,
as the *Athens Daily Post* revealed in August 1967, quoting the Minister of Public Order, a certain Mr. Totomis, under the headline, 'Name
Dropping No Use'. According to reports reaching his Ministry, said
Mr. Totomis, gravely, 'certain people calling at police stations for
various matters make use of the names of prominent people of the
state to have special servicing by the competent authorities. In that
connection Public Order Minister Totomis has addressed a circular
to all Royal Gendarmeries, Police and Fire Brigade services, stressing
that such actions by citizens, due in most to bad habits of the past,
are unacceptable for the post April 21st situation [i.e. after the military *coup d'état*] which among others has set as its aim the creation
of a good administration from all points of view'. Good for Mr.
Totomis; but I fear that his efforts may have met a predictable fate,
like those of all his predecessors.

Greek history is stuffed with such parallels. When Aristotle asked
his pupils to draw up a constitution for their ideal state, for example,
he got 158 different drafts. When Brigadier Pattakos asked the
Greek people 2,500 years later for their comments on the constitution
he and his military colleagues had just prepared for their ideal state
after their *coup d'état*, he was inundated with replies. When Pisistra-
tus seized power in Athens by a *coup d'état* in the sixth century B.C.
his first act was to win over the rural citizens to his side by a new
and generous set of land laws. When Colonel Papadopoulos seized
power in 1967 his first act was to woo the villagers of Greece by
cancelling farmers' debts and increasing farmers' pensions. When
Themistocles returned in triumph to ancient Athens after defeating
the Persian challenge he was promptly deposed and exiled by his
peers for his presumption. Many outstanding Greek politicians in
modern times have suffered a similar fate. From this practice the
ancients gave us the word for banishment, which they called ostra-
cism, derived from *ostrakon*, or potsherd, on which the citizens of
Athens wrote the names of those they wished to exile. The unfortu-
nates usually served their banishment, as many thousands of Greeks
have done more recently, in the Aegaean Islands.

In their religion, too, the Greeks contrive to repeat past patterns with extraordinary facility. True, most religions in the world are based in some way on previous faiths. Few have sprung from virgin spiritual soil. But few, also, seem indebted quite so clearly and in such detail to their predecessors as is the Greek version of Christianity to the pagan beliefs of Hellenism. Half that great gallery of Christian saints, whose white-washed chapels stipple the Greek landscape and whose icons adorn every Greek home, consists of the ancient pagan pantheon in disguise. Some of the gallery have scarcely so much as changed their names. Who is the saintly Dionysios but the older Dionysus of the Bacchic myth, sharing the same old patronage of wine? Who is St. Elias but the sun-god, Helios, with his shrines scattered everywhere across the hilltops so as to be nearer to the divine presence? And when 30,000 Greeks descend on the island of Tinos every year in August to crawl on hands and knees, in penitence and supplication, to the monastery of the miraculous Virgin on the hill above the harbour, it is not just the Mother of Christ they are paying homage to but Poseidon, who presided at the very same shrine before her, and Asclepius the god of health, who—according to some accounts—was there even before that. The Christian God Himself is not safe from such corruptions of the antique Greek past. When the Greek farmer of today hears a clap of thunder and declares that God is rolling his wine barrels about—as I have been assured that he often does—he can hardly be thinking of our austere Christian Father which art in Heaven: plainly, and certainly far more appropriately, it is rollicking old Zeus that is in his mind.

Plus ça change, plus c'est la même chose. That is really the only possible epitaph for the Greek experience, the only possible comment on the way the same general spirit of Greek-ness has survived all the detailed vicissitudes of the material body of Greece. But in that opposition of the intangible and the tangible there is an important guide to the nature of Greek identity as a whole—which is surely, as I suggested at the start, best seen as a constant oscillation between just such opposites as these. The spirit and the flesh, ideal and reality, triumph and despair—you name them and the Greeks suffer or enjoy them as the constant poles of their being, swinging repeatedly from one to the other and back again, often contriving to embrace both poles simultaneously, but above all never reconciled, never contented, never still. This perennial sense of tension between diametrically opposed forces is the essence of their existence—the one absolutely consistent feature of their identity since Greek history began. In the phrase of the Cretan novelist, Kazantzakis, they are truly double-born souls.

We can detect this dualism in the very bones of Greece, in the abrupt contrasts of its landscape and its light and the perpetual interweaving of its land and sea. We can trace it in classical Greek art, in what Mr. Stewart Perowne calls 'that never-ending motion of the pendulum swinging constantly between the representational feminine genius of the Ionians and the formal, masculine conception of the Dorians'[7]—the two strains that were most important in the racial composition of the early Greeks. We can discern it in such classical legends as that of Odysseus and Penelope, whose images contain the eternal themes of exile and return, each as characteristic of Greece today as they were in Homer's day. And we can certainly see dualism of the most extreme kind in the shape of classical Greek politics, with tyranny and anarchy performing their customary Punch-and-Judy show and the authoritarianism of Sparta and the democracy of Athens existing side by side. The Greeks of those days might have urged moderation upon each other and talked of the golden mean, but only, one supposes, because they acted so often like fanatical extremists.

As the centuries and millenniums pass, this dualistic quality of Greek life not merely persists but proliferates, as it were, finding new poles of opposition and new forms of expression, until in our own day there seems almost no aspect of Greece and the Greeks that is not profoundly ambivalent. If we ask, for example, whether Greece is a 'western' or an 'eastern' country we are obliged to admit that it is a bit of both. Three thousand years ago, when Greek life evolved from the oriental patterns of Egypt, Mesopotamia, Anatolia and the Levant, it gradually acquired what we recognize as in some ways a 'western' character, developing among other things those capacities for natural observation, clear description and precise classification that are still accepted as the distant roots of western science and western rationalism. But 1,000 years of Byzantium and four centuries of Turkish rule re-emphasized the oriental heritage. When Greece was reborn in 1832 in the form of a modern nation-state there was, in consequence, a fundamental ambiguity about her entire national character.

The Greek nation-state was a product of western political intervention—'the fatal idea' as Arnold Toynbee once called it, of exclusive western nationalism impinging upon the multi-national traditions of the eastern world.[8] By extension, therefore, at any rate in theory, it was a child of the Renaissance and of western rationalism, some of whose inspiration was derived from classical Greece; and its western sponsors naturally saw the moment of its creation as a rebirth of 'true' or classical Greek-ness in the land to which that heritage rightfully belonged. But the Greeks themselves had few such thoughts. They had known no Renaissance; and the thread of their classical past had long been woven into the oriental web of Byzantium. Their recovery of political independence was to most of them far more a matter of restoring the power of that Greek Christian empire than of rebuilding ancient Hellas. So double meanings and numberless misunderstandings were built into the very fabric of the modern state; and they have not yet been resolved.

Typical of this is the inspissated confusion that still surrounds the name of Greece. For who was it that bestowed this title upon the modern nation-state, and who now thinks of its inhabitants as Greeks? Not, I fear, the Greeks. They may well once have had a word for everything, as the antique legend says, but 'Greece' and 'Greeks' have rarely figured in their vocabulary. Officially, Greeks call their modern state *Hellas*, after the classical world of 2,000 years ago, and by the same token they are officially known as Hellenes, which implies descent from their illustrious classical forefathers. But at the same time, colloquially, they call themselves *Romios*, derived from *Rum*, or Rome, and signifying that they are citizens of the eastern Roman Empire whose capital was Constantinople—in short, that they are really the children of Byzantium. 'Greece', on the other hand, is derived from the Latin *Graecia*, the province of the western Roman Empire which stretched south of Mount Olympus through the peninsula of Attica and the Peloponnese. Its international use to describe the sovereign state that currently occupies that territory is merely a reflection of the fact that 'Greece' in this modern sense is literally a western invention.

Thus, in Greece today, we have the fragmented and purely local traditions of the classical city states compressed together with the wide-ranging and multi-national pattern of the eastern Roman Empire into the mould of a modern nation-state which has nothing structurally in common with either and whose only internationally recognizable name is equally foreign to both. Here is material evidence of a spiritual struggle of titanic proportions, both within Greece as a whole and within every individual Greek, between the poles of pagan classicism and Orthodox Christianity, western rationalism and oriental mysticism, Mediterranean clarity and Balkan obscurity and a great deal more besides. Its bewildering oscillations and dense ambiguities inspire much of the mental and some of the material turmoil of modern Greece.

This was, indeed, what Kazantzakis was getting at when he wrote of the double-born soul of Greece. He saw it as essentially an enormously complex juncture of eastern and western characters, related to Byzantium and Hellas respectively, or as he called them the oriental and the native Greek, 'sometimes flowing side by side, never joining, sometimes meeting and struggling furiously, and even, rarely, joined in organic union. The modern Greek loves life and fears death, loves his homeland and is simultaneously a pathological individualist; he fawns upon his superiors like a Byzantine and torments his inferiors like an Aga, yet he will die for his *philotimo*—his personal honour. He is clever and shallow, with no metaphysical anxieties, and yet, when he begins to sing, a universal grieving leaps up from his Oriental bowels and breaks the crust of Greek logic; all at once the East, all darkness and mystery, rises up from deep within him.'[9]

Mr. Patrick Leigh Fermor has elaborated a similar idea in his theory of the 'Helleno-Romaic Dilemma', whose corner-stone is 'the supposition that inside every Greek dwell two figures in opposition'. The Romios is, as it were, the reality—the cunning child of poverty, oppression, the Turks and Byzantium, the man with the oriental streak. The Hellene is something nearer to the golden image of the classical legend—a sort of official Greek, altogether a nobler, more pompous and less convincing fellow than the Romios, but equally influential. The Romios distrusts the law, the Hellene respects it, the Romios loves the recent past, the Hellene reveres the remote past, the Romios—naturally—glories in the dome of Santa Sophia in Constantinople, the Hellene—of course—worships the columns of the Parthenon in Athens. Mr. Leigh Fermor has listed no fewer than sixty-four of these conflicts of thought, emotion, tradition and institution, down to such illuminating divisions as a Romaic preference for the demotic tongue against Hellenic support of *katharevousa*, and a Romaic fondness for smoking narghiles (water pipes) as opposed to Hellenic disapproval of the same 'for obvious (i.e. anti-oriental) reasons'.[10]

But, of course, these ideas are not always mutually exclusive. They can be and often are held simultaneously in the same mind, for no Greek is wholly Romaic or wholly Hellene, any more than Greece itself is so. Indeed, as it seems to me, the whole point of being Greek is that the poles *must* exist together in the individual mind as much as in the corporate state because only then can they generate the tension, the sense of perpetual motion between them, that is the distinctive feature of the Greek identity. This is surely what makes Greece so hard for most non-Greeks to understand—and for writers like me to get a grip on, for that matter. If it were only a matter of a country being divided between one group of people and another, whose predilections might roughly be defined respectively as eastern or western, Byzantine or classical, Romaic or Hellenic, or what-you-will, it would all be simple enough. If these could be linked convincingly with other group interests such as, say, farmers—who might be Romaic, etc.—against townsmen—Hellenic, etc.—we should all be home and dry. If we could somehow discover even in individual Greeks a roughly consistent set of attitudes, so that a man who, say, smoked a narghile might assuredly be set down as oriental, Byzantine or Romaic in all other ways as well, we might see our way clearly through the Greek darkness. But there is no consistency. Greeks defy this sort of categorization. They live in a state of total and permanent contradiction of each other and of themselves. This has the advantage that if you do not like what they do or say today you have only to wait until tomorrow to find them doing the opposite; but it can be uncommonly hard on the nerves and is a rich and continuing source of misunderstanding and mistrust.

The constant inconstancy of the Greek character implies, I think, a vision of life unlike that normally held in the western world. The West does, in fact, tend to categorize facts and ideas, to seek definitions and logical progressions. In Greece, on the other hand, there is a perennial tendency for facts and ideas to change shape, and definitions—like Greek frontiers—to blur. In the western tradition, for example, history is usually seen in a linear perspective as a record which starts at point A, faintly discernible in the more or less distant past, and progresses through a series of events to points X, Y or Z, more or less clearly visible on our contemporary horizon. This is what might be called the palimpsest interpretation of the past, where each succeeding year or century not only absorbs but in so doing obliterates a little of its predecessors, layer after layer, until we almost cease to be conscious of, and certainly cease to care about, our remoter origins. Our past becomes at best a row of milestones we have left behind along the road; which probably accounts for our peculiarly western notion of 'progress' and its assumption (until just now, anyway) that man and his society are perfectible if only we travel far enough. At heart, your true westerner has to be a bit of a Coué-ist, believing that every day in every way, things are— or at any rate ought to be—getting better and better.

Not so, by and large, the Greeks. They do not travel this western kind of point to point, starting here and progressing there past the milestones of 'improvement'—nor, for that matter, past those of 'decline'. They have their historical ups and downs, it is true, and none have been more dramatic; but they see them in a different perspective, not receding in apparently ordered gradations like some eighteenth-century landscape painting, from the here and now to the distant there and then, but all jumbled up together instead, like certain modern paintings and most Byzantine icons. Everything remains in the foreground, as it were; everything is potentially of equal importance and everything is always relevant. Thus, the Greeks seem to experience history not as a palimpsest of century piled upon century but—and here we see their characteristic dualism at work again—as something both more fragmentary and more pervasive; a cross between a kaleidoscope and a seamless web. The kaleidoscope represents the shattered aspect of their past, the seamless web its continuity. In the one is mirrored those seismic transformations in the form of Greece, from the Hellenic world to Byzantium, from Byzantium to the Turkish occupation, from the occupation to the independent nation-state of modern Greece. In the other we see old qualities continuing in new guises, as the gods of Olympus have survived in Christian vestments. But while the two may be distinguishable, they are never separable. They are not even to be described as the two sides of one coin, for they are both on the same side, merging and dividing and merging again throughout history, rather like one of those modern 'op' art paintings in which a single arrangement of shapes and colours on the canvas suggests now one picture and now another in the eye of the beholder.

The same contrast between Greek and western ways appears in their disparate notions of society and government. It is often remarked that the Greeks have never developed a true aristocracy, nor have their governments contrived to build sound administrations around the hierarchies of rank and office that are commonly accepted in western societies as essential to the functioning of the state. Greeks do not like such social distinctions. In fact, they do not really like distinctions at all—which is why, of course, they so frequently throw up governments that feel obliged to enforce some. Even the Greek Church, in spite of its antiquity and its social influence, has no real hierarchical tradition. The Patriarch of Constantinople today lives in not much greater state than one of Greece's more prosperous village priests. To compare him to the Latin Pope, as is sometimes done, is to misunderstand both his authority and his style. A mere suffragan Bishop of the Church of England, indeed, would expect to be surrounded by more pomp and circumstance. But that is because the Orthodox Church, in true Greek fashion, has always maintained a mystical, all inclusive view of itself in contrast to the exclusive and highly institutionalized forms of its western counterparts. 'In the West', says Sir Steven Runciman, ' "the Church" came in ordinary parlance to mean the hierarchy and the priesthood. In the East the Church always meant the whole body of Christians, past, present, and future, including the angels in heaven. The priesthood was not a class apart.'[11]

Yet, of course, social and functional distinctions are constantly being made, just as the continuity of Greek history is for ever being disrupted. In government they tend to be distinctions of sheer power; in other words those which are of necessity temporary and can be, and frequently are, reversed as everyone strives to become king of the castle in his turn. In the Church the distinction is between the earthly and the heavenly aspects of each individual; so that while everyone remains piously convinced that virtue in this world is only the prelude to glory in the next, everyone is simultaneously free to practise what Runciman calls 'a self-seeking, cynical and often unscrupulous handling of mundane affairs'.[12]

Here, as ever in Greece, we see life shaping itself again as an oscillation between opposites. No sooner have we defined one aspect than its reverse is automatically conjured forth, and so on for ever, each pole inert without the other, but between them generating the leaping spark of tension that is the only certain characteristic of Greekness. Tension, movement, change, process; these are the essence of Greek life. Stability means death. In this sense, Greece seems a curiously contemporary country. Just as modern art tries to create tension by exploiting many planes at once, just as modern music is multi-tonal and modern literature increasingly concerned with multiple echoes and meanings, so Greece is chronically in a state of fission and yet remains mystically united. A mathematician might say it belonged to the world of Einstein rather than of Newton because its linear measurements are less important than the interplay of its relative forces. A sociologist might find its lack of established hierarchies and distinctions a splendid example of that fashionably 'unstructured'

C

society that hippy communes, anarchists and students of group dynamics aspire to. And no doubt Mr. Marshall McLuhan, that most contemporary of prophets, could view it as an eternal land of the psychedelic—although the practical uncertainties of the Greek power supply might deter him from describing it as electronic—where the medium is always the message. Greece, in short, might be defined as not so much a place, as a happening.

But there, yet again, is the rub. For the point about happenings is that they are indefinable. They defy measurement of the orthodox kind that depends on the acceptance of certain fixed points or values because it is their nature not to be fixed at all. They move—and that is just about the most precise thing that can be said about them. Greece is like that, too; a maddeningly mobile, elusive, paradoxical world, where there seems nothing solid enough to grasp save splinters, yet where no part is less than the mystical whole and where past and present, body and soul, ideal and reality blend and struggle and blend again with each other so that the most delicate scalpel can scarcely dissect them.

Which brings me back to where I started—the practical difficulty of beginning a book on Greece. It is not a difficulty that I have invented, for I am by no means alone in experiencing it. Many respectable writers about contemporary Greece, far more knowledgeable than I am, have encountered the same problem and have sought to answer it roughly as I have by asking themselves and their readers in one way or another, what is Greece? Inevitably, their answers vary; but it is striking how the question sets them all galloping off to distant frontiers and ancient times in search of clues. Some simply take the most straightforward chronological answer, beginning 3,000 years ago and working their way steadily onwards to the present day. Others begin with the Emperor Constantine and the founding of Byzantium, a mere 1,600 years ago—and then have to hark backwards to the Hellenic world in order to explain the significance of Byzantium. To begin with 1821 and the War of Independence is, of course, a commonplace in studies of modern Greece; yet often, almost before the authors seem to realize what they are at, they are forced to scavenge in far remoter centuries for evidence on this one.[13] Who would feel the necessity to approach contemporary Britain or the U.S.A. in such a way? We do not as a rule imagine that an account of the Union of the Crowns or the Boston Tea Party is indispensable to an explanation of the current state of these two countries—even upon reflection they may be granted only a distant relevance—and we certainly do not bother our heads with the Roman conquest or the voyage of Columbus as preliminary material for a study of British or American politics in our time. This is not just because writers about current affairs or modern history in Britain or America can take for granted a certain minimum of earlier historical knowledge in their readers. They would, indeed, be most unwise to do so—although, to be sure, their expectations may be justifiably higher than those of writers about Greece, who are likely to be confronted with blank incomprehension in most non-Greeks at any reference to actual history except a few clichés about Lord Byron or 'the glory that was Greece'. Nor is it only because Greece has more history to cope with than either Britain or America—or any other western country—that there seems to be a compulsion to summon immensely distant centuries to testify on the most contemporary affairs. No; it is because with Greece, as I have suggested, the perspective really is different. Everything seems genuinely relevant all the time, and one is constantly harking backwards simply because one must.

But this, too, has its dangers. For the writer it raises the spectre of historicism, the assumption that history is somehow alive and sentient in itself, directing men willy-nilly into predetermined paths. For the visitor, especially if he has swallowed—as most westerners have—a pre-digested and unsuspected dose of 'Hellenism', it can mean a hopelessly unbalanced view of Greece today. As you wander through the country with half a million other tourists, hearing the insistent guides jabbering from the temple steps at Delphi or being hustled round the Athens museum from the gold of Mycenae to Poseidon's statue, it is all too easy to accept the legends of ancient Greece as more real than present reality. You may be ready to believe, as you blink in the blinding sunlight at the white perfection of the Parthenon, that the chorus in Euripides' *Medea* was right:[14]

The people of Athens, sons of Erechtheus, have enjoyed their
    prosperity
Since ancient times. Children of the blessed Gods,
They grew from holy soil unscorched by invasion.
Among the glories of knowledge their souls are pastured;
They walk always with grace under the sparkling sky.
There long ago, they say, was born golden-haired Harmony,
Created by the nine virgin Muses of Pieria.

But all of Greek history belies this legend. The sky may sparkle, the people may sometimes walk with grace, but golden-haired Harmony, if she ever existed, was raped long ago by war, conquest, and invasion, *hubris*, jealousy and murder, as well as by the ceaseless ravages of the ubiquitous Greek goat, stripping the stony hillsides over the centuries of their thin, protective vegetation. The reality of Greece today, indeed, is that she is an immature, insecure and poor nation with an unmanageable and bitterly divided legacy of historical glory. Socially and economically she remains largely under-developed, but historically she is, so to speak, over-developed and unable, therefore, to treat herself, or to be treated by others, on her present merits. So national pride becomes a substitute for performance and every step forward has to be taken with a confused and confusing backward glance.

Here our problems of external comprehension pale beside the difficulties of the Greeks who must live in and with their eternal paradoxes. Not long ago I came upon a remark in a totally different context that seemed to me to summarize this aspect of their plight. It was in a story by Scott Fitzgerald, appropriately called *The Crack-Up*, and it said: 'The test of a first-rate intelligence is the ability to hold two opposed ideas in the mind at the same time and still retain the ability to function.' With due respect to what that great historian of Greece, George Finlay, once called 'Messrs. Homer, Plato & Co.', Greeks by and large boast no more first-rate intelligences than the rest of us, yet they are stuck with their eternally opposed ideas. It is not surprising, therefore, that their lives, their state, indeed the very concept of Greece, seem so frequently to crack up. 'Things fall apart, the centre cannot hold,' wrote Yeats; and that is surely the most persistent Greek theme of all, because from Pericles to Papadopoulos there runs throughout the structure of the nation not a core, such as more fortunate nations cherish, but a fissure—a permanent abyss at the centre of the Greek soul. Double-born, indeed, the Greeks have always wrestled with—but never yet mastered—that uniquely challenging inheritance.

Chapter 2

SUPERGREEK

God is a Graecophile.
(GEORGE PAPADOPOULOS)

It hardly required Colonel Papadopoulos to tell the Greeks that God was on their side, for in one way and another they assured themselves of that a very long time ago. In antiquity their oracle at Delphi was literally, to them, 'the navel of the world', and they called all other peoples barbarians. Their classical philosophers, including Plato and Aristotle, devoted much energy to proving that Athenians in particular were inherently better than other men; and the most renowned of their ancient leaders, Pericles, became so partly because he reached such remarkable heights of eloquence in praise of the unique Athenian virtues. His famous speech to the citizens of Athens during the Peloponnesian War has become a standard text of this general Greek conceit: 'Our constitution is called a democracy, because the government is in the hands not of the few but of the many,' he told them, blithely disregarding the fact that the citizens of Athens at that hour owed most of their democratic privileges to the work of a large slave population. 'Our laws secure equal justice for all in their private disputes, and our public opinion welcomes and honours talent in every field of achievement,' he went on, with equal disregard for the unhappy fate of such men as Socrates. 'And as we give free play to all in our public life, so we are free from suspicion in our private dealings, and we have no black looks or angry words for our neighbours if they enjoy themselves in their own way, nor do we give affront in ways which, though they may leave no mark, cause pain. Open and friendly in our private intercourse, a spirit of reverence pervades our public acts, and we are restrained from lawlessness by respect for authority and for the laws. . . . We are lovers of beauty without extravagance, and lovers of wisdom without unmanliness. Wealth for us is not a vainglorious display, but a means of making achievement possible; and we think it no disgrace to acknowledge poverty, but it is disgraceful not to try to overcome it. Our citizens are en-

grossed in both their private and public affairs, and those who attend
to business have no little insight into political matters. We alone
regard a man who takes no interest in public affairs, not as a harmless
drone, but as utterly useless; and we decide public matters for ourselves. . . . For we have this superiority over other men: we are the
most daring of men, and at the same time we are the most given to
reflection before the action.' Not for nothing, evidently, did the classical dramatists see *hubris* as the besetting Greek sin; for however we
may admire the Periclean rhetoric we must surely wonder, in view
of the Greek record before and since, what possible connexion it ever
had with reality. Yet the speech has survived through two-and-a-half
millenniums not just as an overdrawn picture of Utopia but as one of
the pillars of the classical Greek legend, frequently taken as evidence
that the Athenians in their heyday really were like that. In so doing it
has helped to colour both the way the world looks at Greece today and
the way the Greeks look at themselves, by holding up to modern
Greeks an image of their ancestors that no mortals could honestly
match and by implying, nevertheless, that in some mysterious way
Greece still must hold the secret of that ideal, Athenian republic. In
short, what Pericles and his contemporaries once fed to the world in
their vanity, the world in its innocence has fed back to their descendants. The result is the myth of Supergreek.

Like most national myths Supergreek is an exceedingly confused
affair, embodying more than one source and assuming more than
one shape. But in two things Supergreek is remarkable: his stamina
over so many centuries—extending even to our own day when myths
of any sort are apt to wilt under critical examination—and his enthusiastic acceptance by people who are not themselves Greek. Let
me quote, as preliminary evidence of both these points, a splendid
exchange in the columns of the *Times Literary Supplement* only a few
years ago. It began with a lengthy review—anonymous, like all
reviews in that distinguished journal—of several books about Greece
under the title, 'The Greek Kind of Glory'.[1] According to the reviewer the books expressed in various combinations of prose and
pictures the familiar, established image of Greece as the land of
Periclean perfection. Exasperated with all such effusions, he proceeded to blow the whole classical legend sky high. Let us have done,
he cried in effect, with all these reverent genuflections to the Greek
miracle. Let us instead have '. . . a deliberate and equally exaggerated
counterblast . . . a sumptuously produced volume in which all temples
were photographed through a torrential sheet of Greek autumn rain,

with a text that damned Pericles as an imperialist warmonger and high-minded megalomaniac, Plato as a homosexual snob whose theoretical authoritarianism came hilariously unstuck in Sicily, and Socrates as a mock-modest, meddlesome, disruptive ass, whose pupils' subsequent unsavoury careers amply vindicated the death-sentence passed on him by his sorely-tried fellow citizens. . . .' This 'anti-ideal treatise', he went on, would have sections on the 'vapid and aesthetically repulsive' fifth-century Athenian sculpture; 'dirty political in-fighting under the cloak of high moral idealism'; 'the windy aphoristic platitudes of Greek tragedy'; and a reminder that the main legacy of Greece, 'apart from a lot of hot air about Truth and Beauty, was a tradition of intellectual *haute couture* so prejudiced against the banausic[2] or practical application of abstract thought, so static in its concepts, so aristocratic in its social assumptions, that it held up technological progress for over 2,000 years, fostered a cheerful acceptance of slaves as "animated tools", laid down the blueprints for every kind of totalitarian government and led countless generations to despise the Romans because they put a premium on efficient sewers, roads and water supplies'. Only at the last moment did the reviewer draw back to reveal, presumably in an attempt to protect himself against the retaliation of enraged philhellenes, that part of his tongue was in his cheek. 'If such a book were published,' he added a trifle lamely, 'it would be howled down, and rightly, as a tendentious, distorted, and malicious version of the truth'—although little more so, he implied, than the familiar, admiring nonsense he had just been reading. His caveat was prescient, but did not protect him, for he was shortly howled down himself in most irascible fashion. This 'iconoclastic epistle', wrote a certain Mr. Thomas Anthem of Liverpool, in particular, was no better than 'a futile attempt to be different, such as whitewashing Hitler'; and he called several distinguished names in evidence to prove it. There was 'that outstanding Hellenist, Nietzsche, who proclaimed the Greeks to be "The only people of genius in the history of the world".' There was 'that great scholar and English saint, the late Dr. William Temple', a former Archbishop of Canterbury who had proposed a toast to Plato before the Classical Association of Great Britain as ' "The Master Mind of the Ages" '. There was Hildebrand, who had described Plato as 'a Christian before Christ'. Homosexual snob, indeed! 'No, sir,' Mr. Anthem concluded, with the air of a man putting his case beyond all possibility of refutation, 'No, sir, you and your kind, on deeper reflection, will have to agree with the greatest English classicist of his time, the late Dean Inge, "There is nothing that is great and beautiful in western civilization that does not come from Greece." '3

Here is the modern Periclean voice in all its absurd splendour, thrusting Christianity and Judaism into a contumelious limbo, and dismissing the native achievements of Rome and Constantinople (for we may be sure that Mr. Anthem and *his* kind are not thinking of Greece in connexion with that Greek city), Florence and Venice, Vienna, Paris, London and New York as mere pallid derivatives of the divine, omniscient Hellenic genius. Without subscribing too seriously to the hypothetical hatchet job of the reviewer in the *Times Literary Supplement*, it still seems reasonable to ask how on earth such patent nonsense can be entertained by otherwise sensible men in the second half of the twentieth century. Most of all, why should it so afflict people who are not themselves Greeks? For if it is one thing for the Greeks to believe that their ancestors were gods, it is something else for other people to take the legend at face value, and it is hard to think of another instance where one people who have actually dismissed others as barbarians have found so many of the barbarians themselves enthusiastically espousing the idea.

As far as Britain and its Mr. Anthems are concerned we may, perhaps, approach an explanation by noting first the relevance of the Greek legend to the former workings of the ancient British universities of Oxford and Cambridge and the allied public school system. Throughout the nineteenth and early twentieth centuries both were largely occupied in training a gentlemanly élite in the hierarchical culture proper to the rulers of a great empire. The classical tradition which dominated these institutions then, and which through them later infected the rest of British higher education, provided an intellectual mystique appropriate to this purpose. The 'dead' languages of Greek and Latin afforded, by definition, a closed system of reference among the few who were privileged to be instructed in them. They became, as it were, the tools of trade and the badge of office of the British witch-doctors—cherished beyond their merits by those who could share them and undeservedly respected or envied by most of those who could not. Thus the whole classical legend—and especially that of Greece, which was so much more remote and intellectual in every way than that of Rome—was identified with authority. To uphold it became practically synonymous with maintaining law and order. To attack it was tantamount to subversion. Hence, perhaps, the often exaggerated response of any classicists to criticism, and the tenacity with which they still fight to impress the rest of us with their mysteries.

This is probably a partial explanation of the apparent power of the Greek legend in Britain; and it may apply in modified ways to other western European countries. It is suggestive, in this connexion, that the legend has usually seemed weakest in the 'banausic' culture of the United States where, with a few exceptions, élitist concepts of education have been unpopular and 'dead' languages, by and large, have remained just dead. But even in Britain the public school theory is the merest beginning. How did the public schools acquire the legend in the first place, so many centuries after the demise of the original classical culture? And what gave the legend its astonishing staying power?

Aside from the genuine merits of ancient Hellas—and I suppose I, too, had better say that, in the context of the time, these were obviously considerable—there is surely a Freudian element in the answer. This is revealed at once, I think, by the extent to which the legend has prospered through the suppression of unpleasant but pertinent facts. In the exchange between Mr. Anthem and the *Literary Supplement*'s reviewer, for example, Mr. Anthem objected to the connexion made by the reviewer between Athenian military power and Athenian cultural achievement. ' "The glory that was Greece," ' he wrote, 'was erected on her incomparable culture and art, not the military excesses which were common to the times.' Reasonably, I think, the reviewer replied: '. . . there is surely something disquieting in the view (by no means restricted to Mr. Anthem) that Greek history and culture are unrelated phenomena, which can be studied without reference to one another. The building of the Parthenon and, say, the Samian Revolt are more closely linked than many people care to admit.'[4] For the benefit of non-classicists like myself, I should explain that the Samian Revolt was a rebellion against Athenian rule in the island of Samos in 440 B.C. It was suppressed with a proper imperialist firmness and Athens continued to exact handsome tribute from Samos and many other Aegaean islands for several decades thereafter—tribute which helped, among other things, to build the Parthenon.

Few guide-books to Greece ever mention such things, however solemnly they appear to present Greek history; and some of their other usual omissions—including, like Pericles, any reference to Athenian slavery—are so blatant as to amount to deliberate suppression of the truth. Has anyone ever heard of a regular tour of classical Greece today that included a visit to, or even a hint of, the

silver mines at Lavrion where the slaves laboured in the damp and
darkness to produce the bullion that underwrote the ambitions of
Pericles and his fellow-citizens? I have not; yet the mines can still be
visited, not far from the ruins of Sounion, whose Byronic 'marbled
steep' is a standard port of call for any half-day bus tour from
Athens. And what Greek guide-book, even in these allegedly permissive days, is not coy about ancient homosexuality? In that delicate
matter the fashion of discreet silence was set long ago by Dr. Thomas
Arnold, a noted classicist and—surely significantly?—the founder of
the nineteenth-century public school ethos in England, who believed
that no man should read Plato until he had passed the dangerous age
of forty, lest he be corrupted. So rigorous an exclusion of possible
blemishes from most western accounts of ancient Greece suggests to
me a powerful narcissism, as if what we were really doing in maintaining the legend was to improve our own image even more than
that of the Greeks. They, we declare eagerly, were *our* ancestors,
fathers of our western civilization, founders of our western democracy and so on. The more marvellous we can make them appear the
better must we seem ourselves, even at several long removes—and,
heaven knows, the removes are long enough, for the organic connexion, as distinct from the theoretical and ex-post facto link, between
classical Athenian democracy and the democracies of the current
western world is almost non-existent. So we engage in an unconscious
conspiracy to paint a picture of a Greece that never was in order to
see ourselves reflected there in a state of hallucinatory perfection. If
at first this seems far-fetched, let us ponder the evidence of much
contemporary tourist advertising about the charms of Greece which
relies upon exactly that self-flattering appeal. 'You were born in
Greece,' said one characteristically glossy effusion not long ago, 'and
it happened almost three thousand years ago. Greece's warm sunshine nurtured the ideas and the ideals that make you what you are.
Solon created democracy in Athens. Aesop made morals entertaining
and Homer wrote the original best-sellers. Thespis stepped out of the
chorus to stardom. Amateur sports and the spirit of fair play were
kindled at Olympia. And the climate, the landscape, had a great deal
to do with it. Come to Greece and see for yourself. Be reborn in the
same clear air. Sail the same blue waters as Ulysses, to storied islands
and sandy bays basking through a long, glorious Mediterranean
summer. Tan as dark as antique bronze and taste food fit for the
gods. Hear the splendours of Sophocles in the moonlight at Epi-
dauros, or revel with the music of bouzoukia players among im-

passioned, hospitable Greeks in the friendly tavernas. Remember, you're one of the family.'

We should not take such advertisements seriously as a source of information. The advertisers have an axe to grind and public relations experts to do it for them, and if they choose to suggest that visitors will actually enjoy going as green as most antique bronzes, or find most Greek food fit for anything but stoic acceptance, that is their affair. All the same, the angle of their approach is instructive. *You* were born in Greece, they say; and as one of the family you will naturally prefer to see your ancestors in the nicest possible light. A Greek light, of course—that 'clear air' that does, indeed, exist in Greece at certain times of year and that has inspired many a purple passage of foreign prose. But above all it must be the light of perfection, obscuring all blemishes and blinding the eyes of the innocent faithful with its shimmering, holy radiance. The sheer one-sidedness of the general picture of ancient Greece that results from this persistent 'family' bias should be enough to start any alert observer wondering how and by whom the dirt has been swept under the rug. But to discover that, we must go back far beyond the revelations of modern advertising campaigns, or the nineteenth-century traditions of classical education in the West, to the conquests of Alexander the Great and the Greek diaspora of the fourth century B.C., when the golden image of Periclean Athens was first exported to a wider world. A brilliant account of how this happened, and of the image's subsequent development, was offered a few years ago by Mr. Philip Sherrard in his introduction to an anthology of other people's writings called *The Pursuit of Greece*,[5] and as I could not possibly improve upon it I make no excuses, except to Mr. Sherrard, for briefly paraphrasing it here with a few interpolations of my own.

The world that emerged in the wake of Alexander, he says, was what is known as Hellenistic—not so much Greek as Greek-influenced. It was the world whose ruins we can trace today throughout the Near and Middle East, from Ephesus and Pergamum to Antioch and old Alexandria. These cities were commercial agglomerations, culturally rootless and imitative, and because the language of their trade and high society was Greek they sought to mould themselves in the image of fifth-century Athens. 'They adopted the language of the past, they tried to think in categories of the past, to fit their lives into the framework of a bygone, outmoded age,' producing 'glossaries of difficult poetic words, glossaries of Homer, systematic grammars, vast tomes on Attic metaphors and on comic and tragic diction'.

Immediately, inevitably and unwittingly they began to drift into cultural rigidity, obsolescence and sterility. C. P. Cavafy, the modern Greek-Alexandrian poet, for whom, alas, Mr. Sherrard's anthology does not find a place, described the process with his usual cool irony in a verse wryly entitled, *Philhellene,* and most delightfully translated here by Rae Dalven:

> See that the engraving is artistic.
> The expression serious and stately.
> The crown had better be rather narrow;
> I do not like those broad Parthian ones.
> The inscription, as usual, in Greek;
> not exaggerated, not pompous—
> lest the proconsul who is always poking about
> and reporting to Rome misconstrue it—
> but nonetheless of course dignified.
> Something very special on the other side;
> some good-looking discus thrower in his prime.
> Above all I charge you to see to it
> (Sithaspes, in God's name, let this not be forgotten)
> that after the words King and Savior,
> there be engraved in elegant letters, Philhellene.
> Now don't try your clever sallies on me,
> your 'Where are the Greeks?' and 'Where is
> anything Greek behind Zagros here, beyond Phraata?'
> Since so many others more barbarous than we
> write it, we too shall write it.
> And finally do not forget that at times
> sophists from Syria visit us,
> and versifiers and other wiseacres.
> So we are not un-Greek, I reckon.[6]

Anyone who has visited a modern colonial or ex-colonial territory will recognize the process Cavafy describes. It is not the British in Britain, for example, who make the biggest fuss about remaining true to their glorious past, but the British in places like Rhodesia—beleaguered, as they believe, by the modern equivalent of the barbarians and standing pat upon their privileges in Royal Air Force ties. It was the same with many of the pillars of the British Raj in India, who ordered their lives in stiff, and ultimately self-defeating, imitation of those that had once been lived by their families at home, with clubs that grew steadily stuffier and hierarchies that became progressively harder as the years of nostalgia lengthened. Today there is not much more left of them than a few dwindling communities of colonels' daughters in places like Simla and Ootacamund, where they huddle over their cucumber sandwiches and lantern-slide lectures in genteel remembrance of times past. But the culture that they and their predecessors imported into India has been taken up and fossilized by some of the Indians themselves, as the Greek culture became fossilized in the cities of Asia Minor. In the halls of the Belvedere Library in Calcutta, or at a presentation of *As You Like It* at one of Delhi's private schools, it is tempting to imagine that if Britain were conquered by some foreign power tomorrow, if its libraries were destroyed and its academies closed as those of Greece were eventually by the Romans, the Franks and the Turks, the most dynamic vision of London to survive might be rooted in Bengali interpretations of the novels of Dickens and Shakespeare might never be heard again, save in the lilt of what is known as Bombay Welsh.

Roughly speaking, that is what happened to the culture of ancient Greece, after the time of Alexander. Life and literature, as Mr. Sherrard puts it, fell apart. 'Cut off from its living roots; divorced from all historical reality; set apart from the present; its gods turned into vacuous man-made effigies, effete literary fictions or devices of a dreamlike etiolated prettiness, ancient Greece became a kind of lost paradise, a great golden past in which souls too timid or trivial for anything else could find relief from the horrors and afflictions of contemporary megalopolitan life.'

So the colonial vision of ancient Greece acquired its own impetus, to be adapted and enshrined in the empire of Byzantium, partially absorbed and modified by the great Arab movement, until at last it was passed into the consciousness of western Europe through the Crusades and the Renaissance. Then, says Mr. Sherrard, came the cry of 'back to the classics' as the new humanists of the Renaissance sought a cultural basis for their revolution. They went back to them with a vengeance. Petrarch, for example, decided that literature—true literature, that is, not just your hand-me-down vernacular stuff such as any old Chaucer might produce—could only be executed in Greek or Latin. Unfortunately, they were not the classics pure and simple that the men of the Renaissance turned to, but the classics as already idealized and fossilized by the later Hellenistic world. There was, after all, nothing else left to them by then; for it was not until modern techniques of archaeology and comparative history were

developed that the life of the ancients could be envisaged in something closer to its original, less-than-flawless form.

The scholars whose job it was to cull the classics for current use
inevitably acquired vested interests in their task. They became the
privileged purveyors of an ideology to a whole new civilization, distinguished and respected men who, little by little, grew fossilized in
their turn; so that by the eighteenth century they were encased in a
sort of crystalline growth of classical learning, that was held to
represent all that was good and beautiful and true for the new,
European world. That it was also a potent source of pecuniary
reward may not have been unimportant, either. As a certain Oxford
divine, the Reverend Thomas Gaisford, reminded his university
flock in a Christmas Day sermon well over a century ago, 'the study
of Greek literature . . . not only elevates above the vulgar herd, but
leads not infrequently to positions of considerable emolument'.[7]

It was through such classical eyes, by now so elevated above the
vulgar herd that they might as well have been made of glass, that
modern Greece was measured when it began to impinge on western
consciousness and western consciences, as its people struggled to
free themselves from the declining empire of the Turks. To the classical legend of perfection then was added the romantic vision of freedom, of which Lord Byron was destined to become the symbol. A
sort of archetypal, aristocratic hippy, with a handsome profile and
a famous club-foot as well as a genius with the English language,
Byron in Greece caught the imagination of western Europe just when
its young intellectuals and gentlemen were beginning to break out
again after the restrictions imposed by the Napoleonic wars. His
death at Missolonghi must have been a godsend to the orthodox
philhellenes, not only because it evoked much sympathy for their
cause, but also because it removed a potential scourge, for he was
never one to tolerate their pretentious excesses. Pressed by a friend
to visit antique sites in Thrace he is reported to have answered with
a snort, 'Do I look like one of those emasculated fogies? Let's have
a swim. I detest antiquarian twaddle!'[8] He does not seem to have had
many illusions about what sort of Greece he might have been fighting
for, apparently liking the Greeks for what they were rather than for
what he thought they should have been. Most of his contemporaries,
on the other hand, loved the Greeks less for themselves than for their
imagined ancestors—and in this respect, as that redoubtable historian H. A. L. Fisher wrote, 'the gentry of England' were in the van.
'English nationalism they enjoyed. Irish nationalism they had sup-

pressed, Indian nationalism was in a distant future. Education made them philhellenes, public life made them parliamentarians, their sympathies as sportsmen went out to a small nation struggling to be free. . . . No-one stopped to ask how much of that ancient Hellas, which young men were taught to admire in the halls of Oxford and Cambridge, still survived in the herdsmen, the brigands and the sea pirates of Greece and its islands.'[9] As far as they were concerned, the romantic vision of freedom was the classical legend in new guise: the cradle of democracy, Periclean Athens itself, seemed about to be reborn. Shelley's poetic drama, *Hellas*, as Mr. Sherrard points out, was the perfect expression of this new view. 'We are all Greeks,' says Shelley in his preface, with an enthusiastic prevision of that later, anonymous copy-writer who cried, 'You Were Born In Greece'— 'We are all Greeks, and the modern Greek is the descendant of those glorious beings whom the imagination almost refuses to figure to itself as belonging to our kind. . . .' Now, with these descendants fighting for their freedom again after centuries of imprisonment, darkness and despair, a great new light was about to burst upon the world:

> *The world's great age begins anew,*
> *The golden years return,*
> *The earth doth like a snake renew*
> *Her winter weeds outworn;*
> *Heaven smiles, and faiths and empires gleam,*
> *Like wrecks of a dissolving dream.*

> *Another Athens shall arise,*
> *And to remoter time*
> *Bequeath, like sunset to the skies,*
> *The splendour of its prime;*
> *And leave, if nought so bright may live,*
> *All earth can take and Heaven can give. . . .*

Poor Shelley. Impossible to read this now, surely, without a twinge of sadness on his behalf, that such exalted expectations should have been so totally falsified. Yet how could it have been otherwise? For while on one side there was what Mr. Sherrard calls the 'legend-wrapped Greek', on the other there was the awful reality of a man who was 'conspicuously lacking in those virtues and features with which classical legend had entrusted the ancient Greek. He wasn't rational. He wasn't enlightened. He knew little of his ancestors and cared less for their monuments.' Even worse, he was a victim of the obscurantism of his oriental religion—that Eastern Orthodox version of Christianity which, in the view of the most enlightened gentlemen of the western world, had inspired all the dark barbarities of Byzantium. How 'mischievous and contemptible' the industrious Gibbon had declared, scribbling out the story of the Roman Empire's *Decline and Fall,* were those 'ambitious and fanatic' eastern monks.[10]

So hideous a reality might have killed stone dead a weaker legend, but so powerful was the combination of the classical myth and the romantic vision that together they not only survived but even began to improve upon the reality by two contradictory devices. The first was intellectual, and consisted of assuming that the Greeks who were now revealed to a breathless world in all their poverty, ignorance and discord were not really Greeks at all. They might be Slavs, mongrels or what-not, but they were not and—for the sake of all that was divine in the ancient legend and all that was noble about the fight for freedom—could not be 'true' Greeks. Only the ancients had the right to that name. The second device was more practical, and highly appropriate to western Europe's growing opinion of itself as the torch-bearer of civilization for the world. It was to assume that if only these people could be exposed to the true light again they would, after all, recapture the virtues of the ancients—from which it was only a short step to actually imposing upon them the standards and attitudes of the classical world, as currently re-interpreted in the West. Thus, after the Great Powers of Europe—especially Britain, France and Russia—had been compelled reluctantly to support the Greek liberation struggle for reasons of state, they much more ardently helped to saddle the new Greece with men and institutions that had little connexion with contemporary Greek reality. Western philhellenes, with Shelley-an enthusiasm, espoused the dream of the new Athens, and exiled Greeks, themselves long converted to western ways, came home to show their erstwhile countrymen how to run their affairs in a properly civilized fashion worthy of 'true' Greeks. One of these in particular, a schoolmaster from Smyrna called Adamantios Korais who spent most of his life in Paris, was responsible for what must rate as one of the most successful and at the same time disastrous pieces of practical philhellenism ever perpetrated. He it was who, at the end of the eighteenth century, invented a new Greek language in the image of the old and thereby hung a dreadful cross of pretension around the neck of the emerging state. The point of the exercise was to re-introduce the benighted Greek peasants to their own history—by which Korais, of course, meant classical history as passed through the ossifying centuries of scholarship and preservation. Realizing that the modern Greek tongue offered little access to the works of Homer, Plato or Sophocles, and contemptuous of its capacity to render them in its own way, he created a language somewhere between the two which might make them 'understandable' without being less 'respectable'. This was *katharevousa*, the 'pure' language, which later became and has remained the official tongue of modern Greece. Its adoption was a triumph of classical philhellenism over common sense, of Cavafy's 'serious and stately' image over reality; and as we have already noted, it has not ceased to be a divisive and stultifying force in the contemporary Greek state. No wonder that no less an authority than Sir Steven Runciman has latterly described Korais as 'an evil genius'.[11]

At the time of modern Greece's birth, however, such problems were scarcely foreseen. Indeed, in the face of all this passionate worship from afar, there were many in the new state itself who felt obliged and even eager to assume as much as possible of the character other people sought so hard to find among them. Instead of forging their own account of the past or their own vision of the future, they were persuaded to see their history through the eyes of others and to chart their tomorrows in foreign paths. They not only adopted a neo-classical language for their new government, but erected neo-classical buildings in their new towns—those of the Athens University and Academy still dominate the centre of that city—and strove to emulate their classical ancestors in the practice of a supposed democracy with whose ways they were painfully ill-acquainted. In general, especially as far as their educated men were concerned, they played pupil to all the hoary-headed schoolmasters of the western world, so that while one side was flattered by its apparent influence and authority, the other was equally delighted by the attention it received.

For both sides this relationship was to be a snare and a delusion, as the last century and a half have often demonstrated; yet so far neither has been able to reject the assumptions on which it was based. In spite of recent social and political changes in the West, which have combined with new academic studies to revise many of the old assessments of Greek history, the classical-romantic legend still provides the prism through which modern Greece is most commonly, if unconsciously, viewed by western minds. Next to the Greek beaches and Greek sunshine it is still what sells Greece in the burgeoning tourist markets of the world, as the Greek National Tourist

D

Organization is happily aware. It would be a strange travel writer in
the Sunday supplements who did not make his ritual bow to the Parthenon or Delphi—*en route*, of course, to 'getting away from it all'
in some miraculously simple and elegantly whitewashed Aegaean
island room. Nor is it altogether irrelevant, I fancy, that 19th April
is still marked every year in England by the insertion of the following
advertisement in the 'In Memoriam' column of *The Times*:

> 'BYRON—George Gordon Noel Lord Byron, died nobly for
> Greece, at Missolonghi, April 19, 1824.
>
> > "*When Love who sent forgot to save
> > The young, the beautiful, the brave.*"
> >
> > (From "The Bride of Abydos")
>
> Sir Walter Scott, speaking of his death, said:
> "It is as if the sun had gone out." '

What other long-dead poet inspires such strange devotion?

But in any case western culture generally is so over-weighted by
now with classical and romantic references to Greek virtue that any
other view of Greece has a hard time surviving in the wine-dark
sea of antique allusion—and illusion—in our minds. Browsing
through the latest edition of *The Oxford Dictionary of Quotations*
recently, for example, I discovered thirty-three index entries under
'Greek' or 'Greeks', another fourteen for 'Greece', twelve for
'Athens' or 'Athenians', two for 'Hellas' and one for 'Hellenism'—
sixty-two entries in all, nearly every one of which refers directly or
indirectly, and usually in admiring terms, to ancient Greece. Among
others, they involve many of the major poets of the English language,
including Matthew Arnold, Robert Bridges, Robert Browning,
Byron, Dr. Johnson, Ben Jonson, Keats, Poe, Pope, Shelley and
Swinburne. There is even a special 'Greek Index' with 141 entries in
classical Greek; and no doubt there is another, and still greater,
multitude of quotations in the volume whose obeisance to the classical legend is just as direct but less easily discoverable because they
are indexed under other headings. Yet, to take an obvious comparison, under the headings 'Byzantium' and 'Constantinople' there are
but four entries and under 'Byzantine' there are none at all. Thus, for
a thousand years of Greek life from the founding of the city of Constantine to its capture by the Turks, when much of the modern
character of Greece was formed, we can probably assume there are

not more than half a dozen references in the dictionary to compare with a minimum of 200 inspired in some way by the preceding classical period.

I admit this is a rough and ready measure, and as quotations take some time to become sufficiently established for entry in a dictionary it is bound to be slightly out of date.[12] Current writing about Greece in English certainly shows a far stronger interest in Byzantium than before, and there are several recent books about modern Greek affairs that give due weight to the non-classical heritage. But even now, especially among the picture books and guide-books with which our anonymous reviewer in the *Times Literary Supplement* had such fun, encomiums of the classical past are still the standard product; while in the mass media of newspapers, magazines and television, an inevitable tendency to think in clichés and write in shorthand phrases has probably helped to disseminate the old stereotypes to a wider audience than ever, especially in the political field. All in all, therefore, it seems fair to say that the superimposed visions of ancient Greece as 'the cradle of democracy' and of modern Greeks as the first people to fight for their freedom from colonial oppression, with the help of Byron and all that, are still subliminally embedded in many western minds as the unarguable basic data of Greek experience, by which all else in Greece today should be measured.

In Greece itself, however, the situation has always been more complex, for while Greece's foreign friends began by believing 150 years ago that they could help to re-create a new Athens, an increasing number of Greeks were emboldened by their sympathy to pursue the ghost of the old Byzantium. As the nineteenth century proceeded, the two concepts became increasingly entangled in what was known to the Greeks as the *Megali Idea*, the Great Idea, of recovering Constantinople and restoring a Greek Christian empire in the lands so long occupied by the Turks. In this new kind of nationalist expansionism Hellenism and Orthodoxy were not seen by the Greeks as opposed to each other, as most westerners, in their innocence, believed. On the contrary, they were assumed for the purposes of political argument to complement each other as expressions of the national character. Inflated talk of the 'Hellenic-Christian tradition' swiftly crept into the Greek vocabulary and, to quote Sir Steven Runciman again, the Greeks once more saw themselves as 'a Chosen People'.[13] In this way the classical notion of Supergreek resulted in a perilous mutual misunderstanding, with the Periclean rhetoric echoing down the centuries through the mouths of Greece's western friends to underwrite a programme of modern Greek aggrandizement of whose true and more oriental sources most of those friends profoundly disapproved.

One result of this misunderstanding was the catastrophe at Smyrna in 1922 when the Greek dream of a revived Byzantium ended in the expulsion of over a million Greeks from Asia Minor by the Turks—and Greece's western friends declined to come to her rescue. Yet salutary as that was for both sides, many of their mutual misapprehensions survived. In western minds the classical-romantic image remained the commonest measure of Greek affairs, while in Greece itself the dual—and far more complex—tradition of Hellenism and Orthodoxy continued to be held aloft by many as the true light of modern nationalism. Between the two the figure of Supergreek, in one guise or another, continued marvellously to prosper. General Metaxas, in his dictatorship of the 1930's, frequently proclaimed his high-minded attachment to 'Hellenic-Christian' ideals of national destiny; and in the Cyprus crisis that rumbled so ominously from 1950 onwards similar invocations always fuelled the passionate Greek cause. Most notably, the colonels of the 1967 *coup d'état* produced Supergreek at once from their propaganda box in his Hellenic-Christian costume. All Greeks, they proclaimed, echoing General Metaxas, must be worthy of their 3,000-year-old history. All Greeks must be honest, efficient, hard-working and good Europeans, true descendants of their classical forefathers, devoted upholders of Christian ideals and a good deal more besides. Immorality and corruption must be eschewed for they were un-Greek—and to emphasize the point, writers who dared to mention classical pederasty were threatened with retribution as 'revolting traitors against the National Heritage'.[14] Yet again, apparently, all Greece was to be remade in the image of a visionary past—with schoolteachers, in particular, becoming 'the guardians of the sacred depository of our national traditions' who must 'guide our youth towards the eternal values of our Hellenic-Christian civilization'.[15] The Greek Foreign Ministry even replied to western criticism of the new dictatorship by directly invoking the West's own image of Greece: 'Let it not be forgotten', an official release proclaimed, 'that this people has been for 3,000 years the one that taught the world what is democracy; who defended since the dawn of history on the mountains or seas of this small land, western civilization and eternal values. . . .'[16] So don't, they implied, lecture *us* about democracy.

Opponents of the colonels, on the other hand, were using the same material to do just that, both inside and outside Greece, exploiting Supergreek's classical-romantic persona to justify their fight in the eternal cause of Greek democracy and freedom. Wreaths were laid ostentatiously at the foot of Byron's statue in Athens. The speech of Pericles to the Athenians was recalled; and all over the western world solemn references to the cradle of democracy appeared afresh in the pronouncements of liberal politicians and leader-writers, peering with eager narcissism into the dream-like past for evidence to use against the current nastiness. There was, of course, much about the new military regime in Greece that was objectionable, but what was revealing was not the fact of the objections so much as their volume and their premises. That Greece was in some way regarded as a very special case was immediately apparent. At its first meeting after the *coup d'état* the Council of Europe—from which Greece was later to be obliged to withdraw in disgrace—was assured of that fact by one Herr Bruno Bitterman, a socialist deputy from Austria who declared that 'the members owed it to the Greek people, who gave the world the organization of the democratic state which was today banished from their country, to do everything to help them'.[17] Only one delegate to that meeting, the Marchese d'Aprigliano, a distinguished Italian opponent of Fascism, was sufficiently detached from the general emotion to point out that this was not the first time the Council had been faced with a military dictatorship in a member-nation. Turkey, he reminded his colleagues, had suffered a far bloodier *coup d'état* only a few years before, when half the elected cabinet had been stood on kitchen chairs and hanged, but nobody had bothered much about that. He might as well have saved his breath. To those who cherished the classical-romantic legend dictatorship was not merely undesirable but actually un-Greek; and that, it almost seemed, was the greater sin of the two. One group of letter-writers to *The Times* even quoted that Greek tourist advertising whose narcissism I have already dwelt upon, calling attention in tones of the highest moral rectitude to 'the Greek tragedy, with its peculiar and shocking significance for us as Europeans', and going on to say: 'As the publicity of Olympic Airlines [*sic*] continues to remind us: "You were born in Greece." They mean democracy. . . .' Such Shelleyan echoes reverberated everywhere. A distinguished American newspaper editor visiting Athens a year or so after the *coup d'état* declared to a colleague of mine that he felt so strongly about the offence of dictatorship in Greece that he could not climb the Acropolis and set foot in the Parthenon until the colonels were removed from power. I wonder

if *he* knew how the Parthenon was paid for? Even those who sought
to qualify such innocent reactions to the latest in the long (but
apparently forgotten) line of Greek dictatorships found it prudent to
make obeisance first to the exclusively democratic western image. 'I
speak with some feeling on this,' said the British Foreign Secretary,
Mr. Michael Stewart, in a characteristic passage in the House of
Commons in 1970, 'because I think all of us feel a sense of distress
that it should be Greece of all countries, with her dazzling history,
who is estranged from the democratic countries of Europe. (Cheers.)
It gives to many of us a sense of deep distress that Greece should be
estranged from European countries who owe so much to her heritage. . . .' Those who chose to omit such propitiatory offerings and
submitted instead some account of the characteristic aspects of
Greek history that might help to explain the country's latest misfortune, were often peremptorily howled down.[18] The dream was
dead, long live the dream!

Thus, in rich confusion, the image of Supergreek has gone marching on. From Pericles to Papadopoulos he bestrides the Greek stage,
sometimes 'Hellenic' and 'free', sometimes 'Christian' and 'disciplined', often all four at once and always worthy, wise, noble and enlightened, a peerless and indestructible example for us all. Like
Cavafy's philhellenes, the Greeks and the western world between
them have done their work well. They have made sure that the
'engraving is artistic, the expression serious and stately', and we have
all been immensely impressed. So much so that Greeks in real life
nowadays seem to me to be in an impossible position. They are like
a crowd of ordinary human beings in one of those fairground halls
of mirrors where every image is distorted—but with this difference:
that instead of seeing themselves reflected as the rest of us do, too fat
or too thin, too tall or too short, or otherwise risibly misshapen, they
look out of all-too-human eyes and see only the image of a god. It
is a burden that no people should ever have had to bear.

Chapter 3

TERRITORIAL TENSIONS

*Greece . . . though a small country, is in
reality many Greeces.*
(GEORGE SEFERIS)

In Greece the facts of physical geography stage a permanent dialectic.
East and west, north and south, land and sea, mountain and valley
—the tortured skeleton of rock that we call Greece is torn between
many worlds. It is the end of Europe as well as its beginning, and
Athens is that continent's last as well as its first port of call. Corfu
may seem to the western visitor cosily familiar because it is more
than half-Italian, with its lakes and pine forests and religious paintings in the westernized style bred of the Renaissance. But Crete has
none of these soothing western attributes, in spite of centuries of
Venetian rule. It reaches farther south than Gibraltar and as far east
as Istanbul, and the particularly angular melancholia of its icons and
chapel frescoes speaks of other, non-western worlds. Sometimes, in
one of the arid coves of Crete's southern shore, where the tiny cubes
of the peasant houses and the feathery branches of the tamarisk trees
are scattered with a terrible sparseness among the rocks, you might
think you were already upon the desert coast of Africa. More often,
as nearly anywhere else in Greece, you can sense the approach of
Asia in the wailing quarter-tones of the *bouzouki* music, in the pun-
gent smell of lamb's meat roasting over charcoal, in the water pipes
and minarets of Islam left over from Turkish rule. Fashionable
Greeks who can afford to travel for pleasure still unconsciously
acknowledge their eastern heritage by saying they are off to 'Europe'
when they visit Rome, Paris or London; and although Her Britannic
Majesty's Ambassador in Athens nowadays does not care to pub-
licize the fact, one of the principal members of his staff, whose particular job it is to follow the intricacies of Athenian politics, still enjoys
the title of Oriental Secretary, like his counterparts in many a less
equivocally eastern capital.

North and south as well as east and west contend for the body and soul of Greece. In these days of ardent, pale-faced sun worship it is too easy for someone from more northern latitudes to think of Greece as simply a Mediterranean country of eternal summer. The truth is that it is just as much a Balkan country of far more wintry aspect, with a long-embattled, northern frontier to hold against the millennial onslaughts and infiltrations of the Slav. The blue skies and purple seas of the travel posters dominate the popular foreign image of Greece now because most people only go there in spring and summer to enjoy those virtues. Seeing, as we all do, only what they want to see, such visitors discover Greece in only one mood, with its southern seashores embalmed in gentleness, offering a jasmine-scented dream of whitewashed cottages and crystal clear water, marred only by an occasional attack of diarrhoea. But this is not only a far cry from the ten-foot snowdrifts of winter on the Albanian frontier; it is a false picture of Greece's Mediterranean life as well. There is nothing like a January passage upon Homer's all-too-wine-dark sea to explode the notion that the sun always shines in the Greek islands. To arrive in Mykonos from Piraeus in the off-season, with the rain driving horizontally across the harbour against the shutters of deserted cafés and the famous postcard windmills furled and shuddering in the gale, like sheep on a Scottish moor, is to say farewell to a few common illusions about Greece.

The contrasts and challenges of Greek geography are witnessed also in the character of the land itself, which seems more divided than united, and threatens more conflict than peace. The balmy summer vision is belied every time you lift your eyes to the hills—and they are never very far away in Greece. Indeed, all the earth's natural elements—sea, sky, lowland and mountain—are so intimately contrasted and so starkly opposed in Greece that they acquire a curiously symbolic, theatrical quality as if they were intended more to make some god-like statement of the absolutes than to support mere human life.

Many writers have remarked on this, and although I have sometimes felt they were simply peddling another version of the old Greek dream, I must confess that I have experienced it several times myself. I think particularly of Crete, where by some histrionic alchemy, both the scenery and the people seem to have sharpened all the ordinary Greek contradictions into a more than usually dramatic polarity. There is, for instance, behind the crumbling Venetian port of Khania, the Cretan capital, a valley of extraordinary lushness and tranquillity, where the water runs from spring to aqueduct and from aqueduct to river in a tinkling idyll of rural contentment and orange groves wrap the road in a perfumed cloak of green. At the head of the valley a village stands on a shelf—a scatter of whitewash above the glittering green groves. There are two little Byzantine chapels on its flanks, and a café or two in the middle where the men can gather for a talk under the vines. No more peaceful place could be imagined in the world. Yet right above it is the stony mass of the White Mountains, as haggard and menacing as death. No gradual ascent separates the two, no mist of distance or of atmosphere softens the contrast. On the contrary, the slopes are fiercely steep and, especially in the dazzling air of spring-time, when perspectives are foreshortened and outlines clarified as though with a telephoto lens, the valley and the mountain seem superimposed upon each other in almost unnatural symbolism. The valley is the essence of all valleys that ever were, the mountain is the distillation of all mountains. In such surroundings it is possible to believe that Greece's physical structure provides a fitting backdrop, and even a natural source, for profound philosophy and sublime drama. 'Is it the climate? Is it the race? I can't tell,' says the Greek poet, George Seferis. 'I believe it's really the light. There must surely be something about the light that makes us what we are. . . . An idea becomes an object with surprising ease. It seems to become all but physically incarnated in the web of the sun. On the other hand, at times you cannot discern whether the mountain opposite is a stone or a gesture.'[1]

But whichever it may seem to be in the mind's eye, the Greek mountain is ever-present as a formidable physical obstacle—a major cause of the country's poverty and disunity. Only one-sixth of Greece's surface is level enough to be easily cultivated. Two-thirds are too mountainous or rocky for anything but the hardiest of sheep and goats.

Traditionally the mountains may be the home of the gods, but that is probably because mere humans find them so forbidding. Generally they are empty except for a few monks and summer shepherds—who are often one and the same—yet because they stand grey guard over every precious nook of lowland green they are always present in the Greek mind. They rise out of the sea in cruel palisades and scatter the coasts with jagged offspring to trap unwary sailors; and their spiny heights, mingling with the sea's long arms, divide the inhabited lowlands into a thousand impoverished fragments. No country in Europe is more savagely splintered. Of more than 6,000 separate communities in Greece only a handful can be counted as more than overgrown villages or modest market towns, and only three contain substantially more than 100,000 people. Between them, however, these three have grown in recent decades to a position of extraordinary dominance. Athens, Salonika and Patras now account not only for nearly 70 per cent of all Greek townspeople, but also for a third of the entire population of the country, with Athens alone containing one-fourth. Compared, say, to London which has in or about it something like a fifth of Britain's population, this Athenian dominance may not seem so remarkable. But Britain is a highly industrialized country and, although London dwarfs the other cities in sheer size, there are many other towns, cities and conurbations of national or regional consequence in which most of the other four-fifths of Britain's people live. Greece, on the other hand, is still basically a peasant country; and between the overbearing mushroom of Athens and the myriads of tiny, infertile spores of settlement scattered over the rest of the country there is little to interpose but the modest growth of Salonika and Patras. Comparing like with like— Greece, say, with other Balkan countries—this provides a pattern of urban domination and rural fragmentation far beyond the norm. Belgrade, for example, has scarcely 15 per cent of the urban population of Yugoslavia and not five per cent of the country's total population. Sofia has barely 30 per cent of Bulgaria's urban population and 10 per cent of the whole. Greece today is both splintered and consolidated to a far greater degree than either; and because—as we shall see later—this is a specifically twentieth-century phenomenon, it has posed immense new social and economic problems in Greece.

The fact that Athens has grown so swiftly, however, both reflects and emphasizes all the more the abiding handicaps of the traditional rural communities in which the vast majority of Greek city-dwellers, including most Athenians, still have their roots. Until now, the comparative physical isolation of these communities from each other and the extreme poverty of most of their land have hindered both strong central administration and effective economic growth. Instead, physical separation has promoted human separatism and uncompromising stones have produced uncompromising minds. So the true pattern of Balkan instability is endemic in Greece. Passionate local loyalties and rampant individualism have led sometimes to outright war and often to banditry; and they have only been modified, or occasionally suppressed, by the shared sense among Greeks of their superiority to all other people and a correspondingly deep resentment of foreign rule. The city states of classical Greece, based on the minute divisions of the Greek landscape, displayed a passion for mutual rivalry and internecine violence that often led to their downfall or decay. Unity visited them rarely and fleetingly: once in the Trojan War, again during the invasions of the Persians, when the Spartans protected Athens as well as themselves by their stand at Thermopylae, and a third and last time under Philip of Macedon and his son, Alexander, who took advantage of the disastrous effects of the Peloponnesian War to seize control of most of the peninsula. Otherwise the city states lived in such a state of atomistic strife, both external and internal, that the wonder is their inhabitants found the reserves of energy and talent to achieve as much in the way of art and science as they did. Their quarrels have had many subsequent parallels. Byzantium was more than once racked by civil war as well as by recurrent religious schisms. The fierce rivalries of the Greek leaders in their struggle for independence from the Turks almost brought their cause to disaster; while in the Civil War of the 1940's the Greeks killed many more of each other than the Germans did in four years of military conquest and occupation.

Athens and Salonika, also, have always in modern times represented fierce rival trends in Greece—the first legitimate and on the whole conservative, the second revolutionary and on the whole radical—as during the First World War when Greece was actually split down the middle between the monarchist, pro-German regime of King Constantine in Athens and the republican, pro-Allied coalition of Eleftherios Venizelos in Salonika. On a smaller but no less revealing scale, Mr. Patrick Leigh Fermor has vividly described the characteristic warfare that was endemic not too long ago in the stony, inhospitable peninsula of the Mani, where rival barons in the same village erected fortified tower houses from which they bombarded each other, sometimes at point-blank range, to the terror of the rest of the population.[2] The tower houses are still there, rearing out of the rocky moonscape in bunches, like broken teeth; and although the fighting has ceased, the passions on which it flourished have not. In 1966 the town of Kalamata at the head of the Mani and the village of Kalavryta on the other side of the Peloponnese conducted such a spirited battle in Parliament and the press over their rival claims to have been the first place in Greece to win their freedom from the Turks, a century and a half before, that they almost brought down the government in their mutual hostility.[3] It was a nice, and characteristic, demonstration of the ancient Greek art of threatening to destroy Greece itself by being all-too-fiercely Greek.

If the harsh and divisive Greek landscape has helped to make national unity the exception rather than the rule, it has also been the prime cause of the permanent Greek diaspora that has become in modern times both a physical and a psychological burden upon the nation's development.

Poverty uproots the Greeks and the sea carries them away. With persistent warfare and banditry at home, with only poor soil and thin crops to nourish an exiguous life, overseas trade and exploitation have always been the best guarantee of Greek survival; and because the Greek earth itself is so desperately fragmented, the sea has always been the natural mode of Greek movement. Most of Greece has to be a seaborne country, for its multitude of gulfs and numberless islands give it a coastline five times longer than that of France for a land area less than a quarter of France's size. Even in the northern mountains, where the sea may be as much as forty or fifty miles distant, it is often easier to travel to the nearest beach or fishing port than to cross the surrounding peaks and watersheds to reach a village only five miles away as the crow flies on the other side of the range. The Greeks, therefore, are an outward-looking people by force of circumstance—which may well account for their famous curiosity about the lives of others. It is certainly no accident that all their sizeable modern towns are seaports (for Athens with Piraeus is essentially that) nor that one of the most intelligible pronouncements of the Delphic Oracle to have been preserved for posterity is the one that advised the ancient Greeks to go forth and colonize other lands. They did—and many of both their greatest men and their greatest legends are associated with their consequent wanderings. Ulysses, called Odysseus by the Greeks, whose twenty years of travelling in the pages of Homer have turned his name into a universal noun for a spiritual as well as a bodily voyage through life; Jason and the Argonauts in search of the Golden Fleece; Alexander, marching into Asia and leaving as his legacy a whole new world; these are the archetypal Greek heroes. Others, lesser-known, followed their example. As early as the eighth century B.C. Greek communities were scattered from one end of the Mediterranean to the other. Five hundred years later, many more Greeks trod in the hurried footsteps of Alexander and took their language and ambitions on to India even after he had turned back. 'They came as wandering philosophers and seaborne traders, as artists and ambassadors, as administrators and princes. They founded kingdoms and cities, and the list of Greek kings and queens who reigned in India and on its borders is as long as the list of kings and queens who have reigned in England since the Norman Conquest.'⁴

The words will serve as the epitaph of Greeks nearly everywhere in the old Eurasian world of 2,000 years or more ago, and they could almost as well be applied to Greeks in the present day. There may not be many Greek princes left around the world, except in Europe's dwindling royal families, but there are certainly plenty of Greek administrators, philosophers, artists and traders. In Mr. Spiro Agnew, Greek-Americans have seen one of their number elected to the Vice-Presidency of the United States. In such figures as Madame Callas and Dmitri Mitropoulos Greek exiles have contributed powerfully to the contemporary international world of the arts. And who does not recognize Messrs. Onassis, Niarchos, Livanos and the rest of the Greek shipping fraternity as among the greatest, or at any rate the wealthiest, of the seaborne traders of our day? Just as in ancient times, too, the big names have been accompanied by a flood of unknown emigrants. Greeks in America, Australia, Canada and South Africa afford a substantial leavening of the old Anglo-Saxon immigrant stock. Tens of thousands of Greeks have helped to keep labour troubles away from the booming factories of West Germany since the 1950's. In Britain the Greeks of Cyprus have joined Italians, Indians and Chinese in recent years in transforming British habits by opening their little greengrocery shops on Sundays, and by refusing to close their coffee and kebab houses until long past what used to be the dead hour of midnight. The dispersal is perennial and has never been wholly arrested—an everlasting haemorrhage of the life blood of the highlands and islands that are Greece.

The significance of this outflow is manifold. As well as robbing Greece of many of its best minds and men, it has contributed greatly to that curious confusion of identity that is one of the characteristic afflictions of modern Greece, by rendering ordinary territorial definitions of the nation insufficient to satisfy Greek minds. When and where, we may ask ourselves, is a Greek not a Greek? The answer is practically never; not in ancient times, when Greeks ruled for twenty generations in northern India and still were Greeks in every way, nor in modern times when a Greek may leave his homeland as a child and spend his entire life elsewhere without sacrificing one jot of his Greek-ness. The sense of exile, although deeply embedded in the collective psyche of the Greeks, remains only partial. Indeed, according to a recent Greek writer, the word for it is strictly untranslatable. 'It is *xenitia*, which is not exactly exile because it can be self-imposed and not estrangement because there is no spiritual estrangement. *Xenitia* is simply the loss of the native land.'[5] It is not the loss of the nation, which Greeks carry with them for ever in their unshakable conviction that to be Greek is a superior state of being. It is true, of course, that most people, whether individually or in groups, exhibit some similar conviction because a touch of it is necessary to sheer survival. But the Greeks, being a people who have survived more vicissitudes than most, also seem to feel more strongly than most the sense of being special—or perhaps it is because they feel it so acutely that they have managed to survive their many chapters of calamity. Certainly for all their many dispersals around the world, they remain as a rule among the least assimilable of immigrants. Chameleon-like, they adapt to any environment, but they rarely disappear. Their government gives legal recognition to this tenacious sense of Greekness by decreeing that a Greek need never cease to be a Greek even unto an infinity of generations, so long as he is christened in the Greek church and registered with an appropriate official of the Greek state. Where he is born or where he lives, what passport he may hold or what foreign causes he may serve are immaterial. Like a Jew who 'returns' to Israel from anywhere in the world, even after a lapse of 2,000 years, a Greek of whatever nationality on paper assumes automatically all the privileges and responsibilities of a Greek citizen whenever he sets foot again in Greece. There are even cases on record of respectable Americans of Greek extraction being arrested as they entered Athens airport on holiday because they had never done their 'national' service in the Greek armed forces;[6] and among genuine Greek exiles it is remarkable how many return in old age to their native villages from half a century in America, Australia or wherever and promptly appear to forget—as I have often discovered—all but the barest scraps of any language but Greek, as if their sojourn abroad had been no more than a long irrelevance in their real Greek existence. This stubborn hold on their communal identity has combined with the dispersals of three millenniums around the eastern Mediterranean to bring the Greeks perennially into conflict with their neighbours, especially in modern times, when the new idea of 'Greece' as a nation-state has led directly to irredentism and war on all of Greece's frontiers in the inescapable but unattainable aim of trying to unite all Greeks under one national flag.

When this aim took its most grandiose form in the Great Idea, born out of a confusion of ideal Hellenism with atavistic Byzantinism, it led to a calamitous dissipation of Greek energy and spirit among the inextricable muddle of peoples, cultures and interests in the Near East. The muddle arose equally from the multiplicity of physical divisions in Balkan and Mediterranean geography and from the traditionally multi-national structure of the two great empires, Byzantine and Ottoman, that had ruled in the Near East for the previous 1,500 years. These eastern empires were essentially religious, both in their overall inspiration and their internal divisions. What mattered most among their inhabitants was whether a man was a Christian, a Muslim or a Jew, and next to that which branch or sect of these communities he belonged to. Only thirdly did the ethnic or linguistic divisions seem important—that is those communities whose members enjoyed a common language with all the shared historical experience that implied. But the western idea of nationalism that the Greeks were the first to acquire in the Near East reversed this order of priorities, making ethnic or linguistic identity the basis of political consciousness and proclaiming, in the words of a distinguished historian of the Near East, that 'every state should contain only one nation and the whole of a nation should be included in a single state'.[7] With the mingling of communities that had taken place in the old religious empires this was nowhere easy to accomplish in the Near East. In the Balkans, especially, where the splintered terrain multiplied the communal and ethnic distinctions, it was impossible without fierce and prolonged dispute.

When the national ambition of the Greeks was extended from the rump of the Peloponnese, which formed the first independent state of Greece, to embrace not only the neighbouring Greek-speaking areas immediately to the north, but also the ancient Greek diaspora across the sea in Anatolia, it seemed, as a British observer remarked, that a country with 'the dimensions of Switzerland' also enjoyed 'the appetite of Russia'—a situation that could not fail to provoke hostility all round.[8] Whether Christian or Muslim, the other communities with which the Greeks were interspersed were not prepared to submit to a revived Christian empire that would be administered on expressly Greek national lines. Thus the Great Idea led directly to war with the Christian Serbs and Bulgars as well as with the Muslim Turks, and contributed to the fearful ramifications of the Macedonian question, in which no less than four separate linguistic groups were in mutual opposition. It encouraged the hostile nationalist movement of the Young Turks, who realistically eschewed the Greek ambition of trying to transform a new state into the semblance of an old empire and sought instead to create a modern nation out of the remains of an empire that had failed; and although the Great Idea was supported by Russia to begin with, as a means of weakening the Ottoman Empire, it aroused Russian opposition in the longer run by conflicting not only with Moscow's own ambition to control the Turkish Straits but also with Russia's growing interest in its own great idea—Balkan pan-Slavism. Moreover, by encouraging an excessive pursuit of nationalist war and adventure which inflamed the individual *hubris* of one Greek leader after another, the Great Idea led Greece repeatedly into situations beyond her own control which compelled other, greater powers either to rescue or to abandon her—and in either case to humiliate her. In the end it led to unequivocal catastrophe, with the collapse of the Anatolian campaign against the Turks in 1922 when one-and-a-quarter million Greeks were expelled from Asia Minor, where their ancestors had lived for 2,000 years or more.

Happily, the Great Idea in its original form died with that disaster; but some of its echoes lingered on. In Cyprus, Greeks and Turks are still at loggerheads in a struggle that holds profound symbolic meaning for both sides. In the Epirus, Greeks and Albanians took until 1971 to resolve old clashes, when the military regime of Colonel Papadopoulos and the communist government of Enver Hoxha at last agreed to resume diplomatic relations between their two countries. The frontier between the two had been closed since the Civil War in Greece and a state of war had formally existed between them since 1940 not only because the Albanians had helped Mussolini's invasion of Italy, and not only because Albania had afterwards become the most unrepentant of all Greece's communist neighbours, but also because Greece had obstinately maintained a claim to southern Albania— known to the Greeks as northern Epirus—dating back more than half a century to the Balkan Wars. Even in 1971 that claim was not abandoned. Rather, it was shelved—and the Balkans being what they are it would be no surprise if, one day when tempers rise, it were dusted off again.

In Macedonia, too, old questions of identity still smoulder. The Macedonians themselves are a small and sturdy Balkan people with their own Slav dialect, a strong sense of their own importance and a long history of irredentism. With 40,000 of them inside her northern frontiers, Greece has always refused to recognize the existence of any Macedonian 'minority'. Let other Macedonians be what they will, those in Greece are officially neither more nor less than Greeks. Bulgaria, on the other hand, has traditionally claimed that all

Macedonians are really Bulgarians: a position for which scholars are said to have found some historical and linguistic justification, although none in law or contemporary politics. Yugoslavia, however, recognizes a specifically Macedonian identity within her own borders and from time to time in recent years has exploited this recognition either to counter the effects of Bulgarian claims to the Macedonian districts inside Yugoslavia or with the deliberate intent of fostering political schisms inside Greece. But as the Greek Communist Party has more than once discovered to its cost, in trying to follow the pro-Macedonian line as sometimes laid down by Moscow, one result of this Macedonian confusion has been to ensure that, to this day, any individual or group who takes up the Macedonian cause automatically sacrifices Greek support. Conversely, of course, anybody who chooses to suggest that the Macedonians do not exist is likely to receive the Greek hand of friendship.

But all these echoes of old territorial battles, menacing as they sometimes can be, fade into insignificance beside the effects of the Anatolian disaster on the very heart and soul of the Greek homeland. In general, a Greek historian has observed, these were 'even more disastrous than the fall of Constantinople and the overthrow of the Greek Empire in May 1453. The Turkish conquest of 1453 did not result in the uprooting of the Greek race from the European and Asiatic regions where it had dwelt since the dawn of history. . . . But the Anatolian disaster resembled a tidal wave. . . . It uprooted and swept all the Greeks, not to mention the Armenians who shared their fate, out of Asia Minor and eastern Thrace, where they had been settled for centuries, and deposited them across the Aegaean, never to return . . . Greece (became) a homogeneous Hellenic state, in fact more homogeneous and compact than she has ever been at any period of her previous history.'[9]

She became Hellenic, however, only in the limited, ethnic meaning of the term and homogeneous only with many qualifications and at fearful cost. The refugees from Asia Minor came 'home' to a Greece that for them had never really existed. Their Greece had been an empire of the mind, a folk ideal compounded of grand historical and cultural associations. The Greece they landed in was a small, impoverished Ruritania with neither power to help them nor room to put them. The enforced transfer of 400,000 Turks from Greece to Turkey at the same time, under an agreed 'exchange of populations' which set the seal upon the Greek defeat, did little to increase the ability of successive Greek governments to resettle the Anatolian

E

Greeks. The refugees were equivalent to a quarter of the entire population of Greece at the time. Most of them were penniless, having lost everything in their flight; yet many were more skilled and had previously enjoyed greater prosperity than the Greeks upon whom they were now so abruptly imposed. It was all the more embittering to them, therefore—farmers, merchants and professional men as many had been for generations—to find that there was nothing for it in their beloved Greece but to beg, sweep the streets, or starve. The ancient diaspora had come home to roost with a vengeance and it soon added yet more schisms to the multiple divisions of Greece. There was a new rivalry between the indigenous Greeks and their formerly exiled cousins who, resentfully, had been thrust among them. There was also a sudden and parallel deepening of what until then had been only an incipient gulf between the countryside and the capital; for it is from this moment, half a century ago, that we can date the contemporary inflation of a handful of Greek towns— especially Athens and the port of Piraeus where the majority of refugees landed and many of them stayed because there was nowhere else to go. Even now, when the second and third generations have taken over from those first, shocked arrivals, the Anatolian Greeks are still not quite assimilated. Outwardly they are indistinguishable from other Greeks, but inwardly, sometimes, their passions still seem to burn brighter than most with the forced draught of their uprooting. It is among them, inevitably, that the old Greek quarrel with the Turks has been most vigorously kept alive, and it was in their sense of displacement and injustice that communism eventually found its most fertile soil in Greece.

What has happened to other parts of the Greek diaspora in more recent years cannot be compared with the Anatolian disaster, but much of it has been unpleasant enough. As the western concept of nationalism has spread throughout the world since the Second World War, many more old Greek communities abroad have been forcibly uprooted in the name of national sovereignty. Under Turkish pressure, amid the conflict over Cyprus, two-and-a-half thousand years of Greek life in Constantinople have flickered as near as can be to an end. Even the Greek Orthodox Patriarch there, symbol as he is of 1,500 years of Greek tradition, has been compelled under Turkish law to adopt Turkish citizenship; and the number of true Greeks left in what was for so long the greatest of Greek cities probably does not now exceed four figures. In Alexandria, whose Greek-ness in modern times was as distinctive as of old, when Alexander gave the place his name and Greek scholars and craftsmen made it the most cultured city in the world, a similar fate has overtaken the Greek community. Since the middle 1950's, when President Nasser's Egyptian nationalism began to squeeze the foreigners out of Egypt, scores of thousands of Greeks have left. The ornate villas of the nineteenth-century Greek quarter are shuttered and dusty or turned into schools for Egypt's own young; and the cotton exchange where quick, Greek voices were raised at auction only a decade or so ago, has been silent since Nasser nationalized its trade. The solitary Greek traders of Africa and Asia, too, who once tended their stores in the remotest corners of those continents, have often found life sadly difficult in recent years. Fleeing in their battered motor cars from the threat of murder in the Congo, or civil war in the Sudan, or watching —as Greek friends of mine did in Aden a few years ago—the work of generations of family trading destroyed in a day or two of revolutionary robbery and arson, they have all discovered that in a world of exclusive national sovereignties there is sometimes no place for Greeks except at home. It has been a harsh discovery for a people with so long a history of emigration and so little to succour them in their homeland.

Yet paradoxically, but necessarily, and in greater numbers now than ever, Greece still drives her people out of poverty and confinement to live on their sharp wits in the far corners of the world. Greek artists in Paris, musicians in New York, shipowners in London, shopkeepers in Johannesburg, mechanics in Melbourne, factory-hands in Frankfurt, barmen in Toronto, rich or poor, they still scatter themselves around the globe because they must and still look back to Greece with pride and longing because they cannot help it. Like Greece itself, they are torn between many worlds; and because of that, perhaps, their lives often seem the most characteristically Greek of all. Born of the tensions of their barren and divided homeland, they are set squarely in the tradition of other Odysseys long ago—sad, perennial comments on the condition of a country that today, as always, compels so many who love it to leave it in order to live.

Chapter 4

THE TWO-HEADED EAGLE

In the tangled lanes of old Stamboul, just above the black and
scummy waters of the Golden Horn, a visitor blessed with luck and
perseverance—and preferably an obliging taxi-driver, too—may discover a little courtyard that is for ever Greece. It is hard to find and
disarmingly modest when you get there, hidden behind a yellow
ochre wall, with a small pantiled church on one side and a plain
stucco villa on the other. There are potted geraniums on the window
sills and straggly carnations in the little garden, just as there might
be in any village square in Greece; and on the top floor of the villa,
overlooking this familiar scene, is the spare and homely office of His
Holiness the Ecumenical Patriarch of Constantinople, first among
equals in the Orthodox Church and true inheritor and defender of
2,500 years of Greek history on or about this spot. Once, a few years
ago, I visited the current occupant of this high office and found him
to be a truly patriarchal figure. His name was Athenagoras, and for
all that he had long passed the Biblical span of years he stood immensely tall and straight and was most marvellously bearded, with
a wise and merry twinkle in his eye. He also had a decidedly orotund
way with the English language as he declaimed to me a brief history
of the Greeks in Istanbul. 'For twenty-five centuries', he boomed at
me, cheerfully, spreading his great arms wide as if to catch within
them the immensity of that span, 'we Greeks have been here in this
great city. We were the founders of Byzantium, and we are the children of Byzantium. This is our inheritance. Today *you*, my son, call
this city Istanbul. But of what do *we*, the Greeks, think when you
speak of Istanbul? Do we not think of Constantinopolis—the city
of the Emperor Constantine himself? Yes, for that and no other
is where we are; the very city of Constantine, the father of our
Church!' He gestured with a great sweep of his black robes towards

the window and the multitudinous domes and minarets of Islam that surmount Stamboul's famous skyline. 'For five centuries now,' went on the Patriarch, warming to a theme that was obviously close to his heart, 'for five centuries we have lived here with our brothers, the Turks. For five centuries we have lived with them in friendship. We have had our difficulties, but these—with God's grace—we have overcome, because our brothers have shown us much tolerance and our hearts have learned to meet. May they do so always!' It was a moving and impressive speech and when, a little later, I rose to go and the Patriarch folded me to his great chest and blessed me in a sudden suffocation of mingled robe and beard, I could almost have believed that this splendid and obviously sincere man had told me no less than the truth. Yet a different history reasserted itself almost at once, for the next day the local papers were full of the latest bloodshed between Greeks and Turks in Cyprus, and that evening I heard the other side of the Greek story from one of the few remaining members of the Patriarch's dwindling flock in Istanbul. He was a rheumy old waiter in a restaurant by the Bosphorus who recognized me as an Englishman and a likely fellow-Christian and promptly offered me his bond. He did it swiftly and surreptitiously by thrusting his hand into his shirt and pulling out a small gold crucifix. For a second he held it, trembling slightly, before my eyes. Then he pushed it back again, buttoned his shirt and mustered a wan smile. 'Christian,' he whispered; and then, with an almost imperceptible movement of his head towards the other customers, and a contemptuous curl of a stubbly upper lip, 'not like them.' An ancient and resentful voice had spoken and said all it thought there was to say.

Yet the waiter had no more told the whole story than the Patriarch about the meaning of Constantinople and the meeting of Greek and Turk. Each had offered only a selective impression and behind the two versions lay the far more complex truth that Greek Christianity has been caught for many centuries in a deep and many-faceted ambivalence, between the jealousy and betrayals of the western Christian churches and the unacceptable eastern encroachments of Islam, as well as between the demands of the Greeks as a nation and the commands of their universal faith. Symbolically this ambivalence was foreseen even before Islam emerged when, in 330, at the very moment of establishing the Eastern Roman Empire of Byzantium and espousing the Christian faith, Constantine took for his standard the imperial eagle of Rome and added a second head to it. One head for old Rome and the empire of the West, the other head for what he called the 'New Rome which is Constantinople' and the Christian empire of the East. The two-headed eagle remained the standard of Byzantium for the next thousand years and in practice if not in law it is still the emblem of the Orthodox Church. Accurately if fortuitously, it has expressed for the last sixteen centuries one of the fundamental conditions of the Greek faith and Greek life—that they have been compelled to look both east and west at once, to secular as well as to spiritual aims, with both national and universal significance.

Like so many other aspects of Greece's intricate inheritance this is not much understood in the western world, outside academic circles. By and large, we know little of Byzantium and care less; and our usual version of the fall of Constantinople to the Turks in 1453 is simply that of a great centre of western civilization being overrun by eastern barbarians. It is true, of course, that Greeks sometimes seem to see it that way themselves, like my Istanbul waiter. Certainly, they have neither forgiven nor forgotten the Turks for their presumption. Even now, few Greeks can bring themselves to speak of Constantinople as Stamboul or Istanbul—the forms into which Turkish tongues have corrupted the honoured name. To most of them, as to the Patriarch, it is still Constantinopolis, the city of Constantine—or else it is just 'the city', plain and unadorned, because it is so immediately dominant in the Greek imagination that it requires no further identification. That it has been in Turkish hands for the last 500 years inevitably has brought a widespread conscious acceptance of its loss, especially since the Anatolian disaster, but in the depths of the Greek unconscious a spectre still walks, like the ghost of Hamlet's father, crying for revenge—and inducing Greeks to seek western friends for the purpose. Yet at the same time those western friends are suspect, because although the Byzantine empire was Roman in name and theory it was in reality part Greek and part oriental, and its final conquest by the Turks was preceded by centuries of betrayal and invasion by the 'barbarians' of the West. Even when under Ottoman rule the Greeks did not forget this western treachery, frequently preferring the Sultan's favour to the uncertain friendship of western powers; and it was not until the classical myth was re-created by the West before and during the War of Independence that Greeks were accepted as 'natural' members of the western community of nations and their defence of Constantinople became in retrospect a heroic stand on behalf of western values against the oriental hordes. Thus, the real heritage of Byzantium is immensely complex; and to grasp its significance for the modern state of Greece we shall have to dis-entangle a few strands of historical truth as best we can from the nineteenth-century western fantasies in which they are still entangled. Two early strands are especially important for our purpose. Firstly, that although the Byzantine Empire was largely Greek its rise was accompanied by the decline and fall into abject poverty of most of the motherland of the Greek peninsula. Secondly, that the funda-mental East–West ambiguity of the imperial situation was built into the geography of the old world in which all the great civilizing forces tended to advance towards, break upon and retreat again from the reefs of the Levant. The rough quadrilateral bounded by the Straits of Constantinople and the Peloponnese on one side and the Fertile Crescent on the other, with Cairo and Alexandria to the south and Trebizond and the Black Sea to the north, was the focus for both the fusion and diffusion of some of the world's major cultures for well over 3,000 years—and arguably it still is. As one of the fundamental elements of this crucial region the Greeks were, therefore, born into ambivalence even in the classical 'golden age', and they have con-tinued in it down to our own time with ever-increasing complexity. The story of Byzantium and its downfall is the greatest, but by no means the only, part of that permanent Greek see-saw.

It begins with the emergence of the classical city states in peninsular Greece as the westernmost vanguards of civilization, inheriting, fusing and improving upon the earlier oriental cultures. It continues with the eclipse of the city states under Alexander and his subsequent march into farthest Asia when the Greeks in effect turned their backs upon a still barbarian West and forfeited a western destiny. In a sense, Alexauder was only taking Greek culture back where it had come from, but as we have seen already his great adventure marked the start of the classical decline, when innovation gave way to preserva-tion and the early dynamism of Athens and the other city states was dissipated in eastern imitativeness. The effervescent Greeks spread their talents too far and too thinly in Alexander's wake, and as the centre of Hellenistic life shifted eastwards to cities like Alexandria and Antioch the old peninsula of the Greek motherland sank into comparative obscurity until eventually it became a mere fief of the western empire of Rome—the insignificant *Graecia* from which we take its contemporary name. But when the Roman Empire grew in its turn, stretching the arms of its centurions and the roads of its en-gineers north and west as well as east and south, from the Scottish borders to the mountains of Yemen, it, too, surpassed its own strength. From diffusion, disintegration followed; and by the third century the Roman Empire was already divided in fact if not in name. Rome itself ceased to be an effective capital as successive emperors fought from other, more strategic, centres to secure their crumbling frontiers. That one of the strongest challenges came from the tribes in central Europe, aiming their thrusts directly at Rome itself across the Alpine barrier, only emphasized the inadequacy of this nominal capital of the Empire. It was too vulnerable and at the same time too far removed from the main sources of trade and culture which were still concentrated in the east. When Constantine selected the growing town of Byzantium on the Golden Horn for his capital he was recognizing where the true centre of gravity of the Empire now lay. Tactically, the site was magnificently defensible. Strategically, it governed what the succeeding sixteen centuries have proved to be one of the most sensitive military and commercial crossroads of the old world; and as Rome and the western territories were in due course overrun by the hostile Goths and Vandals from the north, Constantinople and the eastern lands gained steadily in power and significance.

This eastern empire had woven into its complex texture many strands that could be identified as 'western'. It inherited Roman laws and military traditions and for a time, at least, Latin remained its imperial language. Embedded in its common life also were the Greek language and memories of the classical Greek literature which had once been the most 'western' of cultural manifestations and which were to re-emerge after another thousand years as among the chief ideological inspirations of the western Renaissance. In these matters the imperial eagle looked rightfully westwards, but in all else it was the East that held its gaze. While Latin remained the language of administrators and churchmen in the West, Greek soon displaced it in Byzantium and over the succeeding centuries the Greek inheritance itself was orientalized.

The chief agency of both these changes was the Church, with which the empire came to be identified. As an institutionalized bond for a heterogeneous collection of peoples, the Church had a value that, in the beginning at any rate, far surpassed its theological message. Constantine seems to have seen this clearly, recognizing Christianity less as the most convincing revelation of the divine truth than as the most highly organized of many such revelations that happened to be competing for adherents at the time. But by his formal acceptance of the Christian faith he made certain that his empire would acquire not merely a Christian but a Greek ethos, for Greek was already the language of the Church in these eastern lands. As his successors built upon his foundation, faith and calculation advanced hand in hand and Greek became the language of Byzantine administration as much as it was of worship. At the same time, however, because the eastern sections of the Church were serving the aims of a powerful lay emperor, they moved naturally on a course opposed to that of the Church in Rome, where the Pope had assumed imperial authority in his own right in an attempt to fill the vacuum left by the collapse of the western empire. Theological differences accompanied the inevitable secular rivalry. While the Latin Church grew more concerned with its temporal authority and official hierarchies, the Greek Church seemed increasingly mystical and, in western terms, other-worldly, fostering what one Greek writer has called 'an oriental cult'.[1] Through a tortuous series of doctrinal schisms and partial reconciliations the two steadily diverged until, at last, the formal excommunication of the eastern Patriarch by Pope Leo IX in 1054 set the seal on Byzantium's eastern destiny.

While this overall schism was developing between the western and eastern worlds, the Orthodox Church and the Byzantine emperors were collaborating in the deliberate suppression of that part of their Greek heritage which might be thought most 'western'. Although they maintained the Hellenic language, they equated the style and substance of classical Hellenism with paganism and were determined to eradicate it. Fired with Christian zeal, as well as a characteristically Greek taste for rule by decree, the Emperor Theodosius II in 435 ordered all his subjects to demolish their temples, eschew their heathen gods and, among other things, cease forthwith that inane and godless form of competition known as the Olympic Games. A century later the Emperor Justinian dealt the final blow to the old classical world when he closed the last of the Athens academies in the name of Christian rectitude. The effect of these restrictions was most profound in the original Hellenic homeland of peninsular Greece where, in spite of many centuries of provincial stagnation and decline, the classical traditions had remained important to the inhabitants. Now, with their deliberate suppression, the peninsula's social and cultural decay accelerated. More of its people left, either to jump on the new imperial band-waggon in Constantinople or to seek a less arbitrarily restricted life elsewhere. Plague and invasion in succeeding centuries did the rest.

From the sixth century onwards the Slav tribes of eastern Europe descended in their thousands across the Balkan passes upon the old

Greek motherland and for two centuries the peninsula was almost wholly cut off even from the new Greek power of Constantinople. Ist villages were overrun, its people overwhelmed and Athens itself was reduced to little more than a crumbling village—in which state it remained for the next thousand years. By the time Constantinople reasserted its authority there, Hellenism in the old sense had been destroyed in its birthplace. There was little of it left but a corrupted language and the folk memory of the ancient gods transmuted into Christian saints. The Church and the Emperor between them were able to re-establish undisputed sway.

But not for long, for soon the two-headed eagle of Byzantium, which had represented to begin with a hopeful fusion of east and west, acquired a new and more troubled significance as the emblem of an empire that was to be ground remorselessly to destruction between the millstones of eastern and western power. To be sure, this threat had existed previously in the challenge from the Persian Empire in the east and the Slav and other barbarian invasions from the north and west. But although these caused many fluctuations in the imperial frontiers they did not seriously threaten Byzantium's existence. That privilege was reserved for two new movements—the rise of Islam in the east and the growth of Roman Christian militancy in the west which between them led to the long religious and commercial saga of the Crusades in which the Greek world of Constantinople met a treacherous but probably inescapable end.

The original Islamic conquests by the Arabs were astonishing but not decisive. Within a century of the death of Muhammad in 632, the Arabs had swept clean through North Africa into Spain on one side and right across the Middle East into the northern plains of India on the other. France was almost in their grasp, Jerusalem had fallen and Constantinople had been besieged. Yet the last battles on both sides were won by their Christian enemies, and as the Arabs fell to that vicious internal squabbling that has distinguished their society ever since, less exciting but more persevering peoples gradually assumed the leadership of the challenge to Byzantium. From the east, the Turks—newly converted by the Arabs to Islam—pushed out of Asia towards the Mediterranean. In the west, the Latin Christians were slowly recovering from the collapse of the old Rome and beginning to reach out for new forms of dominion. Between these two the fate of Byzantium and the Greek people was to be decided, with the Greek peninsula as their decisive battleground.

The Greek rulers in Constantinople helped to prepare the peninsula for its war-torn fate by their own repressions and exactions. Once their rule was re-established there after the Slav invasions, they imposed the strait-jacket of Orthodoxy with more determination than ever and squeezed even more taxes out of its already impoverished people, to whom their attitude was one of bigoted suspicion mingled with metropolitan contempt. According to one source, they regarded the motherland of Hellenism not as the birthplace of the empire, as in so many ways it was, but rather as 'an utter hole'[2]—much as some Greek exiles appear to view it today, indeed, when they return on holiday to their humble little villages from the concrete jungles of New York or Sydney, and cannot rest until they have told their erstwhile compatriots how inferior are all their ways of doing things. The results of this attitude and the exactions it encouraged were yet more poverty, depopulation and unrest, so that as the power of the Latin West revived the peninsula seemed an inviting target for interference and expansion. The earliest western efforts there, however, amounted to little more than the organized piracy of the Normans from Sicily. Not until Venice began to develop its commercial strength did Greece re-emerge from the limbo of Byzantine oppression as a desirable western stepping-stone to the riches of the Levant. Then, with commercial interest reinforced by Christian conviction, the rising Latin states of the West joined forces in a long series of assaults upon the eastern strongholds of Islam that inevitably brought them into conflict with Byzantium as well. Venice and Constantinople, in particular, became rivals in trade as much as Rome and Constantinople were already rivals in faith; and it is a nice point whether, especially after the excommunication of 1054, either of the Christian parties fought the Muslims with as much zeal as they attacked each other. The climax of their rivalry was disastrously self-destructive. In 1204 Franks and Venetians joined in the notorious Fourth Crusade when, instead of attempting to capture Jerusalem from the Arabs, they descended unexpectedly upon the Bosphorus to capture Constantinople and wreck the Byzantine Empire. Carved into eleven different pieces, the empire was doled out like doubloons to the piratical hands of some of the premier families of the West. There was Count Baldwin of Flanders, elected ruler of an imperial rump around Constantinople, and Boniface of Montferrat who became 'King' of Macedonia and central Greece. There was Othon de la Roche from Burgundy, first Duke of Athens and, therefore, unwitting founder of Shakespeare's court in *A Midsummer Night's Dream*. There were the gentlemen of the Order of St. John who became the

Knights of Rhodes, Geoffrey de Villehardouin who became Prince of Achaia in the Peloponnese and Marco Sanudo, a nephew of the Doge of Venice, who won a state out of the islands of the Cyclades. Their traces are dotted all over Greece to this day, in great fortresses like those of Monemvasia or Methoni, in crumbling former palaces like those on the waterfront of Khania in Crete, in place names like Frangokastro and family names like Marcopoulos. Here and there, also, pockets of the Latin faith remain as mementoes of this first moment of modern western imperialism. On the island of Naxos, where Sanudo set up his capital, a tiny but stubbornly persistent Roman Catholic community, distinguished by an assortment of Italian names, lingers on under ornate Venetian doorways and stone armorial crests in the alleys of the old town; and on Sunday mornings you can even sense a little of the hostility their ancestors must have aroused when they huddle self-protectively on the steps of the Roman church with their priest while the rest of the town seems to turn its back on their apostasy.

This Venetian segment of the eastern Roman Empire was the longest-lived of all the enforced divisions of 1204, lasting until the seventeenth century in the islands of the Aegaean, up to 1715 in Crete, and even to the brink of the nineteenth century in the Ionian islands on the more accessible western side of Greece. Most of the others enjoyed only a brief life under western rule, before they were caught again in the cross-tides of commercial rivalry and religious war. But the Fourth Crusade and its aftermath had ensured that the Byzantine Empire would play an increasingly feeble role in these conflicts. Although Frankish rule in Constantinople lasted only fifty-seven years and the city, together with a sizeable core of the empire, reverted to Greek control before the century was out, the old Byzantine power had vanished. New forces from the north as well as from the east and west now contended fiercely for the spoils; and as the kingdoms of Serbia and Bulgaria snatched great chunks of territory in northern Greece and pressed closer to the western approaches of Constantinople, the imperial rulers turned for help, in desperation, to their old eastern enemies. So it was that, in the fourteenth century, the Ottoman armies crossed the Hellespont into Europe for the first time not as the enemies but as the allies of the Greeks. Invited by the Emperor, Cantacuzenos, they crushed the Serbian and Bulgarian forces and within a few years had subdued much of the Balkans and northern Greece. It was the first practical expression of that harsh Greek choice which, paraphrasing Voltaire, was later to be described succinctly as 'better the turban than the mitre'; but though it saved Constantinople and the Greeks from western envy it delivered them into eastern bondage. Long before the city itself fell to the besieging Ottomans on that fateful Tuesday in the month of May, 1453, much of the rest of the empire was already in Turkish hands. By 1461 the Ottomans controlled almost all of mainland Greece as well. Soon they were pressing still farther into Europe, exacting a kind of poetic justice for that western hostility to the Greeks which had opened the door to them in the first place, while for the better part of the next four centuries they were able to keep the Greeks themselves in subjection, willy-nilly, to their eastern ways.

The Turkish occupation remains today, in Greek eyes, what Mr. Leigh Fermor has called a 'boundless limbo'. Yet in some ways westerners seem more aware of it than they are of the preceding history of Byzantium, possibly because western actions in respect of it were slightly less discreditable. Forgetting that western powers were partly responsible for the Turkish conquests in the first place, they take pride in the fact that the West later helped to rescue fair Greece from her distress and so set the pendulum of Greek affairs swinging away from the East again for the first time in 2,000 years. But the cost to Greece in the meantime was severe—although hardly as bad as the Greeks themselves are wont to say, believing, as a tourist guide on the Acropolis once told me, that the Turks are 'the reason for everything bad in Greece'. Basically, what the Turkish occupation achieved in Greece was to complete the economic and cultural decline of the peninsula that had begun as far back as Alexander and to corrupt still further the already enfeebled sources of Greek leadership. But it did so less by deliberate repression than by the unthinking continuation of those Byzantine methods of government which had previously brought much hardship to the Greeks of Greece. In structure and administration, indeed, the Ottoman Empire was largely that of Byzantium itself pressed into the service of the Muslim Allah instead of the Christian God. It was equally religious in inspiration, equally multi-national in character and, if possible, even more loosely-knit—more like a vast and shifting encampment than a coherent, stable state. War in pursuit of converts to the faith was its first preoccupation; and while its armies were ceaselessly on the march and its frontiers were never fixed, its Sultans were happy to leave most of the business of governing their motley crowd of subjects in the hands of those who best knew how to do it—the officials of Byzantium.

At the top of this traditional bureaucratic pyramid were the

Church and its minions, whose most characteristic representatives—outside the priesthood itself—were to become known as Phanariotes after the district of Phanar, near the headquarters of the Orthodox Patriarchate in Constantinople where they had always lived and worked. Especially in the seventeenth and eighteenth centuries the Phanariote Greeks became the most influential servants of the Ottoman state. At the bottom of the pyramid were such persons as the tax-gatherers and traditional local 'notables', called *archontes* by the Greeks, who remained responsible under the Ottomans as they had been under the Byzantines for the good order of their local communities. Thus many of the offices of the Turkish Muslim empire, both high and low, were occupied as often as not by Greek Christians. Unhappily but inevitably, however, the interests of the rulers diverged from those of the ruled; and whereas in the past the Phanariotes and others had at least been Greeks in the service of a Greek and Christian empire, they were now the servants of an infidel foreigner who had set up his court in the greatest of all Greek cities. Often, it is true, they protected their fellow Greeks from the direst pain of the Turkish lash when that was threatened, but in the nature of things they got small thanks for it. In the eyes of ordinary Greeks there remained something faintly treasonable about their activities, and however they might seek to modify that image by cunning or kindness they became objects of frequent suspicion and resentment, so that after three centuries of Turkish rule many of the primary sources of native leadership seemed tainted and Greek had been set against Greek even more than before.

The chief sufferers in this process, however, were the Orthodox Church and its Patriarch upon whom the main burden of Greek leadership was imposed by the nature of the Ottoman system. In the *sharia* or sacred law of Islam, Christians and Jews are specifically exempt from forcible conversion by the faithful because they are 'People of the Book' to whom the One God has also revealed himself, even though they have had the misfortune to be denied the final and perfect revelation of the Prophet. It was not mere generosity or diplomacy, therefore, but strict adherence to the Prophet's law that caused the conqueror of Constantinople, Sultan Mehmet, to confirm the Orthodox Patriarch as head of the Orthodox Christian community and thereby make him responsible for the behaviour and welfare of all Orthodox Christians within the imperial domains. He did the same with the Grand Rabbi of Constantinople and with the Armenian Patriarch, who became respectively the supreme authorities for the Jews and the Armenian Christians throughout the empire. On the face of it this division of the empire into religious communities, or *millets*, in which members of each faith were made responsible for their own affairs, displayed an admirable tolerance on the part of the Turks, but in practice it placed the Orthodox Patriarch in a series of insoluble dilemmas. Unlike his two non-Muslim colleagues he was already, by Byzantine tradition, both the spiritual head of a universal Christian community and the national vicar of a largely Greek empire. Under Muslim domination he was forced to choose —or deliberately to avoid choosing—between the national and the universal role. On the one hand the Patriarchate of Constantinople continued to be regarded by all Greeks as the focus of their political as well as their religious life, from its long and intimate association with the former emperors of Byzantium. Whoever was Patriarch, therefore, could command obedience in secular as well as religious affairs from the Greek Christian flock and was consequently regarded —by Greeks at any rate—as the natural, national leader against the Muslim Turks. On the other hand, no Patriarch could lightly encourage any of his flock, Greek or otherwise, to defy the Ottoman authorities for that would not only invite immediate reprisals on those who were defiant but probably cost the Patriarch his head as well. Acceptance of Ottoman rule and the preservation of Greek ethnic pride, therefore, were equally mandatory but mutually contradictory.

Uneasily the Church did its best to find a compromise on this issue. But as the decades of ambiguity stretched into centuries it retreated into a kind of paralysis. It was both the only protector of 'Greekness' and the chief instrument of its betrayal. It was neither truly national nor properly universal. It defied the Christians of the West, yet was resentful of the ruling Muslims of the East. In such circumstances it was not surprising that leadership was replaced by intrigue and scholarship by rote, or that Church schools and monasteries which had replaced the classical academies in Greece fell gradually into decay. This slow pollution of the Church which for more than 1,000 years had been the highest expression of Greek-ness, was accompanied by a further decline in the physical conditions of peninsular Greece. Under Turkish domination the population there was reduced again as war between the Ottomans and the Venetians continued sporadically over its various appendages and brigandage and piracy alike increased. In Constantinople the Phanariote administrators viewed the peninsula with more disgust than ever and turned their backs upon its troubles to luxuriate, instead, in the struggle for worldly preferment at the Sultan's court. Even the Patriarchate itself became a political football to be kicked about between the Sultan of the day and such prelates as were willing to conspire for the office. In one period of sixty-three years in the eighteenth century, forty-eight different Patriarchs were appointed to the see of Constantinople.

By then, although the Ottoman Empire was beginning visibly to decay and the first rumbles of Greek national rebellion could be heard, the Patriarchate was the prisoner of its multiple inhibitions. As the eighteenth century neared its end and the fever of western nationalism infected more of the Sultan's subjects, the Patriarch of the day committed what seemed to many Greeks the final betrayal of their national interest. In a theological exhortation he called upon all Christians to support the empire and respect the Sultan whom God had set over them as the best means of preserving Orthodoxy. Political freedom, he declared, was 'an enticement of the Devil and a murderous poison destined to push the people into disorder and destruction'.[3] As Sir Steven Runciman has pointed out, this position was not theologically unsound for 'Christ Himself had distinguished between the things which are Caesar's and the things which are God's,' and it was no business of the Church, therefore, to indulge in subversive national activities.[4] But the practical result inevitably was to sever Constantinople from the Greek national movement and to split the Orthodox Church itself.

In Greece the priests and monks were the only organized repositories of 'Greek-ness'. In maintaining the memory of Byzantium in their chapels, their monasteries and—above all—their language, they could not help but emphasize the national, rather than the universal, character of their Church. Moreover, the fact that 300 years of intellectual vacillation and physical neglect had reduced their institutions to poverty and themselves to ignorance only increased their readiness to retain what influence they could among their flock by supporting them in the fight against foreign—and heathen—rule. Not to have done so would have been to abandon not only their old glory but their power as well, and to have put the whole future of Orthodox Christianity at risk among the very people who had invented it. Slowly and fitfully, but in the end decisively, they identified themselves with the Greek nation and abandoned the universality of Constantinople's tradition. In April, 1821, it was the monks of Lavra in the Peloponnese who raised the flag of rebellion against the Turks and began the War of Independence—although paradoxically, it was the Orthodox Patriarch in Constantinople who paid the highest price for their presumption. He who had urged the Greeks to honour the Sultan for the sake of their Church was hanged at once outside the gates of his palace because they had disobeyed him for the sake of their nation. Twelve years later when the battle was won and Greek independence had become a fact it was the Orthodox Bishops of the new state who established the final irony of their Byzantine heritage. Declaring that they could not accept the primacy of a Patriarch who sat in a city still under Turkish rule, they proclaimed the Orthodox Church in Greece to be autocephalous and consigned Constantinople to a powerless limbo. There, in effect, the Ecumenical Patriarch has remained to this day, Greek as the city in which he sits, in name, spirit, history and appeal, yet shrunk almost to a cipher in the blast of modern nationalism.

In rejecting the leadership of Constantinople, however, the Greeks opened the door to new confusions. Materially weak and spiritually divided, they were compelled to look elsewhere for inspiration and support. Effectively, they had two choices. One was Moscow, the self-styled 'Third Rome' of Orthodoxy, where the ruler had assumed the style of Tsar, or Caesar, and claimed the true succession to Constantinople's supremacy soon after the Ottoman conquest. By the middle of the eighteenth century this claim was strengthened by the presence in Russia of many Phanariote Greeks who had left the Muslim empire of the Turks to serve a growing Christian polity in whose realms they saw restored again some of the glory of the earlier Holy Roman Empire. But, like the Patriarch in Constantinople the Muscovite leadership suffered from the in-built ambiguity that the more it supported a specifically Greek national movement, the more it threatened its own authority in other Orthodox communities, while the more it maintained its universal Christian appeal the less interesting it was to the Greeks. Even so, as the Russian Empire grew and increasingly threatened the Ottoman hold on southern Europe, Moscow became another important pole of Greek existence that not only was to last throughout the nineteenth century but would be transformed and continued even in the twentieth under the guise of Soviet communism.

The second choice before the Greeks, however, was both more radical and, to an influential minority of westernized Greeks, more truly 'Greek' as well. It was to turn westwards again ostensibly to recapture the thread of their classical tradition which the Greeks

F

themselves had begun to lose with Alexander but which others, more fortunate, had preserved and elaborated for them in the development of the western Renaissance. To most ordinary Greeks this had no appeal whatever. Their priests had kept alive the memory of Byzantium, and in emphasizing its Greek-ness had fostered the belief that Constantinople 'again, one day, again it will be ours'; but the classical world from which the Empire had descended had vanished from popular consciousness. Its revival, as we have seen elsewhere, was essentially a western intellectual concept. Yet within the Ottoman domains a small but growing community of Greek administrators, merchants and professional men, whose duties brought them into contact with the western world, were increasingly aware of the possibilities offered by the strictly secular life of its new nation-states. Outside, Greek exiles like Korais, the creator of *katharevousa*, were by this time scattered through every western capital, where they eagerly accepted the new classical humanism and revelled in the legends of its Greek inspiration. To both groups, western rationalism beckoned as the answer to the intellectual failure of eastern Orthodoxy and western nationalism presented itself as the escape from the universal obligations of the Christian faith. Most powerfully, too, with the rise of British and French imperialism, western commercial, diplomatic and military interests seemed naturally to support these new Greek visions in the struggle they presaged with the Turks. A new wave of conquest was on its way to the eastern Mediterranean, more powerful and revolutionary than any other in history, and it was to pile upon the impoverished peninsula of Greece the last and most burdensome of its historical ambiguities: that while most of its people were emotionally moved by a longing to restore the Christian glories of Byzantium, many of their leaders and all their western friends and allies were intellectually inspired by the notion that they were fighting for the ideals of classical Hellenism as expressed in a Greek nation-state.

Thus modern Greece was born in an unprecedented welter of ambivalence. Its people were made a nation, yet retained a universal soul. They had lost a Christian empire and adopted in its place a pagan legend. They were the defenders of Christendom against Islam, yet had been betrayed by Christians. They therefore hated the Turks while resenting the Europeans. They were also suspicious of their own Church because it had let them down, yet were proud of the priests who had led their fight for freedom. They respected Moscow but detested the Slavs; and having abandoned the great city that had been their pride and joy they still yearned for its restoration to them. Above all, perhaps, they were caught between their longing for those great Greek centuries when faith was all, and eager anticipation of a day when the nation should be everything. In the many convulsions that were to follow their attainment of political independence these infinite contradictions gave the two-headed eagle of Constantine a new and still more complex significance as the emblem of an unattainable future and a past irrevocably lost whose conflicts could not be reconciled.

Chapter 5

THE SCORPION AND THE FROG

Two Greeks will do badly what one will do well.

(W. Miller)

The scorpion, who could not swim, was sitting on the river bank wondering how to cross to the other side when the frog came swimming by. 'Dear frog,' said the scorpion, in his friendliest tone, 'how happy I am to see you! Please will you carry me across the river on your back?' But the frog was cautious and demurred: 'Scorpions are known for their stings,' said he. 'How do I know you will not sting me if I carry you?' 'Because', cried the scorpion, 'if I sting you, you will sink and I will be drowned. Surely you can't imagine that I want to commit suicide?' This logic convinced the frog, so he took the scorpion on his back and set off with good, stout leg strokes across the river. But in midstream the scorpion stung him, after all; and as the poison paralysed him and they both began to sink, he croaked to the scorpion, 'Now we shall drown, just as you said! Why did you do such a foolish thing?' And the scorpion replied, as they both went under, 'Because I cannot help it. To sting, O frog, is my nature!'

I first heard this venerable folk-tale somewhere in the Middle East where it was applied, with justice, to the endlessly self-defeating quarrels of Arab politics. To sting, it was suggested, was the Arab nature; so that no matter how much Arab called fellow-Arab brother each would react eventually as the scorpion did to the frog—with a gesture of involuntary betrayal. But the parable is just as applicable to the Greeks, whose mutual stings seem equally deadly. It is scarcely possible to review the Greek record of internecine warfare, crumbling governments, fissile parties and bickering oppositions, *coups*, plots and counter-*coups*, without suspecting that all these things are at least as much an expression of the fundamental character of Greekness as the result of mere historical misfortune. Their cumulative message, at first glance anyway, is of a compulsive urge to self-destruction; and if one accepts even as a half-truth the popular adage that people tend to get the government they deserve—or, as Plato put it, that the political structure of the state reflects the soul of its people—then the Greeks must appear singularly undeserving of good government and their souls must be supposed to be in a state of unusual torment. Yet paradoxically—and how often one encounters paradox in Greece!—part of the trouble is that where politics are concerned the Greeks usually try too hard. They are, for a start, ardent constitutionalists who, as we have seen already, have never been short of new ideas for administering the state according to proper legal forms, whether under the tutelage of Aristotle or Papadopoulos. Indeed, constitutions sprout from their agile minds as leaves from a vigorous tree—and are usually blown away as freely by the winds of change, or Greek contentiousness. It is a striking fact that virtually every Greek regime since the early days of the modern independence struggle, whether ostensibly democratic or dictatorial in character, has taken enormous pains to equip itself with a formal constitution: but it is equally striking that none of these elaborate parchments has been able to contain the effervescent Greek spirit without, in the end, becoming an instrument of oppression or a gateway to anarchy. More than once the mere business of reaching initial agreement upon the form of the constitution has itself been enough to rip the state asunder; and even in the lengthiest periods of comparative acquiescence in one constitution or another at least one Greek faction has usually devoted itself with unfailing zeal and towering self-righteousness to the fundamental revision of whatever the legal structure of the state has happened to be. The characteristic Greek attitude to any constitution, in fact, is to change it as soon as it ceases to be of personal advantage. Thus the rules of the political game are in constant dispute and play is as often paralysed by the teams walking off the field in protest at the law's alleged irrelevance as by their setting about each other with fists and boots in contempt of the law's provisions.

At bottom, as I have just remarked, the problem is that Greeks do so often try too hard. Their ideal state would appear to be one in which every voice is raised all the time in a kind of permanent plebiscite—and while that might have served for classical Athens where the citizens were so small in number that they could all assemble in one place (a circumstance that Aristotle promptly made into a principle, as being the only way democracy could work), it is not exactly the easiest way to run a modern nation of several million people. Contemporary circumstances suggest, rather, that a certain popular indifference to the affairs of state is indispensable to their effective conduct; but that quality remains largely absent from the Greek character. Cherishing, as they do, a high opinion of themselves and a correspondingly low regard for each other, most Greeks are easily convinced that only *their* special contribution can save the state from ruin. Mostly, therefore, they like to be in a state of permanent and passionate engagement with the affairs of the nation. Indeed, if 'participation' were the magic key to true democracy, as some of our theorists nowadays seem to think, then the Greeks certainly would be nature's democrats and their state ought to be a model of functioning democracy, for they will all participate in anything, given half a chance. Their coffee-houses, when not infested with police informers, reverberate morning and night with the rattle of political argument as much as with the clatter of dominoes and trictrac counters. Their newspapers, when not strictly censored, are choked with column after column of political comment, news and gossip of the most shamelessly partisan and often scurrilous kind. Even under a police regime, many Greeks cannot be kept away from politics by anything short of solitary confinement. Not for them the docility of the Slavs across their northern borders, nor the comparative stolidity of their old Turkish enemies. Volatile and unquenchably argumentative, the Greeks devote themselves with endearing openness to outwitting authority on principle even—or especially—when it wields a heavy truncheon; for, as we have seen already, they are apt to take most unkindly to anyone among themselves who sets himself up (or is set up by others) as their superior.

Greeks are, indeed, not only natural participators but compulsive egalitarians as well, ever ready, in the words of Bernard Shaw, to treat a duchess as if she were a flower girl or a flower girl like a duchess. Rank, class or status mean little to them as a rule, except as indications of the personal advantage that may be gained from striking up an acquaintance with a person of title or connexion—such as the proverbial tax-collector as mentioned by Edmond About. Normally they expect everyone from the Prime Minister downwards to maintain an open door to them at all times; and I suspect that one of the principal reasons why kings have usually had such a hard time of it in Greece is precisely that they are, in the nature of things, so much harder than politicians either to approach or to humble. For if Greeks cannot do the one with their leaders, they usually try to do the other— a state of affairs which does much to account for the extraordinarily sharp and frequent reversals of fortune among Greek political figures. From Aristides who was exiled because his fellow Athenians were tired of hearing him called 'The Just', to Constantine Karamanlis and George Papandreou a few years ago, the Greek record suggests that success is more likely to arouse opposition than admiration. As a distinguished Greek politician once said to me, musing on the qualities required for leadership in his country, 'Leaders are not recognized in Greece by what they achieve, but by how many enemies they acquire. To prove you are a great man in this country you must be vilified—every day if possible!' From which, I suggested, it ought to follow that the best way to cut a too-successful or presumptuous Greek down to size would be to praise his achievements as studiously as you ignored his faults. 'Yes,' said my informant, like the scorpion to the frog, 'but no Greek is capable of such restraint. To attack each other is our nature!'[1]

Here, I think, we return to the heart of the matter—that sense of tension or perpetual opposition without which neither Greece as a nation nor the Greeks as individuals seem fully to exist. Historically we have traced this tension in such relatively abstract matters as the tug of East against West, of classical Hellas against Christian Byzantium, and of the national against the universal tradition of the Greek Church. Culturally we have witnessed it in the opposition of the Greek ideal to Greek reality. Geographically it is evident in those polarities of landscape and position that identify the territorial character of that piece of the globe we call Greece. But it is in Greeks as individuals that it is most sharply and concretely focused, reflecting—or, perhaps, inspiring, according to how you look at it—all the tensions of the collective Greek identity in the personal state of being. As with the Arabs, its effects are most apparent to outsiders in the chronically unstable nature of Greek politics, from the repeated conflicts of the classical city states, through the autocracy, civil wars and murderous intrigues of Byzantium—barely a quarter of whose Emperors died a natural death—to the perilous discord of the present century, when Greece has suffered one civil war, two foreign occupations, ten major military *coups d'état*, several bouts of internecine fighting, a host of minor military upheavals, and a change of government on the average nearly once a year.

At the social level, however, the Greek inability to co-operate effectively or to maintain collective institutions is just as marked. 'Again and again,' wrote Dr. Miller of the *Morning Post* seventy years ago, 'the daily life of Greece shows examples of the impossibility of forming clubs, companies or anything which requires co-operation and the subordination of the individual to the whole. Two Greeks will do badly what one will do well.'[2] Nobody who has observed the Greeks today could fail to recognize that portrait. It is true that nowadays, when Athens is so much bigger than it used to be, clubs of a kind are more a part of its teeming popular life than they were in Dr. Miller's day. But they are mostly inward-looking gatherings inspired by common roots—men or families from the same village, for example, assembled in mutual protection against the feared anonymity of the city. They are less often groups of like-minded people sharing hobbies or other occupations in amiable concert.

By and large Greeks seem to find sharing surprisingly difficult among themselves even though they may share their last penny with a foreigner. On the contrary, there is a pronounced streak of abrasiveness about most of their relations with other Greeks and a sense of exaggerated independence about their least endeavours that often seem to imply total egotism. You very rarely see groups of drunken Greeks, for instance, as you may see groups of drunken British, American, Germans or Japanese propping each other up in mutual delight or collective stupor. But you will quite often see a solitary Greek drinking himself into private bliss. Even when Greeks dance —that most sociable of occupations in many countries—they frequently prefer to dance alone. The most striking figure of the dance floor or the *bouzouki* bar is not so much the little group joined by the twirling handkerchiefs of the traditional folk-dance as the soloist who, in sublime unself-consciousness, practises his own variations to the music in isolated rapture. This small-scale but revealing individualism is equally noticeable in larger matters. It is surely no accident that all Greece's best and biggest business-men work exclusively as lone wolves. The idea of 'going public', with all its corporate responsibilities and restraints, is anathema to them. Similarly, the Greek trade union movement has never established a reliable collective tradition; indeed, its habit of spontaneous fission has been carried to such lengths that the movement has been rendered all but useless as a means of economic advancement for Greek workers.[3]

Greeks operate as individuals or they hardly operate at all; and while there is something very endearing about that in a world increasingly given over to the big battalions, it is the root cause of Greek political instability. Put two Greeks together and you have three political parties, as the Greek quip goes, because it humbles and even dehumanizes a man to agree too easily with another. Co-operation, save as an expedient, is not merely rejected but despised. As a stone dropped into a pool becomes the focus of an ever-expanding set of ripples so an individual in Greek society is at the centre of an ever-widening set of frictions; himself against the land, fate and the gods first of all; then, typically, with his family against the neighbours; after that, perhaps, with his village or his street against the next village or the city; then with his province or his city against the state; and finally with his nation against the world. But except for the family, to which loyalty is ordained by blood and honour, and the nation, to which it is bound by historical pride, the alliances are less important than the contests that create them. Like the Arabs again, the Greeks believe that 'the friend of my enemy is my enemy, and the enemy of my enemy is my friend', so that they are ready to make, dissolve and remake coalitions every time a new enemy heaves in sight; and as the prospect of life without an enemy generally seems intolerable to them this means in practice that their relationships are in a constant state of flux.

The sociologists call this the 'agonistic' quality of Greek life—drawing yet again on those ancient Greeks who are supposed to have had a word for everything—and one of the most illuminating accounts of it that I know is contained in an American study of a small Greek village called Vasilika, where 'perpetual struggle, principally outside the family, is a part of life'.[4] The ultimate aim of the struggle, as the author sees it, is nothing more or less than the assertion of individual identity. 'One learns to know oneself primarily by contrast with others; and therefore the maintenance of some difference is a necessity. Contrasts and the tensions contrasts create, become expected and desired. Without change and variation the villagers lose their sense of life . . .' Apart from fostering the sense of individual existence, this process of constant change appears to have little meaning. 'It would seem that it is not the outcome but the continuing *aghonia* that gives a village man or woman the feeling that he is a functioning human being, that he has an identity, that he is alive. "*Perazmena, ksehazmena.*" "What is past is forgotten", the villagers say, and although they say so mostly in connection with unpleasantness, the saying is equally applicable to victories. For both victory and defeat are shortlived; a new area of battle constantly supersedes the old.'[5] This sketch of the principles of Greek village life is instantly applicable to other expressions of Greek identity. Note, for example, the similarity between the villager's determination to maintain a sense of 'difference' and the strong collective idea of the Greek nation as a 'chosen people' that I have already referred to. Compare, also, the idea of 'perpetual struggle' as a means to self-identification for the villager with the idea I have quoted above that the status of a leader in Greek politics is determined by the number of enemies he acquires. It is, in fact, remarkable how regularly Greek politics have thrown up leaders who seem committed to divisive policies or attitudes for no very apparent reason other than a desire to irritate their rivals and thereby bolster their own self-esteem. Dr. Miller drew a very apposite picture, in this respect, of a certain Monsieur Delyannes who was over sixty years in public life and enjoyed five 'short and stormy' spells in office as Prime Minister of Greece in the late nineteenth and early twentieth centuries. 'Energy, force of character and ceaseless activity are all represented in the person of M. Delyannes,' wrote Dr. Miller, ' "the grand old man" of Greece, the "Grandfather" as he is colloquially called. No one can help admiring the physical and mental powers of this veteran politician . . . who, in spite of the eighty-four years which those who know him best ascribe to him—for there is some doubt as to his exact age—walks far younger men off their feet in rambles about Kephisia, sits up all night during a budget debate in the *Boule* [Parliament], is never missing at any public function, and at the last election traversed land and sea—and that sea the Aegaean—in winter to make political converts. . . . M. Delyannes is never tired of avowing himself a supporter of the Constitution, and declaring it to be in danger—when he is not in office. During the last election, while their revered leader was uttering these admirable sentiments from his balcony to students, bootblacks, and others, and adjuring them to be "vigilant guardians of the Constitution", others of his followers put his constitutional doctrines into practice by tearing up a number of boards used for fencing off buildings in course of erection, and beating members of the less aggressively constitutional party upon the head with them. . . . He has recently advanced the remarkably frank opinion that "obstruction does not dishonour, but honours, parliamentary government". . . . M. Delyannes has made little mark as a constructive statesman, but he is a consummate "old parliamentary hand", who knows all the arts by which democratic assemblies are governed. He has, however, shown marked want of tact when dealing with the Crown, as, for example, when two years ago he allowed his Minister for War to introduce a measure abolishing the military office held by the Crown Prince, without previously acquainting the King with its contents.'[6] Students of contemporary Greek politics will not need me to draw the obvious parallel in our own day with this 'grand old man' of seventy years ago; but lest others are in any doubt, they may refer at once to later pages in this book (especially Chapters 11, 12 and 13) which recount some of the events in the last years of Mr. George Papandreou's career as a 'grand old man' of Greece. The similarities are uncannily exact—the 'energy, force of character, and ceaseless activity', the equivocal and expedient attitude to the constitution, the skill in parliamentary dealings combined with an absence of constructive effort in government, the 'marked want of tact when dealing with the Crown' (especially in military matters), the 'short and stormy' tenures of office, even the doubt about his exact age—every one of these characteristics of M. Delyannes was to be noted in Mr. Papandreou. In his last disastrous spell as Prime Minister, Mr. Papandreou also went on record with his own version of the 're-markably frank opinion that "obstruction does not dishonour, but honours, parliamentary government" '—only he put it still more personally and plainly. 'Power bores me,' he declared in 1965, 'only struggles stimulate me.'[7]

This distaste for the constraints of responsibility and the contrary yearning for the zest and freedom of battle is a constant factor in Greek political life. I remember an Athens newspaper editor telling me once that he could not recall a day of his life when he was not in opposition—'and on the bitter end of it, at that'. At one level this was a statement of the simple fact that in the thirty-odd years of his adult life he had never known a government in Athens that he supported. But at another level it was a revelation of his psychology—and, I believe, of a characteristically Greek psychology—for he spoke with neither bitterness nor disillusionment but rather with relish, as if opposition had been for him the breath of a rewarding life. This was borne out not long afterwards, when the government was changed and Mr. Papandreou became Prime Minister after nearly twenty years in the wilderness. Until that moment the editor had been a convinced supporter of Papandreou and his paper had been campaigning for him furiously, as if his election would certainly herald the millennium. Within a few months all was changed. The editor and his paper were back in opposition, campaigning with equal vigour against Papandreou and his government.

Such individualism and independence can be admirable, of course —especially, perhaps, in a newspaperman. But they are death to any democracy when carried to excess because they destroy the basis of group loyalty and group confidence on which democracy must rest. Unhappily, albeit sometimes appealingly, the Greeks are great ones for excess, especially in their individualism, so that their democracies are forever poised on the brink of anarchy and frequently end by toppling over it. The end result, of course, is tyranny—as Plato several times pointed out and as his countrymen have demonstrated on numberless occasions.

There is not, perhaps, much difference between democracy and anarchy in theory; they both cherish the same fundamental notions of equality and freedom for the individual. What distinguishes them is their practice. In a functioning democracy it is generally true that at any given moment some people are more equal than others and everybody has to sacrifice some of his freedom in order to ensure that all shall have some freedom left. Anarchy rejects both these qualifications, demanding instead the absolute articles of freedom and equality, neither more nor less. That is the Greek attitude—not to pursue the legendary golden mean, for that requires compromise, forbearance and a consequent loss of identity, but to grasp at the absolute because that way lies the fullest expression of the ego. The ancients had a name for that too, as I have already remarked in these pages. They called it *hubris*, for which some of my scholastic friends tell me there is no exact translation possible, because it describes such a peculiarly Greek vice. But overweening pride, or arrogance, will do; and it is no sooner so named than we can recognize it as the other profile of individualism—the end result of a search for self-assertion that challenges everything and defies everyone, that recognizes no loyalty but to itself and its own, and that accepts no restraint but that which others can impose. Its results in Greek history are plain to see, in the long catalogue of disasters that have overtaken the Greek people at the hands of hubristic leaders, from Pericles embarking on the Peloponnesian War to the miscalculations of Eleftherios Venizelos before Smyrna or, more recently, George Papandreou following a policy in Cyprus that nearly led to a new Greek war with Turkey and contributed to his own downfall.

Yet, although they may feel regret at their failures, whether at the personal or national level, Greeks typically feel no remorse about the follies that may have led to them. On the contrary, they usually blame their disasters on other people. Here, too, a sort of *hubris* is at work, but among modern Greeks it has another name: they call it *philotimo*. Like *hubris*, *philotimo* is a difficult concept for foreigners to define, especially in the guilt-ridden mists of the English language, but as we are fairly embarked here on a whole series of generalizations about national character I shall be brief and call it self-esteem—a term that sounds the proper overtones of egocentric pride and slight pomposity. Its essence is familiar in most Mediterranean countries in the personal codes of honour which regulate the behaviour of their men and it implies, as a Greek observer called George Skleros noted half a century ago, that '. . . to the Greek, moral behaviour is limited usually to three matters: first, the conduct of his wife, which he judges very peculiarly in a patriarchal manner; second, the honour and pride of his family; and third, certain personal obligations which involve close relationships with friends and individuals . . . all in all, a very modest and wholly eastern interpretation of the social code.'[8]

In practice, the Greek concept works like a fierce and sometimes barbaric form of the bourgeois social code of keeping up appearances. It defines what is and is not done, but does not much concern itself with ethical morality. It has nothing to do, therefore, with feelings of remorse or guilt, for those are matters either of inward communion between an individual and his God, or else they arise out of a social contract between a man and his fellows. In the egocentric code of *philotimo* neither of these is at issue. Shame is the only sanction and good form is the only guide. Thus, a young man may be required to avenge his sister's 'dishonour' with death or a shotgun wedding, but he is not expected to promote, or even to consider, his sister's happiness. That is a matter for the fates to take care of. Nor is he expected to take any responsibility for whatever else befalls thereafter as a result of his actions, because his actions are pre-ordained by the requirements of his *philotimo*. If he has done what the code demands his *philotimo* has been satisfied and he is as much entitled to reject any blame for subsequent misfortune as he is to claim credit for any subsequent success. Indeed, he is usually *expected* to do both, for—as the author of *Vasilika* relates—'just as in [the village] the avoidance of self-blame does not have the connotation of irresponsibility, so self-praise does not have the connotation of boasting', because both are a necessary part of the maintenance of self-esteem.[9]

Here again we can see how closely the traditional forms of village conduct are related to those of Greek society as a whole. Greeks do appear to 'boast' about all kinds of things in a way that often seems to western visitors either embarrassing or ludicrous. Sometimes it is a matter of utter triviality. A perfectly straightforward report in a London newspaper in 1970, for example, about the danger to the Parthenon of atmospheric pollution, brought forth an indignant official chorus of rebuttal in the Athens press the next day, saying 'the report does not reflect the true situation. The atmosphere in Greece is amongst the healthiest and cleanest in the world and the atmosphere of Athens is far cleaner than in any other large cities.' Someone in London had evidently pricked the national *philotimo* and whether his facts were right or wrong, whether the danger to the Parthenon was real or imagined, he had to be put down. Sometimes the 'boasting' takes the form of apparently harmless rhetorical embroidery to make actual situations seem grander, more significant and more self-flattering than they really are. Somewhere—and I hope I will be forgiven for genuinely not recalling where—I once read a characteristic little story of an old shepherd on the Island of Skyros who, being asked whether he had ever met the English poet, Rupert Brooke, who was buried on the island during the First World War, replied: 'Of course! I knew him well—a very distinguished old gentleman, he was, with a long white beard, so.' In fact, Brooke died very young of an infected mosquito bite aboard an Allied naval vessel lying offshore and the shepherd could not possibly have remembered him with a beard of any kind, let alone one that was long and white. But it made a much better story that way, not only more entertaining for both the shepherd and his listener, but more self-flattering, too. A similar embroidery, in its own way even more revealing of Greek attitudes, is to be found on the stone that marks the real Brooke's grave. 'Here lies the servant of God,' says the stone, 'sub-lieutenant in the English Navy, who died for the deliverance of Constantinople from the Turk.' Alas, he died for nothing of the kind; but it is immensely pleasing to the Greek spirit to imagine that he might have done, so why not say that he did? That is the way that myths are born and Greece is nothing if not mythopoeic, especially when the myths are flattering to personal or national pride. The Utopian rhetoric of Pericles, for example, is just as much in this 'boastful' tradition of the myth as the more recent emphasis of Papadopoulos on the virtues of the Hellenic-Christian heritage.

The characteristic acceptance of self-praise as a legitimate means of maintaining the Greek *philotimo* is, however, a harmless foible when compared to the other side of the coin—the avoidance of self-blame. The absence of any real sense of individual or collective guilt or responsibility that results from this second trait is one of the most striking features of Greek life. At a trivial level it may be witnessed at any Athenian bus stop where queue jumpers are wholly indifferent to rebuke—seem surprised indeed, to have it suggested that there is anything wrong about arriving at the last minute and elbowing or sidling their way aboard a bus in front of a score of other people who have been waiting longer. In such matters it is a case of every man for himself and devil take the hindmost, and that is all about it—as, in fact, it might be in a good many countries south or east of the Alps. But the conviction of blamelessness that lies behind such everyday scenes is conducive also to other, far more damaging aspects of Greek life and politics—particularly the characteristic search for scapegoats and the passionate addiction to conspiratorial interpretations of events. If self-esteem demands that a man cannot and should not accept blame for failure there must be alternative explanations available. Among villagers, according to the author of *Vasilika*, there is 'a tendency to attribute failures to some outer conditions rather than to any personal inadequacy. If anything goes wrong, a man is most likely to say he did not have the proper equipment to do the job, or he says . . . "How was I to know?" or it is the fault of the government, or he has been deceived. . . . "*O Kakomiros*," "the ill-fated one", the villagers may say of a man even in connection with routine mishaps.'[10] At higher levels of Greek society where the excuse of 'the fates' may wear a little thin, the conviction of blamelessness is sustained very happily by recourse to unbounded fantasies of other external causes, from malice and conspiracy to simple misfortune.

I once witnessed an educational experiment in Greece which illustrated this tendency precisely. It was the occasion of the national high school examinations for the Greek equivalent of the *baccalaureat*, when, under normal circumstances, the results were generally known to be open to manipulation through the good offices of Members of Parliament, senior civil servants, or any second cousin who happened to be highly placed. The corruption had, indeed, become a national scandal; but this time the Ministry of Education had decided to put a stop to it. Great precautions were taken against cheating and elaborate devices were set up to prevent the traditional exercise of patronage. Fifteen different sets of examination papers were drafted and lodged in bank vaults all over Greece. The final choice of papers was made by lottery in the Minister's office on the morning the examination began and announced in a special radio broadcast to the waiting schoolmasters throughout the country. The chosen papers were withdrawn from the banks and presented to the candidates. Girls were required to leave their handbags outside the examination room. Boys had their pockets searched. Books and papers were totally forbidden. Several different examiners marked each candidate's papers, and a careful system of numbering prevented any of them knowing either who the candidate was or what marks other examiners had awarded him. Only when all the examiners had finished were the marks compared and the candidates' identities revealed. Then, utterly fair and impersonal to the last, the results were fed into a computer which alone was able to decide who had passed and who had failed. Given the necessity of examinations to begin with, it was difficult to conceive of a system more likely to bestow justice, or one where personal partialities or any other human failings had so little chance to influence the results. But it altogether failed to quieten the suspicions of the students of Greece. When the results were posted on the school notice-boards there was acrimony and agitation among the failures, but no remorse and no contrition. They were ready to accept that their examiners had not cheated them; but the computer, they decided, was another matter. Plainly, this new-fangled instrument was the source of their humiliation. What unknown idiocies might it not have committed behind its gleaming front? What failures of electric current, what dark conspiracies of faulty programming might not have robbed them of their desired, and therefore deserved, pass? The Ministry of Education was swamped with angry letters of denunciation and appeal and Members of Parliament, who had thought to be freed for once of the onerous duty of wangling a pass for the idle or bone-headed son of a loyal voter back home, were besieged as usual by indignant parents demanding that the computer be thrown on the scrap heap as a manifest liar and a cheat.

It is in politics, however, that the Greek search for a scapegoat is most intense and the Greek addiction to the conspiracy theory of history most sophisticated and fantastical. It is, of course, a truism that politicians anywhere will always avoid blame for their mistakes if they can; so much is simply human. But in Greece they do so with a determination and consistency that amounts to both personal and national self-deception on a colossal scale. Elections are never honestly won in Greece in the eyes of a losing candidate; they are rigged. National disasters are never caused by miscalculation; they are created by the malicious conspiracies of foreign powers. 'International communism' and 'Soviet imperialism', or 'NATO-inspired fascism' and 'the C.I.A.' become the standard excuses for each fresh calamity, the choice depending only on which end of the political spectrum a man happens to inhabit. Once more I am reminded of the Arabs here, for they are addicts of the same drug. No fantasy of 'zionism' or 'imperialism' is too wild for them to swallow as a pain-

killer for their manifest misfortunes. Admittedly there is some connexion between these attitudes and the objective facts of the world
in which Greeks and Arabs live. Both have suffered actually as well
as in their dreams from the sharp end of other people's interests.
Both can recall a supposedly glorious past from the standpoint of a
relatively inglorious present, for both once ruled the world as they
knew it and afterwards declined into insignificance as the chattels or
protégés of newer and greater powers. Now both have re-emerged
from centuries of stagnation to find—if I may adapt in an unkindly
way an old Arab proverb—that the caravan of civilization has moved
on, leaving them as dogs barking in the wilderness. Both in recent
times, therefore, have been confronted with a profound challenge to
their traditional conception of themselves as being somehow the
elect of God; and both have tended to take refuge from the challenge
in a denial of responsibility, becoming grand masters of the circumstantial excuse. It is their way of protecting their national *philotimo*,
of maintaining at all costs their collective self-esteem.

Unfortunately and demonstrably, in both cases, it is an escapist
and essentially self-destructive way, that perpetuates at the highest
levels of national politics the vices of the village coffee-shop, where
the anonymous fates are always in command and nothing is ever
what it seems. It puts a premium on fantasy instead of upon fact,
and encourages rumour and speculation at the expense of honest
inquiry, as anybody who tries simply to report Greek political affairs
soon learns from bitter—or farcical—experience. In any moment of
Greek crisis, one well-spent night in Athens will produce more fabu-
lous tales of plot and conspiracy than any other place I know, except
perhaps Beirut. Every journalist who has ever worked there has his
favourites. My own is a simple little tale confided in me one night
by a Greek editor at the time of the marriage of Crown Prince Constantine (as he was then) to Princess Anne Marie of Denmark in
1964. That, you would have thought, was a straightfoward enough
affair. The young man could reasonably be expected to want to marry
someone, for no one suggested that he was not the marrying kind.
The Greek royal family was of Danish origin, the Princess was pretty
and there were not many of her age, rank and eligibility left among
the dwindling royal houses of Europe. Surely, then, an eminently
sensible match in every way? Not so, said my informant. There was
more to it than met the eye. Had I forgotten that Queen Frederika,
Constantine's mother, was German? Did I not know her fascist
reputation? Was she not always poking her fingers into everybody

G

else's pie? Well, he had it for a fact that she was acting in this matter as an agent of the new German Nazi Party by marrying her son into the Danish court, where he could assist in a deep-laid plot to secure control of the Baltic Sea for Germany in time for the Third World War.

Laughable, even at midnight, no doubt—yet among Greeks that is the kind of story that is apt to be heard and even accepted because they have made for themselves a world of Chinese boxes, containing deception within deception within deception, where any nonsense may win an audience because nothing can really be believed. In short, just as unchecked individualism leads to tyranny, so total scepticism may induce utter credulity; and as the first two are the perennial poles of the collective Greek existence, so the second pair provide the framework for most Greek political argument. Lest anyone think that, as a foreigner, I am being altogether too harsh, let me quote again in my support the judgement of that trenchant Greek commentator of half a century ago, George Skleros: 'To this day, our people have been wallowing in a vast sea of subjectivity and a form of self-deceit which leaves no room for self-criticism and precludes any straightforward self-evaluation. This compels them to overlook reality, to give exaggerated explanations of the most simple and human events, and to become swamped by an endless flow of pompous self-flattery about their ancient heritage and their so called incomparable attributes. . . . A direct result of this personality make-up is a frightful mistrust and suspicion that pervades our people, that is to say, we suspect any acts of others as being motivated solely by the desire for gain and we cannot conceive of the fact that an act can be motivated by unselfish and higher human ethical forces. . . .'[11]

These are harsh words, indeed, such as perhaps only a Greek should—or could—use about Greeks. Yet stripped of the moral judgements with which Skleros has invested them, they are not much different from that sober sociological account of the little village of Vasilika. Both, in fact, are describing to perfection what is nowadays sometimes called a *noyau*—a society bound together by its mutual animosities where, in the words of Robert Ardrey in his book, *The Territorial Imperative*, individuals or groups 'could not survive had they no friends to hate'.[12] This seems to me to express the essence of Greek society. A deep current of rivalry and suspicion, leading even to violence, does indeed run between Greek and Greek; yet it is just that current that seems to provide some of the greatest social and personal satisfactions. Just as the scorpion would have betrayed its nature if it had not stung the frog, if Greek did not struggle with Greek each would lose his sense of identity. Once that is understood, the rest follows: the persistent engagement in competitive one-upmanship, the exaggerated sense of self-esteem, the taste for tension, the high regard for the process of events rather than for their outcome, the refusal to admit self-blame—all these stem from the basic requirement of conflict as the evidence of being. At its most primeval source, therefore, the Greek soul is 'double-born' in this everlasting opposition of Greek against Greek, each needing the other to define himself by in a perpetual process of conflict, reconciliation and yet more conflict, in the midst of which the individual discovers his identity through the knowledge that the *aghonia* is all.

PART II

MATTERS OF HISTORY

Chapter 6

THE TUG OF WAR

*When Greeks joined Greeks, then was the
tug of war.*
(NATHANIEL LEE)

Traditionally the birth of modern Greece is represented as the fruit
of a love match between heroic Greeks fighting to regain their heritage of freedom and western philhellenes hopefully presiding over
the revival of classical virtues. In fact it was much more the result of
a shaky marriage of convenience between Greek ambitions and
western power amid the complex entanglements of what came to be
known as the Eastern Question. We have already seen in what
mental and historical confusions the first idea was rooted and to
what persistent misunderstandings it has given birth. It is time now to
turn to some of the more practical ambiguities in which the second
union resulted by adding the shifting oppositions of Great Power
rivalry to the multiple tensions of the Greeks themselves in an intricate interplay of mutual exploitation and betrayal that has lasted
down to our own day.

At the opening of the nineteenth century no western traveller
could doubt that the Orient, in all its imagined romance and actual
barbarity, was in full command in Greece. It was not just that the
Ottomans were its rulers—the very incarnation of eastern power. It
was that the Greeks themselves appeared to western eyes so
thoroughly, and often shockingly, oriental. They ate oriental food
and played oriental music, wore eastern clothes and flourished
eastern daggers; and although they remained resolutely Christian,
their worship was of a garishly eastern and mysterious sort unacceptable to decent gentlemen, and their priests were knavishly
dirty and rebellious fellows, who seemed as ready to fight as to pray.
Moreover, and conclusively, the Greeks were widely reckoned to be
dishonest, and their land was patently in a most lamentable state of
division and decay. 'The natives here', wrote the Russian Admiral
Orlov in 1770, during an abortive attempt to assist a minor rebellion

against the Turks in the Peloponnese, 'are sycophantic, deceitful, impudent, fickle and cowardly, completely given over to money and to plunder.'[1] Other visitors, less directly involved in Greek affairs, could afford occasionally to be more charitable, but the overwhelming impression recorded by them at the time was that poverty was the common lot and cunning, intrigue and factionalism its universal accompaniments.

There is no cause to question the validity of these judgements. Peninsular Greece by 1800 was, indeed, in a sorry way. Whatever prosperity it had once enjoyed in the heyday of the classical city states had been ruined and forgotten long ago—wrecked by repeated invasions, dispersed by perpetual emigration, suppressed and drained of all remaining substance by centuries of Byzantine exactions, Frankish and Venetian conquest and Turkish misrule. What remained was one of the poorest of Ottoman provinces, where banditry was rife, the administration was corrupt and local governors and village chieftains disputed with each other for the spoils of power. Only in the islands was the picture more cheerful. There the Greek tradition of mercantile adventure had been maintained under both Venetian and Turkish authority; and in places like Syros, Hydra, Chios and Kasos, shipowners and sea captains who were half traders and half pirates enjoyed a life of comparative wealth and privilege.

Distressed as the condition of mainland Greece might be, however, it was little worse than the state of the Ottoman empire as a whole. Since the Turkish army was defeated at the gates of Vienna in 1683, the empire had been retreating steadily into physical disruption and moral lassitude, while 'the fatal idea' of western nationalism against which the Turkish wave had broken had begun to seep with the backwash into all the Ottoman provinces. By the beginning of the nineteenth century the process was well advanced. In Egypt the Albanian adventurer Mehemet Ali, was profiting from the shock of Napoleon's expedition to create a state that was effectively independent, although still in nominal fealty to the Sultan in Stamboul; Serbia rose against the Turks in 1804, and in the Epirus a local Ottoman governor named Ali Pasha was asserting his independence of the Porte. With this manifest decline in the old eastern order, the Great Powers of Europe were forced to contemplate, in mingled greed, fear and confusion, the possibility that the Ottoman Empire might soon cease to exist. Cautiously, therefore, and often reluctantly, Britain, France and Russia began a three-cornered struggle for the inheritance of Turkish power, while Austria-Hungary—in the prudent person of Chancellor Metternich—kept a nervously watchful balance between them. The long wrangle of the Eastern Question had begun; and for many decades Greece was to be one of its chief arenas.

For the Greeks, this new stirring of western interest in Ottoman affairs offered the first real prospect of salvation from their own sad condition. There had been plenty of minor rebellions in the peninsula in the eighteenth century, but none that the Turks had been unable to suppress and none in which the other powers had shown more than a perfunctory, and often timorous, interest. But when the decline in Ottoman power forced itself on western eyes the Greeks took heart and their leaders—especially those of westernized education or experience—did their best to inflame by flattery and action the new urge to intervention in the Sultan's provinces that flickered uncertainly at first in London, Paris, Moscow and Vienna.

The western philhellenes gave them an eager audience. Inspired by their self-imposed debt to the classical past they presented the benighted, oriental plight of Greece as the first great international affront to the new liberal conscience of the West; and although at first their success was limited, Byron's martyrdom at Missolonghi enabled them eventually to transform the untidy squabbles of Greek nationalism into Europe's most fashionably romantic cause. This was undeniably fortunate for the Greeks, for it saved their movement from the sort of blank incomprehension, neglect or disapproval that most western capitals still displayed at that time towards equally restive nationalists among the Serbs and Bulgars. But on its own the philhellenic lobby could do little except spread emotional propaganda and inspire a few idealists to join the Greek guerrilla bands. To establish their national freedom as a fact rather than a dream the Greeks had to await the action of the governments of the Great Powers—and for all their attempts to provoke it that was painfully slow in its arrival.

The reasons for the early reluctance of the powers to intervene even after the Ottoman Empire had plainly begun to crumble were not unlike those which have helped to preserve the peace of Europe since the Second World War. Then, as now, the one thing on which all the powers were agreed was that stability was the prerequisite of their diplomacy. The French revolution and the Napoleonic wars had shaken them all; and the Congress of Vienna with which the wars ended had established a set of guide-lines and spheres of influence which, although they might not satisfy anyone fully, at least left no one totally without reward. The incipient collapse of the Ottoman Empire threatened this hard-won balance of power almost as soon as it had been created. To the Tsar Alexander I in Moscow and to Metternich in Vienna, insurrection in any of the Ottoman provinces seemed the all-too-likely forerunner of rebellion in their own sprawling multi-national empires, from which they might not recover. To Britain and France, likewise, Ottoman decay posed a threat of renewed strife, but this time in the eastern Mediterranean where they might find themselves at war with each other and with Russia over the division of the spoils. All four agreed, therefore, that the Ottoman structure should be preserved lest its end provoke another European free-for-all whose outcome none of them could foresee. Together, they turned their backs upon the Greeks and piously hoped that the Turks would re-establish their control of the peninsula as quickly as possible.

Yet Great Powers would hardly be Great Powers had they not as sharp an eye for the main chance as for the principal threat; and in their sidelong glances, so to speak, they could see that, when a suitable moment arose, the situation in Greece happened to offer to three out of four of them a tempting prospect of extending their respective spheres of influence. The opportunities were basically the mirror-images of the dangers. On the face of things, Russia both had most to gain and the best cards to play with. The prizes to be won by her out of Ottoman decline were, firstly, the allegiance of the Slav territories, and secondly, control of the Turkish Straits—the famous warm water outlet that has always lain close to the heart of Russian foreign policy. Pursuing these, Russia had been encroaching on Turkish territory for half a century already and Catherine the Great had even flirted with Greek rebellion. The unhappy Admiral Orlov, who found the rebels so awful, was, indeed, her emissary. But there were additional reasons for Russia's interest in Greece that the other powers did not share and which, for a time, promised to give her an advantage in Greece that might even have outweighed the threat of infectious rebellion spreading into Russia's own provinces. One was the natural sympathy between the Russian Orthodox Church and its counterpart in Greece, which persuaded many Greeks—with characteristic over-optimism—that Russia was bound to be their most ardent ally against the heathen Turk. The other was the presence of several distinguished Greeks in the service of the Tsar, which ensured that the issue of Greek independence was never without influential champions in Moscow. Two of these especially did their best to make Greek and Russian interests meet for the benefit of both sides. Alexander Ypsilantis was one: a Phanariote Greek who resigned his commission as a general in the Russian army to become the leader of a Greek 'freedom society'—the *Philiki Etairia*, founded by Greek merchants in Odessa in 1814. Early in 1821 Ypsilantis provided the first foreign military aid for the rebels in Greece when he led a small force across the river Pruth into Wallachia, the northernmost Ottoman province, in an attempt to provoke an anti-Turkish rising there to coincide with the Greek outburst in the Peloponnese where his brother, Dimitrios, had been appointed rebel military commander by the *Philiki Etairia*. John Capodistrias was the other principal Greek figure in Russia: a foreign minister of the Tsar who was President of another Greek exile society and who was widely believed to be a secret member of the *Philiki Etairia*. Capodistrias resigned from the Tsar's service in 1822 to devote himself to the Greek struggle and in 1827 became the first President of an independent republican Greece.

Had Alexander I been less afraid of revolution breaking out again all over Europe he might have exploited these valuable connexions to win an early foothold in Greece that the other powers could not at first have equalled. But his fears were greater than his taste for a gamble. Ypsilantis's adventure was allowed to collapse in utter failure and the rebels in the Peloponnese secured no further Russian aid. Not until Alexander's brother, Nicholas, was enthroned in Moscow four years later did Russia's Greek policy grow bolder when Nicholas sought to use the Greeks as a lever against the Turks. But even then, and in spite of the subsequent Presidential triumph of Capodistrias, it was inhibited partly by Nicholas's strong personal dislike of the Greeks and partly by the daunting disapproval of the other three Great Powers who persistently frustrated the Russian wish to use the Greeks against the Turks by supporting the Turks against the Russians.

This was especially important for Britain and France, who were allied in their desire to keep Russia out of the Mediterranean and therefore to maintain Turkish control of the Straits of Constantinople. At the same time, however, their own Mediterranean rivalry was deepened by their fierce competition for supremacy on the route to India. Napoleon's Egyptian adventure and defeat had sounded the first shots in that war; and now, a quarter of a century later, under the tattered umbrella of nominal Ottoman sovereignty, British and French commercial and cultural agents were snapping at each other's heels everywhere from Alexandria to Aleppo. Any additional influence that either power might gain through helping to create a client state in Greece would obviously be of advantage in this eastern rivalry; and with their growing naval power they were each in a position to assert their strategic claims in the peninsula if and when the right moment came. Only Austria-Hungary could see no profit in helping the Greeks. Apart from fearing that the infection of rebellion might spread to her own imperial provinces, she recognized that if the Ottoman Empire did fall apart she was less likely than any of her rivals to pick up any of the pieces. Unlike Russia she could not appeal to the ethnic sentiment of the Slavs, or to feelings of religious and diplomatic solidarity with the Greeks. Nor could she match the naval strength of Britain and France in a competition for influence on the Mediterranean seaboard. Chancellor Metternich remained, therefore, a firm supporter of the *status quo* and of the Sultan in Stamboul, and for as long as the ambitions of the other three powers were paralysed by their mutual fears and jealousies he was able to dominate his fellow-statesmen. It was not until more than a decade after the first Congress of Vienna and six years after the outbreak of the Greek war that the balance finally was tipped against him, from Great Power inaction to intervention in Greece. The catalyst of change was the physical appearance inside Greece itself of still another power that suffered none of the inhibitions of the European rivals and none of the weary inefficiency of the Turks. Egypt had arrived in the person of Ibrahim Pasha—Mehemet Ali's son—who first entered Greece in 1825 and by 1827 was leading a powerful army in a brisk campaign throughout the Peloponnese on the Sultan's behalf, killing men and burning villages with oriental gusto.

Neither Mehemet Ali nor Ibrahim Pasha was personally concerned one way or the other with the fate of the Greeks. What they wanted was to inherit the Ottoman Empire in the Middle East; and for that purpose they were prepared to fight the Sultan's battles for him until they were strong enough to seize the Sultan's title. Egypt was emerging, therefore, as yet another rival in the eastern Mediterranean power-struggle and Britain and France, particularly, had an interest in seeing its progress checked. Moreover, Ibrahim's intervention in the Peloponnese had given the philhellenes their biggest boost since the death of Byron. Greek captives, it was reported, were being sold as slaves in Cairo and genocide was threatened throughout the Greek mainland. Humanitarian sympathies and reasons of state combined, therefore, to force the European powers into action. The British Foreign Secretary, George Canning, made the first move, characteristically coating the strategic pill of intervention with the sugar of enlightened philhellenism. 'Though he was a Tory by tradition,' wrote H. A. L. Fisher, 'and the member of a Tory government which viewed all rebels with disfavour, he was not prepared to see the most illustrious corner of Europe and the original home of its civilization settled by a population of fellaheen and negroes. Rather than acquiesce in the extermination of the Greeks he invited the intervention of the powers.'² Austria refused his invitation, out of what Fisher called her 'steady hatred of liberty', but really for what might be better described as her usual jealousy of the other powers and her fears for her own security. France accepted for sentimental and strategic reasons akin to those of Britain, and Russia joined in because she could not afford to be left out—and, anyway, by then the cautious Alexander was dead and the new Tsar Nicholas was already urging a stronger policy against the Turks.

Even so, it was a hesitant, mousey little move the three of them made at first. By the Treaty of London, signed in July 1827, they recommended limited home rule for the Greeks in the Peloponnese. The Sultan's sovereignty, they suggested, should remain unaffected, and Greeks beyond the Peloponnese should continue under Ottoman rule as before. It was an attempt to have their cake of Ottoman stability and eat it at the same time and it was no doubt doomed, whatever happened, to the brief life of all such uneasy compromises. In the event, however, its qualifications were swept aside almost at once in a fashion that signalled the end of effective Ottoman power in Greece and the consequent irrevocable immersion of the Great Powers in the bog of Greek affairs.

Among the provisions of the Treaty of London was one enabling the three signatories to establish a 'peaceful blockade' in Greek waters if the Sultan and his Egyptian allies failed to accept the Treaty's terms. Flushed with the success of Ibrahim's campaign, the Sultan rejected them, and ordered the Turkish and Egyptian fleets to maintain a supply route for Ibrahim so that he could finish his job. The two fleets met and anchored together in the great land-locked bay of Navarino, near the south-western tip of the peninsula. There, in October, 1827, the fate of Greece and, to a great extent, of the Ottoman Empire, was settled in a few hours of cannon-shot. Right up to the end there was something diffident and haphazard about the matter for the Great Powers never seemed to lose hope that they could somehow steer clear of embarrassing entanglements in Greece. When the British, French and Russian fleets gathered outside Navarino under the command of the British Admiral Codrington, their brief was still, under the terms of the Treaty of London, to impose a 'peaceful blockade' and persuade Ibrahim to go home quietly, leaving the Greeks to their emasculated home rule. Only Admiral Codrington seems to have asked the obvious question: 'How can we coerce the Turks without hostilities?'[3] There was, and could have been, only one answer, and whether by accident or design it was soon evoked. On 20th October the tripartite fleet sailed into Navarino bay in an impressive show of strength, but flying a flag of truce to show that no engagement was intended. Sliding slowly through the still waters within hailing distance of the Turkish and Egyptian lines they must have looked a thoroughly provoking sight; and it is difficult not to think that Codrington intended them to be so. At all events, when a Turkish vessel fired the first nervous shot, the European ships were ready with a devastating reply. Within a few hours of close engagement they had sent virtually the entire enemy fleet to the bottom of the bay. The bones of the ships lie there still, and in the flat calm of a summer dawn the boatmen of the little town of Pylos on the Peloponnesian shore will take you out to look at them—faint, dark patterns in the sandy seabed, fathoms deep in the clear, sun-and-fish-flecked water. They are not, it must be said, the most compelling vision in the world; and even the most ardent student of Greek history might be forgiven for thinking at that hour that they are not worth getting out of bed for. Yet, phantom and fleeting as they now seem, their significance can hardly be over-estimated, for they commemorate the day when Greece was assured of her modern independence and the Great Powers of Europe were sunk up to their necks willy-nilly in the intricate diplomacy and ceaseless emotion of the Greek cause.

In some ways it was just as well for the Greeks that they were, for like a lot of more recent liberation movements they had been making a sorry mess of the cause on their own. No sooner had they won their first small victories, with the risings of 1821, than they seemed to take their final triumph for granted and fell to quarrelling among themselves with characteristic zest over spoils that were not yet even within their reach. Looked at now through the softening lens of time those internecine fights of the 1820's may seem sometimes farcical; yet they must have been tragic, too, like that macabre scene in Kazantzakis's *Zorba the Greek*, where the village women cluster round the dying 'Bouboulina', and—long before she has breathed her last—squabble and scrabble like jackals over her pathetic possessions. Moreover, to anyone familiar with contemporary Greek politics the parallels between then and now seem both laughably and horribly exact. There was, for example, the chronic inability of the Greeks to co-operate in keeping each other's secrets. The plans and intrigues of the supposedly secret *Philiki Etairia* seem to have been every bit as exalted, as incompetent and as widely whispered as those of most of the resistance organizations inspired by the military regime in Greece in the 1960's. 'The existence of the *Philiki Etairia* and its conspiratorial activities in Greece soon became an open secret,' according to one sympathetic historian. 'The organizers were bold to the point of rashness. They exuded plots and promises for which they had little authority. They intrigued with rebels throughout the Ottoman territories in Europe. . . . In particular they persuaded thousands of their followers in Greece that the Tsar was their secret patron, whose armies would see that they did not fail.'[4] The vainglory and over-optimism are painfully familiar; and they threatened then, as they have done many times since in Greece, to snuff out the flame of freedom at its first flicker.

Factionalism, too, came promptly upon the scene, as the multiple schisms of Greek society found expression in fierce political rivalry. The exiled leaders like Capodistrias, with their sophisticated ways and international contacts, were disliked and distrusted by the local Greeks whose horizons were largely bounded by personal ambitions and family loyalties. The traditional clan and village chiefs of the mainland were suspicious of the merchants and successful shipowners of the islands, and the *klephts*, or bandit leaders, of the mountains—combining bravery, ferocity, treachery and avarice in roughly equal parts—were cordially hated by all. Under the stress of these multifarious jealousies, co-operation was impossible. By the end of 1821 no less than four separate 'national assemblies' had been established, all purporting to represent some sort of popular Greek will. They disputed the disposal of what small funds were available to them, and of other money they had not yet got. They drafted constitutions, with all the eagerness and fertility of those pupils of Aristotle who once produced 158 different democratic plans for their master; yet they were still years away from winning a state to embody any of them. When words failed, as they frequently did, they fell upon each other in civil war with the ferocity of those later Greek guerrilla bands who were supposed to be fighting the Germans in the

1940's, but who spent much of the time fighting each other instead. And in perhaps the most pathetic prevision of their subsequent troubles, the Greeks made monarchy a matter of violent dispute among them before they had so much as created a throne. By 1825 no less than six princelings of western Europe had had their names put in the ring for the non-existent crown of an unborn Greece. Unfortunately, none of them especially wanted the job and none had put forward his own name. They were exclusively candidates of the Greek imagination.

Against such a profligate and divided challenge even the decrepit Turkish Empire was not entirely powerless, and without the disaster at Navarino it is likely that the Sultan would have re-established for a time, at least, some general suzerainty over the whole of Greece. But the loss of both the Turkish and Egyptian navies and the subsequent withdrawal of the Egyptians from the battle left the Empire too vulnerable; and under the protecting wing of Britain, France and Russia, the Greek leaders thereafter were able to redouble their fight not just for freedom—for that, albeit limited, was already as good as won—but for power and recognition.

Capodistrias was the first to seize his opportunity. Under the Treaty of London he had been recognized by the three powers as provisional President of an autonomous state of Greece, and within a few months of Navarino he had set himself up in office at the little port of Nauplion, in the northern Peloponnese, which thereby became the first capital of modern Greece. From there, for what must have seemed like the longest three or four years of his life—and were, indeed, to prove the last—he tried vainly to control his quarrelling countrymen with one hand while striving unsuccessfully to enlarge the boundaries of the infant state with the other.

His failure in both respects was painful but illuminating. Now that the Greeks had some sort of homeland they could call their own again they pursued their internal rivalries with all the more passion. With the authoritarianism of his training and experience under the Tsar, and the feelings of superiority natural to a cultivated gentleman who thought himself among ruffians, Capodistrias sought to discipline his compatriots when he found that persuasion left them unmoved. Within a week he had suspended the state's first constitution and was ruling by decree—a device that predictably aroused yet more opposition. At the same time, he launched fresh expeditions and fomented more rebellions in the Greek-speaking highlands and islands beyond the Pelopnonese in an effort to rally support behind him for the greater national cause. But there, predictably also, he encountered the opposition of the very powers which had just conferred his brief authority upon him. Soon the bitter truth was plain that although the Turks had been obliged to concede defeat after Navarino, it was not the Greeks but the Great Powers who had been the victors, and they were far more concerned about their own security than about the extension of the sort of disorder that evidently passed for Greek liberty. To them it was plain that if the future of the eastern Mediterranean could lie no longer in Turkish hands, it must be taken firmly into their own. What Greeks might propose or Turks dispose was therefore of little moment beside what London, Moscow, Paris or Vienna could or would consent to.

Collectively, that turned out to be as little as possible. Only the Russians supported Capodistrias unequivocally, seeing his campaigns for a greater Greece as an opportunity to force more concessions from the Turks on their own frontiers. Within six months of Navarino, Russia and Turkey were at war; and among the swiftly growing ranks of his enemies inside Greece Capodistrias, with his old Muscovite connexions, was reviled as a pawn of the Tsar. Britain and France were more hesitant than Russia. By their action at Navarino they had helped to make Greek independence an accomplished fact, and they were enviously competing with each other, and with Russia, for influence among the new Greek leaders. On the other hand, they were even more enviously watching the Tsar Nicholas, whose ambitions so plainly threatened their own oriental interests. Supported by Austria, which would have reversed the result of Navarino if it could, Britain and France agreed that if Greece had to be free it had better be small, and ruled by someone biddable. They therefore frowned upon the expansionist efforts of Capodistrias and began, like many of his Greek opponents, to promote the idea of a monarchy in Greece that would end his aspirations by extinguishing the republic.

Quietly, they scanned the royal houses of Europe for a suitable candidate for the putative Greek throne. At the same time, the Greeks were doing their not inconsiderable best to bend the powers to their multifarious wills. They redoubled their appeals, promises and intrigues. Each faction thrust itself upon a foreign patron, so that Russian, French and British 'parties' soon became fixtures of the Greek political scene and statesmen of all three powers were involved, willy-nilly, in the conspiracies of their often self-appointed servants. In this way, for nearly five years the powers and the Greeks trod a jig of tortuous complexity and mutual suspicion while the new Greece

H

slid miserably into anarchy. In 1831, after less than four years of declining authority, Capodistrias was shot down in the streets of Nauplion. His assassins were members of the Mavromichaelis clan who, confidently asserting themselves as members of the 'British' party, were taking revenge for his attempt to challenge by decree their traditional, independent rule in the Mani. Thereafter the chaos deepened until, at last, Russia was persuaded again that the threat of this instability spreading through the Balkans outweighed the advantages to be won from Turkish humiliation. In May 1832, the statesmen of Britain, France and Russia met again in London to complete the work they had begun there five years earlier. This time the document they agreed upon was entitled a convention rather than a treaty, and it set out the terms on which Greece was finally to be free. Although in both sovereignty and territory they were an advance on the Treaty of London, they were still as restrictive as they could well be made after all that had happened since Navarino. Greece was to be a fully independent nation state—but under the formal protection of the three signatories of the convention. Its territory was to be extended north of the Gulf of Corinth—but only as far as a line drawn across the mainland between Volos and Arta, which included Attica and the little town of Athens as well as the whole of the Peloponnese but left all of Epirus, Thessaly, Macedonia and Thrace still under Turkish rule. Most of the islands were excluded also. Corfu and the Ionians remained a British protectorate, as they had been for twenty years since they were seized from the French in the Napoleonic wars. Excepting only a handful the rest remained in Ottoman hands. The structure drafted for this pathetic little rump of Greek-ness was not to be the allegedly democratic republic which, under Capodistrias, had already been tried and found wanting, but a constitutional monarchy with a foreign king—because, it was agreed, the Greeks would surely never consent to any one of themselves occupying the ultimate seat of power.

It remained only to choose the new king. For a decade the non-existent throne of Greece had been hawked around Europe like a chamber-pot at auction, looking for some luckless prince to sit on it. Now that it was to exist, after all, the choice of occupant had to be made with care. Significantly, the criterion proved to be wholly negative—not who was the most suitable candidate, but who was the least unsuitable. The choice fell upon the young Prince Otto of Bavaria—a stripling of seventeen who spoke no Greek, was a Roman Catholic and was accustomed to the distinctly illiberal traditions of the German aristocracy, but who had the negative advantages of being neither a scion of any of the royal families of the protecting powers nor the choice of any significant faction in Greece. In short, he had few friends but—a far greater rarity in Greece—few enemies, either. The enemies would, of course, appear soon enough; but in the meantime, in January 1833, he arrived at Nauplion on board a British warship accompanied by 3,500 Bavarian soldiers to keep the peace and a panel of three Bavarian Regents to help him run the place. Modern Greece had been born at last.

As Fisher observed with his customary elegance, 'this resurrection of Greece, little as it altered the balance of power in Europe, was a most significant fact. It was here that the first successful blow was administered to the autocratic government of Europe by Congress; here that the Ottoman Empire received its most sensible wound; here that the modern spirit of nationalism, destined to govern Italy and Poland, Bohemia and Ireland, and to bring the Austrian Empire to the ground, won its first romantic and resounding triumph.'[5] Yet for the Greeks, more than anyone, their resurrection was inauspicious, holding the promise of trouble for practically every aspect of their new life.

History has amply fulfilled that promise, and contemporary Greek politics have continued the sorry tale. By leaving so many Greek-speaking areas still under foreign rule the frontiers of 1832 were an invitation to fresh rebellion and irredentism—and from Thrace, Thessaly, Macedonia and the Epirus, to Crete, Smyrna and Cyprus, those have duly been inspired and their effects are with us still. The monarchy was as plainly a potential focus of disruption as of unity —and from that day to this it has proved to be so. The intensity of factionalism was clearly a menace to any political system—and repeatedly through the last century and a half that has been the case. Most of all, and perhaps worst of all, Great Powers and Greeks were inextricably linked in a symbiotic relationship of patronage in which the influence and protection of the one over the other were as widely resented as they were eagerly sought. That, also, has not ceased to be true.

Modern Greece was born, therefore, in this single decade of pride and prejudice, like the Pallas Athene of her classical past—full-armed with all the traits of her maturity. Unhappily, these included neither the wisdom nor the power with which the goddess was blessed. Instead, weakness, division, folly and intransigence were to be her perpetual burdens.

Chapter 7

THE GREAT IDEA

The politicians systematically cultivated the deceitful belief that Europe was duty-bound to look after Greece.

(GEORGE SKLEROS)

Like the illegitimate child of some hedgerow affair, modern Greece was born out of, and into, the politics of irresponsibility. At the moment of union between the Great Powers and the Greeks in which the infant state was conceived, neither side had shown much concern for the real character and interests of the other. The result, as we have just seen, was a bit of a bastard. The new Greece was, indeed, wholly new because no nation state of Greece had ever before existed; yet it had behind it supposedly the longest and most distinguished history known to the civilized world, and some of its best friends accordingly urged benefits upon it and expected standards from it that were equally beyond its merits. Its people knew no tradition of western monarchy, yet they were saddled with a foreign king who neither spoke their language nor shared their religion. It was constitutionally free and independent, yet its boundaries left millions of Greeks in servitude beyond them while those within them had to accept the hard fact, embodied in the formal protectorate of the Convention of London, that they had gained their statehood on sufferance only and were neither intended nor entitled to pursue their own interests without permission. Willy-nilly, they had swopped their old position as vassals of an eastern empire for the equally humiliating posture of dependence upon a western alliance. That alliance, moreover, was as riven by contradictory stresses as the new Greek state itself. As Britain, France and Russia pursued their separate interests in the Eastern Question throughout the nineteenth and into the twentieth century, their conflicts made Greece more than ever their battleground while rival Greek statesmen increasingly sought refuge and power in their embrace. Thus, the relationship between the Greeks and their patrons became a classic case of multiple neo-colonial irresponsibility in which each party misled and exploited the others in a vicious circle of intrigue, flattery and deceit. Superficially, it was a happy enough game for the Greeks, as the British traveller Charles Kinglake illustrated metaphorically, by describing how it was played by Greek sailors in the earliest years of independence. 'The first care of the Greeks when they undertake a shipping enterprise, is to procure for their vessel the protection of some European Power. This is easily managed by a little intriguing with the dragoman of one of the embassies at Constantinople, and the craft soon glories in the ensign of Russia, or the dazzling tricolour, or the Union Jack. Thus, to the great delight of her crew, she enters upon the ocean world with a flaring lie at her peak; but the appearance of the vessel does no discredit to the borrowed flag: she is frail, indeed, but is gracefully built and smartly rigged: she always carries guns and, in short, gives good promise of mischief and speed.'[1]

There was certainly mischief enough about the various Greek political factions, and plenty of flaring lies at their peak, as they settled to the game of intrigue with the European powers. But in politics it was to prove a more serious business than in sailing for the cost of it in the long run was an appalling demoralization of Greek public life and a series of national calamities. What most Greek statesmen seemed unable to keep constantly in view was that although the affairs of Greece might be vital to them they were only incidental to the Great Powers. In London, Paris or Moscow, as the British writer, A. P. Herbert once observed, the elevation of 'Mr. Popoulos' over 'Mr. Dopoulos' was a matter of indifference except in so far as it advanced or retarded the respective interests of Britain, France or Russia. To be sure, certain ties of sentiment remained to confuse the facts of power with heartfelt rhetoric. In Britain, the tradition of philhellenism and the memory of Byron combined with the Victorian nonconformist Christian conscience (especially as expressed in Mr. Gladstone's execration of 'the unspeakable Turk') to ensure that the cause of Greek liberty was never overlooked. In France, the new republicanism and an elegant and self-confident culture established a constant pole of attraction for many cultivated Greeks. In Russia the religious bonds of Orthodoxy and the historical links between Moscow and the Phanariotes continued to awaken influential echoes. Even Austria and later on, Germany, established special relationships outside the bounds of simple power politics partly through the family connexions which developed between the Greek and German royal houses and partly because of the legacy of King

Otto's thirty years on the Greek throne, which left a tradition of German training in the Greek army and German learning in the Greek academies whose effects can still be discerned. But with the possible exception of the philhellenic tradition, to which many western politicians continued to pay lip service, if little else, all these links loomed larger in Greek minds and politics than in the chanceries of Europe. There, as always, the fundamental issue was power, to which the affairs of Greece in themselves were peripheral. Britain and France were more interested in India, Egypt and the Middle East, Russia in the Slav lands and the Straits of Constantinople. Greece lay on the fringe of both sets of interest—significant, but hardly a matter of life and death, and certainly not to be pursued or cultivated for its own sake. So while the Greek politicians schemed and orated, persuading themselves and their friends that this or that power was indissolubly bound to them in whatever project they had just conceived (or, alternatively, that it was unalterably opposed to whatever project someone else had just dreamed up), the apparent objects of their esteem or disapproval in London, Paris and Moscow were often more aloof and cautious than they seemed to be.

For a long time this was especially true of Britain, which continued after the War of Independence to be more concerned, as a rule, with maintaining the Ottoman Empire than with fostering Greek national ambitions. With her seaborne trade and swiftly growing eastern empire, Britain's interest was simply to keep the Mediterranean littoral as free as possible from hostile or unstable influences. A moribund Turkey was no great menace. A turbulent Greece might be. The safest course, therefore, was to keep the Ottoman Empire alive as long as possible as a *cordon sanitaire* around the eastern Mediterranean against the thrusts of Britain's rivals. Often this meant that the Greeks were frustrated by British support of Turkey against their own designs, as they had been after Navarino and were again in the aftermath of the Crimean War, yet again in the Cretan struggle for *enosis* towards the end of the century, and even more, in somewhat different circumstances, in the Cypriot campaign for *enosis* half a century after that. Yet in the end it was Britain that emerged as Greece's chief friend and protector for, as Turkish strength continued to wane everywhere, Britain was compelled to assume a more direct interest in the Mediterranean territories. Especially after the cutting of the Suez Canal and the subsequent British entry into Egypt, Greece became more important as a foothold on the northern coast from which to watch the Turkish straits and straddle the east–

west trade route; and although a warmer British embrace did not at first bring any relaxation of British restrictions on Greek action, it did supply a welcome guarantee of Greek security against anyone else's attacks.

This was particularly important along Greece's northern frontiers, where the rising power of Slav nationalism, fostered by Russia, presented a constant challenge to Greek ambitions. By the end of the nineteenth century, as Ottoman authority declined and Moscow's pan-Slavism gained momentum, the Greeks were fighting as many wars against their Slav neighbours as they were against the Turks, and in those circumstances Anglo-Greek friendship became as natural as Russo-Greek hostility. But in the end British supremacy in Greece was a function of the simple fact that Britain was the world's premier naval power. As the Battle of Navarino had dramatically demonstrated, the reappearance of peninsular Greece as an independent entity was irrevocably associated with the superiority of sea power over land power around the Mediterranean shores. At that time the vanquished land power was Turkish. That later it was to be represented by Russia or Germany made little difference to the geo-political equation. When any land power threatened to reassume a dominant role in Greece, independent Greek statesmen were bound to look to Britain for protection. Long before the First World War began, therefore, when Turkey joined Germany against the Allies and what was left of the Ottoman Empire crumbled into the dust of history, an Anglo-Greek partnership already seemed to many statesmen on both sides almost a predestined fact of life.

Only France—like Britain, essentially a maritime power as far as the Mediterranean and the Orient were concerned—boasted a similar set of conjoint interests. Had she, rather than Britain, become the ruler of Egypt and India and the consequent guardian of the eastern lifeline of empire, she might well have assumed Britain's eventual place in Greece. As it was, being only the second imperial power of the Orient, she also tended to play second fiddle in Greece, sometimes endorsing and sometimes opposing British policies there, but never strong enough to replace British influence with her own.

The Russians, on the other hand, suffered more than their two chief rivals in Greece from divided aims and uncertain leadership, veering repeatedly from caution to boldness and back again to caution as the Tsar Alexander and Nicholas had done from the start, in the 1820's. In their anxiety to penetrate the Turkish Empire and gain the Turkish Straits the Russians more than once encouraged

Greek expansionism, as they did after Navarino. Yet early and late, their efforts in Greece were never really successful, partly because the natural alliance with the Greeks against the Turks was increasingly cancelled out by the animosity of the Greeks for the Slavs, but ultimately because, as representatives of a land power, they were unable to bring their full strength to bear in the Greek peninsula. Indeed, compared to the maritime powers, they had far less compelling reasons to do so. In the overall balance of power Russia's vital interests always lay elsewhere—as Alexander I recognized when he chose to preserve the peace of Europe rather than risk it for the sake of Greece, and as his successor, Nicholas, accepted also when he finally underwrote the Anglo-French concept of a small, client state of Greece under the London Convention instead of continuing to press for something bigger at the expense of the Ottoman Empire. Subsequent pro-Greek shifts in Russian policy, such as support for a Greek war against the Turks to coincide with the Crimean campaign, ended in similar disillusioning adjustments when Moscow's ambitions ran headlong into Anglo-French hostility. Nevertheless, Russia's influence in Greece could never be discounted, if only because it was often crucial in determining how much weight Greeks would attach to their British and French connexions.

Thus, as the death watch continued throughout the nineteenth century over the shrivelling body of the Turkish Empire, Greece's self-appointed guardians replaced their brief tripartite alliance at Navarino with an eternal triangle of compromise and dissension. More often than not their compromises were made and unmade over issues far removed from Greece. Britain and Russia were joined against France in 1841 over French support in Egypt for Mehemet Ali who had declared his independence of the Sultan, while forty years later the situation was reversed when Russia and France combined to oppose the British occupation of Egypt. In between, Britain and France fought Russian expansion in the Crimea; and when the new power of Germany entered the eastern lists in earnest with Bismarck's *Drang Nach Osten*, the convolutions became still more twisted. Every possible grouping was embraced and rejected again, as each power sought to gain some advantage over the others, while the others combined to destroy its hopes. Yet although Greece was often only on the periphery of these struggles, her politics inevitably mirrored them, as foreign ambassadors and Greek statesmen wove around each other their webs of patronage and dependence.

Mostly, like Kinglake's sailors, the Greek politicians got the better of the arrangement, for it fitted their character and experience like a second skin. The humiliation of their dependence was deliciously compensated by the flattering interest of their patrons. Wooed alternately by one or another of them, so that they were never wholly without a suitor, they were confirmed, both individually and collectively, in their natural *hubris*; and when things went wrong, as they often did, they were equally confirmed in the comfortable belief that their misfortunes were really the fault of other people, for they could always point to the intervention of the Great Powers as proof that Greeks were literally not responsible for their own affairs. Moreover, they were agreeably conscious that even if they were caught in the extremities of folly one of their patrons would generally find powerful reasons of state for coming to their rescue. In this splendid combination of pride, guiltlessness and comparative security their statesmen could, and zealously did, pursue the most inflated policies of personal and national aggrandizement without a visible qualm.

Unfortunately, a situation better calculated to deepen existing political schisms, inflame ambitions, corrupt institutions and generally delay the emergence of stable government in Greece could scarcely have been imagined. The rot began at once with the young King Otto and his Bavarians. Understandable—even, probably, inescapable—though it was, King Otto's preference for foreign advisers and foreign troops seemed an immediate affront to the Greek leaders of the independence struggle. Klephts and sea captains, merchants and Phanariotes, clan chiefs and Orthodox priests, they had none of them imagined their many-sided battle with the Turks and with each other would end in another form of alien rule. But demonstrably, that was what had happened; and although Otto showed himself as committed as any true-born Greek to the cause of a greater Greece, he could not persuade his new subjects of his Greek-ness. Persuasion, anyway, was not his favoured method. Out of a mingled sense of philhellenic duty and Germanic paternalism Otto and his Regents, like Capodistrias before them, determined that a firm hand was the best hand with such an uncouth people and proceeded to instruct the Greeks, *de haut en bas*, in the manner of administration proper to enlightened governments. They rejected all suggestions for an elected assembly. They disbanded all but a handful of the armed bands and soldiers that had fought in the War of Independence. They gathered all the administration of the country into their hands, sending clerks to confound villagers with the new red tape of bureaucracy and elevating only the most pliant, reliable and westernized of Greeks to positions of consequence in their administration. And they levied, or did their utmost to levy, taxes such as the Turks for a long time had been too idle or inefficient to collect.

It was all too much for the Greeks, and where corruption did not immediately undermine these worthy efforts insurrection soon threatened to overwhelm them. Before long Greek leaders of every persuasion were beating well-worn paths to the doors of the British, French and Russian representatives in Athens, the new capital, to demand still more foreign help against these wretched new foreigners. In doing so they established from the outset a paradox of Greek national attitudes that is still unresolved: namely, that while they claimed to be pursuing a 'true'—i.e. unfettered—independence, they were simultaneously ensuring that their nation's destiny would be still more closely interlocked with the rivalry of the protecting powers. More than a century later in the Cyprus crisis, this conflict between the national desire for 'absolute' sovereignty and the pragmatic necessity for retaining powerful friends was at the root of the eternal Greek dilemma over *enosis*; and just as it helped then to rock more than one Greek government and befuddle more than one opposition, so in these early years of independence it both shook Otto's party and divided his opponents. In the event, Otto survived without serious mishap for a full ten years until, exasperated beyond restraint by his high-minded paternalism and their own exclusion from the spoils of office, the native Greek leaders turned upon him. Enlisting the aid of the Athens garrison—the only Greek soldiers still under arms—they cornered Otto in his new palace in the centre of the city and forced him to accept a parliamentary constitution. The brave new Greece, Shelley's 'nobler Athens', had suffered its first *coup d'état*.

The name of Constitution Square in Athens is one memorial of that day, but there were two other results of rather more consequence. The first was the prompt and continuing corruption of Greek parliamentary life, for in effect what the constitution did was merely to insert into Otto's administrative pyramid a new but wholly native layer of patronage and favouritism in the guise of the National Assembly. The Assembly's powers were relatively small, for the King retained a right of veto and the authority to appoint and dismiss Ministers from among the members of the Assembly without consultation. The King's own power of patronage was therefore practically unaffected: all he had to do was to exercise it through the Assembly, so that those politicians who had previously been so disaffected should get their due reward. Between them, in short, the erstwhile rebels and the King had agreed on a set of jobs for the boys. The second result in many ways followed from the first—the corruption of the Greek desire for territorial expansion into a stepping-stone to office. When kingly patronage alone failed to ensure a man his seat in Parliament or his place in a Ministry, a call for *enosis* with Crete, or Thessaly or Macedonia might do the trick, especially if it could be made to coincide with the interests of one or more of the protecting powers, which might then feel disposed to support not only the call but the politician who made it. It was in these squalid circumstances that the Great Idea was born, to set the bounds of modern Greece wider still, and wider, and to bedevil both the Greeks and the Great Powers for the next three-quarters of a century.

It is hard nowadays for foreigners to take the Great Idea seriously, so patently absurd does it seem, in the second half of the twentieth century, that anyone should ever have entertained the notion that Byzantium could be reborn. As we have already seen, it was a concept based on an inherent—although characteristically Greek—contradiction, for while Greece was seeking to make itself a modern nation-state it could not simultaneously re-create itself as a multi-national empire. The Serbs, Bulgars and Albanians on Greece's northern frontiers felt the same desire as the Greeks to be free, and were not disposed to exchange Turkish rule for a renewed Greek hegemony. The Orthodox Church might link them, as it once had done in Byzantine days, but the new idea of nationalism divided them far more effectively, so that any grand Greek design for expansion was bound to run into immediate and continuing opposition from all of Greece's neighbours. On the other hand, no one could really object in principle to the Greek desire to unite within new national frontiers at least the nearer parts of the diaspora, where Greeks were genuinely in a majority; and if that ambition had been pursued with coolness and realism everyone might have been spared a great deal of trouble. Coolness and realism, however, were qualities conspicuously lacking in Greek politics, then as now. To the passions of factional intrigue the Greeks added their immemorial sense of being a chosen people to whom the world—and especially the western world—owed a decent homage; and they were encouraged in this belief by many of their foreign friends and patrons who, either out of cynical political calculation or sentimental and misinformed phil-hellenism, offered all too many words and gestures of admiration and support. The result was to convince the Greeks that in any

serious conflict with their neighbours they would always enjoy a
moral advantage, so that in a constant spiral of Greek ambition,
factional dispute and foreign patronage the pursuit of a legitimate
national purpose was transformed into a *folie de grandeur*—the
tragically anachronistic vision of a new Greek Empire that would
rise, like the phoenix, from the ashes of Ottoman defeat, and that
ended, inevitably, in disaster.

The *folie* was conceived in the few years immediately following
the constitutional *coup d'état* through the interplay of mutual interest
between King Otto and his new Prime Minister, John Kolettis, on
one side and France and Russia—with some unwitting help from
Britain—on the other. Kolettis, who had been a leader in the recent
coup, has been depicted as the evil genius of the Great Idea, but in
fact he was probably only doing what any other Greek would have
done in his position. Having achieved office, he wanted to stay there,
and he saw the popular advantage he would have over his rivals if
he used his Ministry to further the patriotic cause of Greek expansion. He therefore summoned up from the Greek past the vision of
a new Byzantium, and enlisted French support for his proposals.
Otto also was eager to outwit the other politicians, who had so
recently joined Kolettis in outwitting him in the *coup d'état*. Uniting
his Prime Minister's expediency to his own acquired sense of Greek
national duty he exploited the openings that the British, as it happened, were quick to give to him. As usual, Britain was anxious to
maintain the Turks and restrain the Greeks. A series of small interventions to this end culminated in 1850 in the ludicrous affair of
Don Pacifico, when the British Government demanded restitution
from Greece for the destruction by anti-British Athenian mobs of the
home of a Jew of that name who enjoyed nominal British nationality.
When the Greeks refused and the Royal Navy was sent to blockade
Piraeus in earnest enforcement of London's demands, Otto became
a national hero. He also won the automatic support of the Russians,
who were just as eager to destroy the Turks as the British were to
sustain them, and who therefore encouraged Greek nationalist ambition. Although by then Kolettis was dead his successors had immediately assumed his methods and in the fever of national feeling they
aroused against Britain, with the Russians making capital out of
their Orthodox Church connexions, Greek horizons widened swiftly,
as Kolettis would have wished, to imperial dimensions.

When, in 1853, Russia and Turkey went to war, the moment of the
chosen people seemed to have come again. The French, they reasoned,

had already supported Kolettis in his idea of a greater Greece; and now, with the Russian attack, the Ottoman Empire apparently was tottering to its end. Constantinople itself was surely within the Greek grasp. Quickly Otto arranged a Greek attack across the southern Ottoman frontiers into Thessaly and Epirus to coincide with the Russian campaigns in the north—and just as swiftly the new-born Great Idea turned into a great dream. For what the Greeks had forgotten was that plain lesson of previous years, that the British and French would not tolerate the destruction of the Turkish Empire by the Russians, and the more Greece seemed to be contributing to that end the more certain would be retribution. The retribution was, in fact, cruelly humiliating. In the spring of the following year Britain and France were joined by Austria in alliance with Turkey against Russia in the Crimean War. The Greek troops in the Balkans were routed, British and French marines occupied Piraeus and Otto was compelled to renounce his alliance with the Tsar. The King had backed the wrong horse too heavily, and he paid for his error eventually with his crown. Within six years of the end of the war a new generation of Greek politicians in a new permutation of local factions and foreign alliances provoked another military rebellion and Otto sailed away into exile, as he had arrived thirty years before, on board a British warship.

Henceforth the supremacy of British naval power in Greek affairs was rarely to be in doubt, and in that fact alone there was, on the face of things, a promise of greater stability to come. Moreover Otto's successor, Prince George of Denmark—chosen, significantly, by the British Government—was perhaps a more level-headed young man than Otto had ever been, and enjoyed several other immediate advantages denied to his predecessor. For one thing, he was submitted to the Greeks for their approval, and secured it in public election, so that they were committed to him at the start as they had never been to Otto. For another he was deliberately entitled 'King of the Hellenes' rather than King of Greece, to indicate that he was himself one of the people he was to reign over. For a third, the new politicians were at least accustomed to constitutional ideas, if scarcely yet to constitutional practice, which was more than could have been said of many of the independence warriors whom Otto had so soon fallen foul of. For a fourth, these new men were the first political reflection of a new middle class emerging in Greece as a result of the development of the country in the previous thirty years, and they might reasonably have been expected to show a greater community of interest among themselves than the older, unruly leaders. And for a fifth, George's reign began auspiciously when the new British Prime Minister, Mr. Gladstone, ceded the Ionian Islands to Greece after some sixty years under the flag of the British Raj. Altogether the omens looked surprisingly good so soon after the last Greek humiliation. Yet swiftly the old realities overwhelmed the new promise. Factionalism flourished as ever, irredentism was just as fierce, and Great Power rivalries continued unabated. Between them these three sustained most Greek minds in a state of constant political inflammation. The best that could be said was that the King kept his throne and the Army kept either to its battlefields or its barracks. Otherwise, Greek governments spent most of their time over the next half-century dreaming of the Great Idea and accomplishing little save to bring the country close to bankruptcy and their own reputations into discredit. As one Greek historian remarked, more in sorrow than in anger, 'Many [Greek politicians] were no doubt ardent patriots who also desired the aggrandisement of their country. But they gave the impression of children crying for the moon—as if their whole policy consisted in hanging up a Kiepert's atlas of the Balkan peninsula on the walls of the Greek Foreign Office, seeing how far the Byzantine Empire stretched at the period of its greatest extension, painting the whole thing blue, and then waiting fatalistically for it to drop one day into their mouths.'[2]

In spite of a constant drumfire of war, guerrilla action, uprising and agitation all around her borders, and in defiance of all the intrigue, manœuvre and rhetoric of her politicians, the only significant territorial gain for Greece in these years was the transfer of Thessaly from Turkey in 1881 as a result of another Russo-Turkish war and the combined pressure of the Great Powers. Cyprus had been transferred from Turkey to Britain meanwhile, Crete was officially 'autonomous' but occupied by the Great Powers, Macedonia was a place of such persistent lawlessness that it had become a European scandal, and in Anatolia a million and a quarter Greeks still groaned, as the rhetoric had it, under the vile Turkish yoke. Greece, which laid claim to all these places in the sacred name of the Greek nation and the Greek past, not only had been cheated of all of them, but had seen its undeserving Slav neighbours (for undeserving they certainly seemed to all good Greeks) win new territories and greater independence while Greece continued in neo-colonial subservience to its supposed protectors—a pawn in the Great Powers' chess game. Put like this, as it often was in the heat of Greek politics, it was all too humiliating to be borne; and repeatedly, Greek governments found they could not bear it. Between 1864 and 1908 Greece had an average of nearly one general election every two years and a new administration every nine months. The politics of irresponsibility had entrenched themselves with a vengeance, and the results were dire.

As the twentieth century opened, according to George Skleros, 'All people admitted that the Greek state and Greek society suffered from some deep ailment and that nothing in Greece functioned properly. They saw their political and administrative machinery a complete wreck. They saw the public services lame and inefficient. They saw the Church in a state of conservative inactivity, lacking inspiration, without creative work. . . . They saw the schools and educational system in a wretched condition, full of the scholastic spirit but incapable of preparing individuals to face life constructively and realistically. They saw the University dominated by a medieval and static spirit, a University controlled by a handful of men who in the name of ancient Greece and the shades of their forefathers resisted the introduction of modern techniques of education and the new scientific spirit into the country's institutions of higher learning. . . . They saw the sciences shackled to routine, parasitic work. . . . They saw their literature and art as purely personal and subjective, completely alien to the people.'[3]

Greece had not much improved, it seemed, upon the lamentable state into which she had been born seventy years before. Nor was she destined to better herself substantially for almost as long again, for that depressing picture of Greece in 1900 is remarkably similar to many that were drawn in the early 1960's; and on both occasions the response was similar—a military *coup d'état*. The army *coup* of 1909 was the first in Greece in this century and it set the pattern in many ways for the others that were to come. Its roots ran deed, feeding upon a general weariness with the political and administrative anarchy in Greece; but its immediate cause was the usual matter of national pride—the collapse of a campaign for *enosis* with Crete in the face of Turkish threats and disapproval by the Great Powers. Once more Greece had been made to look like a pawn in other people's games, and this time the Army felt compelled to intervene as the saviour of the nation's honour—a role in which it has cast itself many times since then—by promising to consummate the union that Greeks in Crete and Greeks in Greece so ardently desired.

Ironically and also, as things turned out, most ominously, the catalyst of this new upheaval was the revelation that the western nationalist infection the Greeks had caught well over a hundred years before had spread at last to their old Ottoman masters. The proof was in the military rebellion of the Young Turks in the previous year which had overthrown the moribund despotism of the Sultans and introduced a form of constitutional government to Constantinople. Suddenly, the rulers were leading the ruled in revolution, and within months all the remaining Ottoman provinces, from the Arab world to the Balkans, were shaken either by imitative nationalist revolt or precautionary annexation by watchful neighbours. But when a Cretan assembly seized the occasion to declare that their island would henceforth be united to Greece, the Greek Government seemed paralysed by its fears of reaction both from Turkey and the Great Powers, whose representatives were still in nominal control of the island. The Army, taking its cue from the Turkish officers who had deposed their old Sultan, swept away those fears by deposing the old politicians and—in a moment of inspiration—inviting the leader of the Cretans to come to the mainland and assume the leadership of Greece. The man concerned was Eleftherios Venizelos, whose name is still venerated today by at least half the people of Greece— and might have been revered by all of them had not he, too, like so many others, allowed his personal *hubris* to mingle with Greek schisms and international chicanery to encompass his downfall when he was apparently at the height of his power.

By any standards Venizelos was evidently a remarkable man. Within three years of his arrival from Crete he had managed to seize the initiative in both domestic and foreign affairs as nobody had done before him, reforming the constitution, attacking some of the chronic administrative weaknesses, and forming new alliances to enable Greece to extend her northern frontiers at last. The Balkan Wars of 1912 and 1913 were among the most confused and confusing engagements ever witnessed in that notoriously muddled corner of eastern Europe, with practically everyone taking turns at fighting practically everyone else; but the eventual results for Greece were gratifying. The annexation of Crete to the mainland was finally established. The southern half of Epirus was also seized from Turkey and much of Macedonia was secured. Greece was almost doubled in size and population and Venizelos became a national hero. So, however, did Greece's new King Constantine, eldest son of George I— and therein lay the seeds of rivalry and defeat for both men.

As Crown Prince, Constantine had commanded the Greek armies

in their northern battles with conspicuous success and had then succeeded to the throne in sentimentally favourable circumstances when King George was shot down by a madman in Salonika in 1913 after achieving the truly remarkable feat of keeping his head and his crown for all but half a century. Now, with the joint triumph of the Balkan Wars behind them, both Constantine and Venizelos scented new possibilities of Greek advantage in the opening of the First World War. Unfortunately for both of them, and even more for Greece, their visions were diametrically opposed. Constantine was married to a sister of the Kaiser and was surrounded by military advisers, trained in the German school, who believed that the German Army was an invincible machine of war. In alliance with Austria and Turkey, it seemed to Constantine that Germany must win; and that in any case Greece could do nothing but harm to herself by taking on three such enemies at once. Moreover there were hints that if Germany did win, Greece might be rewarded for a friendly attitude by the transfer of further territory in the north, from Serbia and Albania. Shrewdly, as he thought, Constantine elected to remain neutral and await such crumbs from the German table.

Venizelos, however, took the opposite view. Emotionally he sympathized with the Allied powers who were also Greece's traditional protectors—Britain, France and Russia. He had grasped the significance of British naval strength, and was dazzled by the bait dangled before him by the Allies, described in a Note from the British Foreign Secretary, Sir Edward Grey, as 'important territorial concessions on the coast of Asia Minor'. Once again the Great Idea seemed attainable and *hubris* took command of judgement. Boldly Venizelos elected to support the Allies, promising to crown his magnificent career by restoring Anatolia to Greek rule.

The resulting clash between the two men, mirroring the conflict of the warring powers in the Near East, split Greece down the middle. Territorially as well as politically the nation was divided by the creation of two governments each claiming to represent Greece. In Athens, Constantine and his friends maintained a royalist administration that was officially neutral but sympathetic to the German cause. In Salonika, Venizelos and his supporters set up a republican government and mustered Greek troops to fight for the Allies. On both sides the rival powers intrigued and bribed their way to influence in an atmosphere of mingled farce and tragedy until, at the end of 1916, the French lost patience and landed marines at Piraeus again to settle the matter. Six months later, with reluctant British support,

I

they had virtually occupied the country. Constantine was forced into exile, leaving his second son Alexander on the throne with Venizelos in command of a mortified—and mortally divided—Greece. No one could escape the effects of so deep a schism. Royalism, meaning support for Constantine, and republicanism, signifying the Venizelist attitude, became the all-embracing criteria of political principle and public identity, and Athens and Salonika became the contradictory symbols of loyalty or betrayal. The army, the politicians and the people were torn apart. So deep was the bitterness between the two sides that it was to warp the whole course of Greek politics for the next thirty years and was destined to be reflected even half a century later in the political upheavals of the 1960's.

Yet with the victory of the Allies over Germany and Turkey it seemed for a moment that Venizelos had been triumphantly justified by events; and when Greek troops actually joined Allied forces in occupying Constantinople, Greek enthusiasm was boundless. All that was required apparently to confirm Venizelos as the greatest of Greeks since the first Emperor Constantine was that the Allies should honour their wartime promises and hand western Anatolia to Greece. At the peace conference Venizelos seemed both an heroic and an appealing figure. 'We will win among the family of free nations,' he told the assembled statesmen, 'and hand down to our children a Greece such as generations past have dreamt of, a Greece such as we ourselves foreshadowed in our recent victories in 1912 and 1913.' He seemed the re-embodiment of the Byronic legend, and the statesmen were suitably impressed. In the Treaty of Sèvres, signed in 1920, they duly awarded to Greece almost everything Venizelos wanted. Only Cyprus, Constantinople and the Dodecanese Islands were denied him. The islands were already in Italian hands, and as one of the victorious alliance Italy could hardly be expected to surrender them. Similarly, although the transfer of Cyprus to Greece had once been promised in wartime adversity, the British in victory retained the island for themselves. Constantinople was placed temporarily under an international regime to give the Great Powers more time to deliberate its fate, but in characteristic exaltation the Greeks continued to believe that, having gained so much, this last great prize could not now escape them.

They were more wrong than they had ever been. Not only did Constantinople remain for ever beyond their grasp but the entire Treaty of Sèvres proved almost at once to be a pipe dream. Immersed in their private squabbles and public visions of glory the Greeks had failed to notice that the war had changed not only their status but the rest of the world as well and in the new circumstances the old bonds could not be honoured.

As usual, they were not alone in their blindness, for the Great Powers, too, were evidently living in a dream world. 'It is appalling', the British diplomatist, Harold Nicolson wrote to his wife from the peace conference, 'that these ignorant and irresponsible men should be cutting Asia Minor to bits as if they were dividing a cake.'[4] But of course they could not, and did not, succeed. The old Ottoman Empire had all but vanished, but the new and more coherent nation-state of Turkey under its nationalist leader, Ataturk, was emerging in its place to claim Asia Minor as its natural homeland. Suddenly the powers found they had better things to do than help Greece to dispute the claim. France had won a new Muslim empire in Syria out of the Ottoman collapse and now sought the friendship of Muslim Turkey. Italy wanted Albania as well as the Dodecanese and was in no mood, therefore, to be generous with the Greeks who laid conflicting claims there as well. Many in Britain, too, were reluctant to offend the new Turkish nationalists, partly for fear of Islamic repercussions in places like India and Egypt, and partly because they recognized again, as in the nineteenth century, that Turkish rather than Greek control of the Straits of Constantinople was still the best guarantee against Russian expansion. Russia herself was immersed in the aftermath of revolution, and in so far as the new men in the Kremlin had an active foreign policy they favoured anything that, like the Turkish national movement, seemed to weaken the old European order. The United States, on the other hand, which had signalled its arrival in Great Power councils by inspiring the search for a just peace, had already withdrawn again into semi-isolation with the post-war illness of President Woodrow Wilson and the relief of getting the boys home from the bloody wars of Europe.

Nowhere was there any enthusiasm for another military campaign such as would presumably be required to force the Sèvres settlement upon the new Turkey. Even in Greece there were men who proclaimed it a dangerous business. A certain Colonel John Metaxas, who had been Constantine's Chief of the General Staff and was later to become notorious as a Greek dictator, had advised against an Anatolian campaign on purely military grounds when it was first contemplated by Venizelos during the Balkan Wars. In the post-war circumstances his advice was all the more cogent, and it was reiterated by British generals and accepted by several members of the British cabinet, when the question was put to them in 1920. On a sober assessment, then, this was a moment when Venizelos might have withdrawn from the Greek imperial dream with honour and should have abandoned it from common prudence. That he failed to do so was the result, yet again, of Greek ambition interacting with the interests of a foreign patron. For Venizelos did have one, apparently vital, ally left in the British Prime Minister, David Lloyd George, whose Welsh romanticism responded to the flamboyant character of Venizelos, whose nonconformist conscience told him (like Gladstone) that a Christian nation should be supported against the heathen Turk, and whose domestic political calculations persuaded him that he could present the triumph of Venizelos and Greece as a victory for Britain, its Empire and its loyal friends over the unspecified forces of darkness. While other statesmen stood back, Lloyd George pressed on; and with his encouragement Venizelos determined to crown his career by taking Anatolia regardless. Ignoring all the warning signs along with the military advice he ordered Greek troops in June 1920 to begin a general advance into Anatolia from Smyrna.

At first, the Turks retreated in apparent disorder and before the summer was out the Greeks commanded much of the area they had coveted for so long. Then, with the gods at their most ludicrous as well as their most vengeful, the young King Alexander died in Athens of a monkey bite and Venizelos's embittered royalist opponents seized the opportunity to demand the return of Constantine and force the Prime Minister into a general election. To the astonishment of Lloyd George and himself, Venizelos lost heavily. Perhaps he had begun to take the Greek people too much for granted, becoming too preoccupied with his image as a world statesman. Perhaps too many Greeks were getting tired of war after so much of it. Probably too many had been humiliated by the foreign occupation of 1917 that the actions of Venizelos had prompted. Certainly he had made a host of implacable enemies, and in typical Greek fashion they were all the more determined to destroy him now that he was apparently at the height of his power. They succeeded, for after a national referendum in which Constantine won massive popular support, Venizelos's old enemy returned to Athens in triumph while the defeated Prime Minister went angrily into self-imposed exile in his turn. He was to be gone for nearly eight years.

His departure provided another opportunity to end the Anatolian adventure by honourable withdrawal—yet again it was lost in the vainglory of the great dream and the pettiness of factional ambition, when Constantine and his advisers resumed the folly that Venizelos had begun. Like him they sought to win immortality by restoring the imperial heritage of Greece, and they assumed that Greece's friends would not let them down. But by now Greece had no friends. Not even Lloyd George would support King Constantine—the man who, so he and other statesmen of the victorious First World War powers assumed, had 'betrayed' Greece to the Germans. And, in the meantime, while the Turks had been revitalized by Ataturk's ruthless leadership, the Greek army had been ripped asunder again by the change of government. Venizelos had started the rot in the army by dismissing over 1,500 officers of every rank on suspicion of loyalty to Constantine. Now the King reversed the edict, in a way that was to become painfully familiar in later years, so that the army should again be faithful to him. Thus the Greek tragedy was prepared in a classical pattern of personal *hubris* and retribution. In 1921 the disorganized army resumed its advance into Asia Minor. By the summer it was bogged down at the end of impossibly long lines of communication, 150 miles from Ankara. Through the following winter it held on in increasingly miserable circumstances, while the Great Powers sought a way out of the apparent impasse. An armistice between Greeks and Turks was proposed. The Greeks, in a last-minute return to sanity, accepted, but Ataturk demanded first that they should evacuate Asia Minor. The Great Powers, in a last-minute reaffirmation of their own folly, turned him down. In August 1922, Ataturk took the issue into his own hands and launched a general attack on the Greek positions. Within ten days the Greek armies in Anatolia were routed, Smyrna was reduced to smoking rubble, 30,000 Greeks had died and the great evacuation of one and a quarter million others had begun. It was the end of 3,000 years of Greek life in Asia Minor—the reward for three-quarters of a century of wishful thinking, sentimentality, factionalism and intrigue on the part of both the Greeks and their erstwhile friends. In the words of that trenchant Greek commentator of the day, George Skleros, whose account of the state of Greece at the opening of this century I have already quoted, the politicians of his country had 'systematically cultivated the deceitful belief that Europe was duty-bound to look after Greece'—and Europe, in selfish ignorance, had both connived with them and let them down. Between them now, in their mutual irresponsibility, they had turned the Great Idea into a nightmare and brought Greece to the edge of chaos.

Chapter 8

ANATOLIAN AFTERMATH

*One short clause in the Treaty of Lausanne brought
a Near Eastern Ruritania irrevocably into the headlong rout of twentieth-century politics. . . . .*
(KEVIN ANDREWS)

Outwardly there is not much sign left in Athens today of the disaster
that overtook the Greeks at Smyrna half a century ago. A few names
on the street maps—Nea Smyrna, Mikro Asia—offer a clue to the
sharp-sighted. The wailing lament of *bouzouki* music, when occasionally it can still be heard uncorrupted by later, western influences, is
a reminder of the oriental origins of the tragedy. But mostly the
modern hotels and office blocks of international commerce, the
new roads created by massive public investment, and the whole contemporary cosmopolitan culture of concrete, air-conditioning and
neon lights, have obliterated in the last generation most of the physical scars inflicted on the city after the ending of the grandiose Greek
dream. Yet the mental scars remain, for the generation that grew to
maturity in the aftermath of Smyrna is not yet dead; and many of
the schisms of contemporary Greece are still influenced by the attitudes forged in those chaotic days when Greece was trying to absorb
all at once the shock of a gigantic diplomatic and military humiliation, the shattering of a national myth and the creation of an economic, social and political challenge that came close to overwhelming
the very structure of the state. It is in the two decades after Smyrna,
in fact, between the settlement of one world war and the onset of
the next, that we can see Greece assuming for the first time not just
the general character and outlook but the particular shape and texture of the country we now know, bedevilled by the problems that
current events have made familiar. Physically this was assured, more
or less, by the Treaty of Lausanne, signed in 1923, when the Turks,
the Great Powers and the Greeks at last hammered out a realistic
settlement to replace the dream world they had charted three years
earlier in the Treaty of Sèvres. Apart from the acquisition of the

Dodecanese Islands from Italy, which had to wait until after the Second World War, the Greek frontiers established at Lausanne have remained the confines of the state ever since. The Great Idea was surrendered perforce, as Turkey in its new nationalist guise won the whole of Asia Minor for its territory, together with Constantinople and Eastern Thrace. Greece, in exchange, was awarded Western Thrace; and to avoid a repetition of the irredentism that had plagued the disputed territories of the Near East for the previous century, the powers decreed that the two old enemies should submit to the ruthless form of political surgery known as an 'exchange of population'. While nearly 400,000 Turks were shipped to Anatolia from Western Thrace, one and a quarter million Greeks were dispatched to Greece from Asia Minor. Thus the map was tidied up and the empires of Byzantium and the Ottomans alike consigned to history at last. The statesmen of Europe went home tolerably satisfied but the cost to Greece was staggering. 'Year after year the troops and prisoners of war debarking at Piraeus, still a fishing port, crossing the open plains to Athens, louse-ridden, starving. . . . Relief boats, caiques, warships of allies who had not kept their promise and would break faith again in due time, landing upon Greek soil the descendants of those Ionians who had begun colonizing the Asia Minor littoral around 1000 B.C. . . . the mushroom towns springing up in sight of the Acropolis and for miles around Piraeus, towns made of Shell cans and tarpaper with an average of one water tap and lavatory to twenty families. . . .'[1] Thus Kevin Andrews describes the influx of refugees, equal to one quarter of the existing population of Greece, that was dictated by the Treaty of Lausanne.

The figures of the first national census, in 1928, show the immensity of the resulting problem. Athens then had become a city of nearly half a million people, but of those only 130,000 or less than 30 per cent, had been born there. The rest were either immigrants from other parts of the country flocking into Athens and the other large towns in search of the work and pleasure that the remote Greek villages denied them, or refugees from Asia Minor, in roughly equal numbers. Piraeus, with a total population of a quarter of a million, was an even worse case. Less than 70,000 of its inhabitants had been born there. More than 100,000 were refugees. Altogether, throughout Greece, the census revealed that in the twenty-one towns with populations of more than 20,000, the inhabitants were split almost exactly into thirds: one-third native-born, one-third immigrants from elsewhere in Greece, and one-third refugees from Asia Minor.[2] Leaving aside the separate problem of keeping up with the accelerating internal migration to the towns, which would have been severe enough alone, the refugee problem relative to Greece was, therefore, of a far greater order of magnitude than that of the 'displaced persons' in Europe at the end of the Second World War, or the exchange of several million Hindu and Muslim refugees between India and Pakistan after the partition of India. Rather, it was comparable to the descent of Palestinian refugees upon Jordan after the creation of Israel in 1948, when also the newcomers were mostly penniless and made up a third of the population of the host state.

As that more recent example has also demonstrated, social displacement on such a scale unavoidably promotes economic weakness and political unrest, and Greece was spared neither. Before such a cruel challenge the most popular of governments in the most prosperous of countries would have been hard pressed to survive. In Greece, where a world slump now compounded the other problems left by years of domestic poverty, factionalism and war, the arrival of the refugees as well placed survival beyond the grasp of any government. Administrations swirled in and out of office like leaves in a high wind. One king was exiled, another took his place and soon was exiled in his turn. Army officers followed each other in seizing power and losing it again. A republic was formally declared in 1924, a dictatorship in 1926, a republic again later in the same year and a monarchy once more in 1935. According to the calculations of one historian, dispassionately cutting his way through the jungle of these years, between 1922 and 1936 there were 'nineteen changes of government, three changes of regime . . . seven military revolutions or *coups d'état* and innumerable minor acts of sedition due to the constant intervention of military juntas in the government of the country'.[3]

It was an appalling tangle of national weakness and personal irresponsibility, but hindsight now enables us to unravel from it several threads that are especially significant for the political affairs of Greece today. First, the controversy over the monarchy, which was established in these years as the touchstone of Greek political faith. It is true that the monarchy had been from the start a potential and sometimes actual source of schism. The natural factionalism of Greek politics had amply demonstrated this from the earliest days of the War of Independence and, paradoxically, the attempt to use the institution of monarchy to overcome or circumscribe the factionalism had only deepened the disputes around the throne. Successive Greek constitutions were designed to award the King an umpire's role by giving him unusual prerogative powers both to appoint and dismiss his ministers, but in Greek eyes this only made the King yet another source of power and patronage, yet another target of intrigue and persuasion. Instead of remaining above the battle he was constantly brought down into it, for his legal right to apportion the highest government posts made him appear actually responsible for the most controversial government actions. In moments of extremity, so frequent in the Greek political game, the politicians who were 'out' appealed to the King to do his patriotic duty by dismissing whatever renegade band happened to be 'in'; while those who were 'in' pointed out with equal force that any such action would be an offence against the democratic national will. King Otto lost his throne through his inability to steer a steady course between these conflicting demands, and although King George was both more fortunate and more sagacious he, too, did not always escape the controversy they aroused. The personal clash between Venizelos and Constantine in the First World War, however, and the disaster that overtook them both in Anatolia afterwards, brought a new depth of individual bitterness and national significance to this old issue. The ramifications of what was variously known as 'the constitutional question' or 'the national schism' soon reached into every corner of Greek political life; and as kings came and went and republics rose and fell popular sentiment veered like a weathercock from monarchism to republicanism and back to monarchism again as the Greeks discovered the vices of whoever happened to be in power and nostalgically recalled the virtues of whoever happened to be out.

The plebiscite which led to the return of Constantine, after the defeat of Venizelos in 1920, revealed that nearly all of Greece's one million voters supported the King's restoration at that time. Yet within two years, the final collapse of the Anatolian campaign forced Constantine to abdicate again, and within a few months he had died in renewed exile. He left behind him on the throne his eldest son, George, saddled with a political quarrel that had tragically and abruptly deepened into something like a blood feud. The blame lay this time with a republican section of the army, which had set up a revolutionary council in the midst of the Smyrna débâcle and under the leadership of one, Colonel Nicholas Plastiras, proceeded not only to expel Constantine and seize power in Athens but to court-martial and execute for treason five royalist cabinet ministers and a former commander-in-chief. Venizelos did nothing, although his influence even from his self-imposed exile might have deterred them from such folly. What was worse, two of his erstwhile supporters sat on the tribunal that passed the fatal sentences. Thus in the eyes of royalist Greeks the whole of the Liberal Party that Venizelos led became tainted with blood as well as with republicanism, and reconciliation with the monarchists was made impossible. It did not matter that Venizelos was not in fact a convinced republican, or that he had refused to serve the Plastiras council on the grounds that it was unconstitutional. His quarrel with Constantine had started the affair and the natural polarization of Greek politics did the rest.

For the next twenty years the country was torn between monarchists and republicans and no politician or army officer could escape taking sides in the dispute. Its intensity soon made the position of the new King George II untenable. Little more than a year after he had assumed the throne in his father's place, he, too, was thrust into exile and the Royal Family had all its property confiscated and its Greek nationality revoked. This time, in another plebiscite organized by republican officers, two-thirds of the voters welcomed the formal declaration of a republic in Greece and for the next decade an assortment of military and civilian governments persisted in this rejection of the monarchy. Predictably, however, it did nobody but the exiled monarch much good, for the constitutional dispute was tragically irrelevant to the real problems of the country, squandering energy and ability that should have been devoted to other things.

While refugee poverty and national indebtedness mounted, government degenerated into a plethora of decrees and opposition into a rattle of big talk and small arms. Well-meaning and patriotic men there were in plenty, like the bluff and puritanical General Pangalos who impatiently declared his dictatorship in 1926. But the better their intentions the worse their follies seemed. Pangalos himself was regrettably characteristic. Having strictly censored the outraged (and, as usual, outrageous) press and packed off his opponents to the Aegaean islands, he could think of little better to do thereafter than to prohibit women from wearing skirts more than fourteen inches from the ground. Only Venizelos proved a partial exception to the prevailing rout. When he returned to Greece in 1928, after eight years in exile, he succeeded in forming a republican administration that lasted for over four years, giving the country the only semblance of stability it had known since the start of the First World War. It was arguably his finest achievement; but even he was forced to govern with a stern and repressive hand and few Greeks mourned when he, too, eventually was overwhelmed by the problems of world slump, domestic inflation and the schismatic passions surrounding the monarchy that he had himself done so much to arouse. By 1935, after two or three further years of instability and conspiracy, his career had come to an ignominious end in the failure of an attempted republican *coup d'état* to which he had lent his name. Back in power at last by then, his monarchist opponents took their revenge for the executions of 1922, sentencing Venizelos to death in his absence—happily, he had gone again into exile—and executing two of his less fortunate colleagues who were caught in Greece. With the old bitterness thus given a new twist the Greeks were then invited to pronounce yet again for or against their King. This time, in their third somersault in fifteen years, no less than 97 per cent of the voters were said to have demanded the return of King George II. It is true that this may have been an inflated figure, for there were reports of royalist army officers marching their men from one polling booth to another to record their votes twice over. But by then Greece was accustomed to such chicanery and, in any case, there seemed no reason for surprise if after twelve years of failure, a genuine majority was anxious to renounce the republic and experiment with the blessings of a monarch again.

Alas, the new royal honeymoon lasted little longer than the one before. Within three years King George was discredited again through his hapless association with a new dictatorship. General John Metaxas, who as Constantine's Chief of General Staff had once offered wise advice against the Anatolian adventure, seized absolute power soon after the King's return and celebrated a quarter of a century of passionate adherence to the royal cause by enforcing upon his fractious countrymen another dose of high-minded discipline. By the time the Second World War arrived in Greece, in October 1940, when Mussolini ordered Italian troops to invade the country, Metaxas had made the monarchy once again an unpopular institution; and although he managed to retrieve some of his personal reputation by leading the successful resistance to the Italian attack, King George was not so fortunate. He supported the fight, but he won little of the new glamour that immediately surrounded the General. When the Germans brushed the inept Italians aside and marched on Athens themselves the following spring, Metaxas enjoyed a timely death, acquiring the temporary halo of a national martyr, but King George and his family were left to slip away into exile for a second time, unmourned by a majority of the people they left behind. They, too, were later to recover their position yet again, for in Greece it seems almost a golden rule of politics that absence makes the heart grow fonder; but in the meantime twenty years of disaster, unrest, conspiracy and war had entrenched the Greek monarchy in politics virtually beyond recall. In or out of the country, on or off the throne, no Greek king, it seemed, could keep, or be kept, aloof from factional passion. He was fated to be the fulcrum of the whole tortured struggle for Greek power; and a generation later, in the events of the 1960's, this pattern established in the aftermath of Smyrna was to re-emerge and help to shatter once again the fragile stability of the nation.

Another damaging legacy of these years, closely interwoven with the constitutional dispute, was the confirmation of the Army as the arbiter of political power. Like the arguments surrounding the king, this, too, was far from new. Since their first intervention in politics in 1843, when they helped to force a constitution upon King Otto, Greek military men had often displayed a taste for the game; and in bringing Venizelos from Crete to be the leader of Greece in 1909 they had claimed a specific role as the makers of the nation's leaders and the saviours of the nation's honour. Now, in the succession of republican and royalist *coups* and counter-*coups* which followed the Smyrna disaster, the officers of the Army—and the Navy, too—knew themselves to be more than merely king-breakers or king-makers. Potentially at all times and actually on several occasions they were tantamount to kings themselves. With their assertion of military power, moreover, went the usual corollary: that every fresh *coup* and every new government, whether military or civilian, required another purge of the military ranks for the sake of an ever-elusive security. Political intervention in as well as by the armed forces became, therefore, the accepted practice—a tradition that succeeding years did nothing to eradicate and that was eventually to inspire another collapse of political confidence when the young King Constantine II and his Prime Minister, George Papandreou, disputed each other's authority over the Army and in doing so prepared the ground for the military *coup d'état* of 1967.

A third harbinger of contemporary Greek problems in the aftermath of Smyrna, more obscure but no less significant, was the rise of the Greek Communist Party. Both the communist leaders and the discontents they fed upon were, to a great extent, direct products of the Anatolian evacuation; and at first sight it may seem surprising that the two did not combine to give the party a firmer foothold in Greek politics than they did. Two basic disadvantages beset the party, however. One was the normal Greek rejection of collective discipline, expressed both in the reluctance of most ordinary Greeks to join an organization so restrictive and in the characteristic passion of the party leaders for knifing each other in the back instead of co-operating in the mutual cause. The other was the party's insistence, under Moscow's direction, on specific policies that offended the deepest national instincts of the Greeks. This was particularly true of its Utopian notion of replacing nationalist rivalries in the Balkans by a communist federation of different ethnic groups under Russian leadership. In their earliest incarnation as extreme left-wing socialists inspired by the October revolution of 1917, the founders of the Greek party even suggested that Greece should be divided again, rather as it had been under Turkish rule, into semi-autonomous regions each of which would take its place in a 'Democratic Federa-tion of Balkan States' alongside Serbs, Bulgars and the rest; and after the pure political lunacy of that had been revealed to them they still persisted with the proposal that Greece's Macedonian territories, so lately won in war, should be surrendered again in the interests of a separate, Macedonian nation. Such ideas were almost literally red rags to the Greek bull, so that it is not, after all, surprising that a party which displayed such an unconvincing mixture of ideological rigidity and individual schism won few adherents. As a recent his-torian of the party, Professor Kousoulas, has revealed, the total membership in Greece probably did not exceed 2,500 in the first ten or fifteen years of its existence.[4] Yet it is perhaps the most eloquent commentary of all upon the state of Greece between the wars that a party so few in numbers and so burdened with liabilities could never-theless attain a position of apparent influence that was to prove crucial in the nation's later political development.

Exploiting the weakness of the other political forces it twice secured a position of tactical advantage where it held the parlia-mentary balance of power. The first time, in the 1920's, it made nothing of its opportunities, preferring, Greek-wise, to pursue its internal schisms to destruction. But the second time, ten years later, the equally self-destructive antics of its opponents enabled it to establish a permanent reputation as one of the principal catalysts of Greek political action. Its undeserved elevation to this exalted role was meteoric, and had little to do with the merits of either its ideology or its leaders. Indeed, these still made so little appeal to most Greeks that even at the nadir of the Greek slump the party was never able to muster more than about 50,000 votes in a national election and as late as the spring of 1935 it could still be described as 'no more than a small, though boisterous, force operating on the periphery of Greek political life'.[5]

Three things then radically changed its fortunes. One was a decision by the international Comintern to abandon the Greek party's traditional attitude to Macedonia. The second was the return of King George II from exile under the new monarchist regime, which gave fresh force in traditionally republican quarters to the communist call for a popular, united, social democratic front against what they called 'monarcho-fascism'. The third was a new system of proportional representation, with whose intricacies Greek parties were for ever dabbling in vain pursuit of electoral advantage. This time, unexpectedly, it gave the advantage to the communists who still could win only 75,000 votes in a general election in January 1936, yet were awarded enough parliamentary seats thereby to hold a comfortable balance between the two traditional parties. Within six months this precarious troika had wrecked the parliamentary system yet again as the republicans and royalists stubbornly maintained their feud while the communists, for once eschewing their own private disputes, manipulated the resulting deadlock.

Two events of these sorry months were to acquire special significance for the future. The first was the signature of a secret pact between the communists and the leader of the Liberal-republicans, Themistocles Sofoulis, in which Sofoulis proposed to barter his party policies for communist support in Parliament. The plan failed, but its revelation left a spectre to haunt all supposedly Liberal politicians ever after of men in their ranks who might sell Greece itself to the communists in exchange for personal power. When rumours flew in 1965 that another such plot was in the making, the memory of that pact of thirty years before lent extra credence to the story. The second event was just as prophetic of the shape of things to come. This was the violence in Salonika that immediately preceded the Metaxas *coup d'état*. Thirty years later this was also to be recalled, when similar events there were thought to herald a new left-wing menace to an Athens regime, and a new military *coup d'état* was organized to forestall it. Whether the danger on either occasion was as great as it was made out to be is another matter. Certainly in 1936 it arose far more from the inability of the two main parties to agree and the consequent erosion of any central authority than from the real strength of the communists. But the record permits no doubt that the communists were doing their best then to exploit the follies of their opponents by deliberately fomenting strikes all over the country. In six months there were nearly 350 of them, with the biggest and most damaging centred upon Salonika and Kavalla in the north, where disgruntled refugees from the Smyrna disaster combined with a restive local people, already jealous of Athenian domination, to provide a specially combustible mixture. In May 1936, one set of strikes and demonstrations in Salonika resulted in twelve people being shot by the police and 150,000 turning out the next day for the resulting funeral. Encouraged by this success, the party redoubled its efforts. There were reports of communist attempts to infiltrate the Army and demands in the party newspaper for a 'universal revolt on the lines of Salonika and with the co-operation of the Army'.[6]

Suddenly it seemed that the communist-inspired popular front, whose candidates had gained so few votes in January, had become by May of the same year one of the most powerful forces in the country. The truth was, as Professor Kousoulas remarks, that '. . . the old political parties, unable to overcome their weaknesses and provide the country with an efficient democratic administration, were voluntarily withdrawing to the background of the political stage, leaving the field open to revolution or dictatorship.'[7] It was, of course, the dictatorship that won. In April the elected Prime Minister of Greece died and the King appointed his deputy, General Metaxas, to the post in a last effort to induce the major parties to agree upon an administration. Their failure to do so reinforced the natural inclination of Metaxas to turn to the Army for support. When the communists prepared to make their biggest effort, with a call for a general strike on 5th August, Metaxas forestalled them by issuing the day before, in the King's name and with the Army's support, decrees dissolving Parliament, banning political parties, and instituting martial law. In military terms, Metaxas had made a pre-emptive strike; and this, too, was to set a fateful precedent for a generation in Greece that was then still in its infancy.

The Government of General Metaxas lasted four years before it was swept away by the death of its leader and the German invasion; and in that time we can perceive the emergence of still more threads which were destined to be woven into the pattern of Greek politics throughout succeeding decades. One of them is easily identified—the example set by Metaxas himself in pursuing what he called national regeneration. Disgusted by the selfishness and stupidity of the country's politicians and disillusioned by the consequent breakdown of the parliamentary system, Metaxas deliberately set himself to create in Greece a sense of civic order, duty and patriotism that would befit his own ideal of 'Hellenic-Christian civilization'. Whether his ideal could ever be squared with the facts of Greek history is doubtful, to say the least, but he was a determined exponent of the great Greek myth and with the fervour of an evangelical preacher and the discipline of an army sergeant he sought both to cajole and dragoon his countrymen into conduct more becoming to the exalted status to which history allegedly had called them. As we have seen already, he was by no means the first to try. King Otto and his Bavarians had pursued the same will-o'-the-wisp a hundred years earlier and most of the military predecessors of Metaxas had been vaguely inspired by similar reforming notions. The achievement of Metaxas was to give these old aspirations a new form, to codify them afresh, so to speak, not merely by creating a more specific programme of reform, but also by appealing more directly than ever to an elevated vision of the Greek past as the proper model for the Greek future.

To cajole the Greeks, Metaxas offered them new forms of social welfare and insurance, cancelled farmers' debts, established minimum wage levels, introduced a national programme of public works and ordered the ramshackle civil service to pay swifter and more impartial attention to the affairs of the people they were supposed to serve. To dragoon the Greeks, he censored the press, excised the famous funeral oration of Pericles from the school-books, made strikes illegal, packed off erring politicians into exile and enlarged the security police until they became, to all appearances, the indispensable prop of his regime. In ten years, he said, Greece would be restored to her true Hellenic-Christian self again—loyal to King, country, religion and family, and ripe, if everyone behaved himself, for a cautious return to democracy.

To anyone who has followed Greek politics in more recent times this combination of social welfare, barrack-room discipline and mythological exaltation is instantly familiar. Like a gigantic act of historical ventriloquism, the Metaxas tone of voice, the Metaxas turns of phrase and many of the Metaxas acts of administration were all repeated by Colonel Papadopoulos and his colleagues after the *coup d'état* of 1967. It was even said in Athens at the time that Papadopoulos had dragged some of the Metaxas censors from retirement to show his officers how to impose their new restrictions on the press. Thus, yet another ghost of the inter-war years walked in the lives of a new generation.

Only one more remains to be identified, and that is in some ways the most subtly persistent of all—the birth during the Metaxas period of the characteristically liberal, western view of Greek politics in recognizable, contemporary form. Once again there were older roots, this time in the traditional philhellenism of the nineteenth century which created, as we have seen, the mischievous image of modern Greece as the reborn Hellas.

In the third decade of the twentieth century this image acquired a new gloss to suit the intellectual climate of the time. Those were the days of the rise of Hitler, the Spanish Civil War, unemployment on a scale so vast that it seemed altogether likely to herald the collapse of capitalism everywhere, and of the appearance of the Soviet Union not merely as the legatee of Russian power, then fast being restored to its old significance, but also as the supposed exemplar of a new kind of society. In short, it was the heyday of respectable Marxism, when the most sceptical of European liberals could scarcely avoid seeing the world through pink spectacles. Their gaze was not long or often fixed on Greece, for the Spanish War provided a more dramatic focus for their political interest, but when it was they could not help seeing in General Metaxas another black, reactionary sheep who fitted neatly into their political stereotypes. He was a monarchist when monarchies were out of fashion and an anti-communist when communism was in fashion. He was a dictator when all dictatorships —unless of the mythical proletarian variety—were held, understandably, to be especially anathema. Most sinister of all, perhaps, he appeared to be pro-German. He had been trained in the German Army, had supported Constantine's efforts to remain neutral in the First World War and now, with the Second World War approaching, was flirting with the Germans again by co-operating with Hitler's programme of economic expansion in eastern Europe.

That there were specifically Greek reasons for all his attitudes—including the fact that he was driven commercially into the arms of Germany by the reluctance of Britain to give him any trading credits— was disregarded. In the liberal division of the world as it was seen at that time Metaxas was on the wrong side of the fence and that was all there was to it. But one simplification led naturally to another: namely, that if Metaxas was wrong his opponents must be right. Thus the republicans, whom Metaxas typically dispatched to the Greek islands, soon appeared to susceptible minds elsewhere to be democrats in the 'true', or classical, Greek tradition, while the monarchists supporting Metaxas were obviously anti-democratic

K

and, therefore, 'un-Greek'. This was a marriage of two misunder-standings. First, the old one that the Greek tradition was genuinely democratic, at any rate as that term was understood in contemporary western society. Secondly, the new one that republicans were in-herently more responsive to that tradition than monarchists. In fact, of course, there was little to choose between them in that respect. Generals Pangalos and Plastiras, after all, were fiercely republican but just as dictatorial as General Metaxas—although a great deal less shrewd or efficient. Venizelos, whose name was widely associated with both democracy and republicanism, had never been a republican in principle, was reconciled to the monarchy before his death and was responsible in his republican days for plenty of undemocratic actions, from his acquiescence in the military council's executions in 1922 to his last, sad attempt at a *coup d'état* in 1935. Not for the first or last time, however, the external view of Greece was so confused with the internal realities that nobody could see the situation straight —except, perhaps, the Greek Communist Party which in the long run won most from the confusion.

To some extent Metaxas and his supporters played into the party's hands. They suppressed it with rare efficiency, but that only tended to win it more sympathy outside Greece where people increasingly fearful of fascism were understandably ready to believe that there was nothing really to choose between the communists and the rest of the Greek republicans. All were on the same side so all, presum-ably, must be decent democrats and true Greeks. The conclusion was not rational but instinctive, more felt than expressed; but from its vague beginnings in these last few years of the 1930's, it was to sprout in the next decade into a widely held liberal conviction, and to linger on for another generation after that to play a significant part in the events both before and after the Papadopoulos *coup* of 1967.

Yet although it was under the rule of Metaxas that this confusion was conceived, it was the death of Metaxas, and the occupation of Greece by his supposed fascist comrades, Mussolini and Hitler, that gave the communists the opportunity to nurse it into a major legend of Greek politics. Had Metaxas lived it is possible that he would have retained sufficient stature as a wartime leader to prevent the com-munists gaining control of the Greek resistance movement, and to check the suicidal jealousies within the wartime Greek government abroad. Had the Germans not occupied Greece the local communists might never have fought as actual comrades-in-arms of the western Allies and so powerfully reinforced the previous vague assumption that if they were against fascism they must be all right. But Metaxas died and the Germans occupied Greece for four years; and in the absence of other Greek leaders of similar stature the leadership of the internal resistance passed to the communists while the old politicians maintained their feuds in exile. By the end of the occupation, the legend of a genuine popular front between liberal republicans and communists inside Greece was entrenched in many liberal minds outside; and in association with a natural wartime sympathy for the Soviet Union it almost led to the extension of the Iron Curtain to the Mediterranean shore and the achievement by Stalin of that dominion in Greece for which the Tsar Alexander and his successors had hankered unavailingly more than a century before. Happily this was not the final outcome, yet it was averted only by the unhappiest of events that even the tortured history of modern Greece had known, when the Near Eastern Ruritania of yesterday capped a hundred years of turmoil, twenty-five years of national crisis and four years of foreign occupation with three hideous years of civil war.

Chapter 9

THE TERRIBLE DECADE

Wolves don't eat each other, Greeks do.
(NIKOS KAZANTZAKIS)

The decade of German occupation and civil war was the nadir of modern experience in Greece. Between 1940 and 1950 more than one in ten of the Greek people died through fighting or starvation and their country was literally laid waste around them. The material devastation was matched by social and moral ruin as the fragile structure of administration was wrecked, the political leadership was splintered into still more quarrelling factions, and virtually an entire generation of young Greek manhood was either wiped out or left hopelessly embittered by its experiences. So livid and so painful were the scars that not until another generation came to maturity could they be contemplated with reason or forgiveness; and even then old feuds were to overcome the new generosity in yet another compulsive Greek reversion to the past, when rival memories of communist treachery and right-wing brutality fed the conflict that led in the 1960's to a fresh Greek dictatorship.

The divisions that dominated this truly terrible decade had their origins, as we have just seen, in the aftermath of the Anatolian disaster, but they were both distorted and deepened by the German conquest. The national unity inspired by Metaxas when he rejected the Italian demand for Greek surrender in 1940 was impressive but transitory. Once Metaxas was dead in the following spring and the Germans had completed their occupation of the country after the initial failure of the Italian campaign, the united front broke down in recrimination and disillusionment. Within a few months several different responses to defeat were clearly visible. Inevitably there were some politicians who thought fit to collaborate with the Germans in a puppet government. Some, on the other hand, chose exile with King George, forming another, 'legitimate' government overseas which enjoyed the diplomatic support of the Allies and tried to rally Greeks abroad to fight against the Axis. Within Greece there were still others who chose guerrilla resistance, as well as those—the vast majority—who were at first too bewildered or despairing to play any active role at all. Between the first three groups there soon developed a complex set of feuds reflecting all the old divisions of Greek life, and devoted less to winning the war against the Axis—for Greece's allies were compelled to take care of that—than to securing the loyalties of the fourth group, and through them the fruits of postwar power. The first gap opened quickly between the government in exile and the resistance groups at home. In this Greece merely followed a pattern familiar to most countries under enemy occupation. Even though the exiled leaders were reinforced from time to time by other politicians escaping from the German net, and were sustained by the Allies as the true Government of Greece, those abroad inevitably became increasingly shadowy and remote from the Greeks at home. The resistance groups, on the other hand, had Allied material support and encouragement and, although they mostly did little enough damage to the Germans, their stature among their own people as representatives of the national spirit grew steadily more commanding. Moreover, this natural division was deepened in Greece by its correspondence with earlier schisms. Many of the politicians who accompanied King George into exile at first were the traditionally monarchist leaders who had served in or supported the Metaxas regime. Their departure meant that the organization of resistance at home fell naturally into the hands of traditional republicans whose memories of Metaxas were bitter; and so unassuaged was the quarrel between the two that even royalist army officers who remained in Greece were ordered by the Government in exile to stay away from the republican groups and await the return of the King and his men.[1] Thus, the reputation of the monarchists, already lowered by the King's association with the recent dictatorship, plunged still farther inside Greece as the republican guerrilla bands appeared to bear the brunt of the patriotic struggle while the exhortations of the monarchists were heard ever more faintly from safer havens abroad.

For the first two years of occupation this old division was apparently crucial, but slowly another was superimposed upon it—the gulf between the Greek communists and their sympathizers and the rest. In the beginning this second schism was obscured not only by a common hatred of the monarchists shared by communist and noncommunist republicans alike but also by the characteristically fragmented nature of the early resistance bands. In spite of the fact that most of the groups shared a republican background they seemed incapable of any co-operation. The Germans, naturally, did their best to foster these mutual jealousies and by the start of 1943 there were at least nine separate bands in action. Except in Crete, where opposition was united throughout the island under the republican National Organization of Crete (E.O.K.) most of them were devoting as much effort to defending themselves from each other as to defying the foreign enemy. Most of the groups were small, however, one or two being little more than personal bands, almost akin to those of the klephtic chieftains in the War of Independence; and apart from the Cretan organization only two of any importance survived to the end of the occupation. One was the National Republican Greek League, generally known by its Greek initials as E.D.E.S., and commanded by Colonel Napoleon Zervas, who was an old follower of the former dictator, Colonel Plastiras, and had been involved in a republican *coup d'état* as long ago as 1926. The other was the communist group, called the National Popular Liberation Army (E.L.A.S.), which was founded and controlled by the National Liberation Front (E.A.M.) under the direction of the Greek Communist Party.

In setting up these two organizations the communists profited from their treatment at the hands of Metaxas. Imprisoned by him they had acquired an air of martyrdom among those Greeks to whom any enemy of monarchy was welcome. Released by the Germans in what one recent account has described as 'an incredible act of folly'[2] —but may have been only another attempt to keep the resistance movement in disarray—they were welcomed as patriotic representatives of a republican and democratic Greece against the fascist enemy. Because they were accustomed to working in conditions of repression and secrecy they had a head start on other resistance groups and were able quickly to re-establish on a much wider scale their old popular front with Greek republicans who were now ready to fight the Germans. E.A.M. was the political cover they devised— ostensibly an equal coalition of socialist and liberal groups, and widely accepted as such at the time both inside and outside Greece, but now seen clearly by historians of the period to have been 'Communist conceived, delivered and motivated'.[3] E.L.A.S. was their military arm, largely recruited in the first place by the same deception but later assisted by Allied, and especially British, military supplies and advice and expanded by intimidation, terrorism and, eventually, outright military attacks on rival resistance groups. The aim, to quote again one of the most authoritative accounts of these years, was to prepare for a possible civil war and 'the ultimate seizure of power'.[4] Indeed, the sponsors of E.A.M./E.L.A.S. had been committed for at least fifteen years to precisely this policy. As long ago as 1929 the Greek Communist Party's Central Committee, with far-seeing eye, had assumed the possibility of just such an opportunity one day and accordingly had resolved that its main task should be, 'a struggle against the preparation of war by the Greek bourgeoisie and the imperialists, the defence of our Socialist fatherland, and the transformation of the imperialist war into a Civil War for the establishment of a workers' and peasants' government'.[5]

Abroad, however, the Greek Government-in-exile continued in sublime disregard of this growing menace. Although it was nominally in command of a small army of exiled Greeks, mostly drawn from the middle eastern Greek communities, and although it should have known that unity in its own ranks was the first condition for the maintenance of any influence inside Greece, its members continually displayed just the sort of factionalism and complacency that had so often before brought Greece to disaster. King George himself proved no better than his followers—a stubborn leader, apparently determined to maintain his monarchical prerogatives whatever the cost. While he and his followers indulged their proud rivalries the gap between exiled dreams and domestic reality steadily widened.

Nor could the Allied Governments bridge it. The Americans were too concerned with their Pacific war and preparations for the invasion of western Europe to bother much about the apparently inescapable squabbles of the Greeks; and as far as they had any preferences in the matter they were usually disposed to accept whatever was told them on behalf of the republicans and against the King. The British, on the other hand, were deeply involved, but handicapped by the need to maintain the support of all the Greek factions, exiled and domestic, in the war against the Germans in the Middle East. Secretly, British anxieties about the communists were growing on the strength of advice from their military missions inside Greece and also because of the increasing activities of communist and republican sympathizers in the exiled Greek forces. Yet they could not risk disrupting the façade of wartime unity by public denunciations. Moreover, to have exposed communist duplicity would have run counter to popular western opinion of the day. With the German attack on the Soviet Union in 1941 the liberal complexes of the 1930's had gained a new lease of life, and communists everywhere were more than ever assumed to be on the side of the angels. As far as Greece was concerned, uplifting propaganda about the resistance fighters—or *andartes* as they now were known—combined with a proper admiration for Russian heroism, traditional western phil-hellenism and a natural optimism about human nature in a war that was ostensibly fought for freedom to persuade most people in Britain and America that E.A.M./E.L.A.S. was no more than it pretended to be: the true representative of liberal democracy in Greece.

Not until 1943, when the communists revealed some of their true purpose, was this view seriously challenged. In the summer of that year E.A.M./E.L.A.S., studying the course of military events else-where in the Mediterranean, came to believe that an Allied landing in Greece must be imminent and that liberation was correspondingly near. To prepare for that event and their own assumption of power from the retreating Germans, they launched a series of brisk, surprise attacks on their fellow-guerrillas which knocked virtually all their rivals except E.D.E.S. clean out of the field. In the long run these suc-cesses proved counter-productive, for the Allies had actually chosen to liberate Italy first instead of Greece and by jumping the gun the communists had sacrificed prematurely the element of surprise. Yet they had also won control of most of Greece, outside the German lines. With the collapse of Italy the Italian occupation forces in Greece surrendered, delivering many of their arms to the communists, and by the end of 1943 all that remained beyond the grasp of E.L.A.S. were the main towns and communications, still in German hands, and a corner of the Epirus that Colonel Zervas and E.D.E.S. had con-trived to hold against their attacks. They had struck the first blow in their Civil War, and it was clear that more were bound to come.

With this revelation a new and traumatic polarization of opinion became evident inside Greece and slowly thereafter it forced itself upon the outside world. While some lifelong republicans continued to believe that the popular front of E.A.M./E.L.A.S. was genuine, and necessary to their old struggle against the monarchy, others like Zervas saw the communist threat as overriding old divisions and made their peace with the King. One of these was George Papandreou, once a protégé of Venizelos, whom some Greeks, indeed, had already greeted as a new edition of the old man. At the end of 1943 he escaped from Greece to join the King and the Government-in-exile. Some others, impressed by the superior military strength of E.L.A.S., de-cided to jump on the communist bandwaggon. Still others, both re-publican and monarchist, took the apparently more outrageous step of joining the so-called 'security battalions'—Greek units conscripted by the Germans to help protect their lines of communication from the guerrillas, but which now began to acquire a more patriotic appeal for people who feared that the communists might soon inherit the good, Greek earth. At the same time, under pressure from the British Government, and at last alarmed by the news from Greece, King George was persuaded to offer a sop to Greek anti-monarchist feeling by announcing that he would form a 'fully representative' government after the liberation and that he himself would not necessarily return to Greece as soon as it was free. Thus, within a few months of the first overt communist *putsch*, the lines of the approaching Civil War began to emerge, with monarchists and many traditional republicans being thrust into each other's arms for the first time by the new threat from the left.

Yet the old divisions were potent still, and for another year or so the new balance of forces remained a tentative compromise, riddled with mutual suspicions and racked by repeated upheavals in the Government-in-exile, whose members seemed to think it was only a matter of time before they would return to Greece in triumph and resume their old struggle for power, unabated, upon their native soil. In the spring of 1944, however, they received another shock when communist agents exploited their divisions and helped to foster an anti-monarchist mutiny of serious proportions among the regular Greek forces in Egypt. With the communists already in command of most of the resistance groups inside Greece, the mutiny left the exiled government militarily defenceless, and compelled it to seek through political unity the power it could no longer hope to recapture by force. Once more republicans and monarchists compromised, with George Papandreou assuming office as Prime Minister under the King to form a Government of National Unity. It was a strange and essentially ramshackle affair, constructed only after weeks of complex negotiation, assisted by the pressure of the British and Soviet Governments on their various protégés inside and outside Greece. But eventually seventeen different political parties and resistance groups were reconciled after a fashion and Papandreou emerged as the leader of a government in which monarchists, republicans and communists were all represented in ostensible amity. In fact, of course, there was no amity whatever, and although Papandreou himself seemed genuinely convinced that he could keep his disparate team in harness, his illusions were shattered in a few more months when the communists launched their second attempt to seize absolute power in Greece.

This second round of the civil struggle was merely the logical continuation of the first. It was unavoidably delayed, however, by the
fact that the liberation of Greece anticipated by the communists in
1943 did not take place until the autumn of 1944. Then, with the
German war fronts crumbling everywhere, Hitler at last withdrew
his forces from Greece and Papandreou was able to return to Athens
as the head of the legitimate government, with a small liberating
escort of British and Greek troops. By then, the forces of E.A.M./
E.L.A.S., profiting from the German withdrawal, were supreme
throughout nine-tenths of Greece; and in spite of the popular enthusiasm Papandreou aroused at first in Athens, where Greeks in
their hundreds of thousands cheered his return, it was evident at once
that since the collapse of most of the regular Greek army in the
summer mutiny, the British troops were the only effective obstacle
to an outright communist triumph. Harold Macmillan, who was to
become British Prime Minister some twelve years later, accompanied
Papandreou and the British forces into Athens as adviser to the
Supreme Allied Commander in the Mediterranean, Field-Marshal
Alexander, and subsequently summed up the situation in his memoirs
with characteristic clarity. Outwardly, he wrote, it was calm, but
underneath it was perilous. 'All the classical conditions for a revolutionary situation existed. The Government was weak and returning
from a long exile without authority or prestige. The German occupation, which had been brutal and destructive, had led to a complete
breakdown of the social fabric. The Communist Party was the most
active and the most effective organized body in Greece, and under
the guise of the National Liberation Movement was all ready to
seize power. It had entered on a bitter campaign to liquidate as far
as possible the rival partisan groups. The numbers of British troops
were small and had entered more as a token force than as a truly
military expedition.'[6]

It was still as little more than a token force that the British were
obliged to meet the expected communist challenge when it came, a
few weeks later. The occasion was an attempt by General Scobie, the
local British commander, to enforce an agreement between Papandreou and the representatives of E.A.M./E.L.A.S. in his government
that all guerrilla forces should be disbanded and reformed within
a Greek national army. The cause was the realization by the communist leadership that their chance of seizing power was slipping
away as the weeks went by, and that to accept Scobie's demand
would probably mean an indefinite postponement of the *coup d'état*

for which they had prepared so assiduously. Accordingly, after some hesitation, the communists rejected the agreement and Scobie's ultimatum, withdrew their ministers from Papandreou's government, and disposed their forces for a showdown. It began on 3rd December 1944, at a mass demonstration called by E.A.M. in Athens' Constitution Square. Just who fired the first shot is still disputed. One recent Greek account written from a non-communist, but left-wing stance, claims that 'it is now beyond doubt that it was the police who fired in cold blood and without any provocation' upon the crowd.[7] But Colonel C. M. Woodhouse, who served with the British Military Mission in Greece throughout the German occupation and had close contacts with all the E.A.M./E.L.A.S. leaders, is less sure, and observes in any case that, 'if it had not been this incident which started the revolution, it would have been another'.[8] The Greek Communist Party has admitted ever since 1950 that it planned a December uprising at least two months previously, and the communist forces were certainly better prepared than their opponents for the battle when it came. 'The best units of E.L.A.S. were already concentrated around Athens,' Woodhouse continues, 'ready for immediate action; and their artillery was able to range on General Scobie's headquarters with its first shots.' In the next three weeks they came literally within a few hundred yards of total success for—to quote Harold Macmillan again—'The rebels soon held four-fifths of Athens and the Piraeus; they held all the hills around; they held the harbour; they had captured one airfield and were threatening another.' They were only 200–300 yards away from the British Embassy itself, which was under constant rebel fire, not merely as a symbol but also as the effective headquarters of resistance to the communists. 'There is no heat,' Macmillan observed wryly in his diary at the time '(for there is no electric power to drive the oil-heating apparatus). There is no water (for the rebels have drained Hadrian's reservoir, on which we depended). There is no light (for the rebels have the power station). We have fortunately filled all the baths; we have a lily pond in the garden; and we have found a disused well, which will probably give us at least water fit for cooking and some washing.'[9]

The British troops put it more succinctly, with a popular marching song:

> *Elas round the windows,*
> *Andartes round the walls,*
> *They've pinched our ammunition,*
> *They've got us by the balls!*

They had, indeed—and they held on with determination, compelling the British to send precious reinforcements from the Italian front to lift the military siege and to force King George into more concessions to the widespread anti-monarchist feeling in Greece in order to regain some political initiative. Once again the King proved stubborn. Since his tardy promise of the previous year not necessarily to return to Greece as soon as it was free, he had been insisting that he would, nevertheless, return at a date of his own choosing to resume his throne. As before, this played into the hands of the communists by inflaming unhappy memories of the Metaxas dictatorship, deepening local resentment at the King's apparent arrogance in exile, and encouraging many non-communist Greeks in consequence to accept the authority of E.A.M./E.L.A.S. as the logical opposition to the monarchy. Equally, it weakened the position of Papandreou's government by associating it willy-nilly with the return of the monarch on whose behalf it was supposed to serve. With E.A.M./E.L.A.S. so close to triumph the King's attitude was a luxury that his government could no longer afford; and at a hasty Christmas conference in Athens, attended by the British Prime Minister, Winston Churchill, his Foreign Secretary, Anthony Eden, and less exalted representatives of the United States and the Soviet Union, it was agreed with the Greeks of all parties that the King must announce his intention not to return to Greece without another plebiscite. In his stead, Archbishop Damaskinos, the aged but impressive Primate of Athens, would sit as Regent so that the principle of monarchy might be maintained *pro tem* while its embodiment was kept out of the way. With this arrangement some of the old Greek passions were appeased; and as the British forces grew in strength the E.L.A.S. fighters were forced on to the defensive. By 11th January 1945, the second round was over, and E.L.A.S. had agreed to surrender its arms.

From practically everyone's point of view it had been a tragedy of errors. Instead of jumping the gun as they had in 1943, the communists this time delayed too long. Had they marched into Athens as the Germans withdrew it is unlikely that Papandreou's government, or the British forces, would ever have got them out again. They could have claimed a political *fait accompli* and defied the world. But their leadership was divided, like that of their rivals; and as we shall see presently they failed to receive the support they anticipated from the Soviet Union. On the other hand, King George and the monarchists were mistaken in refusing to accept until the last minute that republicanism still ran deep in Greece—thus needlessly strengthening the communist position. The British were mistaken on at least two counts: firstly in not being better prepared for the military challenge, which they had foreseen. 'I fully expect a clash with E.A.M.,' said Churchill, in a message to Eden a full month before it came, 'and we must not shrink from it, provided the ground is well chosen.'[10] They did not shrink, but that they were not overwhelmed said more for their guts than their planning. Secondly, they should have been tougher, sooner, with the King who evidently derived all too much comfort from Churchill's infatuation with royalty of any kind. Papandreou, too, was characteristically mistaken in his wishful belief that he could either have honest dealings with the communists or else outwit them, when the first was almost by definition impossible and the second was always likely to be prevented by communist command of the guns. In one way or another they all paid their price. The communists lost the battle, the British lost blood and precious strength from the Italian front, the King was humiliated and almost lost his throne and Papandreou was humiliated and lost his job. His successor was, of all people, Nicholas Plastiras, the former republican colonel who had seized power more than twenty years before in the aftermath of the Smyrna disaster. In January 1945, he returned from a ten-year exile in Paris to find Greece sunk deeper than ever before into chaos and on the brink of a still worse disaster whose effects were to poison Greek life and politics for the next quarter of a century to an extent that the people of more fortunate nations still find hard to grasp.

Liberated from the Germans at last, Greece was now shackled by ruin and hatred. Four years of war and occupation, culminating in the scorched earth policy of the German withdrawal, had shattered towns and villages, ports, roads and railways and left the country bereft of any effective administration. Three-and-a-half years of bloody rivalry between Greek and Greek, capping twenty-five years before that of uninterrupted political and social turmoil, had left personal and factional scores to be settled everywhere. In the wake of what came to be known as the December Revolution some of these multitudinous chickens soon started coming home to roost. War-time collaborators of the Germans, and members of the German-recruited security battalions, many of whom had been imprisoned after the liberation, were released and zealously set about exacting revenge for previous injury. The members of E.A.M./E.L.A.S. who had once attacked and intimidated them in the name of patriotism and legitimacy were now harassed and murdered in their turn, and in the same ostensible cause. In the nature of the schism with which this deadly game of tit-for-tat began, most of those now seeking revenge were monarchists, and all were fanatically anti-communist. Among them was one General Grivas, who was later to earn a name as a Greek patriot in the cause of Cypriot *enosis*, but who led, in 1945, an organization tersely known as 'X' whose chief purpose appeared to be the indiscriminate elimination of anyone remotely connected with the old popular front of E.A.M./E.L.A.S.

The Government's security forces, by and large, co-operated. After the 1944 mutiny in Egypt, the Army had been purged of all its left-wing or republican elements; and after the communist-inspired uprising in Athens in December there was little disposition in a weak and ineffective government to be officious in protecting the rights of anyone with left-wing or republican connexions. Within less than a year something like 3,000 people had been condemned to death officially, another 500 or more had been murdered, around 20,000 were in prison and nearly another 50,000 were being prosecuted for their activities in E.A.M./E.L.A.S. This time of the White Terror, as the Greeks called it, took a stage further the new polarization between the communists and the rest that had begun in 1943. At least until the December uprising and the King's reluctant consent to a plebiscite on the question of his return, it had still been possible to believe, however mistakenly, in the idea of a genuine popular front of communists and others in which the others retained some freedom and influence. The new terrorism destroyed what was left of that concept. By acting on the assumption that all members of E.A.M./E.L.A.S. were, in fact, communists it ensured that they became so, to all intents and purposes, in sheer self-defence. The only alternative was to recant entirely and go over to the other side. So, once more, extremism bred extremism. The members of E.A.M./E.L.A.S., under attack, began to look to their weapons again. They were encouraged by some of the communist leaders who had never accepted the second round as the end, and who were soon emboldened to seek more arms and foreign aid to start again. The right-wing took this as proof of its own virtue and redoubled its persecution and its patriotic exhortations: 'He who is not with me is against me . . .' became the creed of both sides; and as the gulf between the two grew bloodier, the choice of one side or other was forced upon everyone in Greece.

The third round of civil strife began in 1946 with new armed rebellions by communist bands in northern Greece, helped from the 'privileged sanctuaries' of Greece's new communist neighbours, Albania, Yugoslavia and Bulgaria. It developed into full-scale war with the Greek Army—slowly and painfully rebuilt in the midst of the fighting—gradually extending its grip until, three years later, the last of the communist-led resistance collapsed and most of the communist leaders themselves decamped northwards behind what had become by then the Soviet Union's Iron Curtain. The direct cost to Greece was 150,000 casualties and the ruin of what little was left of the country's administration and economy. But the indirect casualties were even worse. An estimated 100,000 people, including 23,000 children, were shepherded across the northern frontiers by the communists as hostages. Some probably wanted to go, to escape the vengeance exacted by the Greek regular forces from villages which were thought to have supported the communists. But many were virtually kidnapped, and few were ever to return, for when the communists were ready to let them go back to Greece years afterwards the Greek Government was no longer willing to receive them, lest they should provide a massive cover for a new subversive operation.[11] Another three-quarters of a million people either fled from their villages into the towns to escape the fighting, or were compulsorily 're-settled' by the government forces, so that Athens, Salonika, and other large towns became more desperately overcrowded than ever with uprooted, unemployed and resentful people, adding to the still unsolved problems of the Anatolian refugees of a quarter of a century before.

Inflation spiralled out of control. Fifteen years afterwards a Greek business-man recalled to me the state of the country at the end of this decade in a couple of sentences: 'Can you imagine', he asked, 'that we had to pay thirty *trillion* drachmae for an Athens bus ticket? Everything we owned before the Germans came was not enough a few years later to buy a ride home from the office!' Worst of all was the infection of hate that spread everywhere as new blood feuds were added to the old and both sides in their passion performed sickening deeds of savagery. Writing about them nearly a generation later in his novel, *The Fratricides*, Nikos Kazantzakis became the first Greek to dare to attempt an artistic reconstruction and reconciliation of these dreadful years. The work was his last and, I think, his weakest novel—too blatantly emotional for art, as if even after that lapse of years he was unable to do more than beat his breast in frantic remorse. But behind its extravagantly supercharged phrases there remains a poignant picture of the struggle and a sharp reminder of what it was to mean for the future of Greece. 'Why am I fighting?' asks one of his heroes—a bewildered young soldier in the army of the legitimate government battling against the communists. 'For whom am I fighting? They say we fight to save Greece, we, the Royal Army, the blackhoods as they call us; and that our enemies in the hills—the redhoods—fight to divide and sell Greece. Oh, if I could only be sure! If I only knew! Then all this would be justified—all our atrocities and all the tragedy we spread—killing, burning, leaving people home-less, humiliating them. . . .' The young man goes on to describe how he kicked the wife of a rebel, a young mother with a baby, and how she had looked at him with such hatred that he had been ashamed. 'And I thought to myself, if that woman could, she would set fire to the barracks and burn us all. That baby's no longer going to suck milk from its mother's breast; it's going to suck hatred and scorn and revenge; and when it grows up, it, too, will take to the hills—a rebel; and he will finish off whatever his father and mother left un-done; we will pay heavily and rightfully for this injustice.'[12]

No government could control such hatreds or console such des-pair, least of all the governments provided by the traditional politi-cians of Greece. General Plastiras had quickly proved no more successful at riding the tiger than Papandreou, and his administration fell within a few months of his return from Paris. For the next seven years, before and after the third round in the Civil War, and in apparently endless permutations of the same old names, new ad-ministrations emerged, dwelt for a few weeks or months in futile bickering, and vanished again. Including a comparatively long spell of coalition government during the Civil War itself, there were be-tween 1945 and 1952 more than a score of different governments with an average life of 150 days. Two years after the war was over, thoughtful Greeks were near to despair at their country's plight. 'Greece,' said the most respected conservative newspaper in Athens, 'is a small-scale model of Chiang Kai-Shek's China. Is it really un-avoidable that nothing sound, honest and straightforward can be done in this country?'[13]

It must have seemed so. Yet Greece was just then on the verge of the first and so far only extended period of government in her modern history that was both stable and approximately democratic. Two domestic events were harbingers of this remarkable change. The first was the eventual return of King George from his wartime exile when the promised referendum at last was held, in September 1946, and once more the Greek people revealed their unending capacity for changing their minds about their monarch. By then the choice between the communists and the rest had become inescapable. Fighting had already started again in northern Greece and the Communist Party was boycotting all the political processes by which successive governments had vainly sought to restore some normality. It boycotted the referendum on King George, too, and so made the result a judgement upon itself as much as upon the King. The verdict was clear: two-thirds of the Greeks opted for the King's return. Dismayed by the prospect of further fighting, resentful of the help the communists were now receiving from some of Greece's old Slav enemies, and embittered by the feuds and brutalities of the past five years, a genuine majority of Greeks had come round to the view that republicanism and communism were now apt to mean the same thing —and in that case, they would rather have the King. They were only just in time to give George the satisfaction of coming home at last in a kind of triumph, for six months later he was dead. But his younger brother, Paul, succeeded him; and as the Civil War proceeded to provide bloody confirmation of the fatal fissure between communists and the rest in Greece, the new King and his Queen, Frederika, became accepted symbols of legitimacy for a clear majority of the nation. By 1949 when the war was over they were popular and respected throughout Greece. Perversely, and to their own discomfiture, therefore, the communists had succeeded in thrusting the constitutional controversy on to the shelf for the next generation.

The second domestic herald of stability in the 1950's also emerged in answer to the communist threat. His name was General—later Field-Marshal—Alexander Papagos, who had commanded the Greek Army against the Italians in 1940 and against the communist bands in 1949 and made himself a popular hero in the process. As the politicians tottered in and out of office after the war in vain pursuit of old rivalries, his stature in Greek eyes grew the more commanding by contrast. Yet with a wisdom unusual in Greek military men Papagos eschewed the notion of yet another dictatorial *coup d'état*. Instead he proposed to exploit his popularity and achieve power legitimately. Consciously modelling himself on General de Gaulle in France, he formed a party called the Greek Rally—after de Gaulle's *Rassemblement Français*—and after a first attempt at winning electoral power had been narrowly frustrated in 1951 by the complex permutations of the voting system then in use, he was voted overwhelmingly into office under a simpler system in October 1952.

For the next three years he ruled Greece without serious challenge,

L

and for eight years after that his successor, Constantine Karamanlis, was able to build on the foundations he had laid and remain continuously in office as Prime Minister nearly twice as long as anyone before him in Greece's modern history. In the whole period of eleven years, from 1952 to 1963, Greece had not a single change of regime, only two Prime Ministers and only three general elections. It was literally unprecedented—and there were unprecedented reasons for it.

One of them, although in the long run probably the least important, was that Papagos arrived on the political scene free of many of the domestic encumbrances of other Greek Prime Ministers. He owed no allegiance to old parties and was impatient of old feuds. He was a monarchist at a time when monarchism had become generally acceptable, but he was also independent of the personal patronage of the King. Indeed, his election was a profound shock to both the established politicians and King Paul and Queen Frederika, who were once more engaged in the old routines of favouritism and intrigue with which Greek kings and politicians had exploited each other since the War of Independence.[14] With his massive personal vote he was able to call his own tune to a degree that no Greek statesman had enjoyed since the brief heyday of Venizelos, nearly half a century before. Behind his vote, however, was a far more basic shift in the Greek political situation that was to guarantee, for the first time, a certain stability in the nation's affairs—the establishment of American hegemony in Greece as a result of the opening of the global Cold War, of which the Greek Civil War proved to be only the first of several hot instalments.

Chapter 10

MANIFEST DESTINY

And not by eastern windows only,
When daylight comes, comes in the light,
In front the sun climbs slow, how slowly,
But westward, look, the land is bright.
(ARTHUR HUGH CLOUGH)

As Wellington said of Waterloo, the outcome of the Greek Civil War
was at moments 'a damned near-run thing'. Three times the communists and their sympathizers tried to seize power by force, and on
each occasion they came close to success—so close, indeed, that in a
purely short-range view of their campaign it is tempting to ascribe
the communists' ultimate failure solely to their own mistakes. If only
they had not jumped the gun in 1943, if only they had not delayed
their strike too long in 1944, if only they had not, throughout,
antagonized so many people by their duplicity and brutality—might
they not have triumphed, sooner or later? It would be foolish to
answer with a categorical 'no', for there were plenty of social and
political injustices in Greece on which a party of the left could
flourish; yet a long-term view of the Greek situation suggests that
the communist effort in these years, although hardly doomed to
failure from the outset, was certain to meet more obstacles than were
at first apparent. There was, as we have seen, that Greek spirit that
would not submit easily to any absolute domination and which
racked the Greek Communist Party with divisions almost as much as
other groups in the political spectrum. There was the Macedonian
question, in which communist policy not only offended Greek
national feeling but specifically linked the party with those traditional
enemies of Greece, the despised and hated Slavs. And as time went
on a conscious element of anti-communist choice emerged as well.
That traumatic polarization which began in 1943, when the communist threat was first seen to overshadow some of the old divisions
in Greece, was completed with the maximum of pain and anger some
seven years later, when most Greeks had not merely decided that

they did not want the communists but also had discovered the will to resist them. Many foreigners who witnessed this will in action have paid generous tribute to it, seeing it as the underlying reason why, in fact, the communist challenge did fail even though there were moments when it seemed physically irresistible. 'There have been few more conclusive illustrations of Napoleon's dictum,' says Colonel C. M. Woodhouse in a typical reference, 'that in war the proportion of moral to material factors is as three to one.'[1] Yet more important than any of these obstacles to communist victory was the reassertion in new and more vigorous terms of what we might call, in the American phrase, the manifest destiny of modern Greece as a western protectorate.

Essentially, Greece's western destiny was implicit in the very manner of Greek rebirth, partly because of the influence of western philhellenism and western nationalism both in the War of Independence and in the eventual constitution of the new state, but even more because—in the grand, millennial sweep of history—the return of peninsular Greece to an independent role in the world was bound to be associated with the supremacy of sea power over land power. In all her most vital ancient moments Greece lived chiefly by and from the sea. It is no more than a mild exaggeration to suggest that it was Alexander's diversion of Greek energies into the Asian land mass, away from the sea-borne interests of classical Athens and the Anatolian city states, that began the long story of Hellenic fossilization and decline. It was Byzantium's preoccupation with its eastern provinces and its continental frontiers that continued the tale, the Slav invasions from the European heartland of the north that gave it added impetus, and finally the Turkish conquest—above all the triumph of a land-based power—that confirmed peninsular Greece in its fate of provincial bondage. By the same token, it was the decline of Turkish power that gave Greece its chance to escape in the nineteenth century from the, by then, closed and sterile world of Asia into the arms of the expanding, and once more sea-borne, culture of the West. It was no accident that the crucial battle of the War of Independence was won, not on land, nor by Greeks, but at sea by the combined fleets of Britain, France and Russia, in the bay of Navarino. And from that moment on it was virtually inevitable that Britain, as the principal sea-power of the western world, should gradually establish herself as the chief protector and mentor of the new Greece.

As we have seen, however, this position was not achieved without enormous confusion and constant challenge, for the other powers of

Europe were always treading on Britain's heels and the Greeks were always ready to exploit their rivalries in what they conceived as their own best interests. It was not until the end of the First World War that Britain's effective supremacy in Greece seemed assured, if only because all her old rivals were at that moment otherwise engaged. Germany was defeated, and the Austro-Hungarian Empire destroyed for ever. Russia was too preoccupied by the internal stresses of revolution to pursue an active policy in the Mediterranean or—as Stalin made clear in his early struggle with Trotsky—anywhere else beyond her own frontiers. France was absorbed in her new imperial gains in the Middle East and Africa. So, to a great extent was Britain, but having emerged victorious from the war, with her Empire wider than ever, her control of the sea unchallenged, and her commercial supremacy apparently greater than before—especially in the eastern Mediterranean—Britain, for once, could take Greece for granted. After the Smyrna disaster she did so; and it was only when the Hitler-Mussolini Axis began to threaten the fragile peace of Europe again in the 1930's that Greece, like the rest of the eastern Mediterranean, was sucked once more into the maelstrom of Great Power politics. The struggle assumed a familiar shape, with the land power, represented this time by Germany, attempting to break the strangle-hold of British sea-power. Thus, when it came to the Second World War, it was the British, with their Middle Eastern and Mediterranean interests to defend, as ever, who were forced into the futile effort to save Greece from the initial German onslaught in 1941. It was the British who, having failed in that, armed the Greek resistance movements and sheltered the Goverment-in-exile. And when, at last, the German tide retreated it was the British who formally re-established the position of Greece as a western protectorate through the secret Moscow Agreement of October 1944, wherein Churchill and Stalin, on a famous half-sheet of paper, agreed that Greece should be 90 per cent within Britain's sphere of influence henceforth, in exchange for similar Russian privileges in most of the other Balkan states.

Seen in isolation now this agreement looks like yet another communist blunder. By the summer of 1944 Soviet military advisers had joined the E.L.A.S. forces in Greece and must have known how completely they overshadowed by then the other, non-communist, resistance groups. Stalin himself must also have assessed the comparative weakness of Britain with her forces perilously stretched around the world from Normandy through Italy to India. It might have been

sensible, therefore, for Russia to see the impending German withdrawal from Greece as the best opportunity she could expect for
asserting her own interests there in place of Britain's and thereby
reversing, perhaps permanently, the balance of power that had
evolved in Greece after Navarino.

Yet in a wider context the Moscow Agreement made sense for
Russia as well as Britain as a recognition of the facts of geo-politics
—a realistic appraisal by both parties of just where the vital interests
of the land power ended and those of the circumventing sea power
began. For Russia, as much as for Britain, indeed, it was all of a
piece with traditional policy. Like the Tsars Alexander and Nicholas
a century before him, Stalin saw that Russia's vital interests lay outside Greece. In 1944 they were on Russia's western front, where the
Red Army's advance into central Europe, Poland and Germany
itself promised far more certain and important rewards in terms of
Russia's security and power than anything offered in Greece. Compared to those, indeed, Greece was little but a distraction. A communist takeover there might even have resulted in more burdens than
benefits for Russia. As the history of Yugoslavia, China, Rumania
and Czechoslovakia was later to prove, any renunciation of Soviet
leadership by a country that was once deemed communist could only
be interpreted in Moscow as a major defeat, to be met with persistent
threats of intervention or suppression. Given the notoriously fissile
nature of Greek life and politics, including the Communist Party,
such a renunciation was all too possible there; and given the geographical position of Greece intervention would be difficult if not
impossible. Better, therefore, to stay out, consolidate Russia's interests elsewhere and let Britain re-establish her own influence in
Greece if she could.

Once this decision had been reached, the Russians held to it in the
face of much temptation although they wavered perceptibly once the
war was over and Britain's weakness was left undisguised. Their
military mission to the E.L.A.S. forces in 1944 was largely responsible
for delaying the communist attack on the Papandreou government
and the British troops; and when at last the attack did take place
there was no hint of any direct Russian help to sustain it. Indeed, by
a nice irony, the communists got more help in moral and propaganda
terms, at least, from well-meaning people in Britain and America.
The United States Government was plainly horrified at the sight of
British troops being diverted from what it assumed to be more important tasks in order to fight gallant Greek 'allies' in the streets of

Athens. Was this what the war for democracy was about? Its representatives in Greece were ordered to maintain strict neutrality and its senior military officers in the Mediterranean theatre refused to provide transport or facilities for the British troops. In Britain, the Labour Party was equally dumbfounded and there were angry scenes in the House of Commons as pre-war memories of Metaxas and Franco Spain were called up to support the widespread liberal and left-wing view that Churchill was abandoning all moral precepts in favour of a return to naked British imperialism. In the press, too, both British and American, partisan feeling for the National Liberation Front was expressed with thoroughly Greek passion. In America the traditionally anti-British organs had a field day of pure *naïveté*. 'E.A.M. is agitating for an American-style republic,' wrote the *Chicago Tribune*, expressing what it took to be the pulse of the Republican, empire-hating and isolationist Middle West. 'The Greeks feel that they want to decide for themselves who should govern and how. England however insisted that they should just accept King George, who will rule as Britain wishes. This the Greeks refuse to accept.'[2] The British press, motivated by somewhat different notions —and especially its guilty memories of the 1930's—was little better. The conservative *Times* and the left-wing *New Statesman* joined in denouncing the Government and moved Winston Churchill to public protest in the House of Commons. 'How can we wonder at, still less complain of, the attitude of hostile or indifferent newspapers in the United States, when we have here in this country witnessed such melancholy exhibitions as are provided by some of our most time-honoured and responsible journals? Our task, hard as it has been and still is, has been rendered vastly more difficult by the spirit of gay, reckless, unbridled partisanship which has been let loose on the Greek question and has fallen upon those who have to bear the burden of Government in times like these.'[3] Papandreou, too, was taken aback. He, who twenty years later was to complain somewhat out of the other side of his mouth, cried this time: 'I complain and protest against the reporting of the events of those days in a large part of the Allied press, and not only American but British.'[4] The Russians on the other hand, said nothing and did nothing, permitting the British to extinguish the rebellion and blandly reaffirming, a few weeks later at the Yalta summit conference, their agreement that Greece should remain in Britain's sphere of influence.

This fiasco should, perhaps, have alerted the Greek communists to the significance of Great Power strategic calculations in any further

attempt to seize power in Greece; and one or two of them did afterwards seem more awake to them. Professor Kousoulas quotes a
speech by Nikos Zachariades, who had returned from a German
concentration camp after the failure of the 1944 rising to resume his
old place as the acknowledged party leader, in which he attempted
to explain what had happened by blaming the British. 'Greece', he
told his comrades, 'is located in one of the strategic, most sensitive
and significant points on one of the most vital communications
arteries of the British Empire. As long as there is a British Empire,
this artery will remain, and England will do everything in her power
to preserve it. A realistic foreign policy cannot ignore this fact. . . .'[5]
Yet the party, including Zachariades himself, persisted in ignoring
it partly, perhaps, because only a handful of its members was aware
of the existence of the Churchill-Stalin pact but more, one suspects,
because they could not bring themselves to believe that when the
chips were down and the battle joined with the British as well as
with their Greek opponents, the Soviet Union might—for its own
reasons—once again leave them to their fate. Like those politicians
of the nineteenth century who 'cultivated the deceitful belief that
Europe was duty-bound to look after Greece', the communists
thought Stalin would feel duty-bound to look after them. And
equally, like those predecessors, this self-deluding *hubris* led them to
disaster, in the third and final round of the Civil War.

Yet their delusions seem understandable, even now. When their
third uprising began in 1946, the Second World War was over, the
Red Army was entrenched westwards to beyond Berlin, and in all
Greece's northern neighbours—Albania, Yugoslavia and Bulgaria—
communist regimes were in power. In the east, the Russians were
renewing their old imperial drive towards India and the Persian Gulf,
with a Soviet republic established under Russian guns in Azerbaijan,
the northern-most province of Iran. In Turkey there was new Russian
pressure for control of the Straits, with demands for the cession of
frontier provinces and the provision of military bases. In Greece the
demoralization of war and occupation, added to the bitterness and
confusion of pre-war politics, had left a people who looked ripe for
a determined takeover. This time, moreover, the British were obviously too weak to resist. Mentally and materially exhausted by two
world wars, Britain was near to abandoning her whole imperial
structure, upon which Greece's western destiny had hung for the past
century. A Labour Government was in power, ill-disposed to new
military interventions or commitments. India was about to be relin-

quished. Palestine was soon to follow, and as the violence increased in northern Greece, the British Government announced that there, too, it could no longer carry the old burden of protection. All round the great Euro-Asian heartland a vacuum was looming, much as it had done a century and a half before, when the Ottoman Empire had entered its long decline and Britain had competed with France, Russia, Austria and eventually Germany to prop it up or pick up the pieces. Now, however, there seemed only Russian influence left to fill the vacuum, unless for the first time the power of the United States could be summoned to confront it—and American policy in Athens in 1944 suggested to the confident Greek communists that they need not fear much from that quarter. Surely, they thought, with their Balkan comrades egging them on, their third attempt must succeed and win the open support of Moscow as well?

In fact, they had misread the omens again. The post-war conference at Potsdam in July 1945, might have warned them of the new perils ahead, by its clear evidence that the war-time partnership of the Soviet Union and the United States had already broken down and that American neutrality in Greece or anywhere else could not, therefore, any longer be relied upon. As the Iron Curtain clanged down over Europe in the succeeding months, attitudes on both sides hardened. The Russians feared American nuclear strength and in self-protection consolidated their existing gains in Europe. The Americans feared communism and its aid to Russian expansionism, and sought to contain them both. The Cold War had begun; and as the communists resumed their fighting in the north the Americans gave an open hint that they were preparing to assume the Greek responsibilities that the British could carry no longer.

Appropriately, the hint took the form of a little naval scene, recalling yet again to those with a sense of history the importance of Navarino and the crucial role of sea power in the story of modern Greece. It was the arrival of the U.S.S. *Missouri* in April 1946, off the Greek shore at Athens. 'American and Greek flags were out in the streets of Athens and Piraeus, and crowds assembled on Kastella, the rocky hill overlooking Phaleron Bay, to watch the spectacle of the *Missouri* about to emerge over the horizon. When it appeared the people greeted it with waving handkerchiefs. The sea was sleek, like olive oil. As the warship dropped anchor, its blinkers kept sending out frequent tiny messages of light. In the morning calm, the warship's loud-speakers transmitting orders could be clearly heard from the shore. Seagulls wheeled above. And all around the huge man-o'-war, rowboats flocked, and caiques, full of impatient and curious people, like a joyful welcoming note in the whole picture. Then, all of a sudden, white puffs of smoke burst from the great guns —the cermonial salute, its thunder.'[6]

The *Missouri*'s thunder announced the effective beginning of a new era of western protection and patronage in Greece, but its message was lost on the Greek communists. With what they now grandly entitled the Democratic Army they steadily increased the scale of their attacks in northern Greece until, by the spring of 1947, the Government forces were hard-pressed to contain them. For the third time in four years victory by force seemed almost within their reach. Yet the ultimate facts of power could not be brushed aside; and when, in March 1947, President Truman announced his famous doctrine, that the countries of 'the free world' must be secured from Soviet domination, he virtually guaranteed the communists' third and final defeat. American power entered the vacuum left by the departing British. American money, arms and advisers poured into Greece. The Greek Army was reorganized and successive Greek governments, albeit as shaky and quarrelsome as before, were sustained against total breakdown. Within four years of the *Missouri*'s Greek landfall, the communist insurrection had been defeated, and within six years not only Greece but Turkey as well had become members of the North Atlantic Treaty Organization, extending the long arm of American sea and air power around Russia's southern flank. It was a repeat in modern terms, and with modern speed, of the slower and far more complex process that had established British hegemony in the area in the nineteenth century.

The Soviet Union did little seriously to prevent this outcome. There was, to be sure, an attempt at Potsdam to overlook the secret Churchill-Stalin agreement when the Soviet Government questioned the right of Britain to maintain any troops in Greece. There was also a readiness in Moscow to test American resolution afterwards by encouraging Greece's communist neighbours to supply the Democratic Army with arms, training and sanctuary, without which the third round of the Civil War might not have lasted months, let alone years. And there was a persistent Soviet campaign in the United Nations to prevent effective intervention by international bodies which several times were instructed to investigate the Greek situation, with particular reference to communist actions there. But that was about the limit of Soviet aid. Like his Tsarist predecessors, Stalin was ready to take whatever advantage might be going free in Greece, but in the face of determined Great Power opposition he would not, and could not, play more than a spoiling game. By 1948, with American aid already beginning to turn the tide against the communists, he was urgently advising that the rebellion be ended. 'The uprising in Greece must be stopped, and as quickly as possible,' he told Yugoslav and Bulgarian communists in February of that year. 'What do you think? That Great Britain and the United States—the United States, the most powerful state in the world—will permit you to break their line of communications in the Mediterranean Sea? Nonsense. And we have no navy. . . .'[7] During the rest of that year the lines of power were drawn up all around Europe that were to last for the next quarter of a century. The Russians absorbed Czechoslovakia into their European security system with a communist *coup* in Prague, but their similar design in the divided city of Berlin was defeated by the great Allied airlift. In Italy America's Marshall Plan helped to tip the trembling scales of politics against the communists and in favour of the right-wing government of the Christian Democrats. In Yugoslavia Marshal Tito asserted his independence of Stalin, and in the most uncomradely row that followed with Moscow and his communist neighbours in the Balkans, he prudently began to re-insure himself with the western world by closing the Yugoslav border to the movements of the Greek Democratic Army. For all practical purposes that was the end of the Civil War's third round. Albania and Bulgaria maintained some pressure on Greece, but with the Yugoslav frontier closed, American power inside Greece increasing daily and Russia anxious to reduce her peripheral commitments in Europe in favour of consolidation along her vital central front, the communist rebellion was doomed. A year later it was all over, and Greece entered the post-war world at last—four years later than other nations—with her western destiny not merely manifest again but apparently made more inflexible than ever. Materially and spiritually crippled by the long years of occupation and civil war, she was now totally dependent upon American aid and protection for her existence and recovery. A million American dollars a day fed her treasury and underwrote her ruined currency. American arms equipped and American soldiers trained her military forces. American advisers sat in her ministries and American ambassadors supervised her policies. America's Central Intelligence Agency became, willy-nilly, one of the great characters of Greece's current political mythology, and America's Sixth Fleet became what Britain's Royal Navy formerly had been—the surest shield of her freedom.

Like the U.S.S. *Missouri*, the Sixth Fleet often in later years rode
at anchor in Phaleron Bay near Athens, a shoal of grey shapes breaking the blue water, with the inevitable aircraft-carrier towering like
a fortress above the rest and the white wakes of the liberty boats cutting across the bay, carrying ashore the sailors of the greatest power
in the world, for a taste of Greek land life. In the yacht club and the
fish restaurants of Turkolimano, in the sleazy little bars along the
coast road, where the *bouzouki* music howled into the small hours
and the drains stank, in the cinemas of Piraeus and the basement pick-
up bars around Athens' Constitution Square, the Greeks met them,
entertained them, often fleeced them and always saw them, clear-
eyed, for what they were: the new masters of their country's fate.
Like it or not, under their protection Greece was assured once again
of her place in the western scheme of things; and this time, more than
ever before, there could be no disputing the outcome. With poverty
and wholesale destruction at home and hostile communist states on
Greece's northern borders, there was no room for Greek initiative
or manœuvre. The world for the moment was divided between East
and West, 'communist' and 'free', and whatever the *naïvetés* of that
division Greece was inescapably on the 'free' and western side because that had become the price of her existence. Nor was there much
popular disposition to question this new certainty. The country and
its people were genuinely bankrupt and exhausted. Not even Greeks
could go on fighting each other for ever with the intensity of the
previous fifty years; and, in any case, the communists had won few
friends and made many enemies by the ruthless nature of their
sporadic rule. On the whole, therefore, the Greeks were glad of the
promise of stability under the American umbrella.

Yet the very certainty of this conclusion held its dangers because
it confirmed the old bondage of the Greeks to the politics of irresponsibility. As Mr. Osbert Lancaster remarked, with characteristic wit,
as early as 1946, 'Unfortunately they are all too aware (for even the
average inhabitant of the remoter villages of Arcadia is invariably
better informed about foreign affairs than the by-pass dweller in
England) that their fate is not ultimately in their own hands, and
that their country, lying astride the Iron Curtain, is likely to remain
in the international limelight for an indefinite period. Economically,
this shrewd but dangerous awareness delays recovery by encouraging
the belief that the Western Powers cannot afford to let Greece go
under and that, therefore, it would be a pointless labour to swim to
the shore when the kind Americans will, whether they like it or not,

have to take one there in a comfortable lifeboat; psychologically it induces a perilously *exalté* but highly congenial mood in every patriotic Greek who derives considerable satisfaction from the thought that his country, historically so important, but economically so uninviting, is likely to provide the *casus belli* for the greatest of all wars.'[8]

Mercifully, the realization of that last exalted vision has been denied them; but the rest of Mr. Lancaster's acute perceptions have been amply supported by experience. Under the cosy umbrella of American aid, the old political habits in Greece were perpetuated of relying too much upon others, of soliciting patronage and intriguing for favours and assuming that the real decisions were always being made, conspiratorially, somewhere else. And along with all that came, inevitably, resentment of America's apparently unshakable supremacy and suspicion of America's aims. In short, the political stability of the 1950's fostered by weariness, anti-communism and American aid, was always to some extent, an illusion. For beneath the unwontedly tranquil surface Greek politics continued in a sort of festering, neo-colonial decadence—such as the Irish knew until yesterday on the other fringe of Europe—full of dark suspicions and hyper-sensitivities, concerned more with personal rivalries and malicious gossip than with rational policies or clear argument, and clouded even at their intellectual summit with exalted but misleading invocations of ancient glory. Breathtaking arrogance and squalid conspiracy remained the twin poles of action, and Greek public life was rescued from total bitchiness and irresponsibility, it seemed, only by occasional acts of personal dignity and a real and historically justifiable fear of communism. Above all, having lived throughout their modern history in the shadow of other people's power, and being now more than ever under western protection, many Greeks ultimately were left with the apparent conviction that other people would always decide their fate—so there was really not much point in doing much about it themselves, except sit back and grumble. As a nation, indeed, they betrayed the worst vices of the village coffee-shop, declaring themselves, like the peasants of Vassilika, to be 'O Kakomiros'—the ill-fated ones—and therefore blissfully blameless for whatever might befall. This was at once both an excuse and a recipe for failure; and there was a certain classic inevitability about the way in which, eventually, they embraced that fate.

Chapter 11

STRANGE INTERLUDE

. . . always keep a hold of nurse
For fear of meeting something worse.
(HILAIRE BELLOC)

Once the agony of the Civil War was over the Cold War that succeeded it brought to Greece a measure of political stability un-
equalled in all the previous 120 years of her modern independence.
The reason, essentially, was that it changed the rules of the Greek
political game. Always in the past Greece had enjoyed—or, perhaps
more accurately, had suffered—the luxury of multiple political
choices. Externally, in spite of the gradual growth of British supremacy, Greek statesmen had usually had three or four Great Powers
jockeying for influence among them and they had rejoiced in playing
them off against each other for their own, and occasionally Greece's,
benefit. Internally, they had been able to pursue their personal ambitions unfettered by any restraints save those imposed by periodic
military dictatorships, whose hold on power had proved no more
lasting than their own. The communist challenge and the American
response changed all that. Instead of several Great Powers there
were now just two super-powers carving up the world between them,
and in the midst of the customary factionalism of Greek politics
there had appeared—and, in spite of the verdict of the Civil War,
there remained—the frightening vision of one group, more disciplined
and purposeful than any other, that had come close to imposing its
will inescapably and by force on all the rest. Suddenly, therefore, the
multiple choices had been reduced to the stark simplicity of two:
either the Americans or the Russians; either internal cohesion and
recovery or more instability and another chance for the communists
to take over; either survival in a kind of freedom, albeit compromised
by American surveillance and police restrictions, or submergence in
a far more rigid system from which there might be no escape. For
most Greeks, in the end, this was tantamount to saying that there
was no choice at all, and for the next decade they clung to the Ameri-

can alliance willy-nilly with the same half-resentful, half-fearful air of a child escorted by his nursemaid among the monsters at the zoo. Deep down, they knew the alliance was their only safeguard, yet they were for ever chafing against its restrictions and flirting with those deliciously forbidden but menacing creatures on the other side of the bars—sometimes with alarming results.

Nearly three years elapsed after the end of the Civil War before many Greek politicians were persuaded that the Cold War had genuinely come to stay and they had better adjust their ideas accordingly. Like their ancestors after the Battle of Navarino they seemed so intent upon returning to their old quarrels that they could not exploit the victory others had helped them to win; and the Americans—like the British, the French and the Russians in the 1820's—had metaphorically to knock a lot of Greek heads together before a government was formed that promised any stability. These tactics, which had gone unremarked when employed in the heat of battle against the communists a few years earlier, caused immediate resentment when used in time of peace; and one affair in particular was to rankle for years afterwards as an example of what those who chiefly suffered from it called America's arrogant interference in the internal affairs of Greece—and what those who chiefly benefited from it described as America's wisdom. This was the so-called 'Peurifoy incident', when the United States Ambassador in Athens, Mr. John E. Peurifoy, gave the local politicians a particularly impatient and startlingly public shake on behalf of what it was then fashionable to describe as 'the interests of the free world'.

Peurifoy's impatience was as understandable as his expression of it was indiscreet. The time was March 1952, already two-and-a-half years after the defeat of the last communist bands, yet so far Greece had failed to produce any stable government. To the Americans—as, indeed, to many Greeks—one of the principal reasons for this failure was the voting system then in use: a modified form of proportional representation which allotted parliamentary seats roughly in proportion to the total number of votes cast for each and every party contesting an election. Although on paper more democratic than other systems, because it ostensibly ensured that any party, however small, had a chance of securing a parliamentary voice, this form of proportional representation in practice emphasized all the worst aspects of Greek politics. By encouraging a multiplicity of parties it made factionalism an institution and weak governments an apparently inescapable outcome of every Greek election. As we have seen already, proportional representation in one form or another was partly responsible for the series of political deadlocks in Greece between the wars, including the crisis of 1936 when the small Communist Party held the balance of power in Parliament and induced the paralysis of government that led to the Metaxas dictatorship. It was not far-fetched to envisage a similar outcome from the condition of government and the electoral system in 1952.

Since the end of the Civil War Greece had known nothing but one flimsy coalition after another, whose members enjoyed briefly the spoils of power before parting again under the stress of their own squabbles. American aid was gushing unproductively down a thousand drains of inefficiency and corruption and the currency was still almost valueless. Both the extreme right and the extreme left had already reappeared in new disguises. The communists, whose party had been outlawed since 1947, had created a new party called the United Democratic Left (E.D.A.)—ostensibly yet another attempt to form a popular, united front—and had gained ten out of 250 seats in Parliament. The right wing had formed a new secret organization in the Army known as the Sacred Union of Greek Officers (I.D.E.A.) and rumours of another military *coup d'état* were already gaining currency in the Athens press.[1] The Government in power was as weak as all its predecessors. For the last time in his long career, General Plastiras was once again Prime Minister, at the head of an ineffective coalition of liberals including Sophocles Venizelos, son of Eleftherios Venizelos, who had already enjoyed several short and undistinguished spells as Prime Minister himself and was zealously seeking another. Venizelos and his supporters in the Plastiras cabinet saw their best hope of further elevation in the restoration of simple proportional representation, without even the modifications of the system that had brought Plastiras back to power. Nothing was more likely to splinter the façade of government into yet smaller and more intractable factions; but as Venizelos hoped to control the largest faction he welcomed such a prospect.

Not so the Americans, nor Greece's other new NATO allies. As early as 1950 some of them had expressed their concern about these Greek follies. 'Athens', observed one of the soberest of London weeklies then, 'has nothing to offer Greece. Political programmes, where they exist, are no more than a thin cloak for personal ambitions and parties stand rather by the names of their leaders than anything else . . . their programmes—vague statements about reconstruction and social reform—are irrelevant to their actual behaviour and have no fundamental points of difference.'² Two years later, with the United States and her allies still fighting a savage war against communist armies in Korea, and new threats of communist disturbances arising in Iran after the seizure of British oil interests there by the emotional Dr. Mossadeq, western concern had turned to impatience with the continuing mess in Greece. Clearly, strong government there of some kind was imperative; and by then the Americans thought they had both the means and the man to achieve it. The man they had in mind was Field-Marshal Papagos, whose name was respected throughout the country, and whose new Greek Rally Party had already shown more solidarity than any of the old factions. Conservative, monarchist, anti-communist and realistically eager to co-operate with the United States, the Rally was an obvious instrument for the American purpose. The means was to be the introduction of a simple, single-member majority system of voting, on the British and American pattern—i.e. one which treated every constituency as a separate battleground and awarded outright victory in each to whichever candidate polled the highest number of votes, even when those did not outnumber the total of votes cast for his rivals. This had the disadvantage that a governing party might be elected on a minority of the total vote, but it possessed the corresponding advantage of discouraging splinter groups in favour of two or three big, cohesive parties. Under this system, it was apparent to everyone, the Greek Rally under Papagos was virtually guaranteed to win. All that remained was to get the system adopted and then wait for the next, inevitable collapse of the coalition government and the new elections it would probably bring in its train.

Plastiras, by now an old man with little longer to live, was soon persuaded of his patriotic duty to introduce the new voting system, especially when the American Government repeated an earlier threat to withhold its financial aid unless a stronger government could be assured. Venizelos and his supporters in the Cabinet resisted American pressure, seeing their chances of further office vanishing. In the midst of the resulting Cabinet dispute, Peurifoy chose to make his public announcement. 'Because the American Government believes that the re-establishment of the "simple proportional" election method, with its unavoidable consequences of the continuation of governmental instability, would have destructive results upon the effective utilization of American aid to Greece, the American Embassy feels itself obliged to make its support publicly known for the patriotic position of the Prime Minister Plastiras with regard to this

M

subject.' Tactlessness and inelegance, it seemed, had been unhappily combined in the gobbledygook of an illiterate pro-consul. But the intervention was effective. When the outcry of the liberals and the new left-wing party had subsided, Greece had the electoral system the Americans wanted; and when the Plastiras Government resigned later in 1952 Papagos and his Greek Rally duly won the elections that followed, taking three-quarters of all the seats in Parliament on only 49 per cent of the total vote. E.D.A. was wiped out, the liberals were reduced to a rump. Thanks to the exigencies of the Cold War, Greece had secured a strong, elected government at last and her recovery had begun.

For the next ten years the basic assumptions of successive Greek governments remained unchanged, in the longest spell of comparative political stability modern Greece had ever known. They started from the premise that the containment of communism was the most vital requirement of Greek public life. From that all else flowed: friendship with the United States of America and suspicion of the Soviet Union and its satellites; the tacit support of the Army and the King and continued suppression of the Communist Party, except in its legalized parliamentary cloak as the United Democratic Left; the long-term imprisonment of a hard core of over a thousand party members or active collaborators, many of them convicted of serious crimes against other Greek citizens during the German occupation or the Civil War; and the subordination of certain traditional national interests to the wider demands of anti-communist strategy within NATO. Inevitably, this stable pattern was under constant challenge from politicians who either disputed its basic premise or failed to share in all its benefits. But here good fortune played a part for once in providing Greece with two leaders in succession who were both strong-willed enough to stick to their guns under criticism, yet better able than most of their colleagues to restrain their natural *hubris* with common sense. Papagos was the first—a legitimate national hero who, by some miracle of character, had not let his victories go altogether to his head. But his successor was a dark horse who had never risen farther up the political ladder than the post of Minister of Public Works, yet who was plucked from his obscurity by King Paul to become Prime Minister when Papagos died, in 1955. His name was Constantine Karamanlis, and at that time he had done little more to make his political reputation than to supervise the rebuilding of Athens. True, he had accomplished that with unusual firmness and dispatch, but it was hardly the sort of achievement to establish him in the normal way as a natural Prime Minister. More to the point was the fact that he had impressed the Americans by his performance—especially after some of the men they had been compelled to work with previously in their supervision of Greek reconstruction—and having made sure that he would maintain the Papagos foreign policy they had no hesitation in letting the King know that he was their first choice as the Field-Marshal's successor. All the same, the shock of his preferment was considerable, especially among his senior colleagues in the Greek Rally—as it might be in a British Cabinet if the Monarch were to send for an equally lowly minister to form a government in a crisis—and it resulted in no less than thirty of the party stumping off in dudgeon to join the opposition. But Karamanlis proved equal to his appointed task. He reconstructed both the Papagos Government and the Papagos party, transforming the Rally into a new coalition of broadly conservative interests called the National Radical Union (E.R.E.) with which he proceeded to win a majority in Parliament at three general elections in a row. Varying the electoral system each time, he won at the polls in 1956, 1958 and 1961—and only narrowly failed again in 1963—to remain continuously in office longer than any other Prime Minister in the history of modern Greece.

As these years of unaccustomed stability went by some of the western powers which had been so anxious about Greece's future began to take the change for granted and turn with relief to more pressing problems elsewhere. The decade after 1952 suffered no lack of those, from Hungary and Suez to Cuba and the Congo; and there were many occasions when Greece seemed by comparison a haven of peace, security and contentment under the safe command of Karamanlis and the avuncular guidance of the United States of America. Democracy, it seemed, was working in its legendary birthplace at last.

Yet in many ways there was less to this Greek recovery than met the casual eye. Neither the structure nor the attitude of Greek politics had undergone any fundamental change. Behind the apparently confident screen of government the old weaknesses and passions remained, frozen by the chill of the Cold War but ready to reveal themselves again at the first sign of a warmer climate. On two closely related issues, indeed, they were never more than fitfully subdued—firstly, the argument with Britain and Turkey over *enosis* with Cyprus and, secondly, the disagreement with the United States and NATO about siting nuclear weapons in Greece. Both were aspects of a typical crisis of national sentiment in which the collective Greek *philotimo* was affronted by foreign powers; and together they threatened—or, to nervous observers, appeared to threaten—to push Greece out of America's arms into an incautious neutralism.

Of the two, the Cyprus crisis was the more profound and was fated to remain unsettled, because it raised again the old ghosts of Byzantium, the Great Idea and Greco-Turkish enmity that might otherwise have been laid for ever at Smyrna. To most ordinary Greeks *enosis* between Cyprus and the motherland represented no more than the natural culmination of Greece's modern statehood. That Cyprus was 500 miles from the Greek mainland and within sight of Turkey might impress other, earth-bound, people as an obstacle to union between the two; but to a maritime nation for so long accustomed to the idea of its dispersal over a thousand islands in the surrounding seas, it was wholly insignificant. Four-fifths of the people of Cyprus spoke Greek and only one-fifth spoke Turkish; and that was enough for most Greeks, both in Athens and Nicosia, to see the island as the last, lost outpost of Byzantium to be gathered with all speed and glory into the new Greek fold. There was nothing new in this. In modern times, Cyprus had always been on the list of Greek irredentist territories, and on several occasions in this century its fate had been an issue in Greek politics. Only the fact that Britain, Greece's traditional protector, had bought the island from Turkey in the nineteenth century, as part of her general plan for containing the Russian threat in the eastern Mediterranean, had reconciled the Greeks to its continued exclusion from their new state. But they looked upon Britain as their caretaker in Cyprus and when the British Empire began to dissolve after the Second World War they soon reasserted their own sovereign claims. Unfortunately, Britain's Conservative Governments in the 1950's did not agree. The more the British imperial position crumbled elsewhere, the more doggedly they clung to Cyprus. The British military bases there were said to be essential for the protection of western oil interests in the increasingly turbulent and anti-British Arab world, as well as to support the eastern flank of NATO. They could not be allowed to fall, it was clearly implied, into the notoriously unreliable hands of the Greeks.

This attitude was not at first quite as foolish, or as arrogant, as it later seemed to be. When the question of *enosis* was raised by the Greek Cypriots in 1950, the Civil War had not long ended, the Cold War was in its chilliest phase, and Greece had no government worth the name. To have ceded Cyprus to Greece at that moment would have seemed to any British Government a wholly unjustifiable act of confidence. But within four years, as Greece was stabilized on the one hand and Britain prepared to withdraw from more imperial strongholds on the other, the rigid British position in Cyprus came to seem gratuitously offensive to Greek national sentiment. If India, Palestine and Egypt could get the British out, why not the Greeks of Cyprus, too? Discontent mounted in the island and communicated itself to Greece in the familiar spiral of request-refusal, demand-rejection, agitation-repression and terrorism-reprisal. By 1954 there were riots in Athens and Papagos was forced to make a public statement in support of *enosis*, in spite of his evident misgivings about its effect on Greece's NATO allies. A year later, the National Organization of Cypriot Combatants (EOKA) began its terrorist campaign against the British in the island under the leadership of the egregious General Grivas.[3] By then, too, Turkey was involved, for the British used the Turkish presence in the island as a further argument against Greek *enosis*, and the Cypriot Greeks responded by attacking the Turks with all the weight of their embittered history behind them. Violence in Athens and Cyprus mounted, but suddenly and shockingly in 1955 this was exceeded by murderous anti-Greek riots inspired by the Turkish Government in Izmir and Istanbul.

Then, with the national *philotimo* now thoroughly inflamed, the Greeks discovered—rather as they had done at Smyrna, thirty-odd years before—that their western allies were letting them down again. Neither in NATO nor at the United Nations, where the Greek Government raised the Cyprus issue, did they get the support they expected from their friends, who were far more concerned about the security of the western alliance against Russia than about Greek national ambitions. The American Secretary of State, John Foster Dulles, made it plain, with a blunt, identical telegram addressed to the Greek and Turkish Governments immediately after the rioting in Turkey, that he regarded both countries as equally at fault and advised them to stop squabbling in the interest of allied solidarity. In Athens even the staunchest supporters of the Government were shocked. Greece, said the normally pro-western and conservative newspaper, *Kathemerini*, had been betrayed. Ominously, it added: 'We do not know what the Government wants, but the people want WITHDRAWAL FROM NATO.'[4] It was amid this mood of popular disillusionment that Papagos died and Karamanlis came to power. The liberals, scenting a chance of victory over an untried leader with the Cyprus albatross around his neck, formed a united front with the communist-dominated left to fight him in his first election, early in 1956. *Enosis* was their common platform, contempt their common rhetoric—for a government that had allowed Greek self-esteem to be trampled in the Turkish mud.

That Karamanlis won in spite of these powerful passions was due immediately to two factors. Firstly, he changed the electoral system to suit his own party which, like the Greek Rally four years earlier, obtained a majority of seats on a minority vote. Secondly, the spectacle of a united front of liberals and crypto-communists was enough to frighten a substantial number of Greeks with the image of a renewed 'red peril'.[5] Even so, eighteen E.D.A. deputies won seats in the new Parliament; and as the Cyprus crisis deepened in 1956 with the arrest by the British and exile to the Seychelle Islands of Archbishop Makarios, the Greek Cypriot religious and political leader, the Government was forced into increasingly anti-British and anti-western gestures. There were more demonstrations in Athens, the Greek Ambassador was recalled from London, and the Minister of Education officially suspended the teaching of English in public schools. In the Suez crisis, Greece played an openly neutralist role; and while the Soviet Union and the Arab states supported the Cypriot demand for *enosis* the Greek press avidly discussed the possibility of forming an alliance between Athens, Belgrade and Cairo.

In this heady atmosphere the possibility of installing American nuclear missiles in Greece, canvassed at NATO conferences in 1957, inevitably started another major political controversy about a further infringement of Greek sovereignty. Hounded by the outcry about American neo-colonialism and British perfidy, from Peurifoy onwards to Cyprus and the missiles, the Government was driven into increasing equivocation over its own attachment to NATO. The terms of Greek participation in the alliance, said Evangelos Averoff, the Greek Foreign Minister, were becoming 'untenable';[6] and by the spring of 1958 Karamanlis was forced into his second general election by what seemed to be an overwhelming weight of national feeling on the issue. In the event, his party won a bigger majority of parliamentary seats than before, but only because the voting system had been manipulated yet again. The party's minority vote was lower than ever and, much more alarming, the liberal opposition had been almost squeezed out leaving the crypto-communists of E.D.A., campaigning on an anti-NATO platform, as the second largest party. With 79 out of 300 deputies elected on a quarter of the total vote the extreme left had returned with a vengeance to the political arena from which they had seemed to be expelled for ever only eight years earlier. For the next three years they were to remain the chief spokesmen of opposition in Greece, urging withdrawal from NATO, nonalignment and—with articulate Soviet support—the creation of a 'peace zone' in the Balkans.

That, however, was the pinnacle of E.D.A.'s achievements, for it was enough to frighten everyone else into a series of efforts to undercut the foundations of its success—in short, to settle the Cyprus crisis. Karamanlis himself was the first to move. Secure with his new parliamentary majority, and sensing the alarm both inside and outside Greece at E.D.A.'s fresh advances, he at once reasserted that the basic principle of Greek foreign policy was her loyal membership of NATO. But at the same time he warned the other NATO powers that the Cyprus issue was placing exceptional strains upon that loyalty; and by pointedly looking forward to establishing better relations with eastern Europe and the Arab world he reminded his foreign as well as his domestic audience that there might yet be in the twentieth century—as there had seemed to be from time to time in the nineteenth century—a Greek alternative to the western alliance.

The British Government responded by naming a new and more liberal Governor of Cyprus in the person of Sir Hugh Foot (later Lord Caradon), and proposing tripartite administrative partnership for the island composed of Britain, Greece and Turkey. This was far from what the Greeks wanted, but from the British point of view it was a significant concession and Archbishop Makarios, on behalf of the Greek Cypriots, followed it with a still more important concession of his own. Restored to the bosom of his admiring countrymen after his balmy exile in the Indian Ocean, he announced that he would accept independence for Cyprus instead of union with Greece as a final solution to the problem. The Turks and the British took hopeful note and before the end of 1958 secret explorations of the Archbishop's proposal had begun at NATO headquarters in Paris. The log-jam had been broken; and swiftly, now, the obstacles to a compromise were thrust aside. In February 1959, Karamanlis met the Prime Minister of Turkey, Adnan Menderes, in Zurich and agreed on the creation of an independent Republic of Cyprus in which the Turkish minority would have self-protective rights of veto. On then to London where the British Government underwrote these proposals in return for guarantees of tenure and security for its military bases on the island. Finally, Archbishop Makarios and the leader of the Turkish community in Cyprus, Dr. Kutchuk,

countersigned the package, on the understanding that the Archbishop would be the first President and Dr. Kutchuk the first Vice-
President of the new Republic. The whole process had taken a bare
nine months from the latest victory of Karamanlis at the polls;
and although the settlement was sternly denounced by the Greek
opposition as a betrayal of the national interest—and although it did,
indeed, contain the seeds of its own subsequent breakdown in the
unusually powerful veto rights bestowed on the Turkish minority—it
successfully removed the worst embarrassments of the Cyprus problem for the next few years and permitted the Greek Government to
return to whole-hearted co-operation with the western alliance in
general and the United States of America in particular.

There seemed still to be overwhelming reason for a responsible
Greek Government to do so. Internally, the parliamentary strength
of E.D.A., born of the Cyprus crisis, continued to create a sense of
public tension out of all proportion to the real strength of the communists who operated under its cloak. It provided cover and encouragement for renewed infiltration of agents and provocateurs,
both Greek and Slav, from Greece's northern neighbours. It forced
the other political groups into more extravagant attitudes so that, in
the blissful irresponsibility of opposition, extreme left and extreme
right as well as the splintered liberals of the centre competed in their
vehement rejections of the Cyprus settlement as an abandonment
of national honour. Externally, too, the Cold War still felt frigid.
Soviet influence was steadily increasing in the Middle East, and in
spite of Mr. Khrushchev's famous denunciation of Stalinism at the
Twentieth Party Congress in 1956, and his talk of permitting different
national roads to socialism, most of Greece's northern borders
remained unmistakably part of Europe's great political Styx, across
which wise men trafficked only with the greatest care.

Greek relations with Yugoslavia were correct enough, thanks to
the 'bourgeois revisionism' of President Tito, but even he inhibited
friendship by reviving old antagonisms in Macedonia. His efforts
were actually directed against the Bulgarians rather than the Greeks,
but it was in the nature of the Macedonian question that he could
not stir one pot without causing the other to bubble; and when, in
1961, he encouraged Macedonian leaders in Skopje, on the Yugoslav side of the frontier, to voice a traditional demand for a greater
Macedonian nation, in order to embarrass communist rivals in
Sofia, he inevitably offended the Greeks as well. The Greek Government, professing deep concern, promptly suspended an agreement

it had just signed with Yugoslavia permitting residents on both sides of the frontier to move freely between the towns of Monastir and Florina. It took more than two years and a change of government in Athens to bury that characteristic little Balkan hatchet.

With Albania, Greece had no official relations at all. Ever since the Albanian Government had supported the Italian invasion of Greece, the two countries had remained formally in a state of war; and as the post-war communist government in Tirana had been the last to stop helping the communist armies in Greece, and had since continued even in Soviet eyes in the parlous condition of 'Stalinist deviationism', there was not much likelihood of anything but continued hostility there. As for Bulgaria what sensible Greek did not suspect the worst? From the Slav invasions of centuries past to the guerrillas of the Balkan Wars and the communists of the 1940's, the Thracian borderland had seen too many invasions of the sacred Greek soil. Now, on those bleak uplands behind Salonika and Kavalla, the watch-towers and barbed wire reminded most Greeks that this was still, as ever, the last frontier against the Slav. Nor did Mr. Khrushchev or the Bulgars encourage anyone to forget it, for when the Greek Government at last signed an agreement with the United States in 1959 on the disposition of nuclear weapons, the Bulgarians thundered their displeasure from Sofia and Mr. Khrushchev spoke warmly of the outlawed Greek Communist Party on a visit to Budapest.

Thus, while much of the parliamentary opposition pursued the alluring nymph of neutralism with ever more reckless ardour, Karamanlis and his colleagues maintained their guard against any fresh hint of seduction. They sought to mollify some of their less radical opponents by signing new trade agreements with the communist block—another genuflexion to the old eastern element in the Greek balance of forces—but their greatest energies were devoted to securing the far more important goal of association with western Europe's new Common Market. The negotiations were long and difficult, for even after a decade of American aid the Greek economy was in no state to withstand early competition from the booming industrial nations of the West, and special protection was imperative if Greece's recovery was not to be halted in its tracks. But the decision to seek association with the Market was more political than economic and more emotional than either, being justified in terms of almost mystical significance as the ultimate symbol of Greece's western destiny. When, at last, the attempt succeeded and Greece was accepted as an associate member of the Common Market in July 1961, the satisfaction of the Government and its friends was profound. 'We have rejoined the mainstream of western history,' said their chief negotiator, Mr. John Pezmazoglou, Deputy Governor of the Bank of Greece. It was, he implied, as if 2,000 years of Greek history had somehow been consigned to limbo, and modern Greece was therefore about to take up where its classical ancestors had left off—in the vanguard of human progress once again. On that optimistic note Karamanlis resigned for a third time and offered himself and his party to the people of Greece for, as he hoped, yet another vote of confidence.

He had already displayed his own confidence by changing the electoral law yet again, but this time in a way that, in the view of some observers, might favour his opponents rather than his own party.[7] With the Cyprus issue dormant, no matter how hard his opponents tried to breathe new life into it, foreign policy and Greek honour were not at stake as they had been before and Karamanlis was able to conduct a campaign that was roughly the Greek equivalent of that of Harold Macmillan in Britain, two years earlier, when the British Prime Minister had swept the Conservative Party back to an unexpected victory over Labour with the purely domestic, material and—some said—vulgar slogan, 'You've never had it so good'. Vulgar or not, the result in Greece was similar. Karamanlis won again, and apparently more decisively than ever. His party even gained a majority of the total vote for the first time, with nearly 51 per cent to its credit, while the crypto-communists under the E.D.A. label lost two-thirds of their seats and had their portion of the vote cut from a quarter to one-seventh of the whole. It seemed, on the face of it, the ultimate vindication of nearly ten years of right-wing solidarity and American support, final testimony to the Greek recovery and its democratic ways. Yet it marked the start of a new political and personal crisis that was eventually to wreck the fragile democratic system and reopen Greece to the politics of militarism.

The way this crisis developed is the subject of the next two chapters. Here, I want only to point to some of the ironies and anomalies in which it began. First, there can be little doubt that Karamanlis had in many ways earned his third victory. By 1961 Greece's economic recovery was beginning to have some real impact on many ordinary people. By the standards of the rest of Europe the country was still pathetically poor, but by the Greek standards of ten years before it was transformed; and with plentiful American financial

aid at his disposal to underwrite his government's powers of patronage, Karamanlis was able to spread the rewards of loyalty both
wider and thicker than perhaps any Greek Prime Minister had ever
done before. For those on his bandwaggon it was literally true that
they had never had it so good. By the same token, however, those
who had not joined his bandwaggon were more than ever outraged
by his success. These included many in the Greek villages who had
found that the prices for their farm produce were not keeping pace
with the cost of the new manufactured goods they now saw dangled
temptingly before them; many who had gone to the Greek towns to
look for better-paid work and had not found it; and many who had
been deliberately and often vindictively excluded from government
jobs and patronage because of past political associations with the
communists or their erstwhile allies. They included also some rational
critics of the Government who argued that the recovery could have
gone further and faster if Greece had not been burdened with an
army larger than she needed and a defence budget higher in proportion to her national resources than any other in NATO. Nearly
twelve years after the end of the Civil War, they alleged, the only
explanation for this must be that the Government wanted to retain
the support of the predominantly right-wing Army officers and to
use the Army as an instrument of political oppression.

Given that the armed forces had been purged of their non-royalist
elements ever since the wartime mutiny in the Middle East, there was
probably something in this. But the most important reaction against
Karamanlis seemed, nevertheless, basically opportunist, for it was
led, inevitably, by all those opposition politicians who had grown
up in the old habits of the Greek game, expecting their share of power
and its perquisites at fairly frequent intervals whether they had any
differences of principle with the Government or not. Unable to contemplate without rancour the apparently permanent lease on government of Karamanlis and his friends, they contrived at last in 1961
to unite nine of their splinter groups under a single leader and enter
the election with correspondingly high hopes of defeating Karamanlis
for the first time. They called their party the Centre Union and its
leader was the old Venizelist liberal George Papandreou—the man
who had returned to Greece some seventeen years before as Prime
Minister of the wartime Government-in-exile, only to be forced into
early resignation by the challenge of the communist guerrilla armies.
He had never held office as Prime Minister again, and although he
had been an early ally of Papagos he was a sworn enemy of Karaman-

lis and for most of the last decade he had not served a Greek Government in any capacity whatever. By 1961 he had turned seventy, but
he was recognized as the most formidable of the old liberal politicians: a tall, imperious figure of a man, with the rhetorical style of an
Edwardian actor-manager, and even more the natural heir to the
Venizelos tradition than the Cretan's own son, Sophocles—who was,
in fact, Papandreou's chief rival in the liberal centre of Greek politics.
If there was to be an acceptable, democratic alternative to Karamanlis and the National Radical Union, it was almost bound to centre
somehow upon Papandreou. His experience had made him staunchly
anti-communist; and in spite of expending his rhetorical talents freely
upon the Cyprus affair, in which he still professed to see Greek
honour betrayed, he was on record—like the rest of the liberals in
the last resort—as a faithful NATO man. A liberal government had
signed the original NATO treaty in 1952, and Papandreou could not
in honour go back on that. Nor did he want to. 'History, geography
and the world of ethical values in which Greece believes,' he said,
in the course of the 1961 campaign, had made Greece ineluctably a
part of the free, western world.[8] But, of course, Papandreou promised
to do more than Karamanlis to make the western alliance sing a
Greek tune now and then instead of the exclusively American airs it
had so far been committed to. In short, he offered American security
without American patronage or Greek subservience. Greece would
be an equal in the free world's councils and the memories of Peurifoy,
Dulles and the despised Zurich Agreement on Cyprus would be
exorcized under Papandreou's benevolent guidance.

It was the old Greek dream again of 'true' and 'unfettered' independence—the sort that Greece had never pursued without mishap,
yet to which she was for ever returning in some new and more hopeful guise. Ironically and characteristically, however, it was advanced
this time with greater conviction because Papandreou himself was
the beneficiary of American patronage, albeit of a more than usually
discreet kind. Its origins lay in a new sense of American disquiet at
the apparent growing rigidity of the Greek political structure. Ten
years previously any rigidity had been welcome in preference to
the sterile flux that then prevailed; but those years had radically
changed the points of reference for the Greek political contest. Under
Mr. Khrushchev the Soviet regime had begun to speak of competitive coexistence in place of its old hostility to the West, and a corresponding new mood was apparent in American foreign policy as
well. John Foster Dulles, the blundering old badger of American

anti-communism, was dead and buried and, since the election of John F. Kennedy to the Presidency in 1960, many of his attitudes had been buried with him. There was greater sympathy for the non-alignment of new nations in the emerging Third World, more concern for the political and economic as well as military foundations of western security, and a new readiness to accept the growing demands of trade between the communist countries and the West. A hint of sunshine was in the air, thawing the hard edges of the Cold War, and Greece was not immune to it. But the danger in Greece was that if government continued to be dominated by the conservatives this faint warmth would be frozen again by the familiar process of polarization between extreme left and extreme right, as the liberals became more frustrated and confused by their exclusion from office and adopted more of the left-wing line, while the right-wing grew correspondingly more alarmed and belligerent at the spectacle of their hated 'red peril' rising again from the ashes of defeat.

The advance of E.D.A. in 1958 seemed to threaten such an unhappy development; and to Karamanlis, the Americans and King Paul the first necessity in 1961 appeared to be to cut the crypto-communists down to size and secure at least a more coherent opposition party of the centre that might speak with the responsibility fitting to a possible government of the future. There arose, in consequence, a strange, tacit and in some ways contradictory alliance between these three on one side and George Papandreou and his friends on the other, with the object of defeating E.D.A. and strengthening the centre factions. There is no evidence, as far as I know, of an actual conspiracy between all four to rig the elections with this specific end in view. Indeed, it is unlikely that Karamanlis and Papandreou would ever have agreed upon anything of that sort, for both men wanted to win. But the Americans did put it about in the proper Athenian quarters that they would not be averse to the right kind of opposition victory, as a proof that they were not invariably on the side of the devil; and King Paul also was believed to be ready to accept a new governing party of the centre to avoid being labelled as a puppet of the right and thus reopening the old dispute about the monarchy. The formation of the new Centre Union grouping under Papandreou was, therefore, quietly encouraged by the Americans and the King, and was even observed with benevolent neutrality by Karamanlis.[9] Thereafter, however, the plan fell apart—or rather, it succeeded too well. E.D.A. was, indeed, cut down to size, but the main beneficiary turned out to be the Government instead of the new

Centre Union. Papandreou and his allies won only a third of the vote and a third of the seats, and while that made them easily the second party in the new Parliament it left them as far from government as ever. For Papandreou this result seemed a personal affront. It was unprecedented in Greece for one man and one party to win three elections in a row, and that it should happen when his hopes had been raised so high by the new climate in Washington must have been all the more galling. His reaction was to reject the whole election as a fraud, to boycott the new Parliament, to call the Government illegal and to demand that the King should dismiss Karamanlis and call new elections at once.

The truth of this odd affair is difficult now to distinguish from legend, but a few aspects of it are fairly clear. First, there was Papandreou's own character. Although a man of great natural ability, he was notoriously volatile, quickly carried away by the sound of his own remarkable voice and plainly addicted to wishful thinking. While all these characteristics endeared him to many Greeks, who recognized themselves writ large in him, they served him ill in political calculations. Already by most standards an old man, who had known one moment of glory in 1944 and had never tasted it again, I think it entirely likely that in 1961 he was first and foremost the victim of his own self-delusion—convinced that the Americans actually wanted him to win, he was immediately persuaded that he must win.

On the other hand, there appeared to be some substance to Papandreou's charge of electoral fraud, or at least of irregularity. The votes of the armed forces went in remarkably high proportions to candidates of the National Radical Union. There were mysterious discrepancies in the voting registers, and frequent reports of police in country districts 'instructing' the villagers to vote for Karamanlis. Indeed, E.D.A. candidates were complaining loudly of fraud on these grounds before the election, and although many of their complaints must be discounted as part of their ordinary propaganda, there was enough independent grumbling to support real suspicion. Much of this, however, was routine in Greek elections, where the exercise— or non-exercise—of Government patronage was always one of the deciding factors. Moreover, there was at least a suspicion that Papandreou's Centre Union was actually privy to some of this pressure, as part of the tacit agreement to reduce the E.D.A. vote. Naturally, Papandreou hoped that voters who switched away from E.D.A. would turn to his party, but it was always on the face of things more likely that they would go, instead, to the party that seemed to offer the best returns. In the circumstances of 1961 that must have seemed to many Greeks still to be the party of Karamanlis; and that a genuine majority of them did vote for his return to power then was strongly indicated by the result of the next general election two years later. In the autumn of 1963, when Karamanlis had fallen out with the King and the Americans were making no bones about hoping for a Centre Union victory, Papandreou had another chance in what were generally conceded to be the fairest elections Greece had ever known —yet after a non-stop, country-wide election campaign throughout the two years of the last Karamanlis Government, Papandreou and the Centre Union in 1963 only just scraped home as the majority party, with an overall minority of seats in Parliament. It seems reasonable to conclude, therefore, that while there were probably more irregularities than usual in the 1961 election they were not great enough in themselves to account for the size of the Government's victory; and the impression must remain that Papandreou knew it, but deceived himself into believing otherwise out of pride.

It was a pride that was to prove costly both to him and to his country, for in the next few years it seemed to gain a dangerous ascendancy over his political wisdom. Yet he was not alone in this sad change. In the years since he had been Prime Minister for the first time the normal passions of Greek politics had been contained within the unfamiliar, irksome but steely corset of the new super-power rivalry. That period, however, was now coming to an end. The Cold War was not over, but it had already entered a new phase when the old polarities seemed less important and Greeks could begin to see multiple choices again where for nearly a generation there had been but two. And as the world returned to something nearer normal, so did Greece, with all its febrile nerve ends tingling at the prospect of a new kind of national freedom, when at last the country might loose its hold on the American nurse without too much fear of meeting something worse. Alas, the prospect was to prove illusory. A strange interlude of enforced stability and restriction was ending; but what lay immediately ahead was not a new liberty but a return to tragically familiar political licence and disarray.

Chapter 12

THE UNRELENTING STRUGGLE

Power bores me—only struggles stimulate me.
(GEORGE PAPANDREOU)

On the 22nd May 1963, a left-wing member of the Greek Parliament, who was also a former Olympic athlete and a university professor of medicine, was run down deliberately in the streets of Salonika by a combination motor-cycle and sidecar. Few people outside Greece had ever heard of him until that moment, but before he died of his injuries, four days later, he had become an international martyr ostensibly in the cause of democracy in Greece. His name was Gregory Lambrakis, and the furore that accompanied his last hours marked the effective end of that deceptive interlude of political stability that Greece had enjoyed in the shadow of the Cold War.

No sooner had the news of the Salonika attack reached Athens than the Greek political world was in an uproar. The local police, it was alleged, had acted in collusion with the attackers; and even before it was established that Lambrakis was dying his colleagues in the United Democratic Front were joined by George Papandreou and traditional liberals of the Centre Union in accusing the Karamanlis Government of political murder. Harassed and shaken, the Government at first denied responsibility, then implicitly accepted it by suspending the local commissioner of police, pending investigation. Three days later, police with truncheons dispersed anti-government student demonstrators in the streets of Athens, and the outcry of the opposition was redoubled. By the time Lambrakis died, his fate had become a *cause célèbre* in more senses than one—both a celebrated cause and a cause to celebrate, for at long last the Government of Constantine Karamanlis had been caught plainly unawares.

From the opposition's point of view, Lambrakis was almost an ideal martyr. His sporting reputation and his medical practice had given him a wide Athenian following. His attachment to E.D.A. was believed to be that of a sincere socialist and not just the orthodox cover for communist activities. And although he was not well known abroad he had established links with the left wing of the British Labour Party and with international nuclear disarmament groups that had already taken up the opposition cause in Greece so that his death was bound to excite foreign repercussions. It was no surprise, therefore, that his funeral in Athens was more of a political jamboree than an occasion for real mourning, for while it offered to the Centre Union a splendid—and apparently disinterested—stick with which to beat the Government, it also gave to the communists and their sympathizers the best opportunity they had enjoyed for years to show their strength in the streets of Athens without risk of police reaction. In the event it was difficult to tell just who was who among the political mourners, but the combined strength of the opposition parties brought out tens of thousands of Athenians to jam the narrow streets of the old city around the cathedral where the Archbishop of Athens conducted the burial service. Scores of enormous wreaths were carried in the procession to the cemetery by Lambrakis's political friends and supporters. All the opposition leaders were present, and the Speaker of the Parliament turned up to honour a former member of the House—and was jeered by the crowd for his pains. Left-wing members of the British, French and Italian Parliaments were among the official mourners, a delegation from the Greek Peace Rally bore a banner with the nuclear disarmers' device, and former fellow sportsmen of Lambrakis carried trophies he had won in his youth. Many of the crowd reacted as if they had learned their lines in advance. 'Democracy! Democracy!' they shouted, as Papandreou arrived at the cathedral. 'Down with Fascism!' and 'Lambrakis will live for ever!' they cried, as the coffin was carried out, draped with the Greek flag.

A sprinkling of genuine mourners for the man showed themselves by their tears, but for the rest, it was plain, Lambrakis was no longer a man, nor even a corpse, but a symbol of all the accumulated frustrations of Greece since the Civil War. Alive, he had never been more than a fairly popular but undistinguished politician of the left. Dead he had become a catalyst of action. Within two weeks of his burial Karamanlis resigned, and the political kaleidoscope in Greece was shaken decisively into new patterns for the first time in a generation.

The roots of the Lambrakis affair went right back to the Civil War and the absolute choice between left and right that had then been forced upon Greece. Its development could be traced through the repeated crises of Greek national sentiment in the 1950's, which had so nearly reopened that choice prematurely by giving the left a

N

chance to ride its tempting white horse of neutralism; but its particular symbolic importance in 1963 stemmed from its dramatic timing in relation to the course of two separate but steadily converging political campaigns against the continued monopoly of power by Karamanlis and the right. The first campaign was that of Papandreou and the Centre Union. The second was that of the communists and their sympathizers outside as well as inside Greece.

Until 1961 the two campaigns had remained quite separate, in spite of their temporary common front against the Government in 1956, for while the first group shared most of the Government's fundamental assumptions and objected chiefly to its exclusive occupation of the seats of power, the second began from radically different premises and sought a permanent change in the power structure. This was still true even after the elections of 1961, when Papandreou refurbished his campaign with the charge of electoral fraud and began what he was to call his 'unrelenting struggle' against injustice and for new elections. For all his vehemence he was still, essentially, arguing the old case of the 'outs' against the 'ins'. In specific policies he had little to offer that was not already in the Government's programme, except to say anything they could do he could do better.

He had no intention of abandoning NATO, reversing the decision to join the Common Market, removing the monarchy, or flirting with socialism—let alone with communism; and if he maintained that he would somehow secure *enosis* with Cyprus and so redeem Greek honour, it was more in hopeful rhetoric than in strict intention. He was, after all, no less of an old-fashioned Greek politician than those men of the right whom he attacked, and with most of whom he had worked willingly in harness at one time or another. Chiefly what he wanted—and what most of his colleagues in the Centre Union equally desired—was not a revolution, nor even much reform by the standards of more developed western democracies, but rather the power that for nine unprecedented years had been denied him. This is not to say that Papandreou was unprincipled—only that his principles were naturally those of the Greece he had known all his life: a poor and overburdened country, weak in institutions and strong of ambition, where power at every level of society was generally seen to be in the gift of someone else and where, therefore, its monopoly by one group to the exclusion of all others argued that somebody, somewhere, was being deliberately unfair. Thus, it was natural after his devastating defeat at the polls in 1961, that whatever the rights or wrongs of the matter Papandreou should raise first and foremost a piercing cry of 'Foul!' The precise extent to which the elections had actually been rigged remains, as I have said, unknown; but it soon became, in any case, irrelevant. The explanation satisfied a characteristic—and not always unjustified—Greek penchant for interpreting all political events in terms of conspiracy, and it was quickly established in the minds of all who felt hard done by that if one group of politicians had been able to hold power for an unprecedented length of time it must be the result of an unprecedented conspiracy.

Yet the logic of this thinking eventually forced Papandreou into much more radical attitudes than he had bargained for. If you cry 'Foul!' you can only expect redress by appealing to the referee for a penalty; and in the context this had to mean for Papandreou looking beyond the normal processes of the polls—which, by his definition, were useless anyway—to some suitably omnipotent force that would uphold his idea of justice. Papandreou named the King. Constitutionally, he argued, the King had the right to dismiss a Prime Minister and order new elections. In the light of the allegations of fraud it had become his duty to do so, especially as the elections had been conducted by a caretaker government under the leadership of one of the senior officials of his Royal Court. Thus, whether he wanted to or not, the King was compelled by Papandreou to make a public decision of profound importance and with the maximum amount of publicity. If he turned a deaf ear to Papandreou's appeal he must appear to be the Government's man. But if he accepted the charge and dismissed Karamanlis, he must seem equally clearly to be the Government's enemy. Either way he would be damned by the resulting controversy. Not surprisingly, King Paul chose the devil he knew rather than the devil he didn't, and ignored Papandreou's arguments. Few people at the time seriously expected him to do anything else, yet the sequel was bitter and predictable—a steady rise in the intensity of opposition attacks not only on the Government for its alleged dishonesty but upon the King and his household as well. Thus the old issue of the monarchy was dragged back upon the political stage. It is true that Papandreou himself consistently denied any intention of criticizing the monarchy as an institution, but by forcing the King to make an open political decision he was, in fact, embroiling him again in party squabbles; and knowing the sour history of the royalist-republican quarrel in Greece he might have realized the danger of releasing that djinn from the bottle again. Many of his opposition colleagues were certainly nervous about it for, as they said frequently enough in private, unless Papandreou was prepared to advocate a republic in the last resort—which he said he was not—he was simply helping to discredit the chief political institution on whose neutrality non-communist Greeks should try to agree. The way to deal with the monarchy's partiality, they argued, was to get it out of politics, not to bring it back in. Belatedly, in 1963, Papandreou accepted this argument and eventually reduced his own attacks upon the Palace, but by that time the damage had been done. The King was back in the arena, and with him under attack was what gradually came to be identified as the whole nexus of right-wing power comprising not only Karamanlis and his colleagues but the Administration, the Police and the Army as well, and behind them, ultimately, the sinister figures of foreign investors and the United States Government.

As with the original allegation of electoral fraud from which the campaign started, there was some truth in his melodramatic picture. The structure of government throughout Greece depended tradi-tionally on the lavish exercise of patronage; and when one group had retained power for an unusually long time it was inevitable that their nominees should have taken over positions of influence to an unusual degree. Like the Army and the Police after the Civil War, the Civil Service by the early 1960's had been widely—although by no means wholly—infiltrated by royalist and right-wing sympathi-zers. Karamanlis was known to have been King Paul's personal selection for the office of Prime Minister, which supported the argu-ment that favouritism began at the top; and in so far as the Army, the Police, the Civil Service and the Government, and indirectly even the Palace itself, were all buttressed by the post-war flow of American aid and foreign investment, the United States and foreign capital could be depicted, with apparent reason, as the pay- and puppet-masters of the lot. But if all these groups and institutions did, indeed, comprise a monolithic establishment it followed that an allegation of conspiracy against one of them—namely the Karamanlis Govern-ment—implied an allegation against them all; and although Papan-dreou himself seemed reluctant to press his charges that far, others were not so shy. Where he tended to baulk in his 'unrelenting struggle' they marched on, and dragged him after them, to transform his original campaign of the 'outs' against the 'ins' into an attack on the whole basis of Greek policies since the war.

Several things assisted this transformation, not least the follies and excesses of some of the Greek right wing. Obsessed with anti-com-munism, they reacted to the mildest liberal criticism as if it were the voice of Lenin himself; and in the chain of patronage which descended from Athens down to the lowest level of rural affairs, they did not hesitate to insert their own men and exclude all others, so that local police stations or village councils were sometimes dominated by people who were little better than bully-boys out for what they could get, or men who were still paying off old scores from the Civil War. Instead of trying to close the desperate fissures that ripped apart Greek society in those tragic years, such men actually kept them open; and whether they did so out of greed, fear or simple misunderstanding, they produced an equivalent reaction from the other side as inevitable as it was depressing. At the topmost levels, also, folly was met with folly. The royal family, for example, contributed powerfully to its own difficulties by its inability to remain cool under pressure. In 1949 King Paul and Queen Frederika had gained wide esteem among Greeks outside the communist ranks by their undeniable courage and initiative in helping the victims of the fighting. Some of this, no doubt, had been lost twelve years later through the normal erosions of time and circumstance, for whether they liked it or not they were bound to be associated in many Greek minds by then with the prevailing state of right-wing favouritism. But when Papandreou issued his ill-judged challenge to the King the Palace replied with equal misjudgements, revealing a capacity for political tactlessness that made its semi-foreign occupants seem more Greek than the Greeks. Queen Frederika, especially, showed a choleric sensitivity to public criticism—and became, in consequence, its favourite target. Her German origins were gleefully recalled in the Athens press as explanation of her authoritarian temper. Comparisons were made between Paul and his father, Constantine, who had also married a German princess and led the country to division and disaster. The Queen's Fund, a charity created during the Civil War, and never subjected to parliamentary scrutiny, was said to be feathering the royal nest. Instead of responding to this with a dignified silence, or better still with a gesture of reconciliation or reassurance, the Palace recklessly offered its critics more ammunition. When ordinary Civil Servants were ordered to accept a wage freeze because the economy was faltering, King Paul applied for, and was granted, a large increase in government payments for the royal household. Necessary, some said, for the minimal upkeep of an establishment that, by the standards of British royalty, lived in no more than modest pomp—necessary, but horribly ill-timed. When his daughter, Princess Sophia, was wedded to the eligible but then throneless Prince

Don Juan Carlos of Spain, she committed, in the eyes of many Greeks, three offences in one ceremony—by marrying a Roman Catholic, by associating the fair name of Greece with that of General Franco's Spain and, worst of all in a country still hideously impoverished, by taking some $300,000 of public money as her dowry. On top of that there was even what appeared to be a royal attempt to censor the press, when two Athens journalists were imprisoned for publishing an attack on Queen Frederika based on alleged remarks by her estranged mother. Scurrilous these may have been, but they were scarcely the best grounds for the Palace to pick a fight, especially in a country where respect for the aged sometimes seemed so virtuous as to be a vice.

Old economic stresses as well as old political quarrels also reappeared at this time to encourage the turn to a new radicalism in Greek politics. American financial aid was dwindling to nothing after nearly fifteen years in which it had not only kept Greece afloat, but had introduced many of its people to a brand-new world of small luxuries and big possibilities. Yet new sources of capital had not been found and the perennially precarious balance of payments was starting to wilt. As the Government struggled with one hand to hold back the rising demands of ordinary Greeks it offered favourable terms to foreign investors with the other, tempting them to bring their needed money and expertise into Greece. An already underpaid Civil Service groaned with discontent. Inefficient and undercapitalized farmers winced. Small business-men living on a mixture of wits and credit squeaked with indignation; and emigration rose sharply from 50,000 to 80,000 and then to an unprecedented 100,000 people in a year as the best and brightest young Greeks sought a better life elsewhere, as their forefathers had done before them.

The contrast between this massive export of Greek life and the import of a handful of privileged international enterprises was especially painful. To make matters worse, some of the biggest deals were concluded with successful but self-exiled Greeks who knew their way as well as the next man around the corridors of their country's power and aroused that special jealousy so often reserved for self-made men among those they have left behind. There were Stavros Niarchos, who was building new shipyards not far from Athens; Aristotle Onassis, who took over the Greek national airlines; and Tom Pappas who combined with the Esso Company of America to tender successfully for a huge oil and petro-chemical complex at Salonika. The Government welcomed them and declared it was planning for the long haul, to secure Greek prosperity inside the Common Market. But ordinary people looked at the short haul and asked for a share of prosperity now. Undoubtedly there was something genuinely new in all this ferment that went beyond the old weaknesses of the Greek economy and the old rivalries of Greek politics. With the massive injections of American aid, the whole balance of Greek society had begun to shift away from the peasant farms and villages with their traditional values and demands, towards the towns and especially towards the booming capital, which grew in numbers and in wealth day by day. By 1961, when Karamanlis won his last and biggest electoral victory, the census showed that the urban population of Greece had equalled the rural population for the first time in history. It was rather like the aftermath of the Anatolian disaster or the Civil War all over again, as men and women poured off the land and into the city, to swell the disordered and disorientated throng. They left poverty and discontent behind them and created more where they came to rest as they looked for the promised riches of the brave new twentieth-century world—and usually failed to find them. Rumours spread of corruption in high places; jealousy rose at the growth of the new financial oligarchy; strikes and demonstrations by discontented farmers and disgruntled city workers became more frequent; and opposition promises of more welfare, more pensions, more schools and more money grew bolder, feeding on the enthusiasm they generated. The pendulum of power was beginning to swing after a decade of immobility and, sensing its movement, both Government and opposition grew more excited and excitable.

Reinforcing all this, moreover, as the inspiration of new Greek thoughts was not only the apparent thaw in the Cold War which typified the international atmosphere of the early 1960's, but also the approach to manhood at last of a new generation of Greeks whose minds were relatively untainted by memories of the Civil War. To them, especially, the restraints of the previous decade seemed not merely unnatural but out of date; and to the politicians who prepared to seek their votes for the first time the shared and strictly anti-communist assumptions of the recent past became correspondingly expendable. In this altogether more hopeful mood in Greece, Papandreou's 'unrelenting struggle' found a quick response as the old man stumped the country with a vigour that belied his years in what one Greek writer has called 'almost mystical communion with the people'.[1] But it was a mood in which others, too, could see advantage; and while Papandreou raised his campaign to greater heights of rhetoric the communists, both inside Greece and abroad, shrewdly took up station behind him, exploiting his emotional blasts of protest to promote their own, more specific, ends. In their hands the Greece that Papandreou painted, of social injustice, electoral fraud and royal favouritism, became a monster of police dictatorship and monarcho-fascism, dominated by American imperialism.

There was no formal identification of this picture with the communists; and many sincere critics of the Greek Government, especially in other countries, remained convinced that the attempt by Karamanlis and his colleagues to blame it on the communists was further proof of just how purblind, out of date and reactionary they were. Yet, as one reliable British newspaper reported at the time, there was ample evidence of 'one of the most effective communist propaganda campaigns ever carried out'.[2] It began with the denunciation of Greece as a fascist country at conferences in France and Italy organized by communists and attended by an international smattering of left-wing or liberal intellectuals and politicians. But it took root especially in Britain where the prospect of a Greek royal visit in the summer of 1963 combined with the old, confused philhellenism of a considerable section of Parliament and the press to generate a mood of moral indignation remarkably similar to that of nearly twenty years before when British troops were fighting in Athens against the communist-led forces of E.L.A.S. Three issues were especially prominent, each calculated to arouse maximum sympathy outside Greece.

First came the question of what were known as the 'political prisoners'—those 1,000 or so Greeks who had been detained ever since the Civil War, mostly on Aegaean islands. In vain did the Government protest that they were not in the usual sense of the term 'political' prisoners at all, but men who had been convicted of criminal acts or espionage during the German occupation and the Civil War. In vain, also, did they point out that most of them had originally been sentenced under Governments formed by the present leaders of the Centre Union opposition, before the long period of right-wing dominance had begun; or that some 20,000 other prisoners had been released in those far-off days and that the 1,000-odd who remained were the hard core of criminals or communist saboteurs; or that batches of them were anyway still being released from time to time, so that the numbers were steadily falling without any outside intervention. All this was obscured by two crucial weaknesses in the Government's position; the fact that right-wing extremists guilty of similar crimes were not detained, and that prisoners being released were usually required to sign a kind of loyalty oath expunging their political past. With these a campaign for the immediate release of all the remaining prisoners could, and did, make great play. Suddenly, the prisoners, about whom nobody had uttered a word for years, became daily news and were frequently depicted in London and elsewhere as Simon Pure allies of Britain from the Greek wartime resistance movement victimized by a fascist gang.

At the same time, the two other issues were introduced: a demand for nuclear disarmament in Greece and an assault on the character and motives of the Greek Royal Family, especially Queen Frederika. The first of these enlisted the support of the British Campaign for Nuclear Disarmament, then the most active expression of the British liberal conscience, and led to widely publicized international participation in a demonstration called the Marathon Peace Walk in Greece to protest against nuclear arms in general and, in particular, the American use of Greece as a base for nuclear weapons. The second roused the passions of a more motley crowd, from the left-wing League for Democracy in Greece to some of London's right-wing newspapers which had never forgiven Frederika for being German, or for saying nasty things about Britain (and therefore patriotic things about Greece) during the Cyprus crisis. Papandreou's campaign against the Palace and Athenian stories of the Queen's arrogance and impulsiveness, whether true or false, were splendid grist to this mill. Soon she was being spoken of in London as if she were an anti-British neo-Nazi who should not be allowed to sully British soil—and especially not in a formal royal visit. Labour M.P.s demanded that the visit should be cancelled. Militant nuclear disarmers threatened hostile demonstrations. The campaign reached its first climax when Frederika visited London privately in April 1963, and was assaulted in a scuffle outside Claridge's Hotel, when a well-known British participant in Greek affairs, Mrs. Betty Ambatielos, tried to force upon the Queen a petition demanding the release of her Greek communist husband, Tony, from the imprisonment he had suffered for his Civil War activities. When the British Foreign Secretary offered a formal apology for this incident in the House of Commons he was accused of toadying to fascism by Labour Members, and in the weeks of unofficial but embittered recriminations that followed between press and politicians in London and their counterparts in Athens, the fate of the Greek royal visit to Britain was placed in doubt. Whether the Greeks liked Frederika or not, she was still Queen of the Hellenes and they did not like seeing her pushed about in the streets of other people's cities and dragged through the yellow mud of other people's newspaper columns. Nor were they amused by the cosy British assumptions of moral superiority. Their national *philotimo* had been touched again, as it had been over Cyprus; and Papandreou himself was moved to protest that the attitudes displayed in London were not to be endured by Greece.

It was in this supercharged atmosphere of tension that the Lambrakis affair exploded. Here, it was assumed at once by the critics of Greece in London, was concrete proof of the 'police state' that was alleged to exist in Greece, for it was soon clear that Lambrakis had, indeed, been killed with the connivance of the local police, although it took another three years to make the charges stick in a court of law. In fact, the incident did not really prove anything of the sort, for in a true police state Lambrakis would not have been at liberty, nor would he have been eliminated in such a crude and public fashion. What it did demonstrate, however, was damaging enough—that the extremists of the right, secure within the Government's web of patronage, were taking the law into their own hands. Lambrakis had been on the Marathon Peace Walk. He had also been in London, meeting supporters of the anti-Karamanlis campaign, shortly before the attack on Queen Frederika outside her hotel. He was therefore assumed by the right-wing extremists in Salonika to have had a hand in that vexatious affair and they had exacted retribution, meeting excess with greater excess.

But the repercussions were obvious. The Salonika incident played into the hands of the Government's opponents; and whether Karamanlis was directly responsible or not he could expect no quarter either at home or abroad. Realistically, he warned the King that he could not take responsibility for the royal visit to London which now seemed bound to inspire further incidents and ill will. This was all the Palace needed to terminate an alliance that after eight years of success had suddenly become a burden. Karamanlis had, in any case, forfeited by then much of the goodwill he had once enjoyed at Court, partly because he had been advocating constitutional reforms which might, among other things, help to take the King out of politics by reducing his influence; and partly because he had recently refused a request from Queen Frederika for a substantial State dowry for her second daughter, Princess Irene. Considering the fuss that Princess Sophia's dowry had aroused he was surely right to say no to the Queen; but he earned her hostility by his action and now, in the aftermath of the Lambrakis affair, he was forced to pay the price. Seeing the opportunity to detach himself from a government that seemed to be heading rapidly for the rocks, King Paul rejected his Prime Minister's advice. The visit to London, he insisted, must proceed in the interests of Greece, if necessary with another Prime Minister. 'A postponement or a cancellation', he said, in a remarkable proclamation dissociating himself from Karamanlis, 'would serve the endeavours of those who wish to undermine the security of Greece, and it is neither right nor proper that the Greek people should submit to the pressure of a small number of people who are consciously or unconsciously serving communist aims directed against the state and who do not represent the views or sentiments of our allies and traditional friends, the British people.'[3] Karamanlis in effect had been dismissed, and one of the most remarkable periods of modern Greek history sputtered abruptly to a close.

The immediate result was anti-climax. A caretaker Government was appointed to oversee the royal visit to London and, with much of the sting of criticism drawn by the fall of Karamanlis, King Paul and Queen Frederika stirred little more on their arrival there than a few half-hearted left-wing boos. New elections were proposed for November and meticulous preparations were made under another caretaker Government to ensure that cheating and intimidation at the polls would be impossible. The Americans let it be known that a government of the Centre would be agreeable to them and the Palace, having broken with Karamanlis, was clearly expecting no other. The Centre Union, after a few weeks of power rivalry among its component factions, pulled itself together and forged into the elections with what looked like merited confidence. But there was further anti-climax in store, for the results were indecisive, after all. It was almost as if the normally acute Greek voters had failed to read the signals—as if, perhaps, after eleven consecutive years of one group's rule they could not adjust so quickly to the notion that another might now be given its turn. Papandreou and the Centre Union won, but by no more than a narrow margin, so that they could only form a minority government dependent for its parliamentary survival upon crypto-communist support. It was enough for Karamanlis, who promptly abandoned the stage to his old supporting players by departing, in thunderous mood, for Paris and a retirement which he evidently regarded as a rebuke to his countrymen for their fickleness—and which was to last a good deal longer, probably, than he ever expected. It was not enough for Papandreou, whose situation was too reminiscent of his first spell in office in 1944. After six un-

easy weeks when his Government survived on the votes of the extreme left while exploiting the time-honoured electoral device of
handing out some quick welfare payments all round, Papandreou
resigned to fight for a bigger victory. This time the Greeks had got
the message. In February 1964, they gave Papandreou and the Centre
Union a clearer majority than even Karamanlis had enjoyed and the
old liberal leader took office again amid general relief and a widespread feeling that the wind of fortune was at last set fair for Greece.

Even death seemed to bestow a kind of blessing when, soon after
the second elections, King Paul died of cancer and his son, Constantine, assumed the throne and quickly took to himself a pretty young
Danish bride. The aggravations of Princess Sophia's wedding were
forgotten. Princess Anne-Marie, the fresh young Queen, came—as
the Greeks assured each other in earnest self-congratulation—from
the impeccably democratic background of one of those splendidly
constitutional Scandinavian monarchies. There would be no trouble
with her as there had been with her German mother-in-law, now
relegated to the role of dowager. And anyway, there was good
old George Papandreou to watch over the young couple like a fond
uncle, wise in his years now and benign in his success; and when the
young King talked, in his first speech from the Throne, of the need,
and the readiness, to forgive and forget, the Greeks were eager to say
I-told-you-so. With not a little complacency they settled down to
enjoy their own hard-wrought miracle—a working system of democracy at last. Yet the fruits of their endeavours, within a shockingly
short time, were to be the familiar gall and wormwood.

Chapter 13

THINGS FALL APART

Things fall apart; the centre cannot hold
(W. B. YEATS)

Looking back over the tragic decades of this century, in the optimistic spring of 1964, few people in Athens could recall a time of such promise in the affairs of Greece. The Civil War seemed to be fading in the memory of the older generation and was already over the horizon of history for the young. The ice packs of the international Cold War seemed to be breaking up and small nations like Greece were beginning to test the warmer waters of coexistence. After more than a decade of strenuous reconstruction the country had proudly set course for membership of the Common Market and its acceptance by the world as a truly western nation. The domestic economy was booming in spite of a persistent weakness in the balance of payments; and for all the alarms of the previous two or three years Greek politics seemed to have acquired a new maturity. George Papandreou's liberal Union of the Centre had just been confirmed in power at the second attempt, with the biggest popular vote that any party had obtained in Greece for thirty years, and the conservatives had retired into apparently loyal opposition after eleven consecutive and constructive years in office. An old, experienced and well-intentioned Prime Minister was complemented by a young and inexperienced but equally well-intentioned King, with a pretty and popular princess as his bride-to-be. Greece, so nearly everyone seemed to think, was a going concern at last, and the future was full of exciting possibilities. 'Before the end of the century', one young Greek economist told me at that moment, 'I expect this country to be a paradise.'

Happy dream, rude awakening. Within six months the coffee-shops of Athens were full of rumours of *coups d'état* being planned by right and left. Within eighteen months the structure of parliamentary government had begun to collapse under the impact of a new quarrel between the Prime Minister and the King. In three years it was all over, with the military men in command again, proclaiming

—like others of their kind before them—that they had not come to murder the old democracy but to bury its already rotten corpse and start anew. Sadly, but irresistibly, Greece apparently had reverted to type in a melancholy muddle of conspiracy, corruption, jealousy and ambition that routed all the best intentions.

Many more or less plausible explanations have been advanced to account for this abrupt relapse. It has been seen as the result of a renewal of the struggle between left and right that had been shelved but not ended in the Civil War; or as part of a revival of the old constitutional schism between republicans and monarchists; or as a further instalment of the long Greek conflict between civilian and military rule; or as a response to rampaging inflation caused by the economic policies of a demagogic government; or as the outcome of foreign machinations—whether by the Soviet Union and its communist agents, or the United States and the C.I.A.; or simply as an expression of an age-long alternation in Greece between the poles of anarchy and tyranny. But none of these is adequate alone, and some upon examination prove to be distorted or misleading. Only if we take them all together, mix them with a certain scepticism, and add a large element of personal Greek pride and perversity, can we hope to see the story in its true, and complex, perspective. In the end, much of the damage was done by sheer *hubris*, as Greeks on all sides of the political struggle let their hearts rule their heads and, in a succession of conflicting rhetorical gestures, entrenched themselves in positions of mutual antagonism and equal indefensibility.

Papandreou's economic policies, for example, seemed governed less by serious calculation than by an emotional need to justify his years in opposition with some grand, immediate demonstration that things really were going to be different now that he was in power. He had inherited from Karamanlis a conservative but, by Greek standards, relatively strong economy. Within eighteen months he had turned it into a liberal but weak one. Karamanlis had enjoyed massive American aid throughout most of his administration yet he had always felt the need to restrict internal demand and to entice foreign investors with favourable terms in order to get some ballast into the economic structure. Papandreou, on the other hand, took over when American aid had already ended and chose immediately to reverse all the other economic gears as well. Increased welfare payments and higher farm subsidies were accompanied by expanded social services and tougher terms for foreign investors all in a matter of months, without a commensurate attack on other forms of government spending. The resulting inflation helped in 1965 to hasten Papandreou's downfall and to sustain the subsequent popular unrest.

But the most significant area of conflict, where both national and personal *hubris* played an incontinent and destructive role, was Cyprus—that final, festering reminder of Greece's Great Idea. Since the Zurich and London agreements of 1959 the Cyprus issue had played little direct part in Greek politics; yet by their repeated criticisms of the agreements as a surrender of national interest to the demands of NATO, both Papandreou's Centre Union and the left-wing politicians of E.D.A. had contrived to keep alive the idea that a more 'independent' foreign policy could still secure for Greece the cherished goal of *enosis*. With Papandreou's election in the autumn of 1963 that particular chicken came promptly home to roost in all its dangerous ambiguity and the repercussions of the renewed struggle for *enosis* that followed were felt throughout the whole range of Greek politics. They contributed to inflation by compelling the Government to keep the armed forces permanently on the alert against Turkey; they fed right-wing fears of communist resurgence at home; they inflamed both anti-American and anti-Russian feeling; and they led directly to the disastrous clash between Papandreou and the King over the loyalty of the Army which was the prelude to the eventual *coup d'état*.

The story began at once with Archbishop Makarios. President of the Republic of Cyprus from the start, three years earlier, he was angered by the determination of the Turkish minority in the island to use the legislative veto provided in the Zurich agreement to prevent the Greek majority passing laws the Turks did not like. In effect, the Turks had declared a kind of independence within the law that to the Greeks seemed wholly contrary to the spirit of the agreement. Scenting a favourable wind of change in Athens with Papandreou's victory, Makarios redoubled his pressure on the Turks to modify their veto power. Predictably, the Turks refused, suspecting a new Greek plot. Just before Christmas, however, both Greece and Turkey were left simultaneously with unrepresentative governments. In Athens Papandreou had resigned to seek his second, and bigger, popular mandate, leaving the country temporarily in the hands of a caretaker Government. In Ankara, a coalition Government under Ismet Inonu had just been forced out. Makarios seized this opportunity, when the two powers chiefly concerned were unable to respond decisively, to clinch his campaign for supreme authority in Cyprus. Declaring that the Turkish community's veto had made government impossible, he proposed to govern henceforth only according to the will of the majority in the island. This virtual abrogation of the Zurich agreement in the interests of the island's Greek majority brought the Turkish Cypriots to the barricades at once to fight for what they conceived to be not merely justice but their lives. British troops from the military bases in Cyprus were pressed into a hasty attempt to keep the peace, but sporadic and often fierce fighting continued. After some hundreds were killed on both sides, Britain was forced to lay the whole problem before the United Nations Security Council, with a request for a U.N. peace force. By the time Papandreou was re-elected in February 1964, Cyprus was again a cockpit of international tension, potentially more virulent and damaging than ever; and before he had passed six months in office it was clear that the dispute was once more edging Greece diplomatically and politically towards neutralism and the left.

The nationalist emotion behind this trend was already familiar from the Cyprus dispute of the 1950's, but it was heightened in 1964 because the withdrawal of Britain from her colonial position in the island had left the underlying hostility of Turks and Greeks more cruelly exposed. Every fresh battle between Turk and Greek in the island increased the demand for action in Athens—and Ankara—in defence of Greek—or Turkish—national honour. Yet no decisive action was possible. As long as the Turkish Cypriots were supported by Turkey Papandreou could neither make war successfully nor peace honourably on behalf of the Greek Cypriots. Nor could Turkey enforce a solution against the wishes of her NATO allies. Predictably, the first result of this impasse in Athens was a fresh surge of Greek resentment against the NATO powers, especially the United States and Britain, for their maddening insistence on trying to separate the combatants in Cyprus instead of unequivocally supporting Greece and the Greeks. The second result, equally predictable, was that the 'independent' foreign policy so eloquently envisaged in the past by Papandreou and his supporters, turned out in practice to involve an increasing dependence upon the diplomatic support of the communist and non-aligned nations, and a growing surrender of the Greek Government's powers of decision to the Greek Cypriot leaders in Nicosia.

The thinking behind this policy had a certain logic as a deep-laid game of diplomatic double bluff. Accepting *enosis* as the ultimate goal of both Athens and Nicosia, the Greeks could argue that it was essential to force the hands of the British and the Americans against the Turks by winning the communist and uncommitted nations to their side. But the communist and uncommitted powers would surely reject a campaign for the union of Cyprus with Greece as long as Greece was still a member of NATO. Therefore if Greece was not to leave NATO, the immediate goal to be pursued could only be that of genuine self-determination for Cyprus, free of the restrictions on sovereignty imposed by the Zurich agreements. The communists and their friends could then be persuaded to support Greece and the Greek Cypriots in the expectation that the result would be a fully independent and demilitarized island from which the British bases would be removed in deference to neutralist sentiment. In this way a majority vote for self-determination could be mustered at the United Nations, the British and the Americans would be deeply alarmed and would promptly bear down on the Turks to do a deal with the Greeks instead, whereupon *enosis* would be proclaimed, after all, amid general Greek rejoicing and Greece would remain in NATO and add Cyprus to the alliance as well.

Alas, for such Machiavellian ideas, what actually happened was rather different. The Americans were, indeed, alarmed at the thought that Cyprus might become a kind of Mediterranean Cuba and in the summer of 1964 they sent Mr. Dean Acheson, a former Secretary of State, to propose a new plan which, in essence, offered *enosis* to the Greeks in exchange for a substantial military base for the Turks in Cyprus. The Turks said yes, if the base area was large enough to make it tantamount to a partition of the island which would then be disposed of by the process known as 'double *enosis*'—the union of the Greek side with Greece and of the Turkish side with Turkey. The Greeks said no, fearing just that outcome, and the plan was still-born. Its fate was sealed by the biggest battle so far on the island when, in August, the Greek Cypriot forces launched a full-scale attack on the Turkish enclave around the port of Kokkina in the north-west corner of the island in an attempt to prevent the import of Turkish arms from the mainland and so to destroy the power of the Turks in Cyprus to resist. The Turkish Government responded by attacking the Greek Cypriots with its Air Force and, while the Americans privately warned Turkey that she could not expect their support if the Soviet Union intervened, President Makarios publicly appealed to the Russians for help and received a promise of their aid if Cyprus was invaded.

The Greek Government was placed in a quandary by these events. Unable to intervene effectively in a military sense itself, it was more

o

than ever obliged to remain politically committed to the support of the Greek Cypriots. But in the wake of the Russian gesture and the failure of Athens either to negotiate or to enforce *enosis*, that word virtually disappeared from the Cypriot vocabulary, to be replaced by the more fashionable battle-cry of 'unfettered independence' pursued with the aid of those good friends of struggling peoples, the Soviet Union, Marshal Tito, President Nasser and the rest. With this apparent transformation of Cypriot values, the Cyprus Communist Party (A.K.E.L.) grew steadily more influential, while NATO, the British and the Americans were correspondingly reviled.

At the same time the Cypriot business and professional community was encouraged to believe that it would be better off outside Greece than inside (which was probably true) and Greek leaders who dared to remind the Cypriots that *enosis* was still the sacred goal of Hellenism were publicly attacked for their temerity. On 30th September a secret Soviet-Cypriot treaty was signed for the supply of arms to the Greek Cypriot forces. Soon afterwards there were reports that regular Greek Army officers who had been sent to the island in the summer with some 10,000 men, in the hope of deterring Turkish action and furthering the cause of *enosis*, had been expelled by the Cyprus Government for criticizing the policies of President Makarios. By the end of October the situation in the island seemed so serious in Athens that Papandreou inaugurated a special '*enosis* committee' at the Foreign Ministry and began a new propaganda campaign in the island in favour of its union with Greece.

The pronounced leftward trend in Cyprus, however, was interlocked with and helped to reinforce a similar, although less pronounced, shift in Greek domestic politics. Taking advantage of the Cold War thaw and what he believed to be the fading memories of Greek battles with the communists, Papandreou had campaigned earlier in the year with a slogan saying that he wanted to make communism seem old-fashioned; and one of his first acts in office was to dismantle the old security apparatus of emergency regulations and police pressure which had kept not only communists but anyone of the faintest left-wing tendencies under close surveillance since the Civil War. The Communist Party in Greece remained outlawed, but its parliamentary *alter ego*, E.D.A., was emboldened by the new freedom and was soon organizing public rallies and expanding its youth movement, now appropriately named after the martyr of Salonika, Gregory Lambrakis. Inevitably, E.D.A. adopted Makarios as a folk hero, whose defiance of the Turks and the NATO imperialists revealed the soundness of his true, Greek heart. Inevitably, also, a number of radical deputies in Papandreou's own party began to take more seriously than before the idea of 'true independence', casting a more encouraging eye upon the efforts of their E.D.A. colleagues to steer the country out of NATO, and threatening the old man's parliamentary majority by indiscipline and calculated pressure.

Before the end of 1964 many people in Athens were already convinced that the whole framework of Greek policy since the war was in grave danger. A new permissiveness in the country's foreign relations that might in other circumstances have been welcomed was seen in the light of the Cyprus crisis as an alarming aberration. Trade with the Soviet Union was growing steadily, diplomatic relations with Bulgaria had been restored after a quarter of a century of frozen silence, Papandreou was preparing to make the first visit by a Greek Prime Minister to Marshal Tito and there was even talk of opening negotiations with the Stalinist bosses of Albania. The deputy speaker of the Greek Parliament had visited East Germany with a left-wing colleague and, to the consternation of half their fellows at home, he had announced with neither qualification nor authority that they were a friendly, official delegation from Greece. In domestic affairs the picture was in some ways more disturbing. E.D.A. had doubled the number of its provincial organizations within six months and had just won a third of the votes in municipal elections—more than the left had ever secured before. The Centre Union had been compelled to disown its own student organization because it had been taken over by the communists, and the Lambrakis Youth movement, led by the appealing and popular composer, Mikis Theodorakis, who was also an E.D.A. deputy, was claiming tens of thousands of new members. Mr. Tony Ambatielos, whose wife's activities in London had helped to bring down Karamanlis, had been released from the island where he had languished since the Civil War and was already back in office as a leader of the Greek seamen's union, whose activities—according to the Athens correspondent of *The Times*—were 'already causing some concern among Piraeus shippers'.[1] E.D.A. literature about the Civil War was reported to have found its way into the schools and the deputy mayor of Piraeus had refused to meet the commander of the American Sixth Fleet on a courtesy call, declaring that Greece should get out of NATO.

All this was alarming enough for the impassioned diehards of the Greek right wing, but three other, almost simultaneous events of the autumn of 1964 sent an extra tremor of fear and suspicion through a far wider body of Greek opinion, including many members of Papandreou's own party. One was the dramatic eruption of a new royal controversy, which brought the young King Constantine hurrying back to Athens from his honeymoon in Corfu. The occasion was a public attack on Queen Frederika, the King's widowed mother, by Prince Peter, a cousin of the late King Paul who was at that moment—before King Constantine and his new Queen had any children—second in line of succession to the Greek throne. Prince Peter, it appeared, had a grudge against the Palace; and the Athens press, ever alive to the scandalous possibilities of royal revelations, had eagerly lent him a platform. His complaint was that Queen Frederika had deliberately influenced the rest of the Court against him and had conspired to deprive him of his constitutional rights ever since her marriage to Paul. The reason, he believed, was that he had taken a morganatic Russian wife against her wishes. 'I have been having diffi-culties with Queen Frederika for seventeen years,' he told a press con-ference in the King George Hotel in Athens. 'I thought that conditions would have changed with the new reign. But they did not. Queen Frederika's influence is still strong in this case.'[2]

This was welcome grist to the industrious mills of Athenian gossip, in which the real or alleged sins of Queen Frederika were any-way ground small and often. A campaign against the Palace in general and the Queen Mother in particular, which had been rum-bling ever since Papandreou's election, half-smothered by a natural public sympathy for the new King and his bride, suddenly found full voice. In spite of a disapproving statement by Papandreou, the Prince was hailed by otherwise anti-monarchist newspapers as a true friend of liberalism and democracy and King Constantine was de-picted as a puppet of his neo-fascist mother. 'Greece', Prince Peter had said, with high self-righteousness, 'needs a good King and a good Queen very badly,' but his remarks helped cruelly to ensure that the only way King Constantine could be 'good' in the eyes of half Greece was by disowning his newly-widowed mother. For his filial refusal to do so there was to be no forgiveness; and although Queen Frederika announced her formal retirement from public life soon after Constantine and his new Queen returned from their honey-moon, the campaign against her alleged influence upon her son continued unabated and prepared the ground for the attacks upon Constantine and the monarchy which were to erupt with fresh violence the following year.

The second of the three autumnal events to reveal the envious fears that bubbled just below the surface of Greek politics at this time was the emergence of the Prime Minister's son, Andreas Papandreou, as a major figure of political controversy on the left of the Greek political spectrum. In a way there was some irony in this, for Andreas had spent most of his adult life in America where he had established some reputation as an academic economist; and he had returned to Greece in 1959 with American approval to take charge of a new centre of economic research, partly financed by the Ford Foundation and set up by his father's conservative rival, Karamanlis. Now Andreas suddenly appeared as an anti-American bogeyman who might lead his father's party into the paths of neutralism and the left.

In the second and decisive campaign of the Centre Union he had abandoned the field of economic research for that of political practice and had been triumphantly returned to Parliament as the deputy for his father's old constituency in Patras—a seat which the elder Papandreou had magnanimously surrendered to him to ensure that the magic of the family name would help him to the utmost. As a reward for his success and in deference to his experience, Andreas was promptly appointed to an economic ministry in his father's Government with the title of Deputy Minister of Co-ordination. This instantaneous success of the prodigal son earned him the title of 'the parachutist of politics' and awakened a dangerous jealousy in older and more experienced politicians of the Centre Union which neither he nor his father seemed sufficiently aware of. Andreas, indeed, deepened the jealousy by poaching in the administrative preserves of other Ministers as if he was still an independent adviser of the Government rather than a responsible member of it, so that a mere six months after his election Athens was buzzing with rumours of cabinet quarrels over the Prime Minister's all-too-paternal devotion to the interests of his son. When Andreas usurped the field of foreign affairs in an interview published in *Le Monde* in October 1964, his indiscretions added fuel to the fire set alight by Prince Peter. Greece was a satellite of NATO, he declared, and it was high time she recovered her 'full sovereignty'. In future she should not take orders from anybody; and any attempt to impose a NATO solution in Cyprus would gravely prejudice western prestige and democracy in Greece. The Soviet Union's support for the Greek Cypriot cause, on the other hand, was 'a positive contribution to the maintenance of world peace'.[3] In themselves these views were not particularly startling. Similar sentiments had been expressed many times in the previous thirteen years by the more radical members of the Greek Centre, as well as by left-wing deputies in E.D.A. But at that moment they appeared to be a deliberate attempt to capture for Andreas's own benefit the new leftward tide, and they were greeted like red rags by many a Greek bull. Possibly this was more than Andreas intended. My own impression in talking to him not long afterwards was that he was surprised by the intensity of the Greek reaction—but if that were so it only served to convince his rapidly growing band of enemies that he was unfit for office in any government, let alone that of an indulgent father. The questions stormed passionately about him. Did he mean that Greece should leave NATO? What was his authority for speaking on foreign affairs? Did his father share his views? Soon, the elder Papandreou was forced to silence him; and a month later Andreas resigned his office with an additional threat of personal scandal hanging over him. The scandal was never proved and his allies attributed it later, albeit predictably and without much conviction, to the machinations of the C.I.A. But Andreas Papandreou was thereafter established in the eyes of both his friends and his enemies as the bell-wether of the new trends in Greece; and his increasingly reckless exploitation of that role, regardless of the anxieties and jealousies he aroused, had much to do with the eventual downfall of his father's administration and the lamentable end of parliamentary government in Greece.

The third of these autumnal events that were setting the tone of things to come was the celebration on the hill of the Acropolis of the twentieth anniversary of the liberation of Greece from German occupation. It was also the most ironic of the three, for what began as a deliberate and laudable attempt to wipe out the memories of past divisions in Greek society ended by reaffirming that those divisions were still there, after all. Previously, the country had never dared to celebrate its wartime liberation for fear of the other inflammatory memories that the occasion would evoke—of the communist uprising, the White Terror, and the subsequent Civil War. But to George Papandreou, back in office as Prime Minister for the first time since he led his ill-fated exiled Government back to Athens in 1944, that overwrought interregnum of twenty years was all the more reason for a celebration now. Partly out of his agreeable ambition to make communism seem old-fashioned, partly, no doubt, out of an old man's vanity, he conceived of the celebration, with himself at its head, as a symbol of Greek reconciliation and recovery from the desperate schisms of the past. Accordingly, one sunny morning towards the end of October 1964, he led a strange body of men up the steep paths of the Acropolis to salute the Greek flag on its summit, where in that grim Christmas of 1944, the communist forces of E.L.A.S. had dominated Athens and forced his eventual resignation.

Tall, but stooped with age and visibly weakened by the climb, Papandreou nevertheless cut a noble figure. Behind him shuffled an assortment of portly generals of the Army in dark glasses and foxy little admirals in naval frock-coats. Behind them again came a straggling line of the halt, the lame and the blind of war limping, hobbling and tapping their way towards the Parthenon. At the side of the path stood rows of schoolgirls in neat blue uniforms, chanting rhythmically as the Prime Minister passed, 'Pap-an-*dre*-ou! Pap-an-*dre*-ou!' The old man managed a wan smile and a feeble wave to each new group before pressing on, grey-faced and panting, to the summit. But half-way up there came a rude interruption of this strained, triumphal progress. At a turn in the path the Prime Minister was confronted by a crowd of shirt-sleeved youths and men, throwing tiny blue-and-white leaflets in the air that fell like confetti upon the official parade while they chanted as rhythmically as the schoolgirls, but with a different song. 'An-ag-*nor*isis! An-ag-*nor*isis!' ('Recognition! Recognition!') they bellowed as Papandreou passed; and for them there was neither smile nor wave, but only an angry flush on the old man's grey cheeks, dark and hostile glances from the military men and sullen mutterings from the wounded train.

What this crowd was demanding was official 'recognition' of the E.L.A.S. resistance movement against the Germans; but what they evoked were their battles against other Greek resistance groups and their subsequent exploits in the Civil War that brought Greece to its knees and closed the door to compromise for a generation. To Papandreou, who was the first to suffer from their treachery twenty years before, and who had hoped to exorcise that memory now, it must have been a bitter blow. There were tears in his eyes a few minutes later, when he raised the flag himself on the summit of the Acropolis and cried, 'Long Live Greece!' It may have been just the exhaustion of the climb that put them there, but I do not think so. As I watched him it seemed to me they were the tears of an old man who knew that for all his good intentions he had failed once more to heal the old Greek schisms. Indeed, that celebration on the Acropolis helped to reopen them, for in the Greek context its implications were painfully plain. It was the first time for many years that the communists had dared to agitate so openly in Athens. Even at the funeral of

Lambrakis eighteen months before, they had only appeared under the legitimate colours of E.D.A., their parliamentary stalking horse. But there was no E.D.A. cover on the Acropolis. This was frankly a communist affair; and to demand recognition for the communist resistance movement was, as Greeks of every persuasion knew, only the first step to demanding recognition of the Communist Party itself. To those who had not lived through the Civil War themselves—like the new generation—that prospect might not seem so terrible. But to the Greeks who had undergone that experience, it was like asking that they should forgive the men who had raped their sisters. It was an affront to their *philotimo*; and to see it expressed thus publicly was a new and potent source of anger, suspicion and fear.

With such inflammable material to work on, the imagination of the feverish Greek press—and some of its equally feverish readers— was taxed to its considerable limits. Plots were scented in every foreign chancery, as the Greeks revived again their traditional belief that their destiny was the fruit of other peoples' conspiracies. The Americans, it was said, were working with the Russians to defeat the British. The British were trying to oust the Americans. The Prime Minister was selling out to the communists. His son was attempting to take over the Government. Prince Peter's morganatic Russian wife was an agent of Moscow. Both an attempted communist *putsch*, and a putative right-wing military *coup* were 'reliably' reported in newspapers of opposing political complexion.

To the innocent and impressionable visitor, indeed, Athens might have seemed, less than a year after Papandreou's first election, a city already poised for revolution. One British journalist who discovered a mob of youngsters shouting outside a ministry building one day just then was so excited by his own revolutionary interpretation of the incident that he refused to accept at first what turned out to be the unglamorous truth—that they were only students demonstrating, in their time-honoured way, against the low grades they had been awarded in their examinations. Gradually, however, some of the uproar subsided. Andreas Papandreou became inaccessible to the press. Greece did not get out of NATO. Prince Peter reluctantly withdrew most of his remarks about Frederika and the monarchy. The communist resistance movement was not recognized. The deputy speaker of Parliament was reprimanded for his presumption in East Germany and the deputy mayor of Piraeus was dismissed for his discourtesy to the Commander of the American Sixth Fleet. By the beginning of 1965 Greece seemed to be returning to an even keel, pursuing a more or less balanced course towards a liberal, democratic future. But the appearance was superficial. The events of the autumn had revealed an underlying infirmity of purpose and uncertainty of direction that promised ill for the next crisis: and that was not long in coming.

Chapter 14

WAITING FOR THE BARBARIANS

. . . the barbarians will arrive today;
and they are bored by eloquence and public speaking.
(C. P. CAVAFY)

The final breakdown of Greek parliamentary democracy began, like so many other crises before it, with the perennial agony of national ambition and frustration over Cyprus. Typically, it was heralded by what seemed to many Greeks another betrayal by a Great Power—the revelation, in January 1965, that the Soviet Union had apparently swopped horses in midstream and was now supporting Turkey against Greece by publicly endorsing a proposal from Ankara for a federal, independent republic of Cyprus as a solution to the problem. In fact, of course, the Russians were being reasonably consistent. They had simply called Papandreou's bluff by taking his campaign for Cypriot 'self-determination' at its face value. But the essential confusion of Greek policy was exposed at once: while talking about 'self-determination' Papandreou and his friends had really had *enosis* as their objective. The Turkish plan clearly excluded that and Soviet support for it revealed Moscow as no less perfidious than London or Washington in its approach to Greek affairs. Thus Papandreou's policy, which had already divided Greece by its encouragement to the left was now revealed to patriotic Greeks as worthless, anyway; and the conservatives in Greece rejoiced righteously at the Government's discomfiture, while E.D.A.'s crypto-communists beat a tortuous retreat from their pro-Soviet attitudes under the smoke-screen of new charges against the previous Karamanlis regime of corruption and maladministration.

Folly now was piled on folly from all sides. The conservatives, half alarmed and half elated, saw the hand of communism everywhere and right-wing newspapers made great play with confidential intelligence reports of left-wing plots inside the Army. The Centre Union, on the other hand, tried to regain the initiative by supporting E.D.A.'s parliamentary demand for a formal investigation of the allegations against Karamanlis. Each new revelation and riposte gave another twist to the spiral of rising tempers; and when the Prime Minister answered criticism of his inflationary economic policies by re-appointing his son, Andreas, to the ministry he had been forced to leave only a few months earlier, the opposition's rage was boundless. By this time Andreas was their *bête noire*, for it was his economic policies that were believed to have caused the inflation in the first place and his characteristic left-wing views on Cyprus that were thought to have led to the latest Greek humiliation there. To bring him back into government in spite of this seemed a deliberate insult and was certainly inviting trouble. His enemies soon found the ideal means of making it by revealing his alleged implication in a left-wing conspiracy among Greek Army officers in Cyprus.

The first secret reports of this plot had been delivered to the Government in January by General Grivas, the former leader of the Cypriot liberation movement who had been sent back to the island by Papandreou the previous year to try to check the excesses of the Cypriot armed forces and the apparently neutralist manœuvres of President Makarios. Grivas was still both a dedicated opponent of anything that smelled of liberalism and a fierce exponent of *enosis* and it may be assumed that his reports erred on the side of what he took to be righteousness in identifying left-wing subversion among Greek officers who might be less fanatical than he in such matters. No doubt the Government would have liked to take a sceptical view, and certainly it tried to keep his reports quiet. But soon, as is the way with most secrets in Greece, they were whispered aloud in Athens; and when right-wing newspapers named Andreas Papandreou as one of the leading conspirators the Government was compelled to announce an official inquiry. It was a splendid tit-for-tat for the proposed Karamanlis investigation commission; and the conservatives were determined to draw blood. Thus began the so-called Aspida affair, whose repercussions were to culminate in the overthrow yet again of what passed for democratic government in Greece.

In themselves the activities of the small group of Army officers in Cyprus who called themselves Aspida (The Shield) seemed hardly to justify such dire consequences. Except to the extremists of the Greek right wing, who were accustomed to describing as communism any-thing of which they disapproved, there was no evidence that the officers had any link with the communists. If anything, as their chosen title seemed to indicate, they were passionate Greek national-ists, inclined to neutralism in foreign affairs and republicanism and woolly socialism at home, rather after the pattern of Gamal Abdul Nasser in Egypt and other leaders among the uncommitted nations of the Third World. After eighteen months of investigation only twenty-eight officers were charged in all, with four colonels the most senior among them, and only fifteen eventually were found guilty and sentenced to imprisonment for conspiracy to commit high treason by preparing to overthrow the regime. The extent of Andreas Papandreou's involvement with them was never established, and he was ultimately freed and exiled without trial by the military regime after the *coup d'état* of 1967. Yet if it had not been for the existence of Aspida that *coup d'état* might never have taken place, and Greece might just have contrived, albeit with many an anxious wobble, to keep to her democratic course. For the true significance of Aspida lay less in its actual threat to the established regime than in the almost theatrical fashion in which it focused all the fears and jealousies, conflicts and ambitions of contemporary Greece, upon a single, fundamentally divisive issue, that irresistibly recalled old schisms and remorselessly precipitated new ones. Even more than the Lambrakis affair, which in these ways it resembled, it became the catalyst of action.

The issue was, simply but explosively, the loyalty of the Army and its relations with the King. At this point it is necessary to recapitulate a little of the agonized history of the Army's role in Greek politics, in order to understand the full implications of the affair. Like Greece itself, the Army's past contained conflicting sets of traditions, for it had been at different times both republican and royalist, and both the arbiter of politics and the victim of politicians. Under officers like Plastiras and Pangalos in the 1920's it had established republican dictatorships. Through the activities of the Military League in 1909 it had secured *enosis* for Crete and brought Venizelos to the leadership of Greece. Under Metaxas it had co-operated in establishing a royalist dictatorship; and in its campaigns against Slavs and Turks up to 1922, and against Italy, Germany and the communists in the 1940's it had earned itself a reputation as the Saviour of the Nation. It had purged and been purged itself in turn, now cleansing the political stables of the mess left by the politicians, now being converted by politicians to their own ends. It was, in short, a thoroughly politicized army; and in 1965, after nearly thirty years of largely right-wing rule in Greece, the majority of its senior officers were royalists and right-wing themselves in outlook, dedicated like General Metaxas—to whom some owed their original preferment and from whom they were spiritually descended—to the preservation of the King, the Church, the Family and the glory of Greece.

To Papandreou, however, and still more to his radical son, Andreas, this kind of army was a serious obstacle to necessary reform in Greece. It was too eager to scent communism in the most modest liberal measures and too willing to accept the political restrictions of Greece's NATO membership instead of supporting the legitimate government in its endeavour to construct an independent foreign policy and restore Cyprus to the Greek nation. The Papandreous therefore set themselves to reconstruct the officer corps as their prerequisite for reconstructing Greece by purging its right-wing senior officers and advancing younger, more radically-minded men of Centre Union sympathies to posts of high command. This was a clear reversal of the trends of the previous thirty years and the most direct challenge they could offer, short of popular rebellion, to the assumptions on which Greek policies had been founded since the war. Coming on top of the effects of Papandreou's inflation, the campaign against the Palace, the anti-NATO agitation, the leftward drift in Cyprus and the resurgence of the left at home, it was the last, unacceptable straw not only for right-wing conservatives in the opposition but for the moderates in Papandreou's own party. Thus, when news of the existence of Aspida came from Cyprus it seemed to justify every dark foreboding of national disaster and personal insecurity that had already been aroused, for here in the midst of this new and menacing climate of affairs was a suggestion that the Prime Minister's own son—who had already in the eyes of many been advanced beyond his merits—was actually conspiring to overthrow the regime and become, it seemed, a kind of Greek Nasser. Powerful personal jealousies were reinforced by stout self-righteousness. The monarchy was seen to be in danger, the constitution to be at stake, the free world itself in peril. When the crunch came, in July 1965, two months after the Aspida investigation was to have begun, the Papandreous, father and son, found they had given too many hostages to fortune and alarmed too many otherwise sympathetic men.

Papandreou's Minister of Defence, a conservative who had been appointed originally to reassure the Army and the King that the Centre Union would not tamper with the security of the nation, refused to accept a new list of Army transfers and retirements prepared by the Prime Minister. Papandreou announced his dismissal and informed the King that he would take over the Ministry of Defence himself. The King demurred, saying that he would accept anyone else Papandreou cared to name, but in view of the allegations about Aspida and the Prime Minister's son that were currently under investigation he could not accept Papandreou himself. The Prime Minister retorted that the King had exceeded his constitutional rights and verbally offered his resignation. The King seized the chance to be rid of the old man by accepting it even before it was put into writing, and forthwith began negotiations with other political leaders to form another government. On the next day, 16th July, the mob was in the streets of Athens shouting for Papandreou, and the remorseless disintegration of Greece's fragile parliamentary democracy had begun all over again.

Two views remain as to whether a conspiracy was proved in the Aspida affair. To a Greek, as we have seen so often, a conspiracy can be any policy which he disapproves; and by the same token a policy is apt to be a conspiracy that he happens to like. The judgement either way is expedient and—as the Athens correspondent of *The Economist* pointed out at the time, with two neat quotations—the facts in the Aspida case could bear either interpretation. 'As a leading member of the conservative right wing put it,' he wrote, ' "Would the King's critics have had him keep the Papandreous in power so that he could react against the plot from an exile's home in Lisbon?" Or, as Mr. George Papandreou put it: "Where is the plot? Would 28 officers out of 10,000 have overthrown the regime?" '[1]

It is undeniable, however, that there was an attempt to reshape the Army in the Papandreou image and that, for what they were worth, the Aspida group and its putative links with Andreas were natural, perhaps even inevitable, outgrowths of that attempt. The Papandreou faction argued that what they wanted was simply to get the Army out of politics by eliminating its right-wing bias. Their opponents retorted that what they really intended was to get the Army into politics by making it their creature. Both were half right. The facts were that the Army was already up to its neck in politics and had been for at least half a century, but to try to extricate it by a series of political purges could only re-emphasize its political role. In the event, as one side pushed and the other side pulled, their differences were magnified and their schisms deepened until at the end there was an unbridgeable gulf between them of fear, envy and suspicion.

On both sides, heated memory stoked fresh passion. The Aspida affair and the attempt to infiltrate the Army with Papandreou supporters recalled to the conservatives the left-wing conspiracies in the Army of 1936, when the communists held the balance of power in the Greek Parliament; and they easily jumped from there to the conclusion that now, as then, the liberals who claimed to be pursuing reform were either self-deluded Kerenskys paving the way for the communists, or were actually in secret league with the communists for their own advantage. On the liberal side, the obvious links between the right-wing Army and the Palace recalled the long history of the constitutional feud, going back to Venizelos and Constantine in the First World War, so that the merits of the current argument were overlain and distorted by old parrot cries about republicans and monarchists.

When the final split came between Papandreou and the King, such memories began to dominate the whole, confused scene. Superficially history seemed to be repeating itself and extremists on both sides deliberately fostered that impression. The communists, who demonstrated openly and repeatedly in Athens and elsewhere in support of Papandreou and against the King, kept the constitutional issue of the monarchy boiling. The right wing, on the other hand, responded with persistent allegations that Papandreou's supporters, led by Andreas, had created a *de facto* common front with the communists. As the demonstrations spread and violence visited the centre of Athens almost nightly, a tragically familiar polarization took place across the political spectrum. Racked by its own schisms, jealousies and uncertainties, the Centre Union fell apart. Papandreou's famous rhetoric seemed to rally much of the country behind him, echoing his latest lapidary phrase: 'The King Should Reign, Not Rule'. But his party would no longer follow him. Tempted by offers of ministries in a new, more conservative government, nervous of the intentions and miscalculations of Papandreou and enraged by the swift advancement of his son, many senior members defected and others were only held back by threats of physical injury from the mob. The overwhelming majority that Papandreou had won only eighteen months before melted in the heat of passion; and after a couple of false starts King Constantine was able to form a new administration under the leadership of Stephanos Stephanopoulos, Papandreou's own deputy Prime Minister. Here, too, there was a characteristic echo of past feuds, for Stephanopoulos had led the exodus from the old Greek Rally to join Papandreou on the opposition benches, ten years earlier, when he had been passed over by King Paul in favour of Karamanlis for the leadership of a new Government. Now King Paul's son was reversing the process: to Stephanopoulos it was a belated, if not honourable, amendment to the family history. It was still a near thing, however. With the other defectors from the Centre Union and the support of the former conservative opposition, Stephanopoulos had a majority of only two in Parliament and, although he contrived to survive on this for nearly eighteen months, the cost in the end was insupportable. Nepotism and corruption increased steadily on the Government benches as Stephanopoulos, the King and the Palace advisers fought with every means of patronage and bribery to maintain control. Cynicism and frustration deepened on the other side; and the younger Papandreou, emerging more clearly and determinedly than ever as the prospective heir to his father's political mantle, moved closer to the socialists and neutralists of E.D.A. both in and out of Parliament and delivered increasingly strident denunciations of NATO, the King, and the United States at every opportunity. Parliament degenerated into a babble of mutual insults, punctuated by fist-fights. 'No Greek Parliament ever sank so low,' said one of its senior members later. 'It was a cross between a coffee-shop and a whore-house.'[2] The Civil Service creaked almost to a halt; and as the Government strove to reverse Papandreou's inflationary policies wage strikes became more frequent and in character more political. Once again memory added another twist to the ascending spiral of passion and disorder; for as Parliament declined in dignity and authority, and as the streets rose correspondingly in influence, both conservative and liberal minds were cast back irresistibly to 1936 and the rise of Metaxas—the one half in hope and expectation, the other in outrage and fear. Steadily the prospect of another military *coup d'état* grew more menacing as the politicians rushed, lemming-like, towards collective suicide.

Yet, on a strictly objective assessment, the *coup d'état* still need not have taken place, for when all the political and economic factors have been considered the simple truth remains about these disastrous years in Greece that the principal contestants were separated—at least in the beginning—by only narrow differences of actual policy. What obsessed them and drove them ever farther apart was the subjective clash of pride with insolent pride. Time after time opportunities for tactical withdrawal or sensible compromise were rejected or ignored by one party or another in favour of some gesture, speech or action which deepened the abyss of contention. To select any single starting point for the process must be to some extent arbitrary and unfair. All parties at pretty well all times were guilty, for the relevant emotions of self-assertion were apparently basic to the Greek political ethos. But the moment when the process began to accelerate can, I think, be identified fairly clearly as the start of the elder Papandreou's 'unrelenting struggle' against the crushing results of the 1961 elections. From studying his demeanour and his words in the course of the struggle, there is no doubt in my mind that for all his qualities the old man's vanity then outweighed his judgement. His crusade for 'justice' and 'impartiality' amounted in reality to an appeal for partiality in his favour instead of in favour of his opponents; and his identification of a 'good' King who would help him and a 'bad' King who would not, did more than anything else to reopen in a new way the old schism over the monarchy and to ensure (even against his own wishes) that when the young Constantine succeeded his father, Paul, he would not long enjoy relief from criticism.

Papandreou's initial misjudgement about the monarchy was compounded by similar errors of pride and vanity in other fields. He was, I think, influenced more than most politicians—if that is credible—by the indubitably mellifluous sound of his own voice and the answering echoes it awakened in a people to whom politics was, in many ways, a highly-spiced form of theatrical entertainment. Their cheers encouraged him to promise them too much in the way of material benefits and to guide them too little in the cruel realities of the Greek situation. His attitude to his son, although not uncritical, was disastrously indulgent in political terms, inflaming jealousies that were eventually a major contribution to his own overthrow. His final quarrel with King Constantine over the Army showed a hideous supremacy of pride over practicality. His experience should have told him that the Army issue would be the last straw for the right; and that if he wanted to tackle it at all he would have to offer some tangible reassurances about national security that would at least make right-wing protests more difficult. Instead, he seemed determined to do everything to offend by simultaneously releasing communist prisoners, scrapping the emergency laws, tolerating increasingly left-wing demonstrations, pursuing an apparently dangerous policy in Cyprus and flatly refusing the choice offered him by the King of naming some other member of his government to the crucial Ministry of Defence. His subsequent behaviour smacked of both arrogance and self-delusion. The violence of his attacks upon those who had deserted his party made any reconciliation with them impossible; his apparently complacent acceptance of extreme left-wing support, especially in the streets, played directly into the hands of the extreme right; while at the same time he appeared to believe that if

P

he could only humiliate the King everything thereafter would be lovely. Above all, perhaps, he thrived on the *aghonia*—the struggle—of politics. The sense of argument and opposition was what inspired him and defined his aims, and the biggest reproach to his eighteen months in office was that he ran his Government as if he was still in opposition, always challenging rather than persuading, emphasizing differences rather than similarities. The result was a permanent state of uncertainty and upheaval at the very centre of Greek affairs.

These weaknesses in the elder Papandreou were compounded by similar flaws in the character of his son. Like his father, Andreas was intelligent but unwise. In many ways he was like those returned exiles who are to be found in nearly every Greek village, proud of their Greek-ness, yet often contemptuous of other Greeks. His long exile in America and his American wife and children stamped him as different from, and even in a way more hopeful than, most other Greek politicians. His reputation as an academic economist with a preference for planning, his fashionably liberal turn of mind, going back to Trotskyist flirtations in his youth, combined with the power of his Papandreou ancestry to make him a natural leader for the young, largely disestablished men of the managerial and professional class who had grown up after the war on American money and American opportunity and had come to resent American domination. To them, he was more than just one of themselves—he was a 'new' man who had both the intellectual grasp and the political connexions with which to shape the 'new' Greece; and through him they sought to capture his father's party and Government and turn it into an instrument of radical reform. In this ambition there is no doubt that Andreas and his young colleagues struck a genuine chord in many ordinary Greek hearts. His vision of social justice and 'true' sovereignty, albeit vague and ambiguous, was one that appealed to the intensely egalitarian and parochial sides of the Greek nature. Yet he was never able to translate his support into anything resembling a political party of his own, nor was he able to put his supposedly modern ideas into modern action. As much as any of the 'old' men of Greek politics he was trapped in the traditional patterns of patronage and nepotism, not only because he was himself raised to office by the patronage of his father, but because he, in turn, appeared to play his own favourites with such lack of discretion that he gravely hampered the workings of his own ministry and—most fatally—aroused unquenchable jealousy among his less fortunate colleagues. As time went on, indeed, his inherent Greek-ness seemed increasingly to overcome the veneer of the 'new', detached, scientific man that he had acquired from his academic exile. In the last few months of democratic decay he, too, appeared possessed by the passions that seem always to sway Greek politics. Rhetorical, intemperate, and recklessly partisan, he contributed as much as anyone—yet perhaps with less excuse than most—to the conditions that encouraged the eventual *coup d'état*.

On the other side, however, equal strictures seem to me justified. Quite apart from the general idiocy of the extreme right wing, few, if any, of the conservative leaders in Greece emerged unstained in the years after the defeat of Karamanlis. Even Karamanlis himself, who had behaved with some dignity and restraint for most of his eight years in office, spoiled his record by appearing to take his last failure as a personal insult from the Greek people and abandoning his defeated party in a huff in favour of Parisian exile. His successor as leader of the parliamentary right wing was Panayiotis Kanellopoulos, a man widely esteemed as a modest, scholarly and thoroughly constitutional figure; but in the end he, too, seemed to let his feelings get the better of him. Rather like Sir Anthony Eden in Britain when at long last he succeeded Churchill as conservative leader and Prime Minister, Kanellopoulos was, perhaps, too anxious to prove himself as good as his master. He desperately wanted to assert his independence of Karamanlis and secure the premiership by his own endeavours; and some of his actions in the last six months before the final *coup d'état* suggested that his desperation had taken his judgement prisoner.

Perhaps the biggest culprits on the conservative side, however, were King Constantine, his mother and his palace advisers. Either out of bad advice or else sheer impulsiveness, the King threw away his best card almost at the start of the game and never fully recovered the loss. By anticipating George Papandreou's resignation in the quarrel over the Army he automatically made the Prime Minister a martyr, especially among those who disliked the monarchy anyway, and so made it impossible for those ministers who were increasingly at loggerheads with him to seize control of the Centre Union from inside. Had he left it to the party to deal with the Papandreous, it might have been done more efficiently, for by the middle of 1965 the effects of inflation were beginning to be felt unpleasantly in Greece and the jealousies surrounding Andreas were accumulating rapidly. But when most of the chief rivals of these two defected to form a new Government under the patronage of the King, Andreas and his father were left virtually unchallenged as the new heroes of a popular, republican and vaguely socialist union of the left, and the possibility of a genuine government of the centre became remote. Some writers have suggested that Papandreou actually engineered the confrontation over the Army with just this end in view, knowing that the economic situation was bound to find him out very soon.[3] It is possible but, I think, unlikely. The crisis was far more consistent with that ordinary, comical-tragical state of Greek affairs in which all parties were in the grip of raging *hubris*, unable to comprehend that a compromise in time is the only thing that ever keeps any democracy working.

Having created the crisis by their mutual follies it was always likely that the politicians would find its resolution removed from them by the reappearance of the military men. It was a time-worn, if not time-honoured, answer to Greek problems; and as the strikes increased, as the popular front of the streets seemed to grow more menacing, and the links between Andreas and the Aspida group were mulled over in the coffee-shops and the officers' messes, the possibility grew into probability that the confusion would soon be ended by a right-wing *coup* on the pre-emptive lines established by Metaxas thirty years before. The only question left was, who would do it? Most people in Athens pointed to the Generals around the King. Others, especially in the camp of Andreas Papandreou and the left, whispered that the C.I.A. was already plotting in its own sinister fashion. Few gave a thought, however, to the notion that the denouement might come, like most truly successful *coups d'état*, from a less elevated quarter.[4] But that was to be the answer.

The last, elaborate political manœuvres need not detain us long, for they were quickly revealed as futile. When the King's substitute Government at last ran out of steam, in December 1966, elections apparently became inevitable and a caretaker administration was appointed, in the usual way, to oversee them. There was then a belated and unsuccessful attempt at compromise by Kanellopoulos and Papandreou, both of them evidently frightened by the rising power of the left but neither of them able to swallow their pride sufficiently to join in subduing it. There were still more inflammatory interventions by Andreas, and correspondingly hysterical outcries from the right; and soon there was alleged to be a 'secret' military contingency plan for containing left-wing subversion that was later to be known variously as 'the Generals' plot' or 'the King's *coup*'—and which might or might not have had American support and might or might not have gone into operation if Papandreou had eventually won a big electoral victory and threatened to humiliate the King. Finally, there was a collapse even of the caretaker administration, and at the beginning of April Kanellopoulos took over—Prime Minister at last in his own right and prepared, in the King's name, to hold elections in May and restore Greece, if he could, to some kind of parliamentary sanity. It was too late. All these familiar political shifts and intrigues were rendered irrelevant in the end by men whom scarcely any of the quarrelling politicians had ever heard of.

Taking their cue from the soldiers who had once wrung a constitution out of King Otto, from the young officers of the Military League who had ended the political humiliations of 1909, and from the numerous other military men of middle rank who had intervened in Greek politics after the Smyrna disaster, a small group of unknown colonels appeared and swept aside the whole, frenetic Athenian establishment—generals, politicians, gossiping journalists and all. In yet another echo of history they chose a night just before Papandreou was due to go to Salonika and address a huge mass meeting there. Rumour variously suggested that he would ride into town on a white donkey, like Christ entering Jerusalem; or, if that proved too much for his elderly frame, in a large white car as a kind of modern symbol of the same event. But the colonels were not thinking of Jerusalem. It was the Salonika of thirty years before they had in mind, when the demonstrations there precipitated the Metaxas *coup* against the possibility of a communist take-over. Proclaiming that the same possibility had been resurrected, they donned—with the final and most overweening attack of *hubris* of them all—the Army's old mantle as the saviour of the nation and sent the tanks into Athens in the early hours of 21st April 1967. In three short years of foolish pride and rhetoric Greece had cast away the best chance she had ever had of a democratic advance into the modern world. Not for the first time in Greek affairs, there had been altogether too much eloquence of the wrong kind, and the barbarians could abide no more.

PART III

LEGACIES IN OUR TIME

Chapter 15

COLONELS AND CRITICS

Men of intemperate minds cannot be free.
Their passions forge their fetters.
(EDMUND BURKE)

It is not necessary to carry a torch for the colonels who seized power in Greece in 1967 to suggest that they evoked from the start in much of the western world a sense of shock and hostility beyond their obvious deserts. Their *coup* was bloodless, after all, and scarcely unexpected. Their authoritarian style was more typical than the preceding parliamentary system had been of the prevailing trend in other countries with similar historical, economic and social weaknesses; and in purely Greek terms it could be seen as a comprehensible and characteristic, albeit depressing, response to a genuine national crisis. The changes in the Greek economy which had ensued from the post-war period of reconstruction, the accelerating drift from the land, the startling growth of Athens, the soaring emigration figures, and the termination of American aid had all imposed great new strains upon the country. The Civil Service was grossly overstaffed and sadly incompetent. The educational system was floundering under dead weights of nepotism and tradition. The shadow of the Common Market threatened most of the old Greek ways of business and the tangled affairs of Cyprus had brought Cold War politics back to Greece again in a new and confusing way, reviving the passions of the Civil War without providing any obvious resolution. The traditional political establishment seemed increasingly unable to meet these challenges effectively. Some of its leading figures had shown themselves too venal, many looked too old, and even those like Andreas Papandreou and the young King Constantine, who might have been expected to represent a new outlook better attuned to contemporary demands, appeared on the contrary to be as obsessed as their elders with irrelevant personal intrigues. Parliamentary democracy had degenerated, in fact, into a kind of bourgeois anarchy, too far removed from the growing economic and social

problems of a poor country struggling to come to terms with the
twentieth century and, as so often before in Greek history, apparently
bent upon demonstrating its utter incapacity to renew or reform
itself from within. Thus the fact of the colonels' *coup d'état* was no
great cause for Greek surprise. Rather, it was an occasion for a
familiar despair at the realization that Burke's dictum—and Plato's,
too—about the consequences of too much freedom and too little
restraint had proved true yet again in Greece. As the country's most
successful parliamentary leader, Constantine Karamanlis, was to put
it a year or two later, 'One can say that democracy in Greece was
murdered by a free regime. The colonels simply inflicted a mercy
killing.'[1]

Yet in spite of all these explanatory and even extenuating circumstances, the conventional shorthand of liberal international comment
established virtually overnight that the Greek colonels were fascist
beasts—somehow, indeed, more fascist and more beastly than others
of their kind, just because they were Greek—and any man who so
much as raised an inquiring eyebrow at that description was apt to
find himself looked upon askance, if not practically railroaded out of
decent liberal company. The only morally acceptable attitude in such
circles seemed to be one of instant boycott in which, like a new version of the three monkeys, one neither saw, nor heard, nor spoke
anything but evil of the colonels' Greece. It is not too much to
say now, I think, that while this attitude was emotionally understandable it was effectively futile. Far from making any breach in
the colonels' defences it tended, if anything, to stiffen their resolve
and preserve their unity and it may, as a result, have left the Greek
people on whose behalf it was ostensibly adopted somewhat worse
off than they need have been. Among other things its insistence on
treating the colonels as pariahs compelled Greece eventually to
withdraw from the Council of Europe—the only arena of public
dialogue between the new junta and representatives of western
Europe's more or less democratic governments—and it encouraged
the old Greek politicians to continue in exile or in domestic opposition all the factionalism and *folies de grandeur* that had contributed
so much to their own downfall and that now delayed indefinitely the
emergence of any coherent alternative to the colonels' rule. As a
practical contribution to bettering the state of Greece it failed because
it was based too much upon illusions—about the nature of Greece,
of the regime and of power in the modern world.

This is not, of course, to deny that there were good reasons for attacking the colonels' rule. On the contrary there were many—and some of the best were the most natural: a compassionate revulsion among humane people for the personal hardships caused by political repression; a conviction that 'dictatorship' was wrong and 'democracy' was right, especially in a nation that was a member of the self-styled 'free world' symbolized by NATO and the Council of Europe; and a vague fear, at any rate among some older people, that this might somehow be the start of a repeat performance of the rise of Fascism and Nazism in Europe before the Second World War. On the last count there was—and is—no evidence beyond the fears evoked by memory; but on each of the first two the colonels gave cause for condemnation. Avowedly and demonstrably they were dictators, and although they promised to restore democracy as soon as Greece was 'healthy' enough, describing their regime as merely 'a healing parenthesis', they refused point-blank to commit themselves as to when that might be. Proclaiming that they were rescuing Greece—and, by extension, the rest of 'the free world'—from the menace of chaos and communism, they imposed martial law, censored all publications, prohibited strikes and political demonstrations, and arrested nearly 7,000 people within a few days. Charges of 'communism' or 'subversion' were flung at their opponents with abandon, and swingeing gaol sentences were imposed by courts martial for trivial new offences such as 'insulting the King'. An immediate purge was ordered of the Civil Service and the professions, tests of 'loyalty' were imposed on university students and a bizarre succession of military orders was barked at the populace as if to show that political and social reforms could be accomplished by the techniques of the barrack-room.

Schoolgirls shall not wear mini-skirts. Civil Servants shall answer all letters within three days. Beards and hippies shall be discouraged. The mail shall be delivered. Music shall cease in public places after midnight. No assemblies of more than five people shall be permitted. Those who disobey shall be locked up. To this mixture of the objectionable, the reasonable and the ludicrous, a more disturbing element was added after a few months by stories that began to appear in the western press of torture inflicted on many of the colonels' prisoners. Within a year these stories had become something of a *cause célèbre* in liberal-minded circles in western Europe and North America, and within three years they had become one of the chief instruments of a successful campaign to compel Greece to withdraw from the Council of Europe when the European Commission on

Human Rights examined over 200 alleged cases of torture and concluded that the regime had 'systematically' employed torture to
further its own interests. Understandably, in the face of all this, it
became even harder for anyone outside Greece to say an explanatory,
let alone a good, word about the colonels.

Yet mingled with a justifiable concern over the regime's apparent
severity were other more equivocal reasons why the colonels were
treated from the start with more abhorrence than most other dictatorships in the world today. One, undoubtedly, was sheer ignorance
of the state of affairs in Greece at the time of the *coup d'état*, for in
spite of numerous western press reports about the political upheavals there, remarkably few people outside Greece seemed to have
grasped how far the old political establishment had discredited itself
and how much it had placed the parliamentary system in jeopardy.[2]
Another, as I have already suggested elsewhere (see especially
Chapter 2), was the profound western attachment to the classical-
romantic dream of Greece as the cradle of democracy and the home
of freedom which—paradoxically but characteristically—acquired a
new lease of life in the wake of another Greek dictatorship, persuading many other people who knew no better that the colonels were
in some mystic sense 'un-Greek'. A third, closely related reason for
their immediate acquisition of this ogre-ish, 'un-Greek' image was
that the people who happened to suffer most from the colonels' *coup*
were precisely those Greeks who had the closest links with western
countries—the Athenian political and intellectual establishment.
These were the people who were swept aside, purged or arrested, and
who therefore sounded the loudest lament. They spoke western
languages and read western newspapers, they had attended western
universities and had adopted many western ways. Some of them had
influential western friends and had been accustomed for years to
putting their various views to the world through embassy dinners and
cultural seminars, parliamentary delegations and intellectual salons;
and if the world had not always taken much notice of them, at least
it had some idea of who they were. Accordingly, when they protested
at their fate, they quickly found a sympathetic audience.[3]

The colonels, on the other hand, were quite unknown even to the
majority of Greeks. They spoke foreign languages only with difficulty and often not at all; and even their Greek was apt to cause
mingled pain and laughter in the better Athenian circles. They possessed no cultural virtues discernible to a western eye and their political vocabulary was shocking to the temper of the time. On one

notorious early occasion their leader, Colonel George Papadopoulos, spoke of Greece as 'a patient strapped to the operating table', with himself and his colleagues in the role of surgeons; and their alarmist view of communism as a treacherous and expansionist tyranny intent upon enlarging its domains throughout the world in general and Greece in particular seemed more appropriate to the Iron Curtain world of the late 1940's than to the more complacent coexistence world of the late 1960's—as if they had all been living in a cave for twenty years. The colonels also proclaimed their respect for established religion, upheld propriety of a thoroughly narrow-minded kind, and were almost apoplectic at the idea of 'permissiveness'. Moreover, being military men, they encountered in the West the resistance of an age that, thanks to Vietnam and the Bomb, had grown unusually weary of militarism. In short, whatever their other sins might be, they were hopelessly out of fashion—a cross between Oliver Cromwell and Queen Victoria stepping out into the Beatles' world—and most of their audience outside Greece either did not begin to understand what they were talking about or was resolved never to try.

This basic gulf between the colonels and some of the most politically and intellectually articulate people in the West was deepened by the fact that their victims included not merely the established figures of the centre and left in Greek politics, but most of the traditional right as well. The colonels were evidently right wing in the sense that they were passionately anti-communist, but in some other ways they were less easily type-cast. In particular, they were evidently far from certain or unanimous about the value of the monarchy—that characteristic touchstone of Greek right-wing attitudes. Although they used the King's name to begin with to give themselves a cloak of legitimacy, they purged the most influential King's men from the Army as ruthlessly as even Andreas Papandreou could have wished and increasingly made it clear that they were just as ready to put His Majesty in his place as well. When the King struck back, with a pathetic attempt at a counter-*coup* in December 1967, they swept him contemptuously from the board. The Army by then was theirs, not his; and, after forcing him into exile in Rome, they installed a senior officer, General Zoitakis, in his place as Regent and bent their minds towards producing a new constitution that would in future restrict the Monarch's power in Greece more than ever before. In terms of the old Greek power structure, therefore, they seemed to stand alone, bereft of support—with but a few individual exceptions

—from right, left or centre; and the world, which had accepted that structure as roughly representative for most of the previous fifteen or twenty years, assumed in consequence that the colonels represented nobody in Greece but themselves.

All this produced a climate of opinion in most of the countries of western Europe, and to a lesser extent in the United States as well, that was tailor-made for left-wing propaganda of all denominations. At first glance, the mere fact of a military *coup d'état* whose instigators were both bitterly anti-communist and sternly authoritarian seemed to confirm everything that had ever been said about the menace of fascism in Greece; and left-wing groups all over Europe were soon co-operating with Greek exiles to let loose once again upon the Greek question that spirit of 'reckless, unbridled partisanship' that Winston Churchill had deplored over twenty years before.

Both the old and the new left engaged in this campaign. Established left-wing organizations like the League for Democracy in Greece, which had languished in fellow-travelling obscurity from the Civil War until the last days of the Karamanlis regime, acquired a respectable, liberal halo again in the wake of the *coup d'état*, and their old clichés about fascism, monarchism and NATO imperialism became part of the standard currency of ostensibly liberal protest demonstrations from Stockholm to Washington. Students and others in the new left movement, on the other hand, who had never previously spared a thought for Greece, found the situation there an ideal excuse for their ideology of revolution because it undermined ordinary liberal confidence in western institutions and rational discourse and appeared to justify all their arguments in favour of revolutionary violence. Thus, a mob of students and other youths who invaded a dinner party in a Cambridge hotel in 1970, assaulting policemen, breaking furniture and intimidating guests, found many defenders among apparently sensible men because the dinner had been held in the allegedly offensive cause of promoting trade with 'fascist' Greece. In this atmosphere sober judgement was bemused, and attempts at reasoned explanation or inquiry as to what was really happening in Greece and how best to improve the situation there, were apt to be branded as mere apology.

In fairness it must be said that the nature of the Greek case made it difficult to disentangle the real complaint from the false grievance, for the colonels seemed as determined as any other Greek rulers to be their own worst enemies, continuing—as they had started—to give cause for offence and revealing an impressive inability to understand the first principles of either diplomacy or public relations. Time after time they gave unnecessary hostages to fortune out of either stubbornness or folly. Their wholesale removal of judges who delivered judgements they did not like did more than anyone else's propaganda could have achieved to destroy their high-minded claims to impartiality. Their obtuse political censorship even of such things as the classical Greek dramas, although by no means new to Greece, seemed to many people in the western world proof either of their idiocy or their fear. Their immediate imprisonment of Andreas Papandreou with the threat of bringing him to book for the Aspida affair on charges of conspiracy to overthrow the Government —which was, after all, what they had just done themselves—gained him widespread sympathy as a noble martyr to the cause of freedom and democracy. Mikis Theodorakis, a popular composer and somewhat feckless communist politician, who was previously known to most people outside Greece only for his music in the film of Kazantzakis's novel, *Zorba the Greek*, was transformed overnight into an international cultural status-symbol when the colonels detained him for his political activities and prohibited his music in Greece. And when they deprived the well-known film actress, Melina Mercouri, of her Greek citizenship—a long-practised but self-defeating tactic for dealing with critics in Greece—they guaranteed themselves the well-publicized hostility of all her equally well-known friends.

Yet there was little doubt that the colonels' sins, although so often real enough, were also greatly magnified, both in relation to those of similar authoritarian regimes elsewhere and in the perspective of Greece's own past, by a deliberate campaign of vilification that sought to depict them from the start as an unscrupulous, brutal and metaphorically 'un-Greek' gang acting on behalf of American neo-imperialism. To this purpose some of the Greek exiles and their friends resuscitated two favourite themes of left-wing propaganda in new and more damaging guise. One was the old allegation of NATO imperialism, which had done yeoman service in Greece throughout the Cyprus crisis and was now presented in the form of an American C.I.A. conspiracy to impose the colonels upon Greece. The other was the issue of the Greek political prisoners which had served to blacken the foreign reputation of the Karamanlis regime and was now given a new twist by the circumstantial reports of deliberate torture being applied in the colonels' overcrowded gaols. Each of these contained enough reality to make a plausible case, yet both required more critical examination than they usually received;

and because they successfully influenced the view taken of the colonels in most western countries I must digress at some length to look at them here.

As I have noted already, the allegations of deliberate torture by the new regime became particularly associated with the campaign to expel Greece from the Council of Europe—a campaign led, significantly, by the Scandinavian countries and the Netherlands, whose own histories, governments and societies happened to be about as different as any could be from those of Greece and whose left-wing pressure groups were notoriously powerful. Again it must be said that there were legitimate grounds for complaint, for by suspending the democratic constitution in Greece the colonels had clearly breached the Council's statutes, which stipulated that member governments should be organized in a democratic manner and with respect to the rule of law. It was not enough for the colonels to protest, as they did, that they would eventually restore democracy. The Council wanted a time-table, and the sooner the better. As early as January 1968, its Consultative Assembly passed a resolution threatening Greece with suspension if the new Government did not restore parliamentary democracy by the spring of 1969; and a year later when that restoration seemed as far away as ever, the threat was repeated in stronger terms. Greece, said the Assembly, was 'in serious violation' of the conditions of membership and must take the consequences. When it became clear to the colonels that suspension was imminent, in December 1969, they instructed their representatives to reject the case laid before the Council as being born of misunderstanding and unwarranted interference in Greece's internal affairs and to withdraw voluntarily from membership before the threat of suspension could be fulfilled. Ostensibly, then, the matter was decided on the grounds of the suspension of democratic government and the rule of law in Greece and there were many who argued that on those grounds alone no other decision was possible.

In practice, however, a different decision might have been reached —or at any rate suspension might have been delayed—without the moral pressure of the concurrent campaign about Greek torture. The British and West German representatives in the Council's Committee of Ministers where the final decision had to be taken, certainly shared doubts about the usefulness of suspending Greece and could have swung the issue the other way if they had joined the representatives of France, Turkey and Cyprus in recommending further consideration of the matter. But by then the allegations of torture in Greece had become a political issue in their own countries and they could not afford to be seen publicly defending the colonels. It was only when they let it be known that they would agree to suspension if the matter came to the vote that the Greeks withdrew.

The coincidence between these actions in the Council and the most significant phases of the anti-torture campaign cannot be overlooked. The first reports of torture in the colonels' prisons began to circulate not long before the Council of Europe's meeting in January 1968, when the first threat of suspension was made, and they built up into a crescendo of almost daily publicity in 1969, culminating in an obviously deliberate 'leak' of the conclusions of the Human Rights Commission in November, just before the crucial meeting of the Committee of Ministers. There was, in fact, a hint of orchestration about the campaign that inevitably aroused some suspicion as to the truth of the allegations themselves. Plainly those were extremely difficult to prove or disprove conclusively, as such atrocity stories nearly always are. Equally plainly, some of them were shown to be exaggerated, if not fabricated, when alleged victims of the colonels' torture turned up apparently none the worse for wear and even willing, sometimes, to repudiate what their friends had been saying about their fate. The most notorious such affair took place in Strasbourg in 1968, when the Greek Government produced two prisoners to testify to the Human Rights Commission that they had not been tortured. Before they could do so, the two men disappeared, to surface in Norway a few days later under the aegis of an organization called the Pan-Hellenic Liberation Movement, led by Andreas Papandreou. There they announced that, on the contrary, they had been tortured; but after a few more days they reappeared yet again in Greek Government hands to maintain that they had been kidnapped by Papandreou's men, including twenty 'communists' with guns, and had made their previous statements under duress. Naturally, their erstwhile friends, or captors, replied that it was really the colonels who had kidnapped the men after they had very properly fled from persecution, and that it was their new statement, not the old one, that was made at gun-point. You paid your money and you took your choice; but from such a scene of black comedy it was impossible for any detached observer to draw anything much save, perhaps, a renewed determination to hold hard to his natural scepticism in dealing with Greek affairs.

The case of Mikis Theodorakis provided another example. Theodorakis was several times said to have been at death's door from

Q

tuberculosis owing to lack of medical care in prison, or in the remote mountain village to which he was later exiled, and on at least one occasion it was reported with conviction that he was actually dead. Yet when he was eventually released from Greece three years after the colonels' *coup* he appeared—at any rate for a man who had supposedly been so ill for so long—to be in remarkable health, fully equal to holding immediate and ebullient press conferences with a hundred journalists and to appearing within a week or two at London's Albert Hall to conduct a full symphony orchestra in a performance of his own music. It does not follow, of course, that Theodorakis was treated well or justly. On the contrary, he was treated with quite unnecessary severity, regardless of allegations of physical neglect. Nor does it follow that because many atrocity stories appeared to be untrue or exaggerated, all must have been so. But the inescapable suspicion of perjury and propaganda involved in so many similar stories allegedly coming out of Greece persistently vitiated the worst conclusions about the colonels' torture and cast doubt upon the judgement of the Human Rights Commission.

Equally, however, a decent scepticism rejected the best reports. The regime's frequent disclaimers of the use of torture were certainly not to be accepted at face value—and not because of the hoary notion that there's no smoke without fire (in propaganda matters there often is) but because to have avoided all physical maltreatment of opponents under the circumstances would have been remarkably un-Greek. Here it is necessary to reassert the obvious—that Greece is not always a gentle country, nor are Greeks a gentle people, especially among themselves. On the contrary, there is a persistent undercurrent of violence between Greek and Greek that can, as in the 1940's, lend itself to appalling brutalities and from which neither the police nor the Army has ever been free. It is doubtful whether any Greek government has ever stopped the practice of beating up prisoners, even if they have tried; and that classical form of punishment known as the *falanja*—striking the soles of the feet with a bar— has been well known to the authorities at least since Turkish times. It seems certain that this sort of thing increased after the colonels seized power, for although in public they explicitly condemned or denied the use of torture it was obvious that the witch-hunting atmosphere of their regime, especially in its first year or two, gave implicit encouragement to violence. When, for example, they reinstated the policemen who had been found responsible for the attack on Gregory Lambrakis in 1963 (and later arrested the lawyer who had conducted the case against them) they must have given hundreds of other police-men and security officers a cosy feeling that they might get away with violence, as long as they stopped short of murder. The colonels' preoccupation with security in opposition to the underground resistance movements which appeared from time to time must also have produced a more permissive attitude to official violence. My own conclusion, therefore, for what it is worth, is that there almost certainly was some torture, and probably a good deal of casual brutality, but not nearly as much as the campaign against it suggested and not enough to condemn the regime as uniquely barbaric by Greek standards, still less by the standards of some other countries much less in the news, where political imprisonment, torture and even execution are unfortunately still standard practice.

Again, this is not to condone whatever took place, nor to suggest that it could have been any consolation to a victim to know when he was having his teeth knocked out or his feet beaten, that matters might have been worse. But if we are to approach the truth in these grim affairs I believe it is wiser to recognize that violence of this kind is not, in itself, new to Greece and to see it as a likely—albeit deplorable —response to passion and opportunity rather than to pursue the demonological view encouraged by the propagandists of a systematic policy of widespread, physical intimidation directed from the top by evil men. In the climate of opinion that met the colonels in many western quarters, however, it was the demonological view that won; and a kind of moral intimidation peculiar to good causes made it increasingly difficult for anyone even to try to sketch in the Greek historical and social background by way of explanation—let alone to mention any conceivable justification for the regime's existence— without being accused of defending unprecedented and 'un-Greek' barbarities committed for the sake of 'fascism'.

Whether this intense and selective sense of moral indignation pro-duced any improvement in the treatment of Greek prisoners, as its exponents claimed, was not proven. Most of the 7,000 people origin-ally arrested were released within the first year, before the anti-torture campaign had reached its peak. Within three years, the number of prisoners held on political charges of one kind or another was down to about 1,000—roughly the same as at the end of the Kara-manlis regime—and in spite of fresh arrests or deportations arising from sporadic activity by underground resistance groups, the num-bers were continuing to decline. It is possible to argue that this would not have happened without external pressure. It is equally possible that the nature of that pressure was actually counter-productive, in that it caused the more ruthless or more unthinking members of the junta to dig in their heels rather than seem to be giving in to what, in their eyes, was just another communist plot. The campaign did, however, compel the colonels to produce some named prisoners from time to time as part of their effort to show that allegations of torture were unfounded, and it also helped the International Red Cross and several parliamentary delegations from Britain and elsewhere to secure the junta's permission to inspect Greek prisons and detention centres between 1967 and 1970. For what it was worth (which probably was not much) none of these inspections produced any evidence of torture; but it is possible that they acted as a deterrent to violence or ill-treatment for which it was right to be grateful. On the other hand, by contributing to the exclusion of Greece from the Council of Europe the anti-torture campaign eventually destroyed what was, perhaps, one of the best means of keeping up effective pressure. On the face of things it seemed likely that if the colonels were the sort of fascist beasts they were said to be they would have felt more, not less, free to do their worst once they had been forced out of the Council and that there would have been even more stories about torture as a result. In fact, however, there was a marked drop in the number of torture stories after the Greek withdrawal. This could have been attributed, of course, simply to the fact that many newspapers by then had got tired of publishing them; but it could also have suggested that much of the campaign had been motivated by political rather than humane passions—and that it needed to be looked at, accordingly, only with the greatest care.

Less directly damaging to the colonels' image abroad, but hotly argued by some of their Greek critics and international left-wing groups, was the notion that they were tools of an American conspiracy. At least three preconceptions were involved here: (a) that the United States was or could be the outright arbiter of Greek affairs; (b) that the colonels were so low in rank, so relatively few in number and so uncertain of their reception by the Greeks that they could not have sustained their *coup* without tacit American support and dared not have mounted it without prior American agreement; (c) that there was such a clear coincidence of interest between America and the colonels in the establishment of a right-wing regime in Greece that the Central Intelligence Agency would never have let slip the opportunity of collaborating with the colonels to produce one. Taking the three together, concluded one relatively cautious but widely-distributed account by a young Greek writer, Constantine Tsoucalas, 'The inference may well be drawn that the U.S. could make good use of a government so totally dependent on them that it was to American advantage to help it along.'[4]

On the face of it, this was a plausible argument. The Americans had, indeed, been Greece's chief patron and protecting power ever since the Civil War. The colonels were, by definition, comparatively low in rank and most of their supporters were lower still. Including colonels, captains, lieutenants and all, the full complement of military conspirators behind the *coup* probably did not exceed 300 out of a Greek officer corps of more than 9,000; and as the Greek armed forces were almost wholly equipped by the United States it would be reasonable for them to want to ensure continued American support so that they would retain Greek military loyalties. As for America's interest in a more right-wing government, that had been manifest in the previous two or three years in Washington's distrust of the Papandreous and the shift to the left encouraged by their administration. With the Soviet Union establishing a new strength in the Mediterranean through its successful diplomacy in Egypt and the Arab world and the Cyprus crisis perennially threatening to permit further Russian advances, it was also plausible to suppose that America would back a regime in Greece that would unequivocally favour the NATO alliance, rather than risk a return to the demagogy of the Papandreou period and new uncertainty about the NATO bases in Greece.

This hypothetical case for an American conspiracy was supported, moreover, by certain suspicious details. The fact that the colonels apparently had organized their *coup* along the lines of a NATO contingency plan called 'Prometheus', originally drafted as a defence against internal subversion, was adduced as evidence that NATO—i.e., in this case, the United States of America—had been in some characteristic way implicated in the 'murder' of Greek democracy. It was also pointed out that the leader of the *coup*, Colonel Papadopoulos, had been head of the Greek Intelligence Service which had always had close links with the C.I.A. It was assumed, therefore, that the C.I.A. must have known—and approved—what he was up to. Besides, a certain allegedly senior operative of the C.I.A., a Mr. Richard Barnum, who it was 'known . . . had played an important role' in deposing George Papandreou in 1965, was reported to have been in Athens at the beginning of 1967. 'He operated through the Esso-Pappas concern,' said Constantine Tsoucalas, 'whose interests were at stake' because the contracts they had signed with the Government that succeeded Papandreou, to build an oil refinery and petrochemical complex in Salonika, had been questioned by Papandreou's party. The head of the company, Tom Pappas, was a wealthy Greek-American who 'did not make a secret of his belief that Greece "needed" a military dictatorship. It has been further established that the Boston Pappas Foundation, run by Pappas's brother, was a conduit for C.I.A. money destined for Greece. Characteristically, a Pappas employee, Pavlos Totomis, was entrusted with the key Ministry of Public Order after the success of the *coup*. The contracts of Esso were revised in Pappas's favour soon afterwards. Another detail might help to shape the picture. Tom Pappas is a personal friend and the main financial backer of Spiro Agnew, Nixon's obscure vice-presidential choice, who has been openly supporting the colonels since his nomination.'[5] To his credit, the author of this account went on to say that, 'It is of course ridiculous to maintain that the dictatorship in Greece was purely a product of U.S. intervention.' But there was no doubt of the drift of the argument, and the nuances and reservations which he was honest enough to make were often obscured by others less scrupulous who happily accepted the C.I.A.'s guilt, and forgot about anything else. In reality, however, the evidence was wholly circumstantial and inconclusive.

The 'Prometheus' business was a red herring, for similar contingency plans existed in all NATO countries and there was nothing in principle or in fact to connect NATO as an institution or the United States as its chief power with the use of the plan for ulterior purposes by the head of the Greek Intelligence Service. If the C.I.A. had really been plotting with Papadopoulos, with whom they had such supposedly close contacts, it would hardly have been necessary—indeed, it would surely have been unwise—for one of their senior men to visit Athens, where he was 'known' to suspicious eyes, not long before the intended operation. Pavlos Totomis was notoriously a cipher in the Ministry of Public Order, carrying no weight with the colonels and lasting only a short time in that office. And just what Spiro Agnew might have been doing in the case was about as obscure as the man himself was at the time of the colonels' *coup*. He certainly supported the colonels after he became Vice-President, as he supported many another dubious cause; but that was eighteen months later, and it is asking too much to suppose that the C.I.A. and Mr. Pappas had him ear-marked for the job, with the situation in Greece at the forefront of their minds and the American electorate presumably at their mercy, before they had even ensured the success of their Athenian conspiracy.

Nor was the general inference—of America creating a 'totally dependent' government in Greece—any better grounded. Indeed, it was in some ways self-contradictory, for if the Americans had been so wholly able to take charge of Greek affairs as the inference implied they would presumably have been able to impose whatever regime they chose upon the powerless Greeks. In that event it seemed unlikely that they would have chosen the colonels, if only because they were such unknown quantities that no sane foreign conspirator would have touched them when a suitable alternative was available. A suitable alternative from the American point of view obviously did exist in the shape of the King and his generals, whose favourable political attitudes had been tested by long experience (as those of the colonels had not been) and whose *coup*, had it ever taken place, could have been presented as a far more respectable affair. Springing from within the establishment, it would almost certainly have won the acceptance of a number of right-wing politicians for a 'temporary' suspension of the constitution with the object of refurbishing the parliamentary system and reviving something like the former Karamanlis regime. As such it would have seemed far more open to diplomatic manipulation by the Americans than a junta of little-known junior officers whose reaction to the pulling of strings from Washington could not safely be predicted. The direction of American diplomacy after the colonels' *coup* certainly suggested that a 'King's *coup*' of this kind would have been more welcome—although there is still no firm evidence that it was ever more than a gleam in the eyes of a few Greek generals. The immediate response of the Americans to the colonels was to withhold half their normal military aid to Greece and publicly—through President Johnson and others—to express the hope that democracy would soon be restored. Subsequently, they maintained close contact with the King, especially while he was still in Athens, and with Karamanlis in his Paris exile, apparently in the hope of using the two of them to rally enough traditional support inside the Army and the old political establishment to compel the colonels to widen the base of their government and so create, in effect, the sort of 'interim' regime that might have resulted from the prospective 'King's *coup*'. Their attempts failed, but that they were made at all hardly supported the view that the colonels had been Washington's chosen instrument, and that they

failed seemed equally to contradict the notion of the colonels' 'total
dependence' on American support. But perhaps the best evidence
against the theory of a C.I.A. conspiracy was provided by the
colonels themselves. Most successful military *coups* in Greece or elsewhere have been made by men of their rank or lower if only because
more senior officers generally have too much of a vested interest in
the *status quo* to want to upset it. And most successful conspirators
of this kind prove to be men of great determination and independence of mind. The Greek colonels soon showed themselves to be in
this tradition. Indeed they seemed to be not merely determined but
remarkably obstinate and tactless; and the idea of them hesitating
before their *coup* over their presumed weakness and uncertainty
about American reactions seemed profoundly unconvincing. It was
far more likely that men of their stamp would have gone ahead with
their plans regardless, convinced that righteousness would prevail;
and when a congressional inquiry in Washington revealed in 1970
that Greek military units under the colonels' control had actually
threatened to occupy American nuclear sites at the time of the *coup*,
the idea of any prior American complicity seemed finally to have
been exploded.[6] It was scarcely conceivable that the C.I.A. would
have countenanced such a rash move except as part of a complex
game of double bluff, deliberately to imply that the C.I.A. was *not*
involved. And in that case, it was equally inconceivable that the incident would have been hushed up for three years, since the whole
point of such a cover operation would have been to secure discreet
publicity for it.

For all that, however, the C.I.A. conspiracy theory continued to
thrive, nourished partly by the strident anti-Americanism of European left-wing circles and partly by the characteristic tendency of
many of the deposed Greek politicians to avoid blame and reject
guilt by placing the responsibility for self-induced misfortune
squarely upon other people's shoulders.

In less violently partisan minds a milder but still misleading theory
of American manipulation of the colonels gained wider approval.
This accepted that the United States might have known nothing of
the *coup* in advance, but claimed that Washington had the power
afterwards to dispose of the colonels if it wanted to. Therefore, the
colonels must be American stooges. One of my Greek acquaintances
summed up this one with a touch of unconscious irony: 'Nobody's
ever heard of these colonels before,' he said. 'You can't tell me a
bunch of peasants like that can stand up to the United States!' A

few other Greeks took the implications of this to its logical conclusion for me, asserting quite seriously that Washington could and should have got rid of the colonels at once by simply sending in the Marines —recalling earlier occasions when Britain and France had done so; and although wiser heads agreed that the Marines might have been too drastic a remedy in the 1960's it became the almost universal view of Greek liberals and their western friends that a sterner American moral and material squeeze would and should have brought the military regime to a swift and ignominious end.

The underlying assumption of American omnipotence here was understandable, but mistaken. In a country like Greece, where patronage has always been the essence of politics and independence has rarely been untrammelled, it is hard not to believe that other people and other nations always hold the strings of power; and America's position in Greece after the Civil War had in many ways upheld that conclusion. Yet the decisive period of American hegemony, coinciding roughly with the decade of reconstruction in the 1950's, was exceptional; and by the time the colonels arrived on the scene it had clearly come to an end. The termination of American economic aid to Greece in 1962 removed one crucial lever of power from American hands and the increasingly complex situation in the eastern Mediterranean and western Europe, with the Soviet Union gaining influence in the first area and France and the Common Market countries showing greater independence of America in the second, also reduced Washington's capacity for effective intervention in Athens. By 1967, with the Turkish Government under increasing left-wing pressure and the western position eroded throughout the Arab world by the side-effects of the perennial Arab-Israel crisis, the importance of Greece to NATO in general and the American Sixth Fleet in particular was as great as it had ever been. The colonels were able, therefore, to establish a more equal and more dynamic relationship with America than was widely supposed. They had little fear of being removed from NATO. They could and did respond to America's partial suspension of military aid by threatening to negotiate new arms agreements with France. They could disregard the hostility of the Council of Europe because their trade with the Common Market countries was largely unaffected by it; and they could even overcome their passionate anti-communism sufficiently after a year or so to begin expanding Greek trade with the communist states of eastern Europe. Short of some such miracle as effective international sanctions it was hard to see, therefore, just what instruments America, or any other power, could have used to discipline or remove the colonels once they had made their *coup*, without taking unacceptable risks like sending in the Marines.

Moreover, there was no evidence that greater pressures on Greece would have resulted in more democracy. Given the intricacies of the Greek national *philotimo* they might conceivably have transformed the colonels into nationalist heroes, rather like General Metaxas in 1940, bravely resisting the malign interference of foreign powers. Alternatively, and even worse, they might easily have provoked greater repression, and could just possibly have ended in new civil strife. In retrospect this last fear seems exaggerated, but it must not be forgotten that the colonels' *coup* had followed a period of growing political bitterness and violence and that nobody could be sure, during their first days and weeks in power, what support they enjoyed in the country or in the armed forces.

Precipitate American action to remove them would have required both a greater degree of certainty about their unpopularity than any-one could honestly profess (including, surely, an absolute conviction that their removal would require no bloodshed) and a greater readi-ness to accept direct responsibility for the internal affairs of Greece than any American Government could assume in the 1960's. Lacking such certainties, the Americans inevitably played safe, hoping that the colonels would prove amenable enough to diplomatic pressures to return swiftly and peacefully to some more 'respectable' form of government. Predictably, this pleased nobody in Greece—and not very many people outside Greece, either. The colonels were annoyed but unmoved by America's pinpricks, and their numerous enemies were contemptuous of America's timidity. Yet—and this was the most crucial factor of all in the colonels' evident ability to outstare all their critics—no reasonable alternative was offered, either to American policy or to the junta's rule. Merely to have gone back to the situation prevailing before the *coup* would have solved nothing, even if it could have been done; nor was there much enthusiasm for such a return in Greece outside the circles most immediately affected by the *coup*. On the other hand, the politicians who urged the Ameri-cans to take stronger action proved unable to supply any other alternative for the United States to support with conviction.

One of the colonels' leading critics in the Council of Europe, Mr. Max Van der Stoel from the Netherlands, reported in September 1968, his belief that the only alternative to a perpetuation of the junta was a 'really representative government of national unity in which all the democratic forces of the country would take part'; and he added his personal conviction that such a government could be realized. But it was not. The best that the representatives of 'the democratic forces' seemed able to do was to assert their personal integrity by refusing to co-operate with the colonels. To sink their own differences and construct a genuine common front against them, or to provide a coherent alternative to the colonels' somewhat nebulous long-term plans for redrafting the Greek constitution and reconstructing Greek life was more than they could manage. On the contrary, most of them persisted in envisaging policies that were mutually contra-dictory, such as encouraging armed resistance inside Greece (usually from a safe exile) while at the same time denouncing the colonels for raising the spectre of civil war, or urging the Americans to intervene on their behalf while stoutly condemning 'NATO imperialism' and all its works. Unfortunately, like so many other Greeks before them, from the War of Independence to the Cyprus crisis, they were en-couraged in these essentially rhetorical and self-defeating visions by the respectful attention given to them abroad. Their own sins were forgotten in the eagerness to berate those of the colonels, their *hubris* was maintained by the ease with which they were able to secure publicity for their views, and the petty factionalism which had done so much to destroy them when in power continued unabated in the warm glow of western sympathy.

The traditional right wing was split into three between those who thought the colonels the least of several possible evils, those who con-tinued to support the exiled King or former royalist politicians inside Greece, and those whose eyes turned hopefully towards Karamanlis in his Parisian exile. The centre and the non-communist left were riven by a series of personal and political feuds mostly centred upon the equivo-cal rule of Andreas Papandreou; and while several underground resistance movements made their existence known through the oc-casional distribution of home-made pamphlets and the infrequent explosion of home-made bombs in Greece, none of them could claim any substantial following, and the colonels appeared to have little difficulty in breaking them up and bringing their members before courts martial for summary trial and dispatch to the limbo of the Aegaean islands. Not until 1971, after four years of military rule, was there any hint of solidarity even among these underground groups —and the form that took, of a public declaration that when the colonels were overthrown the resistance would bring to trial anyone adjudged to have co-operated with the regime, seemed characteristically self-defeating since it gave every Greek with a government job the strongest possible incentive to maintain the regime in power.

Even the Greek Communist Party, which might have been expected to seize the opportunity to re-establish a common resistance front like that of E.A.M./E.L.A.S. during the wartime occupation, remained divided into at least three recalcitrant factions—one in long-term exile, supported as a matter of form by the Soviet Union, a second inside Greece of Maoist tendencies and a third, largely represented by Theodorakis, which hardly seemed to know where it stood. Neither the Soviet Union nor any other communist power was interested in giving them any material aid to conduct a battle inside Greece; for, once again, as from Tsar Alexander's caution during the War of Independence to the Stalin-Churchill agreement of the 1940's, Russia in the last resort had no interest in Greek adventurism. Such struggle as there was against the colonels, therefore, boiled down mostly to high words and futile gestures—of which, as usual, there were plenty. Of constructive action, serious thought or chastened silence there was all too little.

Three years after the *coup* the situation was summed up, despondently but graphically, by one of the few exiled politicians who seemed to have learned anything from his experience—Paul Vardino-yannis, a former Minister of the Centre Union Government. 'Unfortunately,' he said, 'after three long and bitter years abroad, I am compelled to confirm the unbelievable yet total failure of the free Greek politicians to establish a common cause and to offer the Greek people a carefully and jointly thought out alternative to the present situation. . . . The time has come when we must all irrevocably close down our personal little political boutiques and purchase with integrity our share in the great enterprise that is really democratic Greece.'[7] To do that, however, it was not only the Greek politicians who would have to learn to think afresh, but their romantic, misinformed or—sometimes—just plain mischievous western friends who so persistently abetted them in their delusions. Meanwhile the colonels remained in power, *faute de mieux*, cherishing other delusions —and forging other fetters—of their own.

Chapter 16

WHAT ROUGH BEAST?

And what rough beast, its hour come round at last,
Slouches towards Bethlehem to be born?

(W. B. Yeats)

Just as no single factor could explain the collapse of Greek parliamentary government in the 1960's, so no one characteristic could wholly describe or account for the nature of the military regime that succeeded it. Dictatorial the regime was, without a doubt; and sometimes stupid and ruthless, too. But in whose interest, from what premises and to what purpose? The beginning of any answer must be somewhat arbitrary but the best way to start, I think, is with the poverty and stern morality of the Greek provinces where most of the leading members of the military junta were born and bred.

Take, for example, a village on the north coast of the Peloponnese called Elaiochorion. It lies west of Patras, on a dirt track off the main road to Olympia. Northwards is the Gulf of Corinth, widening hereabouts towards its mouth. Immediately to the south are the first peaks of the Peloponnesian mountains; and between them and the sea are the fields and terraces of wheat and vines, spiked with cypress trees and patched with olive groves, that provide a rough living for the villagers of Elaiochorion. The village itself is a modest little place of only some 250 people and, to a foreign eye, it is practically indistinguishable from 5,000 or 6,000 other such hamlets in Greece. The whitewashed cottages huddled on the hillside, the dusty tracks and laden donkeys, the girls in shapeless, flowered cotton frocks teasing wool upon their distaffs, the black-clad women stooping under piles of brushwood for their ovens, the little church with its crude icons and brown wax candles and wild posies withering on the graves outside, the café where the men gather for their gossip, the priest in his old, blue house-cassock and the policeman in his trim, olive uniform—all these are the universals of Greek village life. To the visitor they may seem endearingly peaceful, innocent and romantic—a vision of a true Arcadia. But for the people who are born and bred among them they are unlikely to possess such sweet significance.

For them the donkey tracks speak rather of brutal isolation, the stooping women and gossiping men are the outward symbols of a moral code of male supremacy and sexual bigotry, the priest recalls centuries of clerical domination and the policeman is the necessary guardian of strict conformity against the wild, Dionysian elements of violence and fear that for ever threaten the placid, rustic scene. For them, in short, this is not Arcadia but Boeotia—that equally traditional but notably unromantic Greek land of cunning minds and harsh morals, where the peasants must make what shift they can to live under the crushing weight of poverty and tradition.

In this light, too, Elaiochorion is typical of much of Greece. It is, in fact, a good deal less isolated and more prosperous than many Greek villages, for it is only three miles from the main road and—in the last ten or fifteen years, at least—a comfortable daily bus to Athens. Yet there are still a few of the men and many of the women who have never been farther afield than Patras, just a few miles down the coast, and the village itself has a desperately poor and hangdog air when you get past its whitewash and its ornamental pots of basil. Nor is the Dionysian violence very far beneath the surface. Four of the men who gather daily at the café were tortured by Greek communists in the Civil War, the local doctor was killed by the communists and was never replaced and thirteen other villagers were killed just before that by the Germans, or by other Greeks, in the confusion of treachery, heroism, blood feuds and political strife that accompanied the wartime occupation. In just such bitter and blood-soaked soil have the Boeotians under one name or another eked out their lives through nearly 3,000 years of Greek history, despised by the quick city wits of Athens or Constantinople—as provincials are derided by the denizens of capital cities everywhere—yet nevertheless providing an enduring and jealous opposition to Greek metropolitan decadence. In classical Athens, Boeotia was known as the land of dullards. In Byzantine times it was what the gentlemen of Constantinople meant when they dismissed the impoverished old peninsula of Greece as 'an utter hole'. In modern times, it is what the Athenian socialites have in mind when they talk of the *stenokephalos*—the narrow-heads, or country bumpkins, out there beyond the pale of sophisticated city life. Part of the explanation of what happened in Athens on the morning of 21st April 1967, was that some of the Boeotians rose again to rebuke the city slickers with their provincial righteousness. Their hitherto unknown leader, George Papadopoulos, was born—the son of the village schoolmaster—in Elaiochorion.

Papadopoulos's youthful, Boeotian background of material hardship and stern morality was shared by practically all his colleagues. Stylianos Pattakos, the often garrulous brigadier who became deputy Prime Minister to Papadopoulos and a favourite butt of Athenian jesters, was born into a poor peasant family in a tiny village in Crete. Colonel Nicholas Makarezos, the third man of the regime, who was appointed to the senior economics post as Minister of Co-ordination because—so they said in Athens—'he knew how to add and subtract', came from another, not much bigger village on the road to Delphi. Colonel Ioannis Ladas, who was to become notorious in opposition circles as the head of the regime's security services and its so called 'torturer-in-chief', spent his youth amid the characteristically grinding poverty of a mountain village in the Peloponnese. According to one account their breaths 'stank from hunger' in their childhood, and in their early army days Papadopoulos was known to his fellows as 'the rich man' because, as the son of a schoolteacher, the poverty he had endured had been almost genteel instead of frankly brutal.[1] None of them, except Makarezos—who once did a course in economics while serving as military attaché in Bonn—had any higher education, for there was simply none to be had. All of them, like tens of thousands of other young Greeks bred in similar surroundings, learned virtually with their mothers' milk a sour distrust of the well-fed ruling cliques in Athens—often known to rural folk, significantly, as 'the eaters'.

In the Civil War of the 1940's many such Greeks joined the communist guerrilla bands with little more ideological baggage than this sense of provincial resentment, seeing in the promise of battle their chance to get their own back on the traditional 'eaters' and in the vision of social justice their opportunity to escape from the straitjacket of rural poverty. But two other ways of escape were more traditional—emigration and the Army. As in most other underdeveloped countries, the Greek Army in modern times has always been a favourite means for poor boys to achieve material reward and social advancement. At its worst it has supplied an alternative to emigration by providing square meals and a minimal living wage beyond the usual capacity of the hard Greek earth. At its best, for more ambitious youths, it has offered a ladder to influence and office, besides conferring upon those who served in it the prestige fitting to an institution that on so many occasions had proved itself (at any rate to its own satisfaction) to be the saviour of the nation. But in the nature of Greek affairs it was, as we have seen, also a political force.

Although the direction of its politics often varied from *coup d'état* to *coup d'état* and from purge to purge, especially in the long quarrel between royalists and republicans that raged from the First World War onwards, its officers consistently saw themselves as a disciplinary counterweight to the indiscipline of Greece's politicians. Like other politically-minded soldiers, they justified their interventions in highly moral terms which, whether directed towards royalist or republican ends, stressed the military virtues of duty and patriotism in opposition to the corrupt Bohemianism of the Athenian world.

The men who were to become known collectively as the colonels entered upon this tradition at a significant time. Being more or less of the same generation, born soon after the First World War, they mostly came to manhood just before or during the German occupation when the Army under Metaxas had become an essentially royalist and right-wing institution. The experience of the Civil War and the Cold War that followed confirmed this right-wing bias. For the colonels themselves, serving as young officers on the northern front against the communists, the Civil War must have been a searing experience, especially when members of their own families suffered behind the lines from starvation and guerrilla action. Ladas, for example, lost his mother to the communists when they shot her down in the village street and one of the men tortured by them in Elaiochorion was a cousin of Papadopoulos. By the time some of them had also served with Greek units in Korea, fighting with the United Nations force against the communist Chinese and North Koreans, and then had returned home again to see the Greek armed forces integrated into NATO and charged with holding the line for Greece and the West against the nation's traditional Slav enemies, their identification of communism with anything and everything inimical to their own vision of Greece must have been well nigh unshakable.

To this shared social and military background of their formative years, a number of the colonels added a profound and specifically Greek form of religious conviction which was closely linked both with their provincial upbringing and the Army. Born as most of them had been into rural isolation, where the Orthodox Church was still a focus of community life, they were raised in the characteristically Byzantine assumption that the Greek Church and the Greek State were inseparable. This assumption was reinforced in the Civil War by the persistence and savagery with which the communists attacked the Church and its priests as symbols of the order they wished to overthrow. In reaction, many officers of the Royal Army joined the Sacred Union of Greek Officers (I.D.E.A.)[2] whose aim was to prevent any rebirth of the communist threat and whose spirit was expressed, as its title implied, in a passionate devotion to the Church, the Army and the Greek nation they both represented.

To some of its members, without doubt, I.D.E.A. was little more than a political weapon with which to keep the Army solidly right wing and threaten the quarrelling politicians with retribution. To others, however, the religious element was genuinely significant— and many of the men who were later to become the colonels were of that cast. They were, and remained, mostly pious men, devout to the point of bigotry and mistrustful of anything that did not conform to the purest Orthodox tradition. By the same token, however, they were also reformers—fundamentalist, puritanical and equally opposed to the corrosive effects of worldliness in the Church establishment and lack of moral worth in the political servants of the State. Some of them became members of a lay organization founded at about the same time as I.D.E.A. and calling itself the Greek Light (*Ellinikon Phos*)—itself one of several progeny of an older, religious group known as Zoi which was actively promoting church reform and the teaching of the catechism in Greek schools. Historically, Zoi had been a theological response to the decadence of Greek society and politics before and after the Smyrna débâcle, seeking to restore the traditional values of Orthodox Christian leadership to a nation that seemed to have lost its way. But partly because of the necessary unity in the Orthodox tradition between the affairs of Church and State, it became the sponsor of a number of lay movements which—like I.D.E.A. in the Army—flourished especially in reaction to the communist threat during and after the Civil War. The Greek Light was one of these—a movement akin in some ways to Moral Rearmament in the Protestant world, to Opus Dei among Roman Catholics and to some of the offshoots of the Muslim Brotherhood in Arab countries—dedicated to indoctrinating men of potential influence and authority with what it called the 'Greek Christian Spirit'. Among its spiritual godfathers was the priest appointed by King Paul during the Civil War to the influential post of chaplain and confessor to the Royal Household, Kotsonis Ieronymos. Twenty years later he was to emerge under the colonels' regime as the new Archbishop of Athens and head of the Church in Greece, while the aims of the Greek Light were to be transposed into one of the colonels' favourite slogans—'A Greece of Christian Greeks'.

R

Thus, long before they seized power the colonels-that-were-to-be had acquired by instinct, faith and experience most of the significant attitudes of their maturity. We have only to recall again the state of affairs in Greece in the few years immediately before April 1967, to recognize how deep an affront it must have seemed to their *philotimo*. In that frenetic context there needs no recourse to conspiratorial theories about the C.I.A. to see that something like the colonels' backlash was always on the cards.

Set in this social, professional and historical context the colonels looked a good deal less villainous than they were commonly made to seem outside Greece. They displayed plenty of the higher lunacies, to be sure, both in their moral zeal and their political illiteracy. It was difficult not to laugh when they ruled that mini-skirts were immoral, or when they banned the innocent Greek pastime of plate-smashing in *bouzouki* bars (usually performed with faulty crockery bought cheap for the purpose) because it might convince foreign visitors that Greeks were uncivilized. It was just as hard not to wonder sometimes whether Mr. Papadopoulos knew what on earth he was talking about in some of his high-flown ideological essays couched in the most pompous form of *katharevousa*—for nobody else seemed quite able to follow the intricacies of his thought through the tortuous convolutions of his language. But none of this was strange to Greece. Pomposity of rhetoric had been familiar there since Pericles; short skirts had been banned before, by General Pangalos in 1926; and as Kevin Andrews records in his delightful guide to Athens, Greek officials in the 1930's cut down the palm trees in Omonia Square because they thought they looked 'too African' and the police in Mykonos some twenty years later forbade the playing of Cycladic bagpipes there because 'foreigners will think us Mau-Mau'.[3]

In fact, the more closely the colonels were examined the more characteristically Greek did they appear, being not so much fascist as genuinely populist in their attitudes, combining moral conservatism, anti-establishment radicalism and a bombastic, simple-minded nationalism in a fair reflection of the prejudices and ambitions of many ordinary Greeks. However incredulous foreigners might be, for example, about the colonels' early talk of averting a threatened communist take-over, many of their domestic audience reacted differently. For them, the booming echo-chamber of recent Greek history had helped to make the threat seem alive again, however illusory it may have been in reality; and its proclaimed defeat was welcomed

with genuine relief, especially by the wealthier Athenians and many
of the poorer country-folk, who both remembered with a special
bitterness what the communists had done twenty years before. Similarly, the end of chaos—or at any rate the return of order—in both
the streets and the administration was greeted as a special boon by
many ordinary citizens of Athens. 'Believe me,' one fairly humble
acquaintance told me a few months after the *coup*, 'I think it's better
now. I'm not a politician. I'm only interested in my wife and family
—and for me, it's better. When I come to work, the bus is there to
bring me. Nobody strikes, nobody throws stones. Not like before—
that was terrible, terrible!' He was a man I had known for several
years, and when I reminded him that 'before' he had been an ardent
supporter of George Papandreou whom the colonels at that moment
held under house arrest, he shrugged: 'I know. I *like* Papandreou.
But believe me, this is better.'

In terms of material self-interest he was right. Many of the martial
orders issued by the colonels seemed either trivial or repressive, yet
they conveyed a sense of strength and discipline to which many
weary Greeks were willing for the present to respond. A lot of schoolgirls went on wearing mini-skirts regardless of the colonels' disapproval, it was true, and it was not impossible to hear the sound of
plates being smashed in some *bouzouki* bars with as much gusto as
ever: but complaints to Civil Servants did get answered faster than
before, the Athens Post Office was cleared of a backlog of mail that
had been threatening to break through the floors with its weight,
and the barbed-wire entanglements of bureaucracy, nepotism and
corruption that had long surrounded a number of worthy social projects were bulldozed aside by decree. If a few thousand people had to
be locked up for the moment, a great many more were feeling all
right, Jack, as a result of such improvements. Moreover, the colonels
were as quick as any other government to grasp the value of judicious
hand-outs. They were no sooner in office than they discovered that
the previous government of Mr. Kannellopoulos had prepared a
typically inviting little measure with which it had hoped to win the
rural vote at the next election by offering a 70 per cent increase in
farmers' pensions. Within four days of the *coup* the colonels announced this measure as their own, to the understandable satisfaction
of the farmers. Other simple benefits followed. Wages went up, prices
remained stable. Road-building in the provinces and rural electrifica-
tion acquired a gratifying new momentum as the colonels deliberately
courted the favour of their own kind of people back home. Like

Mussolini in pre-war Italy they seemed bent, metaphorically speaking, upon making the trains run on time; and although such blessings were purely administrative and none too certain to last they seemed satisfying enough to many Greeks after the uncertainties and frustrations of the previous few years.

The man who best expressed this instant combination of puritanism and pragmatism was Brigadier Pattakos. Of limited experience and untrained intellect, he was in many ways the archetypal *Romios*: shrewd, humorous, petty, self-important, boasting and magnanimous by turns—the sort of man no café in Greece is ever without. He was the complete antithesis of the sophisticated, well-travelled and well-read intellectuals of Athens who made so much fun of him, but in other quarters he was often given a surprising, almost affectionate welcome. His idea of administration was typical of his numerous kind in Greece—improvisatory and wholly personal, but with an overlay of military and moral authoritarianism that made him see reform and efficiency simply as a matter of discipline. His political philosophy seemed to derive largely from folk prejudice about the virtues of godliness, obedience and short haircuts for everyone and he seemed to spend most of his time either holding rambling press conferences at which he exchanged a good deal of happy, militant or absurd banter with his questioners, or flying around the Greek countryside in a helicopter exhorting, chivvying and boasting to the peasants and officials at every stop. Typically, he displayed a passion for cleanliness and order wherever he went. His desk was always shining and bare, except for a little plastic icon; and among the mayors and police chiefs of rural Greece he soon acquired an ironic reputation as the right hand of God because he was so apt to fall upon them out of the sky and sack them if he found a garbage dump untended or a cast-off beer bottle on the beach. On one occasion he gave chase in his car through the streets of Athens to catch the wife of an American diplomat who had incautiously thrown a cigarette stub into the gutter before his outraged eyes. When he caught her he ordered her back to the spot to pick it up. At such moments Pattakos made satire redundant; yet he did the regime, if not the state, some service by lending it his intensely human—and very Greek—face.

But if Pattakos represented the regime's light relief as well as its *ad hoc* discipline, there were two other aspects of the junta's rule which possessed more serious implications. The first was its peculiarly solemn, evangelical tone, best expressed by the insistence of Mr. Papadopoulos that what he really intended was a popular revo-

lution in the name of our old friend Supergreek. Pride in Greek-ness
was the revolution's motivation, he said, and purity of Greek-ness
must be its goal. Greeks must be true, therefore, to the splendours of
their incomparable past. Three thousand years of glory must inspire
them again to greatness so that they would all be honest, hard-
working, dutiful and efficient as befitted the Hellenic-Christian tradition. Then, and only then, would they be fit for that true democracy
which, in due time, it would be the regime's privilege to restore to the
land of its birth. This was the politics of revivalism rather than of
revolution, but it carried the clear implication that until the Greek
people had changed their ways to accord with the exalted status to
which Mr. Papadopoulos called them, he and his fellow-evangelists
were there to stay.

This prospect of a long-term campaign of moral uplift was complemented by the second serious aspect of the junta's policies: an ill-
defined but firm commitment to political and social revolution that
really would change the face and nature of Greece by transforming
it into a modern state at last. The inspiration for this came not just
from the senior members of the junta, with their military pragmatism
and revivalist nationalism, but also—and in the long run perhaps
more significantly—from the powerful clique of junior officers who
had lent the regime their support. Nobody knew at first just how
many of these there were, but as time went on it appeared that besides an inner military cabinet of some fifteen or twenty officers of
the middle ranks, there was a kind of revolutionary council, sometimes called a 'captains' parliament', of perhaps 150 younger officers
whose ideas were more radical. These were mostly men of similar
social background to the colonels, but of a younger generation, more
like those other officers who had been arrested for their part in the
Aspida affair; and their basic approach was probably not far different
from that of those former colleagues. They had not fought in the Civil
War, they had not experienced Korea, so they had fewer emotional
debts to pay and no particular loyalties to honour. They represented,
therefore, a potentially 'Nasserist' element in the regime, even more
anti-establishment than the colonels and apparently determined—as
far as anyone outside their ranks could ascertain—to impose a revolution of some kind upon Greece whether the Greeks were willing
or not.

When all these strands were pulled together the policies of the
military regime became at least explicable, even if many of them
remained unlikeable or ludicrous. One thing to which all the strands

contributed was the regime's populist appeal to the under-privileged peasants of the provinces and to their cousins of the lower middle class in the town whose numbers had risen sharply as a result of the post-war reconstruction boom. Like General Metaxas in the 1930's the colonels stressed the traditional Greek virtues of loyalty to the Church, the family and the nation; and however out of date this might seem to sophisticated Athenians it had an appeal among many provincial or suburban people somewhat akin to that of, say, *Rule Britannia* for similar folk in Britain or *My Country 'Tis of Thee* among America's silent majority. The re-establishment of law and order, the provision of better pensions, higher wages and speedier rural development reinforced this emotional approach. So, too, did the anti-establishment attitude which everyone in the regime shared. There was little attempt to win co-operation from most of the old politicians or senior professional men in Athens. On the contrary, it was assumed by the regime that most people who had achieved positions of eminence or responsibility under previous parliamentary governments were probably corrupted anyway and it was as well, therefore, to see the back of them. If they did not suffer a spell in prison or Aegaean exile in consequence, they had their jobs and per- quisites removed, their publications censored and their whole life style encompassed by restrictions—a truly Boeotian vengeance upon Athenian cultural and political snobbism. Most senior officers of the armed forces were similarly treated for, however superficially alike their political outlook might be they, too, represented by virtue of their rank and style an era that, in the regime's eyes, had besmirched the fair name of Greece. King Constantine and his family were beyond trust for the same reason. Indeed, by definition they were the very pinnacle of the old establishment; and although some of the senior members of the junta probably would have preferred the King's co-operation to his resistance and eventual exile—out of a combination of past royalist loyalty and present political expediency —many of the zealous younger officers had no such qualms and were glad to see him go.

The Church establishment, also, was not immune, for the men of Zoi and the Greek Light wanted a pure Church as much as a pure State and there was no lack of scandals and abuses in and around the Greek Synod to provide them with genuine cause for its rejuvena- tion and reform. The elevation of Ieronymos to the Archbishopric of Athens was in fact only the first of many Church appointments in which the interests of Zoi and its brand of militant moralism were promoted by the new regime at the expense of some decidedly corrupt elements of the old Church establishment. The junta was quick also to root out some of the familiar Greek abuses of political favouritism and the closed shop in more mundane matters such as the issue of licences for bakeries and taxi-cabs in Athens, where certain professional men had become notoriously wealthy by artificially restricting the market. These and many other egalitarian intimations were solemnly confirmed by Mr. Papadopoulos himself, who announced with characteristic self-righteousness that henceforth nobody in Greece should earn a higher salary than he did, as the Chief Minister of the regime. In their evangelistic, humourless and authoritarian way, therefore, the colonels and their colleagues proved to be ardent levellers, at any rate in the matter of reducing Athenian pretensions; and for this reason alone they were never without popular backing. What seemed merely crude and repressive outside Greece was not invariably unwelcome inside, especially among those traditional underdogs who, like the colonels themselves, had always been excluded from the Athenian charmed circle and had grown tired of its perpetual in-fighting at their expense.

How far this support went was difficult to estimate. Opponents of the regime naturally put it at a negligible figure—10 per cent or less of the Greek people. The colonels, equally naturally, proclaimed that all Greece was behind them—while taking care not to put the matter to the vote. But on a collation of estimates and hunches which was all that anyone had to go on, it seemed in the beginning—especially if the ease with which the colonels pulled off their *coup* was any guide—that the regime might have counted on the passive (although not necessarily positive) assent of three-quarters of Greece. Six months later, when the King's attempted counter-*coup* failed, there was still little suggestion of active opposition to the colonels or support for the King, except in those establishment circles which by then had been suppressed. Even after three or four years when various underground resistance groups had made their presence known there was little evidence of widespread popular support for them. It was true that when George Papandreou died, two years after the colonels' *coup*, huge crowds estimated at up to half a million thronged the streets of Athens for his funeral, causing a momentary lightening of old political hearts at what was taken to be a gesture of defiance at the colonels' rule. But Athens was not the colonels' chosen ground. Out in the provinces they felt better appreciated; and although they continued to reject as premature all ideas of putting their popularity to the vote—preferring, indeed, to maintain martial law—it seemed probable to many experienced observers in Athens that as long as the economy was satisfactorily maintained they might count on about a quarter of Greece giving them active approval, with about the same number actively hostile, while in the middle a passive mass would go along in tolerable ease of mind and body and because it saw no immediate alternative, anyway.

In any case, head-counting was never very relevant to the regime's survival—although it could hardly have survived as easily as it did had the opposition to it been as intense as many of the old politicians suggested. What was more important was the new set of loyalties that soon began to grow around the junta. Greek financiers and businessmen learned to value far more than its strident anti-communism its ability to keep order in the streets and factories, its readiness to cut red tape and its generous tax concessions and big development projects with which it tempted them to bring back to Greece some of the capital they had previously salted away abroad. Conservative rural folk sympathized with its sententious moralism and churchmen generally found their status raised. Civil Servants of the lower grades who survived the colonels' political purges enjoyed occupying the desks of their old superiors and received additional—and usually overdue—sweeteners in the form of better pay and pensions as well. Technologists, managers and other professional men who were prepared to remain neutral in the political battle were grateful to find they could often work with less interference than before, their paths smoothed by young army officers fired by a vision of a new and efficient Greece. And—no doubt most important of all—those young officers also enjoyed their reward: heart-warming new rates of pay, together with promotion, sometimes dizzyingly rapid, to the posts from which their old, politically unreliable superiors had just been retired or exiled. Within a year or two it was noticeable that a new kind of bourgeoisie had begun to find its way to some of the most fashionable Athenian cafés. They were the wives of the army officers who had made good.

The regime was a far more complex and even representative animal, therefore, than appeared at first sight. Its military façade masked many aspects of Greece, both old and new, that were not in themselves militaristic, such as the characteristic provincial resentment of the metropolitan world which, as I have suggested already, is one of the most persistent threads in Greek history from the ancient Boeotian jealousy of the Athenians to the nineteenth-century clash between the native Greeks of the highlands and islands and the more worldly and westernized Phanariote administrators inherited by modern Greece from Ottoman times. If we follow the example of Mr. Patrick Leigh Fermor, whose account of the 'Helleno-Romaic Dilemma' was recalled in the first chapter of this book, we may also identify the traditional opposition of the Romios for the Hellene as one of the inspirations of the colonels' regime. A classification of some of the characteristic attitudes of the colonels and their most vociferous opponents along the lines of Mr. Leigh Fermor's study provides significant parallels. In its simplest terms it would look something like this:

Colonels	Opponents
Provincial	Metropolitan
Anti-bourgeois	Bourgeois
Anti-establishment	Establishment
Disciplinary	Anti-disciplinary
Ardent moralists and Orthodox Churchmen	Basically anti-Church and morally 'permissive'
Generally royalist in sympathy	Divided on the monarchy with a tendency towards anti-royalism
Passionately anti-communist	Largely anti-communist but more tolerant of leftward leanings
Emphasis on the Byzantine heritage and the image of a Hellenic-Christian Supergreek	Emphasis on the classical heritage and the image of a classical-romantic Supergreek

Dimly, perhaps, but unmistakably the narrow-minded, orientalized product of the Byzantine and Turkish past—the Romios—looms through the list on the colonels' side in opposition to the more cultivated, cosmopolitan Hellene who seems implicit in the characteristics of their opponents. But, as we have seen, no Greek is purely Romios or Hellene. Each is an uneasy amalgam of the two, at war within himself as well as with his fellows: and when we examine further the attitudes of the colonels and their Greek critics we find many disconcerting mutations between them. At the cultural level, for example, the colonels appeared to betray their Romaic tendencies by insisting on the use of the high-flown, Hellenistic *katharevousa* while their opponents generally upheld with equal warmth the value of the popular, or demotic, tongue. Similarly at the political level the junta and its critics were apt to appear in some superficially puzzling or overlapping postures. Plenty of the old Athenian politicians were equally opposed to both the colonels and the communists while the colonels soon showed in various ways—such as their readiness to restore Greek relations with Albania—that they were perfectly ready to modify their own anti-communism in the interests of the nation. Again, many of the colonels' critics were actually more loyal to the King than some of the officers who had proclaimed their *coup* in the King's name for, as we have seen already, the generally royalist sympathies of the Army were not by any means shared throughout the junta whose collective indifference to King Constantine's exile increased as time went on.

The longer the colonels remained in power and the harder they tried to build their brave new Greece, the more such confusions blurred the edges of their self-styled revolution and the more their regime seemed to reflect within itself the very tensions and problems which it had promised, or hoped, to overcome. One of the first such difficulties to make itself felt was the old Greek dilemma about 'true' or 'unfettered' independence. As staunch anti-communists the colonels were naturally committed to NATO and the West—had, indeed, seized power partly because they believed that commitment was in jeopardy. As Greek patriots, on the other hand, they vehemently rejected any foreign interference in their affairs—so much so that at times Mr. Papadopoulos sounded like Andreas Papandreou's *alter ego*. 'Greeks must stop being a nation of waiters with napkins over their arms,' was one way that Andreas had phrased his assertion of national independence a few months before the colonels' *coup*. 'We must not seek to become the summer resort of the Great Powers,' said Papadopoulos a few months afterwards. But if this implied for both men that Greece should be entitled to 'her own' foreign policy and her freedom from western restrictions as well as independence of western favours, it also begged the same questions for both: how, precisely, was Greece going to reconcile a genuinely 'unfettered' foreign policy with the security of the western alliance? And how, if the alliance was sacrificed, could she secure her independence?

Like countless other Greek leaders before them, the colonels discovered there were no easy answers to these questions. When they attempted, during their first six months in power, to settle the perennial Cyprus crisis unilaterally—hoping to consolidate their regime with the triumph of *enosis*—they succeeded merely in deepening the crisis again and, predictably, bringing Greece once more to the verge of war with Turkey. They were rescued from imminent disaster only by American intervention and the soothing diplomacy of one of the Athenian establishment they despised—Mr. Panayiotis Pipinelis, a former royalist minister who agreed to serve them by taking over the Foreign Office in the nick of time. The old lesson was again thrust home: that Greece in this matter had to choose between a war she could not win and an alliance that required the indefinite postponement of her eternal ambition to unite all Greeks under one flag. In the Council of Europe a different but equally humiliating lesson faced the colonels. Having—as they claimed—saved the West from anarchy, or worse, in Greece they were affronted to discover that the West did not thank them for it but compelled them instead to withdraw from some of its most intimate councils. 'Total' independence was, as ever, a Greek illusion; and the junta veered, like other Greek Governments had done, between the poles of defiant rejection of all foreign interference in the affairs of Greece and a reluctant compliance with the demands of the International Red Cross or other people's parliamentary missions of inquiry to be allowed to examine their prisons, their law courts, or whatever else took their fancy.

Expediency and the brute facts of life in Greece were constantly at odds with the colonels' high principles. If Greece was to become a modern nation as they wished, worthy of its place in twentieth-century Europe, it needed better education for more people. But by being so resolute in their purge of the old establishment and so strict in their censorship of Greek ideas they alienated many of Greece's best-trained minds; while their emphasis on piety and the Greek Christian spirit led to deliberate distortions in Greek schools and universities where godliness and Greek-ness were equated in a manner reminiscent of the fundamentalism of the American Bible Belt. One of their new elementary chemistry books went so far as to declare that God had made ice to float on the water out of His solicitude for the fish—hardly the best grounding for budding technologists in the 'new' Greece.

Revising the constitution also presented problems that went back to the very foundations of the modern state, starting with the perennial question of the King. Like most of his predecessors at one time or another, Constantine had been shunted into exile; yet the colonels maintained what was officially a monarchist regime with the throne held vacant for reoccupation by him—or by some other member of his family, should Constantine himself prove too stubborn to accept it on their terms. But what should those terms be? The King could hardly return as long as martial law was in force, for that would make him a mere puppet of the colonels and automatically disqualify him as a representative of national unity. On the other hand, if he returned (as he seemed to wish) only on condition that the colonels reintroduced a democratic system again would he not equally risk becoming once more a focus of political and military intrigue and patronage and therefore of factional strife? And then again, if he were never to return at all, what figure or institution could replace him as a symbol of Greek unity? Mr. Papadopoulos and many of the younger military men were believed to see an alternative in the Turkish system, as inaugurated by Ataturk and modified after the Turkish military *coup d'état* of 1961, in which an elected parliament functioned under a President whose ultimate powers were more or less openly underwritten by the Army. But the record of republican forms of government in Greece was at least as disastrous as the record of the monarchy; and there could be no guarantee that the Greek Army would stay united in republican sympathies in the future, any more than it had been able to maintain an invariably royalist outlook in the past. The Greeks had sought a foreign king in the first place, after all, because they could not agree to one of themselves occupying his symbolic role; and there was precious little indication that they had changed their ways for the better in that respect.

Nor was it easy to see how to devise a constitution, whether monarchist or republican, that would honestly combine democracy with discipline in the circumstances of Greece. The regime struggled with every appearance of sincerity to draft laws that might perform this elusive feat, but four years after its *coup d'état* the law was still martial, the press was still muzzled and Mr. Papadopoulos had declared that there would be no return to democracy of any kind until 'I, the bearer of the people's mandate . . . shall estimate that this can be done in a safe, fruitful and useful situation', whenever that might be. Even then his vision of democracy seemed by western standards distinctly partial—more akin to the 'guided' kind known in Africa or Asia than to that heady vision of classical parliamentary freedom which Greece's western friends seemed to think was the only kind appropriate to her history and their susceptibilities.

Behind these two problems of King and constitution, moreover, loomed a deeper issue, familiar to all dictatorships, of how to evolve from an extra-legal to a legal situation, from 'temporary' authoritarianism imposed for the sake of saving the nation from itself to a permanent yet flexible structure of government resting on genuine popular consent. Many of its extreme critics maintained, of course, that the regime had no intention of so evolving anyway and that the only thing to do, in consequence, was to overthrow it by violence. This seemed a counsel of despair that owed more, probably, to the frustrations of the critics than to an analysis of the Government's actions. In fact, there were several indications, apart from their own repeated assertions, that Mr. Papadopoulos and his closest colleagues genuinely wanted to re-establish some kind of democracy some time —even if, paradoxically, they wished it to remain under their ultimate control. One such early indication was the resignation of their Army commissions by Messrs. Papadopoulos, Pattakos and Makarezos soon after King Constantine's departure for Rome. Another, more significant, was the cautious 'liberalization' programme on which Mr. Papadopoulos embarked in 1970, when a few of the clauses of the new constitution (although not the most important ones) were put into effect, more political prisoners were released and a new toleration of public criticism from old right-wing politicians and newspapers became apparent. But more significant still for the long run was the creation at about the same time by Mr. Papadopoulos of a kind of 'White House' team of new and fairly young civilian officials and technocrats directly responsible to him as Prime Minister, whose work seemed to run parallel to that of the formal cabinet which was still dominated by Army officers. This development brought fierce protests from some of the regime's most intransigent military men who scented an attempt by Papadopoulos not only to recast his administration without them but also to develop his own political power base outside the Army with a view to entering an eventual electoral contest. At the merest hint of such a prospect the real problems of 'evolution' became apparent. Firstly, how would the former politicians react—or be allowed to react—if Papadopoulos contrived to form his own political party and eventually submitted himself for approval at the polls? Secondly, what would be the reaction of the officers who were excluded from this development— as some of them would have to be?

Having marched the Army back to centre stage in Greece, Mr. Papadopoulos was under a compulsion to march it off again if he was to fulfil his promise to restore a 'healthy' democracy. But with an Army that had been highly politicized for most of the 150 years of its existence this was plainly a difficult task that might become even more so as time went on and the officers became increasingly accustomed to the perquisites of power. The best that could be hoped for, probably, in the foreseeable future, was something like the Turkish system in which the Army agreed to hold a watching brief while Papadopoulos and his 'civilianized' colleagues cautiously steered the country towards an ostensibly new and improved version of democracy. On the other hand, this meant that the old politicians would probably have to be excluded from the renewal of the democratic processes, if only as the price necessary for keeping a politicized Army in its barracks. Whether this was done by decree, or by subtle legislation in the new constitution, or simply by rigging the elections whenever they took place, it would cast further doubt on the value of the regime's promises in the outside world and maintain some of the old tensions inside Greece.

Two factors, however, suggested that unless a return was made soon to an electoral system most of the old politicians would be excluded from future Greek politics, anyway: their high average age and the arrival at maturity of a new generation of Greeks upon whose loyalties they had no claim. Coupling this prospect with the likely difficulties of persuading the Army to return to its barracks it seemed that Mr. Papadopoulos had strong internal inducements for making the return to democracy in Greece a slow and measured process. Yet in the nature of Greek affairs the slow and measured tread was unlikely to be welcomed indefinitely. The characteristic Greek demand for change for its own sake might easily reassert itself in new and unpredictable ways; while the other old values and old weaknesses of the Greeks would probably frustrate the solemn intentions of Mr. Papadopoulos and his men to remake them in a visionary image of their past. For beyond all the tactical questions of political manœuvre, all the legal niceties of constitutions, all the antique disputes over monarchies and republics, soldiers and civilians, dictatorships and democracies, even Boeotians and Athenians, there lay still more fundamental Greek problems whose nature would restrict the endeavours of any government and determine much of the course of Greek history for as far ahead as anyone could see. It is to these abiding themes of Greek social, cultural and economic life that we must now turn, finally, to see what intransigent material Greece offers today to any kind of ruler—and especially to those who, like Mr. Papadopoulos and his colleagues, proclaim a revolution in the name of Supergreek.

Chapter 17

SAINTS AND PATRONS

*. . . politics in Greece have nothing to do
with principles, but are wholly personal.*
(W. MILLER)

Two images of Greece. First, a village in northern Euboea where a
local saint known as John the Russian is being given his annual air-
ing. Wizened leather and bone are all that is left of him, blackened
and repulsive, but he has a handsomely chased silver coffin and a
stained velvet cushion for his shrivelled head and for a whole week-
end each month of May his corpse is the object of much reverence
and his reputation the excuse for mild *bacchanale*. For miles around
the countryside is thronged with pilgrims. They come not only from
the island villages, but from the mainland towns of Thebes and Volos,
and even from far-away Athens and Salonika, to feast and sing,
dance and pray, to batter the day with bells and dirges, and shatter
the night with fireworks and music. There are death riders and strong
men, dancing bears and fortune-tellers and a woman who is cere-
moniously sawn in half twelve times a day. Ice-cream and meat balls,
balloons, melon seeds, spit-roast lamb and plastic icons are hawked
from dawn to dawn. As the celebration reaches its climax the dusty
lanes are lined with people to watch a procession of priests in gaudy
robes of ceremony carry the Saint in his silver coffin around the pre-
cincts of the parish. For two miles or more the procession shuffles,
chanting, through the dust, embroidered banners held shakily aloft,
the coffin swaying on strained arms and bruised shoulders, bringing
the Saint's blessing visibly to the people. Saucers of burning incense
are laid in its path. An old man with no legs is left flat on his back in
the dust to be walked over while he prays. Women on their knees
stretch out to touch the hem of a priest's golden surplice and fall back
crossing themselves and kissing their blessed fingers. A blind child is
held up reverently so that the lurching coffin strikes its head, and it
vents a howl of puzzled pain. Everywhere hands and lips are reaching
towards the sacred relic, and on the steps of the church, beneath the

jangling bells, as the procession returns from its tour women and children scramble in desperation with glazed eyes and anguished mouths for a last chance to make personal physical contact with the Saint as his guardians return him to his niche for another year.

The second image comes from Athens, a hundred miles away, in the Parliament building overlooking Constitution Square. We are outside the office of the Prime Minister of Greece and three armed guards are manning the barricades against what appears to be a siege. Thirty yards of the high-ceilinged corridor are jammed with people. Elderly countrymen with heavy boots and white-stubbled chins. City gents with brief-cases and pointed, glossy shoes. In one corner a thick knot of men jostles, argues, gesticulates, shouts, and comes alarmingly close to blows. A transistor radio slung over some-one's shoulder wails, unheeded, with *bouzouki* music. From time to time smart young men in immaculate suits and grey, paunchy elders in dark glasses and the gold-braided uniforms of senior officers, thrust importantly through the crowd, rap out a name or an order to one of the guards, and are admitted under the glare of a hundred hostile pairs of eyes to the Prime Minister's office. As the door opens, the crowd surges forward, voices raised in a confused shout, forcing the soldiers to brace themselves against the door jambs to hold them off. Occasionally, one more agile or smaller than the rest slips through like an eel before the door is closed again, and cries of protest go up from those still waiting. It is hot, and the corridor stinks of sweat and garlic. After an hour, or maybe two, the door opens again from the inside, the guards spring forward, shouting, to clear a path, a senior officer emerges, frowning through his dark glasses, an alert young man follows, fingering his brief-case importantly, and behind him comes the Prime Minister himself. At the sight of him the crowd is galvanized. A hail of welcome and a growl of complaint fuse into an echoing roar. Faces are thrust towards him, shouting, hands reach to grapple his, to seize his elbows, to detain and caress him, to touch, to make contact somehow, anyhow. He is instantly the centre of a seething mass of supplicants protected only by the hard core of his guards and acolytes. Slowly he is inched through the mob towards the exit, to his motor-car and his escape, smiling, bestowing a word here, an inclination of the head there, and painfully rescuing his hands and arms from the crushing grips of the faithful. At last he reaches his car. A final wave, a benediction, and he is gone, and the crowd subsides into muttering argument. 'I have been here for two days. When will he see me?' 'I have been here longer. He should see me first!' But the approach of lunch-time awakens new desires and gradually the corridor empties of people, leaving only the smell behind.

Both these images date from the same year, not long before the colonels' *coup*, when George Papandreou was last in office as Prime Minister of Greece. Between them, I believe, we may sense one of the most intractable aspects of modern Greek life and politics, with which every government has had to wrestle and to which all, so far, have tended to succumb. I mean the characteristic dependence of Greeks upon a sense of personal involvement with the sources of political or social power. The similarity in the Greek approach to politics and religion in this respect is striking and far from accidental. They treat saints and politicians in much the same way because both traditionally perform similar roles in Greek society. Indeed, to the sceptical eye it sometimes seems that the chief distinction between the two in Greece is simply their differential sex appeal; for whereas the saints are usually besieged by women for their favours, the politicians are more often importuned by men. In a society still dominated by peasant attitudes this is a natural division of labour. The women, bound to the hearth by the demands of their children and the social code, have neither time nor opportunity for the pursuit of the earthly powers and must perforce confine their appeals for help to the supernatural, whose aid may always be at hand. The men, on the other hand, are relieved of domestic chores and, from the village coffee-shop or the mayor's parlour right up to the office of the Prime Minister himself, they are free to lay suit to the sources of power in this world, leaving the women to placate the divinities of the next.

Both sets of suitors, however, adopt essentially the same techniques and approach their putative patrons with similar expectations. Whether they are men seeking help from the state or women asking favours of God, they are fixed in their belief that only a personal approach will be effective. Unfortunately, both God and the state are difficult to personify. Mere mortals cannot know God, by definition, any more than mere citizens can really apprehend the state—especially in its increasingly complex modern form. Both are abstractions, equally impersonal if not similarly ineffable; and the Greeks, in their warm, gregarious way, find them too aloof for comfort. In self-defence, therefore, they wrap them both in more familiar trappings, embodying God in an immense pantheon of very human saints and the state in a similar gallery of most unstatesmanlike politicians. With these they can establish a comprehensible channel of communication to the fundamentally incomprehensible.

S

I like to think that the characteristic design of Orthodox church buildings expresses this concept physically through the iconostasis, or icon screen, which stands between the congregation in the main body of the church and the sanctuary beyond, where only the priest may go to celebrate the holy mysteries of God upon the altar. The screen is the division between the world of the flesh in which the congregation dwells and the world of the spirit that belongs to God; and the rows of icons that the screen supports offer to the faithful a symbolic bridge between the two. In one aspect the icons are tangible, concrete objects, telling of the familiar personal qualities of the saints they represent, yet at the same time they possess intangible, miraculous and holy properties because they are also part of the omnipotent abstraction that is God. They may be seen and felt, kissed, wept upon or spoken to. Candles may be burned and tribute left before them, and votive objects may be hung beside them to recall to the saints—less they all-too-humanly forget—the particular favours they have been invited to perform. It is all very comforting; but it is also dangerous, because it opens the door to idolatry through the confusion of the saint's powers with those of the mysterious God with whom he communicates, as well as between the saint and the representative object itself. Thus instead of worshipping God and venerating His saints, the pious often turn to adoration of the symbols for their own sake. Relics and icons themselves become their gods, and paganism creeps in by the back door. Some of the fiercest theological battles of the Greek Church have been fought on this very issue, as when the iconoclasts a thousand years ago destroyed most of the icons in eastern Christendom because, they said, the portraits of the saints had led the faithful into just this error.[1] In the presence of such contemporary festivals as that of St. John the Russian, or the frantic worship of the Virgin on the island of Tinos, or the annual fire-walking ceremony in Macedonia, when the dancers among the red-hot charcoals clutch icons to their breasts to protect their feet from burns, it is easy to understand the iconoclastic movement, for idolatry on these occasions is never far away.

As in the Church, so in politics. If we substitute Government for God and politicians for the saints the picture is not far different. We might even liken the Greek Parliament—when there is one—to the iconostasis, simultaneously screening from each other and yet joining together the ignorant populace and the mysteries of state. Certainly the individual member of Parliament is expected in normal times to be as open and obliging to the pleas of his constituents as any saint is to the prayers of his devotees. From this a form of political idolatry often results in which the person of the politician is revered regardless of his policies, rather as holy objects may be worshipped at the expense of God. It is true that Greek politicians tend not to be idolized for long—and perhaps especially not if they are too successful, for some of their erstwhile best friends may then conspire to cut them jealously down to size. Yet although we must not push the analogy too far, it is useful to be reminded again by the likeness between the forms of Church and Government that the highly personal nature of Greek politics up to now is not an isolated phenomenon but an expression of basic social attitudes. At the core of these attitudes is the notion that social institutions of any kind function chiefly through the medium of personal favours given and received, or what is commonly called patronage. In this, of course, Greece is not unique. Many peasant societies hold a similar belief, and most supposedly sophisticated societies often do little more than disguise the same idea with a veneer of social purpose. Dictators generally flourish by promising the earth to all their people and by giving substantial pieces of it to a privileged few; and even the oldest and most stable of parliamentary democracies find that patronage of some sort is a great oiler of wheels, from the Honours List in Britain to the pork barrel in the United States. What is remarkable about Greece, however, is that the role of patronage is so important there that, whether under dictatorship or democracy, politics rarely seems to be about anything else.

It is important here to distinguish patronage from mere bribery, graft or corruption. Inevitably these can, and do, shade into each other, but the essence of the first is a sense of personal relationship, whereas the others satisfy only material desires. The distinction is implicit in the word normally used in Greece to describe the patronage process. It is *rousfetti*, meaning, roughly, personal influence. Whether for peasants or Prime Ministers, this is so widely assumed in Greece to be the normal means of advancement that it creates a kind of state within a state, simultaneously mitigating the ill effects of excessive individualism by creating its own set of social connexions, while promoting chaos in the more orthodox political and administrative world. Thus the whole formal edifice of government in Greece often seems to be rather like a fragile garden trellis that is both overwhelmed and supported by the burgeoning tendrils and sinewy roots of the creeper that grows around it—in this case the complex personal, family and clan relationships that are the real sources of power. Perhaps the key to this, as to many other apparently confusing aspects of Greece, is the characteristically seamless and egalitarian Greek view of life which recognizes no clear distinction between public and private affairs. Like the Arabs, Greeks instinctively recognize the first as merely an extension of the second—and open, therefore, to the same kind of purely personal manipulation. It is surely no accident that the word *rousfetti* has an Arabic root and a Turkish history, for in governmental methods all three peoples exhibit striking similarities. Anyone who has wrestled vainly with the opaque lunacies of administration in Cairo, Baghdad or Istanbul, only to discover that to drop the right name or recall some mutual interest will instantly open doors that previously had seemed closed for ever, will soon learn his way around the corridors of Athens.

Few Greek politicians of any complexion have managed to transcend these traditions for long, and most have never tried to do anything but continue in them with as much success as possible, both seeking and dispensing—or, at any rate, promising to dispense—their share of *rousfetti* with equal eagerness. Its forms are legion and are often linked at the grass roots level with the traditional position of the Greek 'notables'—those men of substance or acknowledged status who are apt to become father-figures in their communities. The notable is not, in the usual sense, an aristocrat, for that would imply too great an elevation above his fellow men for most Greeks to tolerate, let alone to welcome as a badge of leadership. Nor is money usually the key to his status. He may be, instead, more like an old-fashioned English squire—a member of a distinguished local family, generally getting on in years, perhaps of modest means and certainly of no great pretensions. Sometimes, especially in the past, he has been little more than an energetic bandit chieftain—the equivalent, almost, of the head of an old Scottish clan. More often, nowadays, he is a thorough-going bourgeois gentleman, admirably acquainted with the big, wide world and probably trained in one of the traditional professions such as law or medicine in which opportunity and expertise combine to create a paternal relationship with many local families. From some such bases the majority of Greek politicians have been recruited since the earliest years of the independence struggle. Almost the only important exceptions have been some of the Army officers and a few communists who, in more recent times, have climbed the ladder of power through promotion, rebellion or conspiracy—although several prominent Greek communists have also belonged essentially to the 'notable' tradition. In the last

Parliament, many leading members of the two main coalition groups, the right-wing National Radical Union and the liberal Centre Union, had long, dynastic political lines behind them, based on a family tradition of 'notability'; and most of the radicals of the Centre Union and the extreme left came from equally 'notable' or middle-class backgrounds. Out of a total of 300 deputies no fewer than 165 were lawyers, 23 were medical doctors, and 19 were retired officers of the armed forces. Nearly a third of them were between sixty and seventy-five years of age, and only a handful were under forty.

To aspire to power by popular election, however, a politician in Greece must traditionally extend the natural paternalism of his family or professional role by the deliberate exercise of material patronage, beginning as a rule with the multiple acquisition of a peculiarly Greek kinship status known as the *koumbaros*. Here again, although material rewards certainly influence the connexion, the essence of the matter is the sense of *personal* relationship. A *koumbaros* is a godbrother or godfather, a man accepted as one of the family in the sight of God. He often gains his status by acting as best man at a wedding, thus becoming godbrother to the bridegroom; but convention and the course of nature combine to offer more frequent opportunities for becoming a *koumbaros* by standing as godfather to a newborn child. The godfather is then accepted as godbrother to the actual father. Either way, the relationship is considered as close as that of a true blood brother, with all the obligations that implies. To the politician the possibilities of this convention are enormous. At one wedding or a single christening he strikes up an indissoluble alliance not only with his immediate godbrother or godchild, but with all their close blood relatives as well. With any luck, therefore, he may collect ten or a dozen votes a time, committed to him for ever—provided that he fulfils his obligations in return. This proviso, however, is both important and expensive. To begin with, it involves a substantial outlay on each ceremony, with christening gifts to babies and dowries to brides. 'As far as I am concerned,' one distinguished Cretan politician told me a few years ago, 'I've been godfather to about 700 children in the last three years, and every wedding or baptism at which I perform costs me about thirty dollars—sometimes a bit more if the family is very poor and can't afford to pay for any of the ceremony themselves.'[2] His figures were probably characteristic of most rural constituencies in Greece in the 1960's and when the weddings were added as well, at an average of, say, fifty a year, they meant that an M.P. might spend upwards of $7,500 a year on this most literal, but must acceptable, form of patronage.

Some possible consequences of this system are obvious. As the correspondent of the London *Morning Post* observed at the turn of the century, 'One prominent statesman, who had been more than once Prime Minister, has lost all his fortune in politics; another much of his, and all the leading men become poorer by going into parliamentary life. One of the most costly items of a candidature is the duty of standing godfather to the children of constituents. M. Ralles [one of the senior politicians of the day] is said to have a thousand godchildren in Attica, who are doubtless one source of his vast popularity there. . . .'[3] But this is only the beginning of the politician's obligations. The loyalty he has bought through his initial generosity must thereafter be maintained by extending the help that is properly due from the more successful or influential *koumbaros* to his weaker or poorer brothers in God. He must therefore arrange jobs for the men, examination passes for the boys and visas for those who wish to emigrate. He must find hospital beds for the sick and legal aid for those who need it. He must write letters for the illiterate, offer his telephone to all comers, and try not to forget anybodys' saint's day nor omit to send Easter greetings to all. At the same time, he must be open to the appeals of those who are not yet his god-brothers, for the most liberal and energetic of men can hardly hope to win election on the strength of his *koumbaros* connexions alone. Above all, he must be instantly and personally available at all times, for it is of the essence of his position that he is known among his people. To quote the *Morning Post* man again, 'In Greece all falls on the candidate; and if he be a barrister, as he frequently is, he is expected, when he becomes a deputy, to plead gratis for all his constituents. No wonder that one deputy died leaving debts to the tune of 500,000 drachmae.'[4] Not even Prime Ministers are excepted from these rules. Indeed, the supreme influence they can wield only redoubles the clamour of individual supplicants at their door, and although the additional responsibilities of their office force them to limit their availability more than lesser mortals, they would be thought lacking in common courtesy and, perhaps fatally, in honour if they did not in normal times set aside some part of their working day for direct consultation with the multitude.

There is, to be sure, some charm in a system that involves so much personal interdependence and leads its chief practitioners into such straitened circumstances; and in small societies such as those of the

Greek city states, where Aristotle founded his theory of democracy on the fact that all the citizens knew each other, it may work well enough. But in a nation of eight or nine million people, like Greece today, with many of the outward trappings of modernity, where administration is complex and a large bureaucracy is unavoidable, its results are both farcical and tragic. The democratic virtues of consultation and sensitivity become the vices of gross inefficiency and rank favouritism. Under the last parliamentary regime ministerial offices were crowded every day by puzzled citizens and would-be acquaintances who were seeking to circumvent a Civil Service they did not trust by direct appeal to the minister's personal ear. Ordinary M.P.s were under almost permanent siege by constituents claiming their *quid pro quo* for services rendered or votes about to be bestowed. Inevitably, many demands had to go unheard or unanswered, many supposed obligations had to be left unfulfilled, and for those who were disappointed the remedy was at hand of threatening to vote for another man next time. But equally inevitably, an elected member could always do more than his opponent in the wilderness, especially if he belonged to the ruling faction, for he was the man who might hold the key to the treasure chests of government patronage. His word might hire or fire a Civil Servant or a policeman, appoint a schoolteacher, secure a farmer's bank loan, and in a hundred other ways obtain that advancement that every man desired— or even threaten that demotion that everyone feared. Ordinary voters and officials alike therefore had every reason of self-interest to support the government man, as long as he was in office, and—when elections came round again—to assess carefully the chances of the respective candidates and ensure that they climbed in good time aboard the winner's bandwagon.

At first sight it might seem that such a system would have virtually guaranteed any government against defeat, for once it was in office it needed only to exploit its patronage to the utmost to ensure its permanent hold on power. In practice it usually had the opposite result. Instead of power being self-perpetuating it tended to be self-destructive. And this not for any moral reason, like Acton's aphorism about all power corrupting and absolute power corrupting absolutely, but simply because the system rested on everyone having his turn at the trough. No government could satisfy everybody all the time. If it failed to fulfil its promises of patronage it made enemies of those who were previously its friends. If it fulfilled all its promises it would almost certainly go bankrupt; and if it fulfilled some and not others it antagonized the people whom it had set aside. As the months and years of office went by, therefore, it was not the friends but the enemies who multiplied. The men and the parties out of office became increasingly conscious of their wasting assets. Remote from the official sources of patronage they could only survive by feeding the discontent of those whom the government appeared to neglect and promising more when their turn came, with the implication that those who faithfully supported them in adversity would be especially rewarded. Given the Greek capacity for rhetoric, belief in conspiracy, and love of opposition for its own sake, it was usually no time before the situation was depicted in terms of the wildest allegations of corruption and oppression on the part of the rulers of the day, and equally wild visions of the heaven that lay in store if only they could be got rid of. In short, more of the same, only for another lot of people.

The results of all these attitudes compounded their origins in a vicious circle of cause and effect. The mistrust of impersonal administration which led Greeks to make personal helpmeets, mentors and father-figures of their officials and public men only made impossible the creation of an administration that might have been worthy of trust. To satisfy the demands of their supporters, in fact, Greek politicians were often compelled to undermine the very institutions they were supposed to be supporting. 'With a few exceptions,' wrote our correspondent of seventy years ago, '. . . practically every official in the country is liable to dismissal, or removal to a less desirable post, on the accession of every new Government to power. Hence the whole Civil Service of the country is affected by party politics, and every official, however petty, has to follow attentively the political barometer at Athens, because his bread depends upon its movements. . . . Day by day, after a ministerial crisis, the official printing press groans with lists of judges moved to make way for political adherents, of wretched teachers in intermediate schools deprived of their ill-paid posts at the instance of ministerial partisans, of civil servants discharged in favour of others more in touch with the new Ministry. Even the most unlikely posts, such as that of librarian of the National Library, are given for party services. . . . The effect of this system is disastrous to all sound administration, and the Greeks of all parties condemn it—in the abstract—and practise it when they have the chance.'[5]

Not much has changed between then and now. Widespread purges of the Civil Service and of the officer corps of the armed forces have continued to accompany most significant changes of government in Greece as the new men have asserted their rights of patronage. For a few years in the 1950's the habit seemed to some people to have been broken under the conservative regime of Papagos and Karamanlis, but that proved to be an illusion. Indeed, with the massive American economic aid to Greece enjoyed by that regime there was probably more patronage dispensed in those years than in any other decade in Greek history. Karamanlis and his supporters, especially, could build more roads, open more houses, pay more teachers, install more janitors, send more second cousins overseas as students and appoint more godbrothers to the local police forces than anyone had ever done before; and at bottom, I suspect, that may be why they lasted as long as they did, winning three general elections in a row. But when they succumbed at last to the gathering enmity of those who had not shared in this generous dispersal of *rousfetti* the victors turned the tables in the usual way by purging the losers' men and promoting their own. After the military *coup d'état*, Colonel Papadopoulos described as an example of what had been going on the state of affairs discovered by his minions at a small Ministry of Commerce office in Piraeus, where dockers were engaged to work in the port. There were, he announced, with a reasonable show of indignation, '800 employees on the books, none of whom was a labourer. They were all educated persons, and none was on the premises. When the (new) Minister called them together he found himself in a room where the heads were so close together that if a lemon were dropped it could not fall on the floor.'

It was not only at the grass roots, moreover, or within the civil and military services, that patronage maintained political loyalty. The rulers were equally susceptible to its effects. Like the voters who climbed on to the bandwagon of a winning candidate, the men they voted for were often just as eager to get aboard the bandwagon of the winning party—and as ready to get off again at the first whiff of defeat. Half the members of the various cabinets under Karamanlis were in opposition to him at one time or another but were tempted to serve him by the blandishments of office. At this topmost level of politics patronage often stemmed directly from the King, whose right to choose his ministers or to call elections without reference to Parliament was written into all monarchist constitutions in Greece until 1967. The frequency with which most Greek governments crumbled gave successive kings plenty of opportunity to exercise this prerogative—at least, when they were not themselves in exile as a result of exercising it injudiciously—and the recipients of the royal accolade naturally made the best of their brief good fortune by promoting various privileges for themselves. Every Prime Minister, for example, even if he was no more than a 'caretaker' official appointed for a few weeks to supervise a new election, was entitled by law to a chauffeur-driven government limousine for the rest of his life; and at the time of the 1967 *coup d'état* the colonels did not fail to exploit in their favour the fact that there were then at least ten such privileged gentlemen still alive. Similarly, ordinary Members of Parliament who never achieved ministerial office sought their share of patronage out of the workings of the government machine. Not everyone, after all, could afford to spend $7,500 a year on other people's weddings and christenings solely for the honour of sitting on a leather bench and being looked up to by the multitude. Hence, Greek parliamentarians voted themselves privileges that in some other western democracies would have caused a strenuous public outcry. They enjoyed, for example, total legal immunity for anything they said, whether inside or outside Parliament. No action for libel or scandal could touch them. Their salaries, by Greek standards, were extremely generous —£4,500 ($10,800) a year in the 1960's. In purchasing power this was two or three times as much as their British counterparts were earning and was roughly comparable to the pay of a Washington Congressman, although Greece was plainly unable to afford public salaries at American levels—especially as each deputy represented only half as many people as his parliamentary counterpart in Britain. At one time or another they had also voted themselves guaranteed life pensions, free postal, telephone and telegraph services and free travel on all Greek ships, trains and aeroplanes—which, as the Athens correspondent of *The Times* remarked sourly in 1966, 'explains their frequent week-end visits to Rome, Paris and London'. When the colonels' *coup* overtook them they were just about to add to this list the further distinction of being able to buy land on highly favourable terms.

Some of these privileges were probably justified, but they were widely abused. Free postal facilities, for example, may have been necessary to meet the constant demands of constituents for help in writing to government officials or telephoning from Athens to ailing relatives at home. But they also helped in such less obviously pressing matters as sending out an M.P.'s seasonal political greetings. One Piraeus deputy who polled only 12,000 votes in the 1964 elections sent out 22,000 free 'Happy Easter' telegrams to his constituents the following year. In all, the bill for Parliament's free postal services alone came to about £800,000 ($1,920,000) for a single year in 1965 —an average of over £2,500 ($6,000) for each of 300 deputies, and something like 12½ new pence (30 cents) for every man, woman and child in Greece.

Direct graft, in the sense of making hard cash out of dishonest dealings, has usually been less common among Greek politicians, although it was not unusual in later years for M.P.s to be 'retained' discreetly by interested parties outside Parliament, such as wealthy bankers and shipowners. The reasons for this comparative restraint are, I think, deeply rooted in traditional Greek attitudes. In the first place, the individual *philotimo* of politicians is usually no less strong than that of other Greeks, and it does not easily permit them to be outrageously crooked. But secondly, the expectation of financial reward, whether illicitly obtained or not, is not the main reason for most men's entry into politics. To quote again the Cretan deputy who spent so much on weddings and christenings: 'People go into politics because the society is geared towards political discussion and politics in general.' In other words, political success is recognized as desirable in itself—a potent source of prestige and therefore a true satisfaction of an individual's *philotimo*. Yet the chief measure of political success has always been the extent of personal influence that a man can exercise. Accordingly, it was usual for most successful ministers or government M.P.s, after installing a few members of their own family in sinecure posts, to inaugurate some form of public works in their constituency. This form of pork-barrelling is almost invariably the explanation for those curious stretches of tarmac road that still appear and disappear, apparently without rhyme or reason, on the otherwise rough, unsurfaced tracks of the remoter reaches of the Greek highlands and islands. Their construction doubtless gave employment to a number of men and a contract, probably, to some especially important supporter of a local M.P.

Through all these deeds and attitudes Greece acquired an unenviable tradition of what was sometimes called 'the party state'—a machinery of government that was openly and apparently shamelessly run in the first place for the temporary benefit of the men in power and those who placed them there, and secondly—if at all—on behalf of the nation as a whole. It was a state in which the Civil Service was kept in disorder by the constant threat of political purge, where the police could be employed for party purposes, where Parliament was discredited by the ambitions of its own members, where public funds were diverted to private ends and no one from the King to the coffee-boy was expected—or permitted—to remain above the factional battle. Yet it was a state which reflected with considerable accuracy many of the vices and virtues of the Greek society from which it sprang—its intense individualism and corporate anarchy, its human abhorrence of institutional anonymity and its consequent slavery to personal influence and patronage. It may seem to those of us who live in more stable and economically developed societies to have been as politically primitive as that of, say, eighteenth-century England, whose rotten boroughs and patriarchal politicians in some ways it closely resembled: yet it answered many deeply felt Greek needs and it has so far defeated every attempt to change it either by reform or revolution.

When George Papandreou came to power at last in 1963, pledged to clean up what he called the corruption and favouritism of the Karamanlis regime, he was, I believe, perfectly sincere—like many other Greek reformers before him. But it was not long before he had antagonized half his own cabinet by advancing his son, Andreas, as his political as well as his natural heir; and it took him only a little longer, as we have seen, to infuriate the King, the Army and many in the Civil Service by his efforts to exercise his own kind of patronage there. His unusually lengthy spell in opposition had left him with unusually large political debts to pay, and they were paid in the traditional Greek way. When he left office again in the resulting crisis of 1965 his opponents made matters even worse. The King's patronage was exercised more openly than ever to break Papandreou's parliamentary strength, tempting many of his disgruntled associates to abandon him for the spoils of office. Yet many of these 'apostates', as they were bitterly christened by their old colleagues, were not dishonourable men: they were simply working within an old Greek tradition; and if some of them afterwards acquired a reputation for unusual venality as well as political fickleness, that was probably because the fierceness of the passions aroused by then blinded them to some of the system's customary restraints.

Upon this scene of unbridled patronage and administrative confusion, where the welfare of the State seemed forgotten in the welter of personal ambition, the military men descended in 1967 like the iconoclasts of old, puritanically denouncing idolatry. They declared their contempt for the entire system and their intention to replace it with honest, impartial and efficient administration in the sacred name of Greece. But, as reformers and prophets have so often discovered, it is one thing to be against sin and quite another to abolish it. The colonels certainly hastened some of the processes of decision in government and succeeded in isolating senior Civil Servants and their ministers from the direct popular pressure of the crowds who used to besiege their offices. No longer were there daily jams in the corridor outside the Prime Minister's office, like the one I described at the start of this chapter—and not only for security reasons, as the Athenian cynics suggested, but because they would have affronted Mr. Papadopoulos's sense of administrative propriety and con-demned his regime in his own eyes as no different from the rest. The bureaucratic virtues of 'the proper channels', clean desks and empty in-trays were symbols of progress to Greece's new rulers—and heaven knows, one can see why. Yet even where they were enforced their true effectiveness was limited. Most Greeks remained both sceptical and conservative; and although they might welcome the prompt (and sometimes draconian) bureaucratic answer to their complaints and appeals they still craved the personal touch. So nobody in Athens was surprised to find that within six months of the colonels' *coup d'état* some ordinary citizens were beginning to grumble not at the unfairness or harshness of the new regime but simply at the absence of the familiar parliamentary channels of personal influence through which they were accustomed to doing their business with the State. As for the old M.P.s themselves, they too were still seeking old forms of *rousfetti*, wearing out the carpets and the patience of several foreign ambassadors—as their forefathers had done before them since 1821—in urging intervention from overseas on *their* behalf.

More seriously, the colonels reaffirmed the tradition of the 'party state' more rigorously than ever by the way they set about trying to destroy it. Naturally, they argued that only a thorough sweep of subversive or incompetent elements in the administration could per-mit their revolution to go forward; and, naturally, their argument sometimes carried conviction. There were, indeed, plenty of time-servers and place-men who could very well be spared. But the regime threw out so many babies with the bathwater in its obsessive political purges that the overall administration was as much weakened as cleansed. Moreover, in the search for 'reliable' men to take the place of those dismissed both in the civil and military services, old-fashioned patronage crept in again by the back door. The purges were exploited by some officials to satisfy personal vendettas against others, and then to appoint themselves or their friends to the vacant posts. Within a year there were grumbles that increasing numbers of jobs were actually being filled by relatives or friends of the new rulers themselves; and that disproportionate sums of public money were being spent in the home towns of influential Army officers. Within two years one of the regime's most obedient newspapers felt impelled to write, in a moment of comparatively unbuttoned frankness under the colonels' censorship, that when the Greeks saw corruption in their midst they expected their share of the loot: 'When they see their rulers appoint to key posts their own brothers or brothers-in-law, or maintain incompetent bugbears in other positions, or nominate their personal physicians as professors or hospital directors, naturally they are influenced by the evil example and demand similar favours for themselves.'[6]

Naturally. But it would be equally natural to argue that the rulers had been driven into their evil ways by the demands reaching them from the people they tried to rule. Which comes first, the chicken or the egg? Perhaps it does not greatly matter. The expectation of personal patronage is rooted in the whole structure and outlook of Greek life; and just as the iconoclasts did not succeed in eradicating Greek idolatry by force, so the military men have not been able yet to eliminate *rousfetti* by decree. Nor will they, I fancy, until the social life of Greece has undergone a far greater change than anything it has experienced until now.

Chapter 18

THE LOST RENAISSANCE

Hellenism as applied to a work of art is a
big word to use. . . .
(George Seferis)

Stupefied by a surfeit of classical relics, the tourist in Athens usually escapes to the highlands and islands of Greece with such relief that he never realizes he has missed the National Art Gallery. The omission is not surprising, for the building that goes by that name in Athens is a humble little place by western standards. Although new and elegant enough in its contemporary style, it is physically dwarfed by the neighbouring Hilton Hotel, an edifice of much greater significance for the modern, international world; and the modest nature of its contents reflects the poignant fact that until just a year or two ago Athens was almost alone among European capitals in possessing no National Art Gallery whatever.

Much of the story of modern Greece is implicit in that lacuna. The great collection of works by known, individual artists in the style of the Louvre or London's National Gallery is essentially a western invention, created out of the Renaissance and the development of a moneyed society. Until quite recently Greece had experienced little of those transformations. Far away in the distant past there had been the cultural explosion of the classical world, followed after an interval by the oriental flowering of Byzantium. But the rest was silence. When the incipient, new nation-states west of the Adriatic were revelling in their Renaissance, Greece was suffering in provincial vassalage under the Turks. When aristocrats and prosperous burghers from London to St. Petersburg were filling their mansions with paintings and *objets d'art*, Greek culture was in the hands of mountain bandits and village priests. While the Church of Rome was the patron for many a great new individual artist, the Church of Constantinople could do no more than preserve, with dwindling conviction and increasing rigidity, the anonymous traditions of its early fresco and icon painters. And when, in the nineteenth century, the imperial powers of the West were plundering the whole globe for their artistic collections, Greece had just emerged into a troubled new independence, too poor and preoccupied to join the action. Small wonder, then, that there was no proper Art Gallery in Athens for nearly a century and a half. There could be museums of archaeology and Byzantine painting, and of decorative folk culture, too; but there could be no Art Gallery because in the rather selective sense that the western world had come to attach to the word, there was, as near as could be, no Art.

The absence of the Renaissance in Greece, symbolized by this artistic hiatus, has had profound cultural consequences in the Greek intellectual world. On the one hand, as we have seen elsewhere, it led to an exaggerated respect among many sophisticated Greeks for the distant classical heritage which had inspired the Renaissance in the West, and hence to a self-conscious attempt to resuscitate its style as being rightly and peculiarly 'Greek'. On the other hand, it left the traditions of the Eastern Church intact in all their aloofness from—and suspicion of—western thought and action. The two streams of thought were radically inconsistent with each other, and at the same time were equally conservative and backward-looking. Torn between them, as Greece has been throughout much of her modern independence, most artistic creativity faltered into mere imitativeness or inhibited silence. Not until the 1950's, for example, did any Greek sculptor of note escape from the tyranny of the classical style and craftsmanship in marble. Painting was almost totally neglected for over a century; architecture slavishly followed classical patterns—except in the churches, where the Byzantine style was mandatory—and with the exception of a handful of nineteenth-century poets whose names are still treated with respect in Greece, creative literature was largely moribund until after the First World War.

For Greek writers there was a special handicap, directly resulting from the worship of the classical Hellenic legend and its supposedly western attributes. This was the paralysing gulf between demotic Greek, or Greek as it was popularly spoken, and the *katharevousa*, or 'pure' form of Greek as it was supposed to be written—the legacy of Sir Steven Runciman's 'evil genius', Korais. The popular tongue had evolved naturally down the centuries until it was less like classical Greek than modern English is like the language of Chaucer. So when *katharevousa* was adopted as the official language of the new state, as a sign of Hellenic legitimacy, a fresh rift was opened in the Greek body politic between the intellectual, westernized minority who could use it and the majority of ordinary people who could not. The immediate effect of this was a disastrous cultural snobbery. To speak, and still more to write, in the new, 'pure' form was taken as a sign of superior, 'western' culture. To use the popular language was to reveal an inferior, 'oriental' mind. Accordingly, as George Seferis has written, the purists tried 'with touching obstinacy, with sweat and toil . . . to purify the national language from the stains of "barbarism" and hoped that slowly but surely we would attain once more the language and the art of Sophocles and Plato. And their reward was what might have been expected—a destruction and drying up of Hellenism's fairest and truest streams'.[1]

The cultural snobbery of *katharevousa* also acquired political overtones. The 'pure' language was that of the ruling class—the educated minority who had travelled in western Europe and who monopolized positions of power and influence in Athens. It was the language of officialdom, of every pipsqueak mandarin who sought to impress his superiors with his culture and his inferiors with his power. It was the language of the royal court—when Greece's imported royalty learned to speak Greek. It was the language of most of the newspapers, and of Parliament as well. And inevitably it became the compulsory language of the schools and universities, so that teachers and professors were made front-line agents in the international conspiracy to turn Greeks back to their mythical golden age.

But most Greeks were not disposed to turn back—any more than most Irishmen were willing to apply themselves to learning the language of their ancestors when the Irish Republic made the teaching of Gaelic compulsory in its schools half a century ago. Obstinately, but humanly, they went on using the language they had grown up with, and which had grown up with them; and in the natural course of the Greek political struggle the two languages became an issue on the hustings. *Katharevousa* became not merely the language of the ruling class, but especially of its more conservative sector whose members were accustomed to appeal to the idea of authority in all things and who saw the 'pure' language as the embodiment of the national authority that was vested uniquely in the Hellenic past. The cause of the demotic, on the other hand, was generally espoused by the more permissive or liberal politicians. Soon a new symbolism arose from this conflict, whereby *katharevousa* stood, broadly speaking, for conservatives and monarchists while the demotic represented the liberals and republicans. Like most Greek divisions this was by no means clear cut. There were representatives of each group to be

T

found on opposite sides of the fence, for republicans could often be as authoritarian as monarchists and liberals were sometimes as much attached as any conservative to the glories of Hellenism.[2] Nevertheless, like the monarchist-republican schism itself, the quarrel over the language created its own myths and repeatedly divided the nation along apparently irreconcilable lines. The depth of feeling on the issue was intense enough to cause the fall of one government when there were riots in Athens in 1901 over the appearance of a translation of the New Testament in demotic Greek; and many another, before and after, was rocked by the same passions. The rivalry of Venizelos and King Constantine during the First World War was deepened by the devotion of the first to the demotic end and of the second to *katharevousa*. In the Second World War the communists used their support of the popular language to win recruits from their monarchist and right-wing rivals who stuck rigorously to the cause of 'purism', and for many years the communist newspaper *Avghi* ('The Dawn') was the only one in Greece to be printed in demotic Greek. More recently the language was again an issue in the rise and fall of George Papandreou who, in 1964, swept *katharevousa* out of the schools in favour of the demotic—only to see the colonels sweep it back again, three years later, in the name of their Hellenic-Christian heritage. In such an atmosphere of dissension literature could not help but suffer, for while most Greek writers preferred the natural and flexible demotic tongue to the artificial and relatively inflexible *katharevousa*, their use of it set them at odds with a large part of their natural audience among the educated and professional classes of Greece, to whom the 'pure' language was a badge of Hellenic identity.

The confusion and stagnation resulting from these cultural tensions were deepened by other handicaps. In such a small and poor country as Greece no artist could sustain himself on his work alone. There were no patrons for the painters and too few readers for the writers; and most people abroad who were interested in Greece were for a long time too obsessed with the classical culture to care about more contemporary efforts. The constant turmoil of Greek politics was damaging, too, especially in this century and especially to the writers. Quite apart from the vexatious language question, censorship was a recurring threat from one dictatorship or another; and in moments of relative freedom, some of the social and political crises of the nation proved too acute to be transmuted into art. The Anatolian disaster of 1922 spawned no more than a heap of indifferent novels between the wars, I believe, as writers tried and failed to grapple with the immensity of the notion that the last post of Byzantium had been sounded in the smoke of Smyrna. The succeeding traumas of the German occupation and the Civil War went even deeper, shocking most Greek artists into silence. Like Ireland, in James Joyce's phrase, Greece had become by then the sow that ate its own farrow and like their Irish counterparts many of the best Greek artists found exile their only salvation. According to Nanos Valaoritis, a poet who was in his mid-twenties during the terrible decade of the 1940's, the events of those days and their aftermath 'caused an unparalleled panic and catastrophe' in the Greek cultural world. 'A substantial part of the intellectual capital of the country went to live abroad. Those who remained in Greece withdrew into themselves or went to pieces under the pressure of an unbearable atmosphere of collective guilt. The shift of interests into tourism and commercialism increased the general contempt for everything intellectual. The policeman and the hotel-keeper set the tone. . . .'[3] Not until Kazantzakis wrote *The Fratricides* did any Greek writer seriously attempt to deal with the Civil War in a work of fiction. And that was written in exile, like most of the rest of his work, and was only published posthumously, fifteen years after the war had ended.

But if the blight of the Greek past and the tragedy of the Greek present fell painfully upon the nation's artists, they dropped with even more stultifying effect upon the schools and universities of modern Greece. It is true that the schools promoted a level of simple literacy beyond what might have been expected in a country as poor as Greece, for from the very start of Greek independence every child in the country was supposed to be entitled to four years of free education—a noble gesture to the image of Greek enlightenment. It was over eighty years, however, before this became compulsory, another twenty years before Venizelos raised the minimum to six years in 1928, and nearly another forty years after that before Papandreou raised it again to nine, in 1964, to make secondary, or high school, education available to everyone for the first time. Each of these improvements, moreover—like the original provision of four free school years—looked better on paper than in practice. Scattered rural settlements, inadequate budgets, administrative incompetence, poor teacher training and equally poor pay combined to water down the educational gruel so much that even now there are schools in the remoter parts of Greece where one teacher may have as many as a hundred pupils and there is such a lack of books and elementary equipment as might make some nations in Africa or Asia blush. As a result, the literacy figures are not quite as good as they are sometimes made to appear. Most youngsters in Greece today do get enough education to make them more or less literate, but fewer of their fathers did so and far fewer of their mothers. Over a quarter of all the women of Greece are still illiterate, and the proportion rises steadily with age to 70 per cent among those over sixty-five.

The real weakness, however, has been not so much the quantity as the quality of the education. The first was probably as much as Greece could genuinely afford. The second was grievously distorted by the demands of artificial Hellenism. Wedded to the compulsory use of *katharevousa* from the start, the Greek pedagogues of the last 150 years have spent most of their time reviving the classics. Ancient Greek and Latin at school, more ancient Greek with law, theology or out-of-date medicine at the university—these have been, and to a great extent still are, the staple diet of most Greek students. Even in the so-called Science High Schools, of which there are only a handful in Greece, as much time is devoted to the study of ancient Greek as to the Natural Sciences. In the Classical High Schools where the vast majority of Greeks must perforce get what passes for their secondary education, ancient Greek and Latin together command three times as many teaching hours as any other subject. At the universities of Athens and Salonika, too, ten or twelve hours a week must be devoted by everyone to the study of ancient Greek and Latin, and both books and lectures in most of the other subjects are presented in the artificial classicism of *katharevousa*. The students have endured all this because they had to if they aspired to any professional job; yet at the same time, particularly in recent years, they have sought alternatives of necessity. Private academies called *phrontisteiria* have flourished side by side with the public schools, feeding—often exorbitantly and with highly dubious results—upon the students' urge to fill the gaps left by their official teachers. Foreign language schools especially are inundated with paying pupils, for the students know that, however glorious the Greek language may be, it butters no parsnips nowadays in the competitive worlds of international learning and global commerce.

Thousands of the best students end by going abroad, often never to return. This, too, is an old Greek tradition. Ever since the nineteenth century there has been a custom among the Greek élite of starting their children's education with a foreign nanny—usually English—and finishing it at a foreign—and preferably German—

university. Lately the number of nannies has shrunk somewhat, I fancy, although a few can still be seen in the Zappeion Gardens in Athens of a morning, soberly uniformed and agreeably occupied in genteel converse over the heads of their little Greek charges. But the students have multiplied an hundred-fold, until they are found now at practically every university in western Europe and America; for such are the deficiencies of the Greek universities that ever since about 1960 between 8,000 and 10,000 Greeks of college age have felt compelled to study abroad every year—more in proportion to Greece's total population than in any other country in the world. Some return to Greece hopeful of reforming the system and are met, as a rule, by disillusioning administrative obstruction and personal jealousy. Many prefer to escape that experience by joining the permanent Greek diaspora, thus contributing in another way to the vicious circle of inadequacy and reaction that drove them out in the first place.

Maintaining this vicious circle now are not only the outdated image of a past golden age, but a whole series of vested interests. First, the teachers and the mandarin bureaucracy, determined to put each succeeding generation through the same hoops as themselves so as to crush any youthful competition. What, after all, would their own qualifications mean any longer, if the pure spirit of *katharevousa* were to be replaced in official affairs by the corrupted cadences of the demotic, or if ancient Greek were to be abandoned—like the compulsory study of Anglo-Saxon in English universities—in favour of a course, in say, molecular biology or modern economics? More to the point than that, perhaps, who would teach such new subjects? There is not, I am assured, a decent course to be had in a Greek university on contemporary economics, most science teaching has not got beyond the 1930's, and some Professors of History believe, understandably enough, that everything that has happened in the world since 1912 is too politically controversial to be taught at all. Meanwhile, many senior academics have traditionally boosted their not-very-substantial salaries by enforcing their own out-of-date textbooks on their long-suffering students and sometimes by even more dubious means; while provincial schoolteachers have struggled to live on their hopelessly exiguous incomes and besieged such patrons as they could find for a transfer to Athens and the chance to make some money on the side. So educational institutions everywhere and at every level in Greece have continued the sorry round, with bad schools making bad teachers, and bad teachers making more bad schools, and so *ad infinitum*.

Secondly, there are the vested interests of the Orthodox Church which are, at first sight, more obscure but are socially, psychologically and even administratively just as powerful. To this day the Ministry of Education is also the Ministry of Religious Affairs, and the most powerful single body in Greek educational matters is its ministerial council, chiefly composed of elderly theologians and classicists who have devoted most of their lives to defending their hallowed system from the ravages of hopeful reformers. The council's power is as much emotional as institutional, for it is an expression of the simple fact that the Church was for so long the only embodiment of Greece. Admittedly it is fashionable in Athenian intellectual circles to mock the Church nowadays because it represents a rural obscurantism. But with many other Greeks, even now, that remains part of its strength. In the villages the local *papas* is still very often the secular as well as the religious leader of the community, much as parish priests are in other peasant societies of Europe, from the bogs of Ireland to the mountains of Spain. Even in Athens, except among the intellectuals themselves, the strength of the Church is far from broken, although it is obviously weaker. It is revealed in the packed congregations of the cathedral on Sundays, in the constant traffic of solitary worshippers in the little chapels off the crowded streets, and in the instinctive, repeated, gesture of the cross made, it seems, by every second woman in the city as she passes a chapel, glimpses an icon, gets on a bus, or steps safely off again. In affairs of government it is expressed in dozens of ways, from the great state ceremonies of Easter, when the full panoply of the Church precedes and overawes all else, to the local council meetings and even Civil Service seminars which are regularly opened with the blessing of a bishop.

These are far from being mere moments of empty pomp, as similar gestures often are in Britain and some other western countries today. In Greece they are still part of the genuine fabric of life, expressing deep convictions, as much about the nature of Greece as of God. Indeed, in so far as God is represented exclusively by the Orthodox Church—as with rare exceptions He is in Greece today—the two are literally inseparable. A man is not considered truly Greek unless he has been christened with the Church's sacraments. Legally, he can neither be married without its blessing nor divorced without its sanction. On the other hand, the Church's hierarchy is appointed by the state and many of its costs are borne by the state. From the miserable stipends of its parish priests to such exotic matters as the recent renovation of the Orthodox sections of the Church of the Holy

Sepulchre in Jerusalem, it is the Greek Government that pays the piper—even if it does not always call the tune.

In these and many other ways the role of Orthodoxy in Greece is nearer to that of Islam in the Arab world than to that of any church in a contemporary western state. Just as Arabism in the last resort is unintelligible without Islam, so is Greek-ness without the Greek Church. It is true that there are plenty of unbelieving Greeks, as there are unbelieving—and even Christian—Arabs. But their ethos is shaped by Orthodox tradition, whether they believe or not, because from the time of Constantine to the War of Independence the Church was the essential nurse and refuge of everything that was Greek.

Yet in the end, inevitably, time and circumstances have ossified the Orthodox expression of the Greek spirit. The language of the Church's liturgy did not change with that of the people. The traditions of its art grew sterile, and its architecture remained untouched by any innovations of style, material or engineering principle. The Church did not just passively miss the western Renaissance so much as actively turn its back upon it; so that when at last it emerged from the Turkish twilight it became one of the great, conservative forces in the new, independent Greece. An instinctive conservatism is still its dominant characteristic. It is symptomatic of its condition that, like many Greek teachers, Greek priests are infamously ill-educated as well as horribly underpaid. Most of them have had no more than primary schooling and live on little more than £5 ($12.00) a week—a state of affairs which, in turn, discourages the entry of brighter men to the priesthood. Its dwindling communities of monks, on Mount Athos and elsewhere, seem not so much to have renounced the world for God as to have rejected today for a fossilized yesterday; and its bishops are notoriously sceptical of both ecclesiastical and secular novelty.[4] As any visitor to Greece now can see with his own eyes, new churches and new chapels are still being built there in remarkable numbers, many of them financed by exiles who have made good and have chosen this way simultaneously to thank God and be remembered in their native town or village. But whatever new-fangled church buildings the exiles may have seen abroad, still nothing goes up in Greece that does not conform to the traditional Byzantine pattern of miniature Santa Sophias. (And not only miniatures, incidentally. Stylianos Pattakos, Deputy Prime Minister in the military junta after 1967, took the occasion of the first anniversary of the *coup d'état* to announce that the Government intended to build a replica of the original Santa Sophia somewhere just outside Athens. This would, he said, fulfil a resolution passed by the Greek National Assembly in 1829 but never carried out for lack of funds—a typical example of Greek enslavement to the past.)[5]

In bigger things, too, the Church in Greece is generally to be found among the bed-rock reactionaries of modern Christendom. More than any other of the major Christian churches today, for example— unless the Dutch Reformed Church in South Africa be counted among these—the Orthodox Church in Greece has been suspicious of the world ecumenical movement. Orthodox leaders elsewhere, and especially the Patriarch Athenagoras in Istanbul, who is nominally supreme in the Eastern Church, have made friendly noises about ecumenism. But when Athenagoras received Pope Paul in 1967, in the first visit to Constantinople by any Pope since the Middle Ages, the discontented mutterings of the Greek hierarchy were audible and found prompt support in some sections of the Athenian press. 'Greece', said the newspaper *Estia*, 'is as distrustful of references to "the perfect union of the Churches" as she is of the Patriarch's allusions to "our beloved Motherland, Turkey". The Greeks are firmly devoted to their Orthodox faith, and the Holy Synod [of Greece] is fully aware that the Slav Orthodox Churches are only waiting for the Church of Con-stantinople to involve itself in a union of the Churches under the primacy of the Pope in order to claim for themselves the leadership of the Orthodox Church.'[6] Again the echoes of history seem compul-sive and characteristic. The sarcasm at the expense of Turkey and the blatant fear that Moscow, of all places, may one day claim seniority in Orthodox affairs and thus expose the whole of the Eastern Church to the machinations of atheistic communism and the tyranny of the hated Slav—these come from some of the bitterest depths of Greek experience.

Such fears also point to a third vested interest in the archaism of Greek education which in some ways is an amalgam of the other two. I mean the common Greek belief, especially among right-wing politicians and military gentlemen, like the colonels of 1967, that to surrender one jot of Orthodoxy, spiritual or temporal, means opening the door to chaos. It is scarcely too much to say that to these people national survival depends in the last resort upon strict training in theology and philology, for in nothing else but its language and its Church does the Hellenic-Christian tradition exist. They must there-fore be protected from pollution or dilution at virtually any cost. This, in turn, helps to explain why the Church in Greece—with a few individual exceptions—was quick to lend support to the military regime after the *coup d'état* of 1967. Quite apart from the fact that its hierarchy depends upon the state for its appointments and its money and must, therefore, beware of picking quarrels with the government of the day, the Church in Greece instinctively favours conservatism in politics, anti-communism in foreign affairs, and the preservation of the rural communities where its influence is strongest. In all these purposes the colonels of the 1967 *coup* admirably suited the Church's antique book; and their talk of reviving the Hellenic-Christian spirit was pure balm to the souls of many priests who had always believed that to be their duty, anyway.

It follows from all this that the Church's influence is, for the most part, profoundly and deliberately reactionary, and that the aura of musty classicism that still emanates from Greek schoolrooms faithfully reproduces the majority of priestly views. Indeed, to them and to many other Greeks, especially of the older generations, that aura is the breath of the only truly worth-while life: the supposedly golden life of Hellenism preserved in the aspic of Byzantium.

In the second half of the twentieth century, however, such deliberate archaism is challenged from many directions. Few but the sophisticated intellectuals of Athens dismiss it entirely with contempt for, after all, it does involve the vital spark of Greek identity; but very many admit that the resulting educational system urgently needs reform. Indeed, there are few, if any, questions of public policy on which I have found such widespread agreement in Greece in recent years. Many right-wing politicians, as well as those of the left and centre, have canvassed their notions for modernizing Greek education; and economists and industrialists, faced with the realities of international competition, have condemned without exception the traditional institutions as ludicrously inappropriate to twentieth-century needs. Yet so far, most efforts at reform have been frustrated—by the vested interests of God and Mammon, by bureaucratic incompetence and folly, or by jealous political reaction. Vested interests, for example, largely nullified the attempt to create in Salonika between the wars a university which would be more liberal and up to date than the existing one in Athens. In spite of a few lingering improvements, including greater use of the demotic language, Salonika seems to have grown more like Athens with the passage of time, exhibiting the same vices of over-large classes, ill-trained teachers, professional nepotism and indifference to student interests, as well as a heavy concentration of studies in the traditional

—and potentially lucrative—disciplines of medicine and the law. Political jealousy, on the other hand, has several times accounted for the failure of other attempted reforms, whatever side happened to put them forward. When the Karamanlis Government tried to increase foreign language teaching in the high schools at the expense of theology, for example, it was not its own right-wing extremists that defeated it but supposedly liberal members of the Centre Union opposition who supported the theological students in a strike against the Government's proposals. The most crushing defeat, however, was reserved for the most far-reaching attempt at educational reform since Greek Independence was proclaimed—that of the Centre Union Government in 1964–5, under George Papandreou, which not only aroused all the vested interests and political jealousies imaginable, but fell foul of the administration's own impracticality and the Prime Minister's personal *hubris* as well.

In Greek terms Papandreou offered an educational revolution. *Katharevousa* was officially abolished as the language of instruction in the schools. New textbooks were ordered to be written in the demotic. There was to be less ancient Greek, and Latin was even made optional for those lucky few who could obtain admission to one of the Science High Schools. Everyone was to have nine years instead of only six at school and university numbers were to be raised as well. The Government also expedited the plans of its predecessor for a new university at Patras which was to be, so to speak, the new, up-to-the-minute Salonika. Humming with modern technology and swinging with the Social Sciences, it was going to outflank the last-ditch resistance of the Athenian academicians by importing Greek professors from the Massachusetts Institute of Technology or the University of California and by tempting Greek research students in London or Munich to come home and lead their country into the contemporary world at last.

Alas for such hopes. There was too little time and money and too much opposition. Increasing the school years meant raising school numbers, but there were neither teachers to teach the new pupils nor classrooms to put them in. The universities were in even worse straits, for they had already been ordered by the Karamanlis Government to increase their enrolment by a third, and Papandreou's further increase simply submerged their feeble administrations. In self-defence, teachers in schools and universities alike fell back more than ever upon their old-fashioned methods and obsolete learning, while opposition politicians—enraged as much by Papandreou's gathering of political kudos for his reforms as by the programme itself—attacked the Government for its foolish haste and its alleged betrayal of Greek traditions.

Papandreou, in turn, grew more determined to thrust his programme through at all costs; and in the heat of mutual passion practicalities were forgotten. Most Greek students and teachers abroad looked sceptically, as usual, at this scene of their countrymen eating each other and counted their blessings as they were. The official opening of the brave new University of Patras in 1966, a year after Papandreou had fallen from office, was symbolic of the shambles that was evident by then in most aspects of Greek education. For premises the university had been compelled to take over a local girls' school. For students it had only about 250 youths, most of them enrolled in elementary science courses. For the celebration, 10,000 people were invited to a ceremony held in the school assembly hall, which accommodated no more than 300. As if to rub home the lesson that more haste meant less speed, the skies opened on the day with a thunderous downpour of rain. Ministers, officials, ambassadors and professors, even King Constantine, had to fight their way through the crush to their seats. Many gave up and went home. It was a sad climax to a worthy dream—for though the university remained when the ceremonial farce was ended, and has slowly expanded its numbers and its courses ever since, it was tainted, like so much else in Greece, with the flavour of political ambition and acrimony. Twentieth-century standards of learning and efficiency, which it had been supposed to promote in Greece, seemed almost as far away as ever.

The *coup de grâce* was delivered to the Papandreou educational programme by the military junta a year later. One of their first actions was to reduce the years of compulsory schooling from Papandreou's nine to the earlier six. For this they probably had reasonable grounds, for there was evidence that this particular reform, being so over-ambitious, had done more harm than good. But their banning of books and purging of teachers, although painfully characteristic of their kind in Greece, went to wholly unnecessary extremes and were not redeemed by their more commendable efforts to stop university academics short-changing their students with their own old-fashioned texts. Equally typical and in the long run possibly more damaging still was their outright reversal of Papandreou's decree abolishing *katharevousa* in the schools. Appalled at this insult to Hellenism which, they implied, was really part of an atheist-communist plot—they promptly ordered *katharevousa* back again in all its glory and the new textbooks which had been written in the demotic were thrown out in favour of the old. Once more, the Greek past had over-whelmed the Greek present and reaction seemed supreme.

Yet here and there a few reforms had taken root, a few changes had been accepted. It is still possible, for example, that something will be made of Patras University, for even the military men recog-nize the value of modern science and have been anxious to recruit as many technical experts as possible to their administration. Then, too, as the businessmen and bankers feel the increasing draught of ex-ternal competition, especially from the Common Market, they may think it worth paying enough to induce some of the reluctant Greeks abroad to come and help them—which, in turn, might help to pro-mote better education at home. There *are* Science High Schools, although nothing like enough of them, and there *is* a generation now advancing into its thirties which one day must find itself in power and which probably feels with far more unanimity than its predecessors that the glories of the past are of increasingly dubious value to the country and that the strict formalities of *katharevousa* will have to go. Indeed, in recent years the 'pure' language has shown a tendency to retreat, anyway, before other, less artificial ways of writing and speak-ing, such as the language used by some newspapers which seems to be half-way between the popular and the 'pure', and is known as *kathomiloumeni*.

But for the real signs of change we must go back to art and the artists where—at least until the colonels came along with their wither-ing blasts of censorship—they were beginning to bloom to some pur-pose, reflecting the slow emergence of a new kind of Greek society. A more sophisticated and more urban society it was, with more cosmo-politan horizons in which, skipping as best they could the hideous memories of the Civil War, Greek writers were adopting new styles and new subjects. The poets, so I am told (for relatively few of them have been translated yet out of their restricted Greek tongue) had adopted the broken rhythms and images of what one critic called 'total modernism'. The prose writers were turning from the old problem of the end of Byzantium and the peasant society to a livelier concern with modern town life. Among painters and sculptors, whose work mercifully can speak across linguistic barriers—and is less easily censored—both the classical and Byzantine traditions have certainly been abandoned or modified beyond recognition. In the last decade or so, half a dozen young Greek sculptors have emerged, full of strength and character, using a language that is fully contemporary and international. Although it remains true that they find few patrons in Greece—whose rich men prefer, as they have always done, to buy foreign work for reasons both of snobbery and investment—there are now several small galleries in Athens where they can at least get a showing. The new National Art Gallery, although it remains little known, has been designed in the sort of modern idiom that is now displayed in many new public and private buildings in Greece, confirming that architecture, too, has escaped at last from the old straitjackets—the tyranny of the Parthenon on one side and Santa Sophia on the other. Occasionally now, as much under the military regime as before, it achieves a spare, contemporary and internationally recognizable grace and lightness that speaks as eloquently as any book or painting of a new, less hidebound outlook in some minds in Greece.

All the same, these things have not yet penetrated very far. The academic fastnesses of the schools and universities, for the most part, are as tightly guarded as ever. The peasants and the Church, most of the politicians and many of the businessmen stick to their traditional ways. To them, it is not the present or the future but the past that is still supreme—when the rest of the world moved forward while Greece, poor Greece, stood still. It may be a long time yet before many more of them either find the courage or feel sufficient need to follow the artists of Greece in exploring new mental frontiers for their country.

Chapter 19

THE DYING OLIVE TREE

'Tis the grey-leaved olive that feeds our boys.
(SOPHOCLES)

In its economy, as in so much else, modern Greece often seems a confusion of opposites. Rich in talent and poor in resources, developed in its tastes and under-developed in its capacities, it lives perennially in a state of high economic tension. Compared to many genuinely under-developed countries in the world today, Greece looks almost wealthy. What other poor nation of less than nine million people has the same reserves of native wit or such a galaxy of rich, international businessmen? Onassis, Niarchos, Livanos and the rest of the great Greek shipowners—natural successors to the merchant-pirates of the Aegaean who once kept the trade of the Ottoman Empire moving—have made both their private fortunes and the Greek merchant fleet among the largest in the world. The name of Constantine Doxiadis is known and respected wherever planners and architects meet and has been commemorated by now in new capital cities and vast civil projects in at least a score of countries. And even forgetting the money of an Onassis or the reputation of a Doxiadis, it is easy to believe, as you join in the cosmopolitan talk of the Athenian bourgeoisie at the sophisticated cafés around Kolonaki Square, that Greece has already made its way into the twentieth-century world of international culture and affluence. Yet seen from the standpoint of a mature industrial society in the West all this is apt to look peripheral to the true state of Greece—the fancy icing on a soggy cake of urban inflation and rural poverty—and if you happened to be a young man in, say, Ioannina in the Epirus, or any one of a hundred other little towns in Greece, both your mind and your belly would tell you that Greece was still, in many ways, an under-developed country.

They would not be wrong, for in spite of swift economic improvement in recent years, Greece remains at or near the bottom of nearly all the European tables of economic indicators, except the marginal ones of literacy and life expectancy. Compared to the Spanish and the

Portuguese, Greeks are both long-lived and well-lettered. But their standard of housing, at an average of nearly two persons per room, is the poorest in Europe; their average productivity and average personal incomes are not much more than a third of those for the Common Market countries, and in spite of a consistently high rate of male emigration their problems of unemployment and, more seriously, under-employment are traditionally among Europe's worst. Moreover, the internal balance, or imbalance, of the economy is in many ways typical of countries just struggling to emerge from an age-old dependence upon peasant farming. Nearly half the Greek people still live, or try to live, on the land, but they produce less than one-fifth of the country's wealth. For them, as in Sophocles's day, it may still be 'the grey-leaved olive that feeds our boys' because sometimes there is precious little else to feed them. Today Greece is said to have seventy-nine million olive trees—virtually ten to every citizen, man, woman and child—and their profusion makes Greece the third largest olive oil producer in the world, after Spain and Italy. Until only a few years ago the olive crop was probably the most important single factor in determining Greek economic performance. When the crop was good, Greece could rejoice. When it was bad, Greece suffered. In 1961, for example, there was a record olive oil production of nearly 228,000 tons and Greece's gross national income rose that year by 11 per cent. In 1962 the trees, as if in reaction, yielded one of the leanest crops on record, oil production was cut to only a quarter of the previous figure and Greece's total revenues grew by only 3 per cent—a factor which may well have had something to do with the change of government the following year, when George Papandreou vanquished Constantine Karamanlis at the polls after eleven consecutive years of right-wing government. Even now, the olive is so important as a staple food in rural Greece that normally not more than one-eighth of the total oil production can be exported, and in poor years exports may dwindle to nothing—have sometimes even been prohibited—in order to leave the farmers something to live on. No wonder that tourist guides on the Acropolis still point out, with barely a hint of mockery, the first olive tree that sprouted from the ground there when, so they say, the spear of the goddess Athene hit that sacred spot. If only the very gullible are likely to believe the story, it remains an historical truism that without the olive there would scarcely have been a classical Greek civilization; nor could there have been, until very recently, a viable modern state of Greece.

This historical dependence upon the long-lived, drought-resistant olive tree is, of course, a direct reflection of the sheer physical poverty of the Greek landscape. Only a quarter of Greece's surface is officially regarded as cultivable—less than in any other European country—and nearly half of that supports little but the tenacious olive. Only in a very few places, like the plain of Thessaly, does Greece offer large, unbroken tracts of good farmland and even there lack of capital and the traditions of family inheritance are serious obstacles to profitable farming. Sons in Greece usually share out the property of their father on his death, each taking a piece of good land along with some of the bad—or, more likely a piece of poor land along with something almost useless. Daughters, too, must have a wedding dowry which is often yet another portion of rocky soil to be added to that of their husbands. So the land is steadily fractured into ever smaller fragments, becoming a bewildering mosaic of tiny, separate holdings that defy all efforts at rational farming, provoke repeated family squabbles and hinder any attempt to buy and consolidate sizeable areas for redevelopment. When the new town of Aspra Spitia was built in the 1960's, to accompany the erection of an aluminium smelting plant on the Gulf of Corinth, it took two years to buy out the 600 smallholders concerned on a site of only 1,500 acres.[1] Over the whole of Greece the average is somewhat better than that example suggests—8 acres to every family farm. But each of these farms is itself divided, on average, into 6·5 separate plots so that there is nearly one individual landholding to every single acre of Greece.[2]

The result often appeals to the eye but is disastrous for the economy. Driving through the plains of Thessaly, for instance, can still be rather like wandering in a time machine into another century. A Renoir landscape enfolds the narrow, intruding shaft of the road with the sort of pastoral romanticism that a western visitor associates with his grandfather's youth, before the internal combustion engine changed the face of his world. In slow, green streams and shaded pools the cows stand knee-deep and bony-backed among reeds and water mint and yellow flag. The wheat-fields are bloody with poppies or shimmering with yellow marguerites. The roadsides are dusted with the pink of giant thistles and spiked with the royal blue of borage. Troops of horses swish sleepily at the flies and a row of women in full skirts and head scarves may be hoeing an empty field. A flock of sheep ambles down the road before a drover, crook and bundle over his shoulder, and a four-wheeled farm wagon is drawn up beneath a plane tree with a few merry children tumbling in its load of hay. Every cliché of the pastoral idyll is there in beauty and profusion—but to the stern, twentieth-century mind they are evidence merely of inadequate capital and plain bad husbandry. And from those follow, as the night the day, falling farm incomes, apathy and stagnation or bitterness and forced emigration.

Thessaly, however, represents some of the best of Greek farming. At its worst, the combination of man's customs with nature's cruelty has often produced a poverty in Greece of almost Asian intensity. In the isolated valleys of the Epirus, for example, or along the rocky coasts of Mani, a family may count itself fortunate to afford a chew of goat's meat once a year to celebrate the Easter festival. These two regions epitomize all that is most intractable about Greece's problems. Tucked away behind the mountains, one in the far north-west near the Albanian border, the other in the far south behind the towering Taygetus range, they both seem more isolated from the rest of Greece than is Greece itself from western Europe. They share a common tradition of feuding, brigandage and passionate independence—it was Ali Pasha in Ioannina who declared his independence of the Turks at the start of the nineteenth century and the Mavromichaelis clan from Mani who assassinated Capodistrias—and, not surprisingly, they are both historic centres of Greek emigration. In their barren little villages nowadays there is scarcely a male citizen to be seen between the ages of fifteen and sixty. Every year in the Epirus some 4,000 people reach working age, and every year 3,000 of them cannot find a job there. Successive governments have tried since the end of the Civil War to promote regional development in such places, but when you have established a cheese factory for the goats' milk from the mountains and a canning factory for the fruit from the little gardens in the valleys, you have just about exhausted their natural industrial potential. In any case, even where such little factories can be run at a profit they do not provide a man's work in the moral order of rural Greece. Those who seek a steady wage—as well as a touch of the *dolce vita*—prefer, on the whole to do it away from home, where the money is better, anyway, and no stigma of unmanliness stains a wage-slave's job. Most years in the 1960's, up to 2,000 men from the Epirus alone were leaving Greece to seek their fortunes abroad. In one coastal district, near the little port of Igoumenitsa, where the boat leaves for Italy and the fruit gardens provide a living well above the average for the region, the annual remittances from 4,000 local men in West Germany normally exceeded the whole agricultural revenue of the district.

Admittedly, none of this is altogether new. Greece, as we have

U

seen elsewhere, has a tradition of enforced emigration going back to classical times; and the men of Epirus and the Mani today are following naturally in the steps of their ancestors. But although the essential process remains unchanged, the special demands and temptations of the twentieth century have given it a new impetus in that classical contemporary disease of developing nations called the revolution of rising expectations.

This is especially the revolution of the young, to whom modern communications have revealed a world of promise such as their elders never envisaged. They hear it on the radio and see it in the cinema. They find it in the old man who flies back from America or Australia to patronize his native village with tales of good fortune and they see it in the boy who has been to work in a factory in Frankfurt or Dusseldorf and returns for a holiday in a second-hand Volkswagen to become the toast of the village café. Practically everything is grist to this revolution's mill. Every new road brings new visitors from a richer world, asking for beds and hot water. Every new bus from Athens beckons another youngster to go back with it to the bright lights and promises of the city. Only the old are content any more with the daily ritual of tric-trac in the café and family gossip in the evening stroll. The young have learned that life elsewhere can be more exciting and more prosperous, and in recent years they have been packing their cardboard suitcases in unprecedented numbers and taking to the road.

With a booming economy in western Europe to tempt them, an average of nearly 100,000 Greeks were emigrating every year in the middle 1960's—half as many again as the net annual increase in population and enough to denude the country of an entire generation within ten or fifteen years. In some ways this emigration was a blessing. By eliminating any population increase it helped to hold down unemployment to a level that could be tolerated. The money which the emigrants sent back to their families, averaging some £20 ($50) a month from every man in Germany alone, became a major credit item in the Greek balance of payments, equal to the earnings of the nation's merchant fleets and exceeding those of tourism. But in other ways the drain was a curse, for the emigrants included the most energetic young men of Greece, many of them lost for ever to their native land; and their remittances often added another twist to the ever-rising spiral of demand at home, another prod to the revolution of rising expectations.

Moreover, the flight from the villages did not necessarily lead directly overseas. The new buses and the new roads led first to Athens; and many for whom Frankfurt or Melbourne or Toronto seemed too distant settled for the delights of their own Greek capital. But the more they came, the more dubious were those delights. In the decade after the Civil War more than 300,000 people migrated to Athens from the rest of Greece, piling themselves, layer after layer, upon the old refugees from the Smyrna disaster and the tens of thousands who had fled from the fighting in the 1940's. Like an octopus, Athens seemed to spread its tentacles all over Greece, sucking up the wealth of the nation. Its suburbs sprawled outwards along the coast and up the mountain slopes behind in a hasty rash of concrete blocks, inadequate drains and unmade roads. By the mid-1960's the capital contained nearly a quarter of the population of Greece, two-thirds of the country's wealth and four-fifths of Greek industry. It had 40,000 bank clerks and 100,000 Civil Servants, and practically every administrative decision of any consequence in Greece was made within the city's confines. Its growth was both self-generating and self-defeating. The city's services were overstretched, the Government ministries were overwhelmed and the politicians inundated with demands for help. The vicious spiral of bureaucratic incompetence, unemployment and political patronage tightened as the new Athenians advanced their claims to privilege in the city while the people they had left behind in the villages jealously demanded a greater share of the country's wealth.

If the bitter poverty of the Greek earth was the first cause of all this, a second and closely related factor was the deep conservatism of Greek society. At the lower levels, it was the conservatism of the peasant farmer who had never enjoyed money, incentive or opportunity enough to change his traditional ways. At higher levels it was the conservatism of the Greek bourgeoisie, who preferred to invest what money they had in land, gold or property rather than take the risks of the productive entrepreneur—especially in their own country.

The history of political and economic instability in Greece was to them an ugly warning of the pitfalls of any other sort of investment; and if it was not an apartment block in central Athens or a grand new villa in the suburbs of Kifissia that took their fancy, it was apt to be the even more solid virtues of a flat in Monte Carlo and a good Swiss bank account. The characteristic symbols of successful enterprise, indeed, became Onassis's luxury yacht, *Christina*, frequently anchored near Athens, and the everlasting din of concrete-mixers and pile-drivers in the city—the one representing the vital escape hatch and the other the Greek faith in good, hard property. The reluctance of Greeks to invest in other ways in their own country was strengthened by their incorrigible individualism and close family loyalties. No Greek likes to put his money into someone else's hands, or to share the control of any enterprise with another. Even the biggest Greek commercial or industrial firms tended, therefore, to remain family companies, borrowing money from the banks for their expansion rather than marketing shares to the public. Thus, what native enterprise did exist was often throttled by jealousy and the lack of any capital market in which to raise money for productive investment. In consequence, the number of Greek industrialists in the modern sense could be numbered almost on one man's fingers. In 1967, 95 per cent of the country's so-called factories were little more than handicraft workshops, and less than one in a hundred employed more than fifty men.

Nepotism and red tape in the Civil Service placed other barriers in the way of Greek expansion. In 1965, seventeen different notarized documents were required before permission could be obtained in Athens to build a private house; and everyone contemplating opening a business there had to be prepared for anything up to two years' delay in securing the appropriate licences. The parliamentary system compounded all these problems, not only by its excessive dependence upon patronage in general but also by its irresponsible encouragement of special interest groups. Competition for the rural vote, in particular, fostered a process of constant political bribery with the opposition parties naturally seeking to outbid the government with promises of more farm subsidies and higher farm pensions. As long as there was an apparently bottomless well of foreign aid to draw upon this characteristic leapfrog act could be maintained without too much damage. In the decade of the 1950's, when American civil aid to Greece was at its peak, the successive right-wing governments of Papagos and Karamanlis were able to check inflation better than most other European countries. But when the American grants were stopped in 1962–3 the accumulated promises of the political struggle exceeded the Greek economy's capacity to redeem them unaided. In a sense, the whole Greek nation had by then envisaged a future above its proper station and as the 1960's rolled on the gap between economic ideals and realities widened ominously.

It is worth going back briefly to that crucial year of 1962–3 for, economically as well as politically, it was the turning-point of Greece's recent history, when not only did American aid come to an end but Greece began her association with the Common Market and the government of Karamanlis was at last defeated by George Papandreou and his Centre Union Party. The three events were closely linked. The Common Market association was deemed to be the necessary preliminary to the withdrawal of American aid—a new and hopefully a permanent manifestation of Greece's western destiny in which the common interest of the European partners in Greece's welfare would complete the process of economic development that American money had started. The United States Agency for International Development gave the change its blessing, reporting in 1963 that Greece had reached that magic point on the graph of development known as 'take-off'—a precious but ill-defined moment when economic growth becomes a self-generating affair. Reporting to Congress on the performance of forty-one countries which had been receiving American aid, the Agency placed Greece in a category with nine other countries which had 'shown substantial growth and adequate progress in limiting their needs for external assistance where it is excessive'. Accordingly the United States was recommended to close the books on its financial aid to Greece, which amounted by then to the enormous figure of $3,300 million (55 per cent devoted to civil projects) since the outbreak of the Civil War. Henceforth, said the Agency, except for defence aid amounting to about $100 million worth of military equipment annually, Greek economic development must endeavour to be self-supporting. Congress acted readily on this agreeable recommendation; and in both Washington and Athens there was a good deal of self-congratulation on so happy an outcome to the long, post-war struggle in Greece.

At first sight, the statistics marshalled in support of the change offered good grounds for optimism. Since 1950 the average annual income in Greece had nearly trebled, the annual growth rate had averaged 6 per cent—higher than almost anywhere else in Europe— nearly a quarter of the gross national product had been returned to investment, the proportion of total annual investment provided by foreign aid had fallen about 80 per cent to 10 per cent, and the drachma had become one of the strongest currencies in Europe. That Greece was ready to stand on her own feet seemed proven also by simple observation which put flesh on these statistical bones. Athens was being rebuilt almost week by week in the feverish construction boom. New shipyards were opening near Piraeus, the Esso-Pappas corporation was planning a new petro-chemical factory and oil refinery at

Salonika,[3] the new aluminium smelter on the Gulf of Corinth was under discussion and government centres of regional economic planning had been established for the Epirus, the Peloponnese and Crete. Bright young economists, sociologists and statisticians were producing bright new studies of a promising Greek future, chiefly under the direction of Andreas Papandreou, who had not then so disastrously abandoned economics for politics.[4] A small centre of atomic research had just been opened, with its very own nuclear reactor. There was a new Agricultural Bank, under an American-trained economist, to improve the financing of farm credit. And everywhere there was plain visual evidence of a new prosperity—new hotels for the expanding tourist trade, ribbon developments of private villas along the Attic shoreline, shiny new electricity meters on tiny village houses, new bicycles glittering by the hundred in little market towns, and village women drawing water in pink plastic buckets while their men sat at the café listening to Japanese transistor radios. To the traveller the most striking proof of all was the improvement in the roads. At the end of the Civil War it took twelve to fifteen hours to get from Athens to Salonika in buses that were as ramshackle as the tracks they traversed. By 1963 it took only five or six hours in a comfortable Pullman coach along a reasonable facsimile of a super-highway; and in twelve hours you could even reach the Turkish frontier, which had earlier been another full day's drive away.

Plainly, the economic engines were turning faster everywhere; and the terms of Greek association with the Common Market countries seemed eminently reasonable, offering Greece a ten-year period of absolute tariff protection within the Community, followed by a further twelve years of gradual tariff revision until, by 1984, she was to be ready to take her place as a fully-fledged member of the Market. On the face of it, therefore, this was an economically propitious moment in Greek affairs. Yet beneath the glossy surface, the country was still desperately vulnerable. The names of the other nations listed by America's A.I.D. at that time as approaching the point of economic take-off, like Greece, were a warning in themselves. They were Colombia, India, Iran, Israel, Mexico, Philippines, Taiwan, Thailand and Venezuela. However generously their achievements or their promise might be interpreted they were not exactly a comforting lot of class-mates. Rather, they were a reminder that Greece still had a dauntingly long way to go before her economy could catch up with any of the western European nations whose status she aspired to share. Her so-called industries were not only tiny but owed their existence largely to the fact that they enjoyed some of the highest protective tariffs in Europe. Her farmers were not merely subsidized, but subsidized in the wrong way so that they produced large quantities of unsaleable wheat and neglected the cotton, currants and tobacco on which more of them might have made a modest profit. The balance of payments was under constant threat, sustained only by the remittances of the emigrants, the revenue from the great Greek shipping fleets, and the new income from the tourist boom. Had any one of those suffered a serious setback the entire modern sector of the Greek economy might have been endangered. In short, even the massive injection of American aid had failed to alter significantly the country's traditional economic structure; and with the termination of that aid it was all the more difficult for the Greek politicians to do it. Their short-term need was to win votes. The country's long-term need was to be prepared for competitive membership of the Common Market. The latter demanded an overhaul of the economy on a scale that very few Greeks seemed to grasp. The former, on the contrary, encouraged the maintenance of the existing structure through still more farm subsidies and industrial protection. Given the general nature of Greek politics it was always likely that the short-term needs would prevail. Given as well the particular circumstances of Greek politics in the early 1960's it was virtually certain they would do so, for the end of American financial aid meant also the end of that long post-war supply of easy patronage on which successive conservative governments had flourished—and a corresponding increase in the attractions of the opposition's golden promises. The result was the election of Papandreou, but with more commitments and less ready cash than any Greek Government since 1952. Theoretically, no doubt, he should have cut his coat to the new cloth, but few politicians anywhere are capable of such self-restraint for long and Papandreou certainly had not attained power after so many years in the wilderness only to mount a regime of austerity that would assuredly cause him to lose it again. On the contrary, and in Greek terms naturally, he proceeded to fulfil his promises without the cash and plunged inevitably into a spiral of inflation.

In other circumstances many of the policies which led to this inflation could have been justified as more than just short-term vote-catching. Better pay for Civil Servants, more money for education, financial inducements to businessmen to set up businesses outside Athens, and an attempt to satisfy the rural demand for a larger share of national wealth—all these were sensible enough in themselves and they pushed up the nation's economic growth rate by another 2 per cent, so that by 1965 Greece could claim that her economy was expanding as fast as any nation's in the world. Unfortunately, however, the expansion mostly represented just more of the same old things with less of the same old money to pay for them. The property boom continued, with a third of all private investment going into housing. Increased subsidies to farmers produced still more expensive wheat which had to be stored and then sold at a heavy loss at the Government's expense. Within a year of Papandreou's election the money supply had risen by over 20 per cent, and within three years imports had risen so much and exports so little that the perennially vulnerable balance of payments was in serious deficit and the reserves were running down. From 1959 to 1963 the deficit on current account had averaged only $80 million a year. Between 1963 and 1966 it rose to an average of $250 million—a threefold increase. Prices, inevitably, turned sharply upwards; and as wage earners struggled to keep pace with them and the politicians sought to win their loyalty with fresh promises, the drum-roll of strikes grew steadily more menacing and the parliamentary scene more frenetic.

The fact was that Greece, deprived of American aid, could not afford to advance on so many fronts at once, but the politicians could not afford to say so. Nor, apparently, could they afford to admit that Greece's charms for the ordinary foreign investor, whose money might have taken the place of American aid, were something less than dazzling. An amiable belief that Greek sunshine and an abundance of cheap labour would somehow make Greece the California of the Common Market was propagated in several quarters that should have known better.[5] But the big corporations of Europe and America were not as easily deceived as the Greeks themselves. The Greek market was too small, the country's position too remote, the whole structure too ramshackle to tempt more than a very few of them. Foreign capital, therefore, arrived only for highly specific purposes and on distinctly generous terms—like the American money which financed the Esso-Pappas oil and petro-chemical complex at Salonika, in return for monopoly privileges in the Greek market, and the French money which contributed to the aluminium smelting plant on the Gulf of Corinth, where a guaranteed supply of cheap electric power was added to the inducement provided by the local supply of bauxite. These concessions in turn produced an unhappy reaction, as politicians who in one breath demanded the rapid industrialization of Greece to meet the challenge of the Common Market, asked in the next breath why foreigners should be so privileged. Charges of bribery and corruption were bandied about the hustings and the floor of Parliament while the projects languished for want of agreement and other prospective foreign investors were further discouraged by the turbulent Greek scene.

Thus the basic weaknesses of the Greek economy remained unaltered and apparently unalterable—at least, by parliamentary means. The schisms were simply too many and too great: between rural poverty and urban inflation, between the national urgency of preparing for membership of the Common Market and the political expediency of appeasing local pressure groups, between the desire to retain economic autonomy and the need to import foreign capital. This last conflict particularly was significant in a way that no Greek leader seemed fully aware of. On one side was what has been described as the 'political' goal of preserving an essentially autarchic nation of Greeks, politically, culturally and economically independent in every way, while on the other was the economic goal of raising the standard of living in Greece by reducing unemployment, raising consumption and eliminating the inequalities between town and country.[6] The first presupposed a national self-sufficiency that might be economically costly but morally worthy as an expression of traditional Greek-ness. The second implied a dilution of Greekness through continued emigration, rural depopulation and growing foreign investment in Greece. The conflict between the two courses was a restatement in economic terms of the old Greek dilemma in foreign policy—how to attain simultaneously 'unfettered' independence and foreign patronage; and as in foreign policy so in economic affairs the vulnerability of Greece dictated that any compromise between the two would be weighted in favour of the latter.

Indeed, in the long run the existence of true alternatives between which to choose or compromise was probably more apparent than real. If Greece joined the Common Market many of her inefficient industries would be compelled to close or radically change their ways and more of her uneconomic farmers would be forced off the land until the social structure of the country was transformed and Greece became, essentially, an adjunct or annex of western Europe's economic power. If, on the other hand, Greece did not join the Common Market she would still have to adapt to its existence, seeking patronage elsewhere in the form of trade and aid in order to become sufficiently prosperous to retain her people—or else face emigration on a still larger scale and perhaps an eventual political revolution that would do the job of social and economic transformation in some more ruthless way. In any case Greece was due in the succeeding decades for radical social change; and it was arguable at least, that since major changes had to come an authoritarian government might achieve them more effectively than the kind of democratic regimes Greece had hitherto experienced.

Certainly that was one of the hopes attached to the colonels when they seized power in 1967. Unhappily for them, they took over the economy in the middle of the recession which had resulted from the efforts of the last effective parliamentary government to check the inflation induced by Papandreou's policies. The outbreak of the third round of the Arab-Israel war soon afterwards handicapped them further by seriously reducing the tourist traffic throughout the eastern Mediterranean, while the very fact of a military *coup d'état* in Greece, combined with its immediate condemnation in western countries, helped to create a climate of uncertainty about Greek affairs that frightened most private investors for a time and induced western governments to proceed with even more than usual caution in extending aid or credit to Greece. The Common Market countries placed a political embargo on European investment and bank loans and suspended negotiations for harmonizing the agricultural policies of Greece and the Community.

The immediate outlook, therefore, was bleak; and although the military regime swiftly concluded a huge investment agreement with Litton Industries of America, which had been hanging fire for the previous three years, its initial economic performance was barely adequate to keep its head above the rising floodwaters of the chronic balance of payments deficit. The Litton Industries contract proved a dead letter, owing to the company's inability to interest private foreign capital in investment in Greece, and was eventually abandoned by mutual consent in 1969. The tourist trade remained stagnant through 1968 partly owing to Greek exile propaganda and partly to a politically-inspired boycott in the Scandinavian countries; and the upheaval of the Civil Service through the colonels' purges depressed its general level of economic competence. Moreover, the colonels' concern for the welfare of the villages was deeply emotional, as we have seen already, and their increases in farm payments and special attention to rural development projects seemed likely, at first, to result in yet more agricultural wastefulness.

But by the end of the colonels' fourth year in power the picture had begun to change substantially for the better. After an energetic publicity campaign selling Greece to the world as 'The New Place', tourist income was increasing at a rate of between 30 and 50 per cent a year. Emigrants' remittances from overseas had also grown and the national income from the great Greek-owned shipping fleets had been increased, partly through the closure of the Suez Canal—the effect of which on oil tanker and freight rates had more than offset any loss in tourist receipts due to the war that had closed it—but still more because the new government had deliberately offered large tax concessions to Greek shipowners to induce them to move their head-quarters to Athens from overseas, and to transfer many of their ships to Greek registration from Liberian or Panamanian flags of convenience. Prices had been held down successfully, wage levels had risen by an average of 15 per cent, industrial production was rising by 11 per cent a year and, with domestic capital investment growing at an annual rate of 12 per cent the small Greek stock market was booming euphorically. In the countryside, the inflation-ary effects of the rise in farm pensions and credits had been offset by the colonels' decision to abolish the wheat subsidies—an overdue reform that had been too much for any previous government to force through parliament. Public investment outside Athens was higher than before, and on the whole seemed to be showing quicker results. A new electrical power station at Megalopolis in the Peloponnese, for example, was completed from scratch in two years after the *coup d'état*: it had been 'under consideration' before the *coup* for nearly ten. New schools, hospitals, housing projects and roads, like the massive super-highway from Corinth to Patras, had also been com-pleted or extended faster than expected; and the World Bank had contributed a modest loan of $20 million, proclaiming thereby the belief of its officials in the ultimate credit-worthiness of Greece.

In sum, through mingled luck and effectiveness, and by building as speedily as possible on some of the plans laid by previous parlia-mentary governments, the military regime had contrived to make the Greek economy look stronger than it had been at any time since the Civil War. Looking back to the crucial year of 1962–3 it seemed that the take-off predicted by the United States had been achieved. The gross national product had risen by around 75 per cent. Average incomes had nearly doubled, and while farm products and industry had each accounted for about a quarter of the country's wealth in 1962, by 1970 the farmers were producing only 18 per cent and in-dustrial products had risen to nearly 31 per cent of the country's total. These were, indeed, significant and hopeful shifts in an economy which had been so hidebound by tradition and natural poverty for so long.

Yet many of Greece's underlying weaknesses remained to test nerve and skill through at least the next decade and probably longer. Most of the land was still and always would be infertile, most Greek farm produce was still uncompetitive in western markets, and although emigration was falling off as the pool of available young men dried up, the country was still losing up to 80,000 people a year. In spite of comparatively heavy industrial investment most Greek industries remained too small and too protected to have more than a risky future in open competition with the world and Greece's general dependence on foreign capital and invisible earnings from tourism, shipping and overseas remittances was as excessive as ever. Indeed, the old balance of payments problem that had plagued so many Greek governments was still the country's biggest economic cross. The early fiasco of the colonels' agreement with Litton Industries was paralleled four years later by the collapse of a subsequent investment agreement with Aristotle Onassis. In 1970 he and his great rival, Stavros Niarchos, had agreed to invest between them a total of over £300 million (about $800 million) in major oil refinery and power projects; but unfavourable movements in oil prices and freight rates combined with local disagreements to persuade Onassis to withdraw. Although the Niarchos side of the agreement remained in force its future was cast in doubt by this development and the Greek cupboard was again left ominously bare of guaranteed foreign investment.

Over all there still hung the shadow of the Common Market, threatening sterner tests to come. Although the military regime was in disfavour in the Council of Europe, and there had been some accompanying pressure to sever its association with the European Economic Community as well, Greece remained committed to acquiring full membership of the Community by 1984, with gradual tariff reductions beginning in 1972. Officially, Greek businessmen were confident that their new industries would be ready for the shock before it came—and they pointed proudly to the fact that the country's trade with the Common Market had risen by 150 per cent since the Articles of Association were ratified in 1962. Unofficially, however, and in spite of the glossy new surface of prosperity in Athens, there were still many nervous twitches at the prospect of growing competition. More likely, it seemed, some of Greece's highly protected businessmen might withdraw from their little industries and put their money instead into new forms of the old tradition of Greek commerce—the hotels, restaurants, shops and tourist services of 'The New Place', making Greece not so much the California of Europe as the summer resort of the Great Powers; just what Andreas Papandreou and George Papadopoulos alike had not wanted it to be.

These inescapable realities of the Greek situation compelled the regime to abandon many of its earlier, simple attitudes. Ironically, but predictably, the colonels who had come to power in what they claimed to be virtually an anti-communist crusade had changed their tune a few years later in negotiating sweeping new trading arrangements with Greece's communist neighbours. In February, 1971, Bulgaria—that country upon which all good Greeks learned from their cradles to look with malevolent suspicion—proposed 'the most comprehensive plan for economic co-operation ever put forward by a Communist country to Greece, even when Greece . . . was still a parliamentary democracy.'[7] And the Greek Government, chewing over the revolutionary suggestions it contained for co-operative export of farm produce to western Europe, joint investment in manufacturing projects, and a free zone in the port of Salonika for Bulgaria's foreign trade, announced that its response would be 'positive in several fields'. Balkan economics as well as Balkan politics were, it seemed, as inseparable as ever from the future of Greece.

Thus it was clear after a few years of the colonels' rule that the facts of Greek geography and society remained intractable under any kind of government. What the colonels could do—and to some extent had already done—was to provide a period of enforced stability and comparatively swift decision in Greece appropriate to a genuine economic, political and social crisis. For that Greece had some reason to be grateful—although just how much was open to argument. One foreign estimate suggested that it was impossible to detect from the trends of the main economic indicators in Greece since 1950 when any change of government had taken place, including the colonels' *coup*.[9] In any case, what the colonels could not do for the Greek economy was obviously more important than what they could do. They could not reverse the verdict of nature and make Greece wholly independent, fully employed and entirely prosperous. Nor could they escape the deep social change which in some ways had prompted their own rebellion—the decline of Greek peasant life. Willy-nilly, by the time the 1970's opened, Greece had embarked on a kind of revolution that they, in common with most ordinary Greeks, were only just beginning to comprehend. One that might, in the still distant end, denude half the little Greek country towns and villages as thoroughly as those of western Ireland or the Hebrides—and for much the same reasons. It would be painful, and would ensure that Greece would continue to live for many years yet in a state of high economic and political tension, whether open or suppressed; but in the long run there seemed to be no alternative. The grey-leaved olive was no longer enough to feed the boys of Greece. One way or another, the twentieth century was going to usher in the death of the old peasant society—and in the process eventually change the nature of Greece as it had never been changed before.

Chapter 20

FULL CIRCLE

Meanwhile Greece travels onwards
And we know nothing. . . .
(GEORGE SEFERIS)

To end a book on Greece is almost as difficult as to begin, for the country's perpetual oppositions and contradictions no more permit of hard and fast conclusions than they allow of clear commencements. One jumps off the Greek roundabout as arbitrarily as one jumped on to it in the first place—richer, one hopes, for some knowledge of the endless process that is Greece's essence; wiser, perhaps, for the realization that there are few fixed points to steer by; exhilarated, probably, to the point of giddiness by experience of the eternal circles in which Greece moves and has its being; but—let us face it—still pretty baffled at the last by the task of separating the strands of its double-born identity in which past and present, ideal and reality, East and West, coming and going are mingled in an everlasting flux.

Yet in practice a few mundane aspects of existence may be isolated as abiding features of the Greek scene. One, as we have just noticed, is the country's basic poverty—not now so intense as it used to be but severe, nevertheless, by contemporary western standards and always a crippling handicap to the development of more stable forms of government and society. Another is the nature of the Greek character—that endearing but volatile and often self-destructive personality in which vanity so frequently overcomes judgement and which, both individually and collectively, seems to discover its identity only in conflict and its happiness only in continual struggle. A third permanent factor is the geographical and historical situation of Greece between the poles of eastern and western power and culture, encouraging attitudes that veer easily from ardent espousal of western ideas to equally vigorous resentment of western domination. After the Civil War the former attitude was uppermost in Greek national policies for more than a decade as successive governments accepted—

albeit sometimes with reluctance—the necessity of maintaining a pro-western stance in NATO and sought the benefits of western economic strength through association with the European Common Market. But although, as I suggested earlier, this had the air of manifest destiny for Greece in the 1950's, as a logical conclusion drawn not only from the communist threat but also from the fundamental reliance of modern Greece upon western sea power ever since the Battle of Navarino, the western connexion in the form then established never seemed absolutely irreversible. As the events of the 1960's indicated, the more flexible state of international relations that succeeded the stern early years of the Cold War found a quick response in Greece in the growth of those 'neutralist' ideas which played a significant part in prompting the military *coup d'état* of 1967. After the *coup* it looked initially as though Greece was tied firmly once again to her pro-western policies of old but, as we have seen, military regimes are no less subject than their civilian counterparts to old Greek pressures and desires; and it would be rash to assume that the colonels will keep their diplomacy in a western straitjacket indefinitely. The Cyprus problem, still unsettled, may provoke Greek resentment of the West again as it has done so often before. The internal opposition to the military regime is increasingly anti-American because it believes, rightly or wrongly, that the United States has supported the colonels for purely strategic reasons when it could have removed them if it wished. This anti-Americanism may yet find a protective echo in the regime itself. In any case, an assertion of greater Greek independence is implicit in the refusal of the colonels to restore democratic processes before they are ready to do so, in spite of foreign pressure, and in their willingness to expand relationships with their communist and other eastern neighbours.

Moreover, for the last third of the twentieth century the strategic and diplomatic situation in the Mediterranean and the Middle East shows signs of being radically different from that during the immediate post-war years. The growing naval strength of the Soviet Union, the sharp increase in left-wing opposition strength in Turkey and the possibility—one can put it no higher at the time of writing—of some kind of peace settlement between Israel and the Arab states, underwritten by international guarantees and international peace-keeping forces, all promise to change the picture with which the world has been familiar in that sensitive region for the past quarter of a century. Gradually, it seems, the super-power interests are beginning to overlap where hitherto they have been clearly delineated. In commerce and diplomacy as well as in military strategy there is keener competition for influence and friends all round the margins of Europe and the Middle East. It is true that Russian rigidity—as expressed in its actions in Hungary in the 1950's and Czechoslovakia in the 1960's—still threatens to halt this process whenever it seems to cast the slightest doubt upon the Soviet Union's area of hegemony, but on the American side there is an increasing readiness to modify old positions. This change in the American mood was born, no doubt, chiefly of disillusionment with the war in Vietnam but it has led to Congressional proposals to withdraw troops from Europe, to stop military supplies to Greece and even to withhold American support for Israel—ideas which would have seemed inconceivable to most American politicians in the 1950's or early 1960's. The Administration in Washington was bound to take note of this new mood; and when President Nixon announced in 1971 that he had accepted an invitation to visit China it seemed to an astonished world that all the accepted guidelines of the post-war world might soon be in the melting-pot.

Probably this was an exaggeration, but subtle changes are certainly taking place in the old power relationships and they are bound, in the long run, to have their effect on Greece. Among them is the growing importance of western Europe's Economic Community as a third pole of economic and political strength independent of Russia or America and therefore, probably, the more attractive to many people in Greece. Another is the possible reduction of tension in Central Europe through the hoped-for development of West Germany's *Ostpolitik*. A third is the just conceivable success of the super-power talks on Strategic Arms Limitation and a fourth, as I have just suggested, is the possibility of an Arab-Israel peace settlement which might change the whole nature of the Soviet-American contest for influence in the Arab world. If all these changes were to be confirmed, together with China's recognition as a qualified and responsible Great Power, the old ice floes of the Cold War would be broken decisively at last.

As it is, potentially new leads are opening among them in several directions. Marshal Tito of Yugoslavia, for example, has taken advantage of the new climate to suggest that the Mediterranean should become a 'neutral' sea in which neither Russia nor America should assert a special interest and from which both their fleets should be withdrawn. Possibly the Soviet Union will one day welcome such a move, if only as a tactical ploy against the Americans. More likely, many Americans will be tempted by it as a further means of withdrawal

x

from the harsh over-exposure of the post-war years. Certainly it accords with a deeply-held French ambition and it may yet find support in both Italy and Spain, where the rigidity of the American alliance has aroused growing discontent in recent years. The Chinese, too, may foster such proposals as they enter the super-power game ostensibly in support of the world's smaller nations. They may seem a long way from the Mediterranean in purely geographical terms at the moment, but their close political links with Albania, their diplomatic flirtation with Rumania and their ability to maintain a sense of unease, and even menace, on Russia's Far Eastern flank already afford them some leverage in the area. As China's physical power increases and her diplomatic self-confidence swells this oriental influence upon Mediterranean affairs may grow, presenting new challenges and opportunities to the local powers.

With such ideas in the air, Greek adherence to the diplomatic and strategic patterns of the last quarter of a century cannot be taken for granted; and especially not with the arrival of a new generation of Greeks, whether inside or outside the current regime, who have fewer inhibitions of the immediate past to restrict their minds and actions. They may be growing up to a situation in some ways more akin for Greece to that of the nineteenth century than to that of the middle twentieth century—one in which Greece has not just two choices before her, either East or West, 'enslaved' or 'free', as seemed to be the case in 1945, but where the choices are multiplied again so that governments and oppositions alike may think it feasible to return with impunity, if not necessarily with success, to that favourite Greek enterprise of playing off foreign patrons against each other.

This is not likely to encourage the emergence of a more stable Greece, especially if such a development coincides with the deep-seated social and economic changes inside the country such as have been taking place since the Civil War. On the contrary, these things combined could bring new upheavals in their train—and the knowledge of that certainty strengthens the current military regime in its determination to 'guide' the future of Greece for as far ahead as anyone can see. At the moment of writing the regime does, in fact, have the appearance of stability and it would be no surprise to see it continue for another decade or more, especially if its leaders can devise its gradual—almost certainly very gradual—conversion to a system of 'controlled' democracy. Objectively, that may be the best political future Greece can hope for just now, although what its real achievements might be in terms of the 'revolution' the colonels have proclaimed is open to doubt. Perhaps its biggest achievement will be the simple psychological one of affording many Greeks the period of comparative quiescence they seem to need from time to time as an escape from their own excesses.

But this is not a future that can be guaranteed in any way. Internal schisms could easily shake the colonels. 'After all,' as a Greek friend of mine pointed out soon after they came to power, 'you can't expect them to agree for ever—they're Greeks, aren't they?' If the regime should split or be overthrown altogether a period of internal upheaval would probably follow, generating demands for new initiatives in foreign as well as domestic policies. If, however, it retains power it may well discover some political advantage in appearing steadily less amenable to American or west European pressure and this, in turn, could increase the tensions around it in the eastern Mediterranean and emphasize in a different way the new opportunities—and risks—of that region. In any case, the immediate post-war period in Greece, combining diplomatic and political stability and deriving in large part from exclusive dependence on a single patron— the United States—would come to be seen more clearly as something of an aberration in Greek affairs.

There remains another and perhaps even more fundamental question which, in a sense, the colonels set themselves in 1967: can or will the character of the Greeks be changed to match the country's changing circumstances as the end of the twentieth century approaches? That is a question only God or the Greek fates can answer; but the extraordinary tenacity of the Greek character so far does not suggest that a mere generation or two of modest urban affluence and a veneer of international culture will be enough to do the trick. It is true that the peasant life upon which that character has been so largely based for so long is dying now in many parts of Greece; and as this process will surely continue under the pressure of modern economics and contemporary communications it can be argued that the Greek character itself will undergo some modification in time. But that sort of time is likely to be unconscionably long, for even in the twentieth century it remains true that people in general change far more slowly than the situations around them. Historically the Greeks in particular have shown a peculiar aptitude for accepting or surviving radical changes in their circumstances without significantly altering their basic outlook.

Seen in the glass of eternity, therefore, the present period of Greek confinement and apparent resignation may prove to be only a preparation for the next period of struggle. Dualism, above all else, is the Greek inheritance and I find it hard to picture the Greeks sacrificing permanently the agonizing joys of renewed tension in favour of the material benefits of a more docile existence. More likely, they will try again and yet again to have both at once and will experience again and yet again the inevitable frustrations that must beset such efforts. For as far ahead as I can see, at any rate, they are likely to remain, as they always have done up to now, both individually and collectively authoritarian as well as anarchic, cynical as well as romantic, sceptical and credulous, oriental and occidental all at the same time, for ever in flight between the myriad poles of their existence and extracting from each moment both the joyful knowledge that the next moment assuredly will be different and the sombre certainty that it will also be the same. Thus Greece may travel onwards as it has done for as long as the world has known it: onwards and around, neither stopping nor starting, ending or beginning, but journeying as if in circles, for ever. Who is to say that we, of all the numberless generations Greece has experienced, should be the first to see it change?

NOTES TO CHAPTERS

CHAPTER 1: THE DOUBLE-BORN SOUL

1. Miller, W., *Greek Life in Town and Country* (George Newnes, London, 1905), p. 3.

2. Lancaster, Osbert, *Classical Landscape With Figures* (John Murray, London, 1947), p. 33.

3. Miller, op. cit., p. 39.

4. Arnott, Peter D., *An Introduction to the Greek World* (Macmillan, London, 1967), p. 130.

5. Fisher, H. A. L., *A History of Europe* (Arnold, London, 1936), p. 133.

6. About, Edmond, *La Grèce Contemporaine* (Paris, 1860).

7. Perowne, Stewart, *The Pilgrim's Companion in Athens* (Hodder & Stoughton, London, 1964), p. 120.

8. Toynbee, Arnold, see *The Western Question in Greece and Turkey* (Constable, London, 1922).

9. Kazantzakis, Nikos, *Travels in Greece* (Cassirer, Oxford, 1966), pp. 167–8.

10. Leigh Fermor, Patrick, *Roumeli* (John Murray, London, 1966), p. 106 ff.

11. Runciman, Steven, *The Great Church in Captivity* (Cambridge U.P., 1968), p. 7.

12. Runciman, ibid.

13. See, e.g., Kenneth Young's study of Greek politics, *The Greek Passion* (Dent, London, 1969); C. M. Woodhouse's, *The Story of Modern Greece* (Faber & Faber, London, 1968); *Modern Greece*, by John Campbell and Philip Sherrard (Benn, London, 1968); and *The Web of Modern Greek Politics*, by J. P. C. and A. G. Carey (Columbia U.P., New York, 1969).

14. *Medea*, by Euripides: translated by Philip Vellacott (Penguin Classics, London, 1963).

CHAPTER 2: SUPERGREEK

1. The *Times Literary Supplement* (London, 20th May 1965).

2. The reviewer was obviously anxious to establish his own credentials as a classicist, for this word of Greek origin is to be found only in the *Complete Oxford English Dictionary*, where it is described as 'rare' and defined as meaning 'mechanical'.

3. T.L.S., 24th June 1965.

4. T.L.S., 24th June 1965.

5. *The Pursuit of Greece*, ed. Philip Sherrard (John Murray, London, 1964).

6. *The Complete Poems of C. P. Cavafy*, translated by Rae Dalven (The Hogarth Press, London, 1961).

7. Quoted in *The Oxford Dictionary of Quotations* (Oxford U.P., 2nd ed. 1955).

8. Byron, Robert, *The Byzantine Achievement* (London, Routledge, 1929), pp. 21–2.

9. Fisher, op. cit., p. 879.

10. Gibbon's *Decline and Fall of the Roman Empire*, Ch. LXIII.

11. Runciman, Steven, *The Fall of Constantinople* (Cambridge U.P., 1965), p. 190.

12. It is worth noting that of the eleven poets with classical references in *The Oxford Dictionary of Quotations*, all but one—Ben Jonson—belong to the eighteenth or nineteenth centuries when the classical legend was supreme. A hundred years from now, shall we, perhaps, find Yeats in there, with extracts from 'Sailing to Byzantium'?

13. Runciman, *The Great Church in Captivity*, p. 383.

14. The *Sunday Times* (London, 25th August 1968).

15. *The Times* (London, 13th October 1967), reporting a circular issued by the Greek Ministry of Education.

16. Official Circular from Greek Foreign Ministry, 12th May 1967.

17. *The Guardian* (London, May 1967).

18. This happened, e.g. to the distinguished historian, Professor Hugh Trevor-Roper, at the University of London in 1968.

CHAPTER 3: TERRITORIAL TENSIONS

1. Seferis, George *On the Greek Style* (Bodley Head, Londou 1967), p. 171.

2. Leigh Fermor, Patrick, *Mani* (John Murray, London, 1958), p. 86 ff.

3. *The Times* (London, 6th March 1966).

4. Woodcock, George, *The Greeks in India* (Faber & Faber, London, 1966), p. 13.

5. Kulukundis, Elias, *Journey to a Greek Island* (Cassell, London, 1968), pp. 8–9.

6. See S. G. Triantis, *Common Market and Economic Development* (Research Monograph Series, No. 14, Center of Planning and Economic Research, Athens, 1965).

7. Hourani, Albert, *A Vision of History* (Khayyat's, Beirut, 1961), p. 71 ff.

8. Miller, op. cit., p. 44.

9. Pallis, Alexander, *The Anatolian Venture and After* (Methuen, London, 1937), pp. 151–2.

CHAPTER 4: THE TWO-HEADED EAGLE

1. Vryonis, Speros, *Byzantium and Europe* (Thames & Hudson, London, 1967), p. 22.

2. Heurtley, W. A. and others, *A Short History of Greece* (Cambridge U.P., 1965), p. 50.

3. Runciman, *The Great Church in Captivity*, p. 395.

4. Runciman, ibid.

CHAPTER 5: THE SCORPION AND THE FROG

1. Spyros Markezinis, in a private conversation (July 1967).

2. Miller, op. cit., p. 7.

3. See, e.g., a report on the Greek Trade Union movement contained in a Special Supplement to the Official Bulletin of the I.L.O., Vol. XLIX, No. 3, July 1966: especially Chapter 7.

4. Friell, Ernestine, *Vasilika, A Village in Modern Greece* (Holt, Rinehart & Winston, New York, 1962), p. 76. For lengthier accounts, substantiating Friell, see also *Honour, Family and Patronage*, by J. K. Campbell (Oxford U.P., 1964) and *Health and Healing in Rural Greece*, by Richard and Eva Blum (Stanford U.P., 1965).

5. Friell, op. cit., p. 76

6. Miller, op. cit., p. 33.

7. *The Times* (London, 27th July 1965).

8. Skleros, George, quoted in *Greek Agricultural Cooperatives*, by John E. Tsouderos (published by Fund for International Cooperative Development, Chicago, 1961), p. xii.

9. Friell, ibid.

10. Friell, ibid.

11. Skleros, quoted in Tsouderos, op. cit., p. xii.

12. Ardrey, Robert, *The Territorial Imperative* (Collins, London, 1967), pp. 167–88.

CHAPTER 6: THE TUG OF WAR

1. Quoted in Woodhouse, *The Story of Modern Greece* (see Ch. 1 above), p. 119.

2. Fisher, op. cit., p. 881.

3. Quoted in Anderson, M. S., *The Eastern Question* (Macmillan, London, 1966), p. 67.

4. Woodhouse, op. cit., p. 131.

5. Fisher, ibid.

CHAPTER 7: THE GREAT IDEA

1. Kinglake, Charles, *Eothen* (Everyman Library, Dent, London, 1954), p. 49.

2. Pallis, op. cit., pp. 197–8.

3. Skleros, George, quoted in Tsouderos, op. cit., p. xiv.

4. Quoted in *The Chanak Affair*, by David Walder (Hutchinson, London, 1968), pp. 67–8.

CHAPTER 8: ANATOLIAN AFTERMATH

1. Andrews, Kevin, *Athens* (Dent, London, 1967), p. 22.

2. See Kayser, Bernard, *Geographie Humaine de la Grèce* (Presses Universitaires de France, Paris, 1964).

3. Pallis, op. cit., pp. 149–50.

4. Kousoulas, D. George, *Revolution and Defeat, The Story of The Greek Communist Party* (Oxford U.P., 1965).

5. Kousoulas, op. cit., p. 96.

6. Kousoulas, p. 116.

7. Kousoulas, p. 121.

CHAPTER 9: THE TERRIBLE DECADE

1. See Myers, E. C. W., *Greek Entanglement* (Hart-Davis, London, 1955), p. 103.

2. Heurtley *et al.*, op. cit., p. 145.

3. O'Ballance, Edgar, *The Greek Civil War* (Faber & Faber, London, 1966), p. 63.

4. O'Ballance, ibid.

5. Kousoulas, p. 27.

6. Macmillan, Harold, *The Blast of War* (Macmillan, London, 1967), p. 593.

7. Tsoucalas, Constantine, *The Greek Tragedy* (Penguin Books, London, 1969), p. 82.

8. Woodhouse, op. cit., p. 253.

9. Macmillan, op. cit., pp. 608–11.

10. Churchill, Winston, *The Second World War, Triumph and Tragedy* (Cassell, London, 1954), Vol. VI, p. 250.

11. This was the Greek Government's view in 1962–3, when an international campaign was mounted for the return of the exiles (see also Ch. 12).

12. Kazantzakis, Nikos, *The Fratricides* (Cassirer, Oxford, 1964), transl. by Athena Gianakis Dallas, pp. 102–3.

13. *Kathemerini*, Athens, 20th May 1951. Quoted in *Greece: American Dilemma and Opportunity*, by L. S. Stavrianos (Henry Regnery, Chicago, 1952).

14. Information from private conversation with Spyros Markezinis, October 1969. Mr. Markezinis was a senior Minister in the first Papagos government.

CHAPTER 10: MANIFEST DESTINY
1. O'Ballance, op. cit., from the foreword by C. M. Woodhouse, p. 15.
2. Quoted in *The Royal House of Greece* by A. S. Gould-Lee (Ward Lock, London, 1948), p. 186.
3. Gould-Lee, ibid.
4. Gould-Lee, p. 177.
5. Kousoulas, p. 223.
6. Xydis, Stephen G., *Greece and the Great Powers, 1644–47* (Institute for Balkan Studies, Thessaloniki, 1963), p. 176.
7. Djilas, Milovan, quoted in Kousoulas, p. 224.
8. Lancaster, op. cit., p. 150.

CHAPTER 11: STRANGE INTERLUDE
1. See Stavrianos, op. cit.
2. *The Economist* (London, 18th February 1950).
3. See above, Ch. 9, on Grivas and the White Terror.
4. Quoted in Couloumbis, Theodore A., *Greek Political Reaction to American and NATO Influences* (Yale U.P., New Haven and London, 1966), p. 77.
5. See, e.g. Jean Meynaud, *Les Forces Politiques en Grèce*, p. 101 ff.
6. Quoted in Couloumbis, p. 128.
7. Heurtley *et al.*, p. 177.
8. Couloumbis, p. 138 ff.
9. Information from personal interviews with members of Centre Union Party and others in Greece.

CHAPTER 12: THE UNRELENTING STRUGGLE
1. Tsoucalas, p. 175.
2. The *Sunday Times* (London, 16th June 1963).
3. *The Times* (London, 11th June 1963).

CHAPTER 13: THINGS FALL APART
1. *The Times* (London, 22nd February 1965).
2. *The Times* (London, 5th October 1964).
3. *Le Monde* (Paris, 3rd October 1964).

CHAPTER 14: WAITING FOR THE BARBARIANS
1. *The Economist* (London, 8th October 1966).
2. Evangelos Averoff, former Foreign Minister and E.R.E. deputy, in a personal interview with the author (July 1967).
3. See, e.g. Kenneth Young in *The Greek Passion*.
4. Kenneth Young quotes Spyros Markezinis as saying, 'I am looking for the unknown colonel'—but not many others were.

CHAPTER 15: COLONELS AND CRITICS
1. *The Guardian* (London, 7th August 1968).

2. I write here from personal experience as well as observation, having tried and failed on several occasions to interest magazine and newspaper editors and television producers in the dangers in Greece in the period 1965–7.

3. This was illustrated with special clarity by the support for Andreas Papandreou in the United States, where his former academic colleagues often led the denunciation of the colonels. They knew Papandreou as a reputable economist and one of themselves. Of his very different and highly controversial role as a Greek politician, however, most of them appeared to have no inkling.

4. Tsoucalas, *The Greek Tragedy*, pp. 206–7.

5. Ibid.

6. *The Times* (London, 24th November 1970).

7. *The Guardian* (London, 24th April 1970).

CHAPTER 16: WHAT ROUGH BEAST?

1. *Time* Magazine (New York, 18th April 1969).

2. See Chapter 11.

3. Andrews, op. cit., p. 17.

CHAPTER 17: SAINTS AND PATRONS

1. Virtually the only important exceptions were the icons at St. Katherine's Monastery in Sinai which was protected from the iconoclasts by its isolation behind the wide new frontiers of Islam.

2. Tsouderos, John, formerly M.P. for Rethymnon and son of an earlier Greek Prime Minister, in personal interview, October 1964.

3. Miller, op. cit., p. 23.

4. Ibid., p. 24.

5. Ibid., p. 29.

6. *Estia*, quoted in a report from Athens in *The Times* (London, 19th February 1969).

CHAPTER 18: THE LOST RENAISSANCE

1. Seferis, op. cit., p. 91.

2. General Metaxas, for example, was a lifelong monarchist and decidedly authoritarian, but he introduced demotic teaching to Greek schools.

3. Quoted by Nikos Stangos in 'Letter to Athens', *London Magazine* (London, August 1966).

4. It was typical of them that, in the summer of 1971, when tourism in Greece was reaching new peaks, they issued an official prayer to end this world scourge. 'Lord Jesus Christ, Son of God,' said the prayer, 'have mercy on the cities, the islands and the villages of our Orthodox fatherland, as well as the holy monasteries, which are scourged by the worldly touristic wave. Grace us with a solution of this dramatic problem and protect our brethren who are sorely tried by the modernistic spirit of these contemporary western invaders.' Echoes of the long struggle between the eastern and western Churches can be detected here, as well as a touch of oriental asceticism and simple nationalist reaction.

5. See *Sunday Telegraph* (London, 20th April 1968).

6. *Estia* (Athens, 19th July 1967).

CHAPTER 19: THE DYING OLIVE TREE

1. *The Times* (London, 21st May 1966).

2. Maddison, A., and others, *Foreign Skills and Technical Assistance in Greek Development* (O.E.C.D., Paris, 1966).

3. See also Chapter 14.

4. See also Chapter 13.

5. See, e.g. Triantis, op. cit., p. 192.
6. Triantis, op. cit., p. 52.
7. *The Times* (London, 16th February 1970).
8. Information from Col. C. M. Woodhouse.

ACKNOWLEDGEMENTS

My first thanks must go to the *Sunday Times* of London, and especially to its Editor, Mr. Harold Evans, and its Deputy Editor, Mr. Frank Giles, for the understanding they showed in affording me time to write this book. They also sent me on several happy and valuable assignments in Greece whose various fruits I was able to harvest twice over—once in the pages of the *Sunday Times* and again here. In earlier years *The Guardian* also provided me with several opportunities to visit Greece on its behalf and to its Editor, Mr. Alastair Hetherington, I owe special thanks for his keen interest in the country which—although he may well have forgotten the fact—helped greatly to extend my own.

Other organizations which from time to time sustained my interest in Greece with their funds, included the magazines *Saturday Evening Post* and *Venture* in the United States and the B.B.C. To Mr. Stephen Hearst of the B.B.C. I am indebted for my title, *Greece Without Columns*, which originally was that of a television documentary we made together in 1964. So many other individuals helped me in so many ways, both inside and outside Greece, that it seems invidious to name any of them. I am immensely indebted to them all. I must, however, thank Mr. Ben Duncan and Colonel C. M. Woodhouse, who kindly read my manuscript and—without, of course, accepting all I had to say—saved me from a number of pitfalls. I would like also to mention my special debt to two recent books about modern Greece: Colonel Woodhouse's own *The Story of Modern Greece* (Faber & Faber, London, 1968) and *Modern Greece*, by John Campbell and Philip Sherrard (Benn, London, 1968). Together with the works of Mr. Patrick Leigh Fermor, *Mani* and *Roumeli* (John Murray, London, 1958 and 1966), and Mr. Kevin Andrews, *Athens* (Phoenix House, London, 1967) and *The Flight of Icarus* (Weidenfeld & Nicolson, London, 1959), I rate these as the best of contemporary general texts in English about Greece and I have milked them shamelessly.

I am grateful, also, to the Editor of the *Times Literary Supplement* for permission to reproduce certain passages from that journal; to the Hogarth Press Ltd. in London and Harcourt Brace Jovanovich Inc. in New York, for permission to reprint C. P. Cavafy's poem, *The Philhellene*, in Rae Dalven's translation; and to Penguin Books of London for permission to use a passage from Euripides's *Medea*, translated by Philip Vellacott.

I must also record how heartened I was by the sheer confidence of my publishers, on both sides of the Atlantic, who waited for this book so patiently, so long; and how reassured I was by my doctor, John Allison, whose professional advice at critical moments of the writing persuaded me that I was not, after all, about to die of my anxieties.

Finally, there is my wife, for whose endurance, faith and affection there is only one adequate form of thanks. I dedicate this book to her.

INDEX